ALL IN A MAZE

ALL IN A MAZE

ALL IN A MAZE

A collection of prose and verse

chronologically arranged by

DANIEL GEORGE

With some assistance from

ROSE MACAULAY

COLLINS

48 PALL MALL · LONDON

PRINTED IN GREAT BRITAIN
COLLINS CLEAR-TYPE PRESS : LONDON AND GLASGOW
COPYRIGHT 1938

Now that the world is all in a maze,
Drums and trumpets rending heavens,
Wounds a-bleeding, mortals dying,
Widows and orphans piteously crying ;
Armies marching, towns in a blaze,
Kingdoms and states at sixes and sevens—
What should an honest fellow do
Whose courage and fortunes run equally low ?
Let him live, say I, till his glass be run,
As easily as he may ;
Let the wine and the sand of his glass flow together,
For life's but a winter's day.
Alas ! from sun to sun
The time's very short, very dirty the weather,
And we silently creep away.
Let him nothing do he could wish undone,
And keep himself safe from the noise of gun.

Thomas Flatman. *Poems, 1674.*

Now that the world is all in a maze,
Drums and trumpets rending heavens,
Wounds a-bleeding, mortals dying,
Widows and orphans piteously crying;
Armies marching, towns in a blaze,
Kingdoms and states at sixes and sevens —
What should an honest fellow do
Whose courage and fortunes run equally low?
Let him live, say I, till his glass be run,
As easily as he may;
Let the wine and the sand of his glass flow together,
For life's but a winter's day.
Alas! from sun to sun
The times very short, very dirty the weather,
And we silently creep away.
Let him nothing do he could wish undone,
And keep himself safe from the noise of gun.
Thomas Flatman. *Pawne (?)*

INTRODUCTION

by ROSE MACAULAY

TURNING over the littered utterances of twenty-four centuries, and half as many nations, for thoughts about peace and war, one meets with such a number that one may well fall into the illusion that these topics have always been man's third main obsession. The shocking recurrent obligation to sally forth with murderous weapons to assault sections of his fellows and be by them assaulted, in no quarrel of his own, has obviously from the earliest times loomed dismally in his mind as a horrid but probably inevitable disaster. Fools rush on war, said Euripides ; and mankind are fools. They struggle in the toils, they protest, reason, denounce, cry out against the monstrous doom, but still, as Gregory the Great observed, " the sword of man incessantly rages," and " the wrong-doing of the opposing party," as Augustine all too truly explained, " compels the wise man to wage just wars," so that if you look into our histories, complained Robert Burton, " you shall almost meet with no other subject but what a company of hare-brains have done in their rage." " These wars," moaned he, " last always and for ages ; nothing so familiar as this hacking and hewing, massacres, murders and deviltries."

This, then, is the scheme and pattern attempted in this compilation ; (attempted, I should add, by Mr. George, for the arrangement is entirely his, the selection of material almost entirely, and the footnotes—with only one or two exceptions—his alone. We began the book in collaboration, but when I flagged, he, superior both in skill and industry, stayed the course, and carried it through to what seems to me, if I may say so, triumphant achievement.) The idea is to illustrate by selected extracts the continual clash between man's sense of the horror, the folly, and the

barbarous waste of this insistent doom, and the recurrent
fits of madness in which he plunges into it with noble,
savage, and often pious cries ; between his impassioned
praises of peace and his angry kickings of the gentle goddess
downstairs ; between, in brief, man's civility and his
barbarity. The Greeks knew that paradox. We begin
with Aeschylus pleading for unarmed arbitrament,
Herodotus complaining of the irrational massacre of youth,
Euripides of war frenzy, Thucydides of rash declarations ;
then in comes Pericles, with his funeral oration on the
sacrifice of the glorious dead and their happy parents, and
the self-flattering age-old error raises its head, the confusion
that has obsessed all those who glorify war by speaking as
if its essence were self-sacrifice and dying, instead of
sacrificing others and killing. The Greeks were steeped in
this intoxicating confusion ; only a few philosophers,
intellectuals and satirists kept their heads clear of it.
The Romans too ; despite Cicero's earnest good sense on
the matter, Ovid's immense preference for a comfortable
life, and the denunciations of many intelligent persons of
war's atrocious crime. Tacitus obviously laboured under
the common delusion (which has made so many history
books dry and tedious stuff) that wars make interesting
history. Then entered the Christians, striking a new note
of moral and religious pacifism, which was not sustained
after Christianity became the imperial creed. Basil already
recedes from it ; but suggests the ingenious compromise
that those who have slain in war might well abstain from
communion for three years ; presumably until they have
forgotten about it. The relations of Christianity to
patriotism and war " were from the first very unfortunate,"
says the grave and patriotic Lecky ; however, they
rapidly improved, and by the fifth century seem to have
been quite in order. By the thirteenth, St. Thomas Aquinas
finds himself able to exhort the clergy to encourage the
troops, for " it is the duty of clerics to dispose and counsel
other men to engage in just wars." The Angelic Doctor
was rather martial : others of his age, or a little later, such
as Wycliffe and the Lollards, were less so ; Wycliffe, how-

ever disputatious a controversialist, disapproved of battle, remarking in a most reasonable modern voice that " many men with right of law withstand their enemies, and yet they kill them not, neither fight with them," and asking impatiently " Lord ! what honour falls to a knight that he kills many men ?—the hangman killeth more, and with a better title." John Gower seems to agree, and indeed over-states the case when he tells King Henry IV. that war is the mother of all wrongs. The " unfortunate " early Christian view seems, in fact, to be increasingly edging in again, religion joining hands with good sense and humanity to protest against the long-drawn-out English adventure in France. According to Pecock, even the absolute pacifist position had to be reckoned with, for " some of the lay party holden that in no wise and in no case battle is lawful " for Christians. To the humane intellectual civility of Erasmus, war was an insanity ; no one has better stated the pacifist case and the war-monger's crimes—" not scrupling to propagate lies of the most mischievous kind, false or garbled intelligence, and the grossest misrepresenta- tion of the enemy . . . each party views its own grievance with a glass that magnifies beyond all bounds." Luther, after deciding that " we must look at the business of war with the eyes of men," comes round later to a kind of dual- personality theory ; a Christian is two persons, a spiritual and a temporal, and, in the case of an assault on his wife (that time-honoured but surely unusual quandary for the pacifist) " I would lay aside the spiritual person and make use of the temporal." But fire-arms he calls cruel and of the devil. Of such divided and troubled minds were most of our articulate ancestors, and even the vulgar multitude, according to that firm militarist, Geoffrey Gates, who accused them (1579) of " maliciously contemning soldiers," in a treatise that might be by a modern Nazi.

So the tides of opinion flowed and ebbed about this intractable, rocky, and ever present topic ; but in the main it seems that writers cried out with Montaigne against that scourge that had " the world topsiturvied, ruined and defaced for the traffic of pearls and pepper.

O mechanical victories, O base conquest!" though the extremer negations were left to odd fanatical creatures such as Lollards, Anabaptists, Socinians, Quakers, and the like strange fry, and there never lacked preachers (Stephen Gosson, Lancelot Andrewes, and many more) to insist that war was "just in reason, in religion and in the practice of the church," and might well be divine, even if only a divine rod. That great theologian Cardinal Bellarmine approved "those religious generals and commanders who teach their men by word and example how to shed the blood of the enemy without offence to God."

It would seem, in short, as if there has been nothing said in these our times that was not said in the times before us ; even down to the abuse by Barnaby Rich's Captain Pill of " our peace mongers," who will not hear of keeping up national defences " till the beacons be on fire about their ears " (incidentally, this reference to peace mongers in 1604 precedes by two centuries the first given in the Oxford Dictionary, which quotes Southey on them and the dishonourable peace they would make) and down to the desire of that great peace monger Emeric Crucé for the abolition of frontiers and passports and the setting up of a League of Nations in (delightful thought) Venice. Yes, and down to Bacon's (alas for our judges !) assertion that it makes without all question for greatness to be for the most part in arms. Against this may be set (for the credit of the law) Grotius's highly civilised views on " this monstrous barbarity " and on the conscientious objector. Though on this last thorny point he does not go so far as the Spaniard, Francisco de Vitoria, who says roundly that " subjects whose conscience is against the justice of a war may not engage in it, whether they be right or wrong."

There has always, too, been the isolationist, the escapist, who would, if he could, live in easeful detachment from the fray, like the " honest fellow " of our epigraph, and like Thomas Carew a generation before him, who complacently remarks,

> What though the German drum
> Bellow for freedom and revenge, the noise
> Concerns us not, nor should divert our joys ;
> Nor ought the thunder of the carabines
> Drown the sweet airs of our tuned violins.

There is, too (but now it would seem extinct), the recluse poet, who asks, " why should we vex at the times' ridiculous misery ? " and (always with us) the embittered scholar, whose complaint is that

> Here books are burnt, fair monuments of mind,
> Here ignorance doth on all arts tyrannise ;

the bluff Christian general, with his " truly I think he that prays and preaches best will fight best;" the Quaker, who will pray and preach, but will lie in gaol and go to stocks and whipping-post rather than fight at all; the garden-taster, wanting only the sweet militia of his flowers ; the needy poet grudging money paid by fools to nourish war ; the nice insister on traditional discriminations between permissible and " base " methods of warfare, such as well-poisoning ; the profiteer in food ; the English patriot who is sure that 'tis Britain's care to watch o'er Europe's fate, and that the smaller nations " bless the wise conduct of her pious arms " ; the ingenious wit who suggests that instead of expensively destroying our foes, we might as cheaply buy them, man by man, and " have a new man for our money " ; the philosopher compassionating the slavish and hungry swarms who dance round maypoles " because their *grand monarque*, at the expense of a million of their money and thirty or forty thousand lives, has acquired a white elephant, or in other words gained a town or a village " ; the patriot-poet invoking the roar of the British lion to fright the nations ; the clergyman thanking God for having " been on our side," despite the regrettable habit of profanity in the Army and Navy ; the urbane eighteenth century man of the world, with his humane and civilised disgust for all such barbarous nonsense ; his more savagely ironic contemporary across the Channel—" if besides killing ten or twelve thousand men, the commander has been so far favoured by heaven as totally to destroy some remarkable place, then a verbose hymn is sung in four parts "— ; the outraged moral sense of a humane lexicographer, with his indignation against war profiteers and false news-mongers ; the kindly female author, with her right-minded and impartial compassion for the suffering foe ; the exultantly bellicose lyrical professor, who can " always feel proud at the sound of a drum " ; the worried (in greater or less degree) Christian justifier of the just war ; the perpetually recurring visionary putting forth plans for leagues of perpetual and universal peace, which only need, as Frederick the Great remarked, " the consent of all Europe, and some other such-like trifles," to be practicable ; the champion of the poor, who asks why should a man die for his country when he hasn't got any of it and won't be given any ; the " superior being " from another planet asking shocked questions about our wicked follies ; the smug political journalist who trusts " that we shall go to war often enough to prevent degeneracy," but not so often as to injure commerce ; the neurotic who sees war as a dispeller of *ennui* ; the *ennuyé* officer who would like to pitch his sword to the devil and return to the pleasanter excitement of gardening ; the fatalist, with his " nothing can banish it " ; the bard invoking angels to celebrate victory with a choral shout and proclaiming that " Carnage is God's daughter " (but this bard is no longer in the British Isles, he is now to be found only in more martial lands, though we may still retain one or two who shout, with Lord Tennyson, " Who fears to die ? Who fears to die ? ") ; the statesman preferring war to " peace without honour " and accepting it as the sole instrument of justice between nations ; the more progressive and imbellious statesman, much worried, protesting against this view ; the sanguine proclaimer of the war that shall end war ; the unprophetic soul who believes that his particular age has " reached the very perfection of destructive and refined cruelty in war," which must therefore perish of its own destructiveness ; the clergyman inveighing against his colleagues of the

cloth who " go forth in their sacerdotals, and, to the
disgrace of heaven and earth, consecrate banners and bid
God speed to instruments of destruction " ; the cynic,
observing that, whatever the parties in a war fight for, " what
after all they get, is widows, taxes, wooden legs, and debt."

There emerges, too, the realist, the horrific describer of
battle-field anguish, blood and stench, of men writhing
away their last moments in ditches ; the writer " would
fain tear asunder the veil from the sore places of war . . .
does it become us to let others endure what we cannot
bear even to think of ? " And increasingly, the hopeful
and rational thinker, who " firmly believes that war, or
the sending thousands of our fellow creatures to cut one
another to bits, often for what they have no concern in,
nor understand, will one day be reckoned more absurd
than if people were to settle an argument over the
dinner-table with their knives." Other intelligent and
humane distastes are seen also to increase : riotous,
rocketting and cannonading peace celebrations grow
to be thought indelicate, " the ugliness of our joy is
so appalling," wrote a Canon of the peace celebrations
in 1902 ; and many felt the same in 1919. Distaste,
too, grows for the half mystical exalted exultation
which has always made some men and women drunk at
the thought of war, like revivalists at a religious meeting,
that exultation which is taught in Germany to-day, and
which made the neurotic, opium-bemused little De
Quincey write of war's " ineffable relation to hidden
grandeurs in man . . . the idea of mixed crusade and
martyrdom, doing and suffering, that finds its realisation
in a battle such as that of Waterloo . . . so that the
tutelary angel of man, when he traverses such a dreadful
field . . ." But enough of these tutelary and sadistic
angels : fortunately the type grows rarer with the years,
though William James was deploring in the present
century the " highly mystical view of their subject " taken
by militarists, which still obtains in some countries to-day.
Less repugnant than this exalted ardour is the hearty manly
contempt of such muscular Christians as Tom Hughes for

" the vain and mischievous clique " who raise inopportunely the cry of peace, or even " the empty and disgusting pageantries " designed to popularise war. These simplicities do not disgust, like Ruskin's joy in the purple blood staining the cross on England's breastplate and in his happy fancy of war-bereaved parents sobbing " the old Seyton war-cry, Set on." But all such dire accompaniments of war we must accept ; they have been its camp-followers in all ages, like " the enormities of the press " complained of from the first news-sheets on, and caused, says the pamphleteer of 1681, partly by writers and partly by readers, though not all thinkers on this grave subject would go as far as the Reverend George Beaumont in his distaste for " a set of men who, with a few exceptions, ought to rank among the vilest of the vile, I mean Newsprinters," whom, writing in 1808, he blamed for most recent wars.

So, among eloquent armies of peace mongers, war mongers, and bewildered civilised thinkers up against barbarism, we arrive at the frightful period 1914-18, of which we have made a scrap-book by itself, which may be omitted by the squeamish, though those interested in human nature will find here matter for study. They will find the oddest utterances, degraded, sublime, agonised, complacent, odious, perplexed ; here is a worldful of people up against a dilemma too frightful for clear thinking, too unbalancing for man's integrity ; the maze has thickened to an intolerable sad mess, and we are all lost in it. There are here some less-known poems by soldiers ; the famous ones are too familiar for quoting ; most civilian verse at this time is better left.

And so to the post-war section, which does not, needless to say, aspire to represent contemporary thought on the subject, or to quote from more than a tiny fraction of many thousands of admirable books. Only a few drops from this vast and swelling ocean can splash these pages, or irrigate the pronouncements of journalists and statesmen which conclude them. These pronouncements, despite a few startling aberrations and shrieks from our contemporary mad-houses, in the main echo one another with a gratifying unanimity, all remarking, " We want Peace—nothing is further from our minds than War " : flocks of vigilant and somewhat nervous doves cooing in the chimneys of munition factories, while " the melancholic eye sees fleets and armies in the sky."

Well, here it is : four-and-twenty centuries of sample twitterings from the mazed world ; four-and-twenty centuries of peace dreams and plans, of war fears and facts, of pacifism, militarism, conscientious objection, martial ardour and odes, propaganda, protests, Christianity (bewildered, complacent, or uncompromising) up against a dire dilemma, the rational voice of intelligence lifted in vain, war preparations, wars to end war, war as medicine, the excellent spirit of the troops, all our old familiar friends, in slightly changing dress from age to age, threading the maze in a pattern which (we hope you will perceive) is not only that of date. We trust you may find them good company ; or, anyhow, a good pageant. Let those who can do so echo as they watch it Pepys's " But Lord ! to see it was strange sport " ; or Charles Churchill's

> Spectators only, on this bustling stage,
> We see what vain designs mankind engage . . .
> Perplex'd with trifles through the vale of life
> Man strives 'gainst man, without a cause for strife . . .
> Squirrels for nuts contend, and, wrong or right,
> For the world's empire kings ambitious fight.
> What odds ?—to us 'tis all the self-same thing,
> A nut, a world, a squirrel, and a king.

Those who cannot achieve such easy detachment must find their own way through the maze as best they may.

The spelling has been modernised. Dates are those of publication, except when writing has occurred long before.

POSTSCRIPT

THIS book went to press before the sinister autumnal events which descended on Europe like the marching of a goblin army. An army whose cloven feet we now hear always in the near distance, marching and marching still. The last-minute additions which we have squeezed into the small space at our command do not pretend to report this, our latest nightmare, with its grim accessories of panic precautions, panic flight, evacuations, billeting orders, food hoarding, hysterical ovations, minatory shriekings from dictators, Prime Ministers winging it to and fro, to and fro, and once more to and fro, bearing glad tidings of peace with honour in our time for which the nations must arm and arm and arm. On the subject of this same peace we have collected a small miscellany of varied comments out of the many thousands which it has evoked. An ignoble peace, there seems small doubt, like most of the peaces of history, which are, nevertheless, though poor, nasty, brutish and short, like human life in yet one other particular—they are better, while they last, than their opposite states.

We regret that we have not space adequately to commemorate the many notable peacemakers who have each been named chief artisan of this peace. Posterity, that acute and chilly observer, will perhaps be able more accurately to spot the winner and adjust the olive crown. We ourselves seem likely in the near future to be otherwise engaged.

As to this future, who knows ? " May you," exclaimed Sidonius Apollinaris, that spirited bishop, writing to another bishop about another ignoble peace which had been negotiated by another Big Four (all bishops that time) —" may you live to blush for a peace without either honour or advantage." Did the bishops live to blush ? Shall we ourselves live long enough to blush, those of us who are not blushing now ? All this is hidden from us in the somewhat grim and dubious future on the nature of which we have assembled a few hints at the close of this book.

HYMN FOR PEACE

HEAR the blessings now we pour
From the heart's abundant store
On your issue, gods of Greece !
Ares, from thy madness cease !
Make not this Pelasgian town,
Burned with fire, to crumble down !
Lover of the lyreless cry,
That in regions far and nigh
Mowest down the human grain
Dripping with the gory rain ! . . .

Let your rulers hold in awe
High degree and holy law,
Swaying with far-sighted skill
Towards wise aims the popular will.
Ere they arm the war's array
For the rash contentious fray,
Let them fair proposals bring
To remove the offence's sting,
Healing what their foes resent
With unarmed arbitrament.

Aeschylus. *Supplices, c. 480 B.C.*
Tr. Lewis Campbell.

A LITTLE DUST

FROM each home once there went
A man forth : him it sent
Each knows ; but what are these return ?
A little dust, an urn.

Aeschylus. *Agamemnon, c.*
458 B.C. Tr. Walter Headlam.

FATHERS AND SONS

No one is so senseless as to choose of his own will war rather than peace, since in peace the sons bury their fathers, but in war the fathers bury their sons. But it was pleasing, I suppose, to the divine powers that these things should come to pass thus.

Herodotus. *History, c. 430 B.C.*
Tr. G. C. Macaulay.

HOPE A CURSE

Hope is men's curse : full many a state hath this
Embroiled, by kindling it to mad emprise.
For, when for war a nation casteth votes,
Then of his own death no man taketh count,
But passeth on to his neighbours this mischance.
But, were death full in view when votes were cast,
Never war-frenzied Greece would rush on ruin.
Yet, of elections twain, we know—all know—
Whether is best, the blessing or the curse ;
And how much better is peace for men than war,
Peace, which is the Muses' chiefest friend
But mourning's foe, which joyeth in fair children,
In wealth delighteth. Fools let all these slip,
And rush on war.

Euripides. *Suppliants, 420 B.C.*
Tr. Arthur S. Way, 1894.

FROM BLOWS TO WORDS

Realise, while there is time, the inscrutable nature of war ; and how when protracted it generally ends in becoming a mere matter of chance, over which neither of us can have any control, the event being equally unknown and equally hazardous to both. The misfortune is that in their hurry to go to war, men begin with blows, and when a reverse comes upon them, then have recourse to words.

> Thucydides. *Bk. I. : History of the Peloponnesian War, c. 410 B.C. Tr. Benjamin Jowett.*

ORATORY

THE sacrifice which they collectively made was individually repaid to them ; for they received again each one for himself a praise which grows not old, and the noblest of all sepulchres—I speak not of that in which their remains are laid, but of that in which their glory survives, and is proclaimed always and on every fitting occasion both in word and deed. . . .

Wherefore I do not now commiserate the parents of the dead who stand here . . .

> *Ibid. Bk. II. : (Funeral speech of Pericles.)*

A HARD MASTER

IN peace and prosperity both states and individuals are actuated by higher motives, because they do not fall under the dominion of imperious necessities ; but war, which takes away the comfortable provision of daily life, is a hard master and tends to assimilate men's characters to their conditions.

> *Ibid. Bk. III.*

SERIOUS THINGS

An Athenian Stranger : What I assert is this—that a man ought to be in serious earnest about serious things and not about trifles ; and that the object really worthy of all serious or blessed effort is God, while man is contrived, as we said above, to be a plaything of God, and the best part of him is really just like that; and thus, I say that every man and woman ought to pass through life in accordance with this character, playing at the noblest of pastimes, being otherwise minded than they now are.

Clinias of Crete : How so ?

An Athenian Stranger : Now they imagine that serious work should be done for the sake of play; for they think that it is for the sake of peace that the serious work of war needs to be well conducted. But as a matter of fact, we, it would seem, do not find in war, either as existing or likely to exist, either real play or education worthy of the name, which is what we assert to be in our eyes the most serious thing. It is the life of peace that every one should live as much and as well as he can.

Plato. *Laws, vii., 345 B.C.*
Tr. R. G. Bury.

THE PROBLEM OF LEISURE

FACTS, as well as arguments, prove that the legislator should direct all his military and other measures to the provision of leisure and the establishment of peace. For most of these military states are safe only while they are at war, but fall when they have acquired their empire; like unused iron, they rust in time of peace. And for this the legislator is to blame, he never having taught them how to lead the life of peace.

Aristotle. *Politics, vii., c. 335 B.C.*

The commentators on old ARI-
STOTLE ('tis urged) in judgment vary;
They to their own conceits have brought
The image of his general thought,
Just as the melancholic eye
Sees fleets and armies in the sky . . .
Matthew Prior, *Alma.*

SOLDIERS' FAREWELL TO WAR

Trygæus :
    If there be any that delights in war,
    King Dionysius, may he never cease
    Picking out spearheads from his funny-bones.

Chorus :
    If any, seeking to be made a Captain,
    Hates to see Peace return, O may he ever
    Fare in the battles like Cleonymas.

Trygæus :
    If any merchant, selling spears or shields,
    Would fain have battles, to improve his trade,
    May he be seized by thieves and eat raw barley.

                    Aristophanes. *Peace, 241 B.C.*
                    Tr. Benjamin Bickley Rogers.

"The Clergy, that is to say, the prophets and oracle-dealers, are represented in Greek Comedy, just as they are later by Erasmus and Voltaire, as more ferocious in their war-passions than the average layman. For example, in the *Peace*, when that buried goddess has been recovered from the bowels of the earth and all the nations are rejoicing, the soothsayer Hierocles comes to interrupt the peace-libations with his oracles: ' O miserable creatures and blind, not knowing the mind of the gods! Behold, men have made covenants with angry-eyed apes. Trembling gulls have put their trust in the children of foxes.' And again, ' Behold, it is not the pleasure of the blessed gods that ye cease from war until the wolf weds the lamb.'"—Gilbert Murray, *Aristophanes and the War Party*, 1919.

OVERRULED

THE pretext for hostilities was given. What advice or remonstrance did I omit, when urging that any peace, even the most inequitable, should be preferred to the most righteous war ? My advice was overruled.

                    Cicero. *To Aulus Caecina,*
                    46 B.C.

A SURVIVOR

WITH thee I saw Philippi's rout, and dishonourably dropped my shield, while courage broke, and bold warriors fell ingloriously to earth. But me, terrified, Mercury bore swiftly through the enemy's ranks in a dense cloud.

> Horace. *Odes, Bk. II., vii., c.*
> *23 B.C.*

POETICAL VERSION

> WITH thee I saw Philippi's plain,
> In fatal rout, a fearful scene !
> And dropped alas ! th' inglorious shield,
> Where valour's self was forced to yield,
> Where soiled in dust the vanquished lay,
> And breathed th' indignant soul away.
>   But me, when dying with my fear,
> Through warring hosts, enwrapped in air,
> Swift did the god of wit convey. . . .

> Horace. *Odes, Bk. II., vii., c.*
> *25 B.C. Tr. Philip Francis, 1746.*

"There is something ingenuous in the poet's recording this instance of his own cowardice, which possibly might never have been known to posterity. Archilochus, Alcaeus, and Demosthenes are examples of the same ingenuity of spirit. Next to true courage, says a French commander, nothing is more brave than a confession of cowardice."—Sanadon.

"That Horace should have been able playfully to impute cowardice to himself is enough, as Lessing pointed out, to prove that he had no fear that others would impute it to him."—E. C. Wickham.

DULCE ET DECORUM EST PRO PATRIA MORI

IT is sweet and seemly to die for one's country. Death also pursues him who flees, nor spares the limbs and cowardly back of the unwarlike youth.

> *Ibid. Odes, Bk. III., ii.*

"Some will retort by quoting Horace's well-known Dulce et decorum est pro patria mori, but they must not forget to quote the following line also: Mors et fugacem persequitur virum, for without it Horace's real meaning escapes us, which is that ' as death strikes even a fugitive, it is always better, when a man is once on the battlefield, to die a fine and glorious death for the Country, than to die as a coward.'"—G. F. Nicolai, *The Biology of War.*

"The design of Horace, in this ode, is to recommend fortitude, in bearing the distresses of war; virtue, in the pursuit of the honours of peace; and silence, in preserving the mysteries of religion."—Dacier.

A GLORY GREATER THAN WAR

COME, Peace, with thy adorned locks wreathed with Actian leaves, and gently abide in the entire world. If only there be no foes, and no occasion for triumph, thou shalt be to our leaders a glory greater than war. Let the soldier bear arms only to restrain arms, and let not the fierce trumpet sound except for ceremonial pomps.

Ovid. *Fasti. Bk. I., c. 1 A.D.*

WHEN MARS LORDS IT

BUT Mars—what dreadful purpose has he, when he kindles the Scorpion menacing with fiery tail and scorches its claws ? For the benign star of Jupiter is hidden deep in the West, the healthful planet Venus is dim, and Mercury's swift motion is stayed ; Mars alone lords it in heaven. Why have the constellations fled from their courses, to move darkling through the sky, while the side of sword-girt Orion shines all too bright ? The madness of war is upon us, when the power of the sword shall violently upset all legality, and atrocious crime shall be called heroism.

Lucan. *Pharsalia, 60. Tr. J. D. Duff, 1928.*

OVERMASTERING AND WIDESPREAD MADNESS

WE are mad, not only individually, but nationally. We check manslaughter and isolated murders, but what of war and the much-vaunted crime of slaughtering a whole people ? . . . Deeds that would be punished by us by loss of life when committed in secret, are praised by us because uniformed generals have carried them out. Man, naturally the gentlest class of beings,[1] is not ashamed to revel in the blood of others, to wage war, and to entrust the waging of war to his sons, when even dumb beasts and wild beasts keep the peace with one another. Against this overmastering and widespread madness philosophy has become a greater effort, and has taken on strength in proportion to the strength which is gained by the opposition forces.

Seneca. *Ad Lucilium, Epistle XCV., c. 63.* Tr. Richard M. Gummere.

[1] "The fact that there are some very simple peoples where war seems to be unknown has given rise to assertions that man is 'essentially' peaceful, and that it is civilisation which is to blame for his present undeniable aggressiveness. . . . Most primitive people are not only not peaceable, but live in a state not far removed from that of baboons."— E. F. M. Durbin and John Bowlby, *Personal Aggressiveness and War* (in *War and Democracy*, 1938).

PYRRHUS AND CINEAS

CINEAS now seeing Pyrrhus intent upon his preparations for Italy, took an opportunity, when he saw him at leisure, to draw him into the following conversation : " The Romans have the reputation of being excellent soldiers, and have the command of many warlike nations ; if it please Heaven that we conquer them, what use, sir, shall we make of our victory ? " " Cineas," replied the king, " your question answers itself. When the Romans are once subdued, there is no town, whether Greek or barbarian, in all the country, that will dare oppose us ; but we shall immediately be masters of all Italy, whose greatness, power and importance no man knows better than you." Cineas, after a short pause, continued, " But after we have conquered Italy, what shall we do next, sir ? " Pyrrhus, not yet perceiving his drift, replied, " There is Sicily very near, and stretches out her arms to receive us, a fruitful and populous island, and easy to be taken. For Agathocles was no sooner gone, than faction and anarchy prevailed among the cities, and everything is kept in confusion by her turbulent demagogues." " What you say, my prince,"said Cineas, " is very probable ; but is the taking of Sicily to conclude our expeditions ? " " Far from it," answered Pyrrhus ; " for if Heaven grant us success in this, that success shall only be the prelude to greater things. Who can forbear Libya and Carthage, then within reach ? which Agathocles, even when he fled in a clandestine manner from Syracuse, and crossed the sea with a few ships only, had almost made himself master of. And when we have made such a conquest, who can pretend to say that any of our enemies, who are now so insolent, will think of resisting us ? " " To be sure," said Cineas, " they will not ; for it is clear that so much power will enable you to recover Macedonia, and to establish yourself uncontested sovereign of Greece. But when we have conquered all, what are we to do then ? " " Why then, my friend," said Pyrrhus, laughing, " we will take our ease, and drink and be merry." Cineas, having brought him thus far, replied, " And what hinders us from drinking and taking our ease now, when we have already those things in our hands, at which we propose to arrive through seas of blood, through infinite toils and dangers, through innumerable calamities which we must both cause and suffer ? "

Plutarch. *Lives : c. 80. Tr. J. & W. Langhorne.*

Rabelais has a similar story. "There was present at the time an old gentleman well-experienced in the wars, a stern soldier, and who had been in many great hazards, named Echephron, who, hearing this discourse, said . . . What do you intend by these large conquests? What shall be the end of so many labours and crosses? Thus it shall be (said Picrochole) that when we return we shall sit down, rest, and be merry. But (said Echephron) if by chance you should never come back, for the voyage is long and dangerous, were it not better for us to take our rest now, than unnecessarily to expose ourselves to so many dangers?"

ALEXANDER AND PARMENIO

IT was about this time that he received a letter from Darius, in which that prince proposed, on condition of a pacification and future friendship, to pay him ten thousand talents in ransom of the prisoners, to cede to him all the countries on this side the Euphrates, and to give him his daughter in marriage. Upon his communicating these proposals to his friends, Parmenio said, " If I were Alexander, I would accept them." " So would I," said Alexander,[1] " if I were Parmenio." The answer he gave Darius was, " That if he would come to him, he should find the best of treatment ; if not, he must go and seek him."

Ibid.

[1] "Longinus takes notice of this as an instance, that it is natural for men of genius, even in their common discourse, to let fall something great and sublime."—Note in the Langhornes' edition.

But see Landor's comment through Penn: "History has reserved all her applause for the destroyers of mankind. Point out to me one single schoolmaster, in any age, who has not applauded the speech of Alexander to Parmenio. . . . Was the man so besotted as not to see clearly that Parmenio spoke in the interests of humanity and in the opinion of all nations, and that he himself spoke not even in his own interests, and directly against the well-being of the world?"

THE ARTS OF CIVIL POLICY

THE Romans, by a strange singularity of nature, are the only people who invade, with equal ardour, the wealth and the poverty of nations. To rob, to ravage, and to murder, in their imposing language, are the arts of civil policy. When they have made the world a solitude, they call it peace.

Tacitus. *Agricola, 97. Tr. Arthur Murphy, 1793.*

THE BEST THING

PEACE is the best thing that man may know ; peace alone is better than a thousand triumphs ; peace has power to guard our lives and secure equality among fellow-citizens. Let us then after so long recall peace to the city of Carthage, and banish the reproach of treachery from Dido's city. If Hannibal has such a passion for war, and disobeys his country when she bids him sheathe the sword, then I advise you to refuse all supplies to such a madman. . . .

Silius Italicus. *Punica, xi. c. 100.*

HISTORIAN'S HANDICAP

I AM well aware that much of what I have related, and still have to relate, may seem of little moment, and too trifling to be recorded. But none can compare my subject with that of those who wrote the early history of Rome. They had great wars to describe, the storming of cities, the rout and capture of kings ; or if they turned to affairs at home, they could enlarge freely on the conflicts of Consuls with Tribunes, on land laws and corn laws, on struggles between patricians and plebeians. My theme is narrow and inglorious : a peace unbroken, or disturbed only by petty wars ; a distressful course of events in Rome ; a prince with no interest in the expansion of the Empire.

Tacitus. *Annals, c. 110. Tr. G. C. Ramsay.*

UNDER THE VINE

WE who were filled full of wars and slaughter one of another and every kind of evil, have from out of the whole earth each changed our weapons of war, our swords into ploughshares and our pikes into farming tools, and we farm piety, righteousness, the love of man, faith, and hope which comes from the Father through Him who was crucified, each of us dwelling under his own vine, that is, each enjoying only his own wedded wife.

Justin Martyr. *Dialogue with Trypho. c. 160.*

AN ENQUIRY ANSWERED

BUT now enquiry is made about this point, whether a believer may turn himself unto military service, and whether the military may be admitted unto the faith, even the rank and file, or each inferior grade, to whom there is no necessity for taking part in sacrifices or capital punishments. There is no agreement between the divine and the human sacrament, the standard of Christianity and the standard of the devil, the camp of the light and the camp of darkness. One soul cannot be due to two lords—God and Cæsar. And yet Moses carried a rod, and Aaron wore a buckler, and John (baptist) is girt with leather, and Joshua the son of Nun leads a line of march, and the People warred : if it pleases you to sport with the subject. But how will a Christian man war, nay, how will he serve even in peace, without a sword, which the Lord has taken away? For albeit soldiers had come unto John, and had received the formula of their rule ; albeit, likewise, a centurion had believed ; still the Lord afterward, in disarming Peter, unbelted every soldier. No dress is lawful amongst us, if assigned to any unlawful action.

Tertullian. *de Idololatria, c. 200.*

"In ch. xi [de Corona] Tertullian expounds still more sharply than in the treatise *de idololatria*, the incompatibility of Christianity and the military calling. Here, too, he discusses the question, what is a soldier to do, who is converted when a soldier (Luke iii, 14; Matt. viii, 10; Acts x, 1 f.)—There is always the possibility of taking all precautions against committing any irreligious action as a soldier. But Tertullian recommends only two ways out of the difficulty: either resigning one's post ('ut a multis actum': as has been done by many) or suffering martyrdom."—Harnack, *Expansion of Christianity*, tr. Moffatt.

SIMPLE AND QUIET SISTERS

FOR he says, " Take no anxious thought for to-morrow," meaning that the man who has devoted himself to Christ ought to be sufficient to himself, and servant to himself, and moreover lead a life which provides for each day by

itself. War needs great preparation, and luxury craves
profusion ; but peace and love, simple and quiet sisters,
require no arms nor excessive preparation. The Word is
their sustenance.

Clement of Alexandria.
Paedagogus. c. 200.

AN ARMY OF PIETY

CELSUS urges us " to help the king with all our might, and
to labour with him in the maintenance of justice, to fight
for him, and if he requires it to fight under him or lead
an army along with him." To this our answer is, that we
do, when occasion requires, give help to kings, and that,
so to say, a divine help, " putting on the whole armour
of God." And this we do in obedience to the injunction of
the apostle, " I exhort, therefore, that first of all supplica-
tions, prayers, intercessions, and giving of thanks, be made
for all men, for kings, and for all that are in authority"; and
the more any one excels in piety, the more effective help
does he render to kings, even more than is given by soldiers,
who go forth to fight and slay as many of the enemy as they
can. And to those enemies of our faith who require us to
bear arms for the commonwealth, and to slay men, we can
reply : " Do not those who are priests at certain shrines,
and those who attend on certain gods, as you account them,
keep their hands free from blood, that they may with hands
unstained and free from human blood offer the appointed
sacrifices to your gods ; and even when war is upon you,
you never enlist the priests in the army. If that, then, is a
laudable custom, how much more so that, while others are
engaged in battle, these too should engage as the priests
and ministers of God, keeping their hands pure, and
wrestling in prayers to God on behalf of those who are
fighting in a righteous cause, and for the king who reigns
righteously, that whatever is opposed to those who act
righteously may be destroyed." And as we by our prayers
vanquish all demons who stir up war, and lead to the

violation of oaths, and disturb the peace, we in this way
are much more helpful to the kings than those who go
into the field to fight for them. . . . And none fight better
for the king than we do. We do not indeed fight under him,
although he require it ; but we fight on his behalf, forming
a special army—an army of piety—by offering our prayers
to God.

> Origen. *Against Celsus. c. 240.*
> *Tr. W. H. Cairns.*

Not all the Christian leaders at this period expressed views to which
sensitive military authorities might take exception. Julius Africanus
dedicated to Alexander Severus an encyclopædia, *Embroidered Girdles*,
with a section devoted to the extermination of enemies by methods
including the poisoning of food, wells and air. Oddly enough, according
to the Military Correspondent of *The Times* (June 10, 1938) "the poisoning
of wells, despite its obvious military advantages, has been extraordinarily
rare in the records of war." See, however, p. 379 for the report of an
incident which has otherwise passed unrecorded.

CRIME NOW A VIRTUE

THE whole world is wet with mutual blood ; and murder,
which in the case of an individual is admitted to be a
crime, is called a virtue when it is committed wholesale.
Impunity is claimed for the wicked deeds, not on the plea
that they are guiltless, but because the cruelty is perpetrated
on a grand scale.

> Cyprian, *Bishop of Carthage.*
> *Epistle to Donatus. c. 250.*

THE JUST MAN

HE must also diligently take care, lest by any fault of his
he should at any time make an enemy ; and if any one
should be so shameless as to inflict injury on a good and
just man, he must bear it with calmness and moderation,
and not take upon himself his revenge, but reserve it for
the judgment of God. . . . Because it will be thought that
he is unable to defend himself, he will be regarded as

slothful and inactive ; but if any one shall have avenged himself upon his enemy, he is judged a man of spirit and activity—all honour and reverence him. . . .

From what source do contests, from what source do fightings and contentions arise among men, except that impatience opposed to injustice often excites great tempests ? But if you meet injustice with patience, than which virtue nothing can be found more true, nothing more worthy of a man, it will immediately be extinguished, as though you should pour water upon a fire. But if that injustice which provokes opposition has met with impatience equal to itself, as though overspread with oil, it will excite so great a conflagration that no stream can extinguish it, but only the shedding of blood. Great, therefore, is the advantage of patience. . . . For this alone causes that no evil happens ; and if it should be given to all, there will be no wickedness and no fraud in the affairs of men. . . . In what respect, then, does the wise and good man differ from the evil and foolish, except that he has invincible patience, of which the foolish are destitute ; except that he knows how to govern himself, and to mitigate his anger, which those, because they are without virtue, are unable to curb ? . . . He who endeavours to return an injury desires to imitate that very person by whom he has been injured. Thus he who imitates a bad man can by no means be good.

Lactantius. *Divinarum Institutionum.*
Bk. VI. De Vero Cultu, c. 300.

NOT EVEN BABIES

WHEN God forbids us to kill, he not only prohibits us from open violence, which is not even allowed by the public laws, but he warns us against the commission of those things which are esteemed lawful among men. Thus it will be neither lawful for a just man to engage in warfare since his warfare is justice itself, nor to accuse any one of a capital charge, because it makes no difference whether you put a man to death by word, or rather by the sword, since it is the act of putting to death itself which is prohibited. Therefore, with regard to this precept of God, there ought to be no exception at all ; but that it is always unlawful to put to death a man, whom God willed to be a sacred animal.

Therefore let no one imagine that even this is allowed, to strangle new-born children. . . .

If, then, it is in no way permitted to commit homicide, it is not allowed us to be present at all, lest any bloodshed should overspread the conscience.

Ibid.

"Nowhere else in early Christian literature do we find more ringing declarations of the illegitimacy of war and of everything like it than are to be found in Lactantius's writings. It is not legitimate, he insisted, even to fight for one's own country, or to attempt to promote its advantages in any way at the expense of other lands [*Institutes*, Vi. 6]. Christianity he was sure was above everything else a religion of peace and brotherhood. This he regarded as its great glory, the feature which must commend it most strongly to the best and wisest of men."— Arthur Cushman McGiffert, *A History of Christian Thought*, Vol. 2, 1933.

A LEAGUE OF CONCORD

CERTAINLY if all who look upon themselves as men, not so much from the shape of their bodies, as because they are endowed with reason, would listen a while unto Christ's wholesome and peaceable decrees, and, not puffed up with arrogance and conceit, rather believe their own opinions than his admonitions, the whole world long ago (turning the use of iron into milder works) should have lived in most quiet tranquillity, and have met together in a firm and indissoluble League of most safe Concord.

Arnobius. Adversus Gentes. c. 303.

A CONCESSION

HOMICIDE in war is not reckoned by our Fathers as homicide; I presume from their wish to make concession to men fighting on behalf of chastity and true religion. Perhaps, however, it is well to counsel that those whose hands are not clean abstain from communion for three years.[1]

St. Basil. *Letter to Amphilochius, 347.*

[1] Leo (440) said: "It is altogether contrary to the rules of the Church to return, after doing penance, to the military service in the world, since the Apostle says that *no soldier in God's service entangles himself in the affairs of the world.*"

JUSTICE EVEN IN WARTIME

How great a thing justice is can be gathered from the fact that there is no place, nor person, nor time, with which it has nothing to do. It must even be preserved in all dealings with enemies. For instance, if the day or spot for a battle has been agreed upon, it would be considered an act against justice to occupy the spot beforehand or to anticipate the time . . .

The thoughts of warlike matters seem to be foreign to the duties of our office, for we have our thoughts fixed more on the duty of the soul than of the body ; nor is it our business to look to arms, but rather to the affairs of peace.

St. Ambrose. *De Officiis, c. 391.*

"Even the unwritten law of war was criticised. This had apparently not been affected by Christian influence, so that crimes committed by soldiers remained, if not technically legal, at least excusable. Against this soldier's privilege Ambrose thundered: of killing in a just war he tacitly approved, but he denied that acts of violence incidental to war —robbery, rape, the killing of prisoners — were any less criminal because committed by soldiers in the field."—Edward M. Pickman, *The Mind of Latin Christendom*, 1937.

EVERY MAN SEEKS PEACE

WHOEVER gives even moderate attention to human affairs and to our common nature, will recognise that there is no man who does not wish to be joyful, neither is there any one who does not wish to have peace. For even they who

B

make war desire nothing but victory,—desire, that is to
say, to attain to peace with glory. For what else is victory
than the conquest of those who resist us ? and when this
is done there is peace. It is therefore with the desire for
peace that war is waged, even by those who take pleasure
in exercising their warlike nature in command or battle.
And hence it is obvious that peace is the end sought for by
man. For every man seeks peace by waging war, but no
man seeks war by making peace.

> St. Augustine. *The City of God,*
> *413-426. Tr. Marcus Dods.*

MATTER OF GRIEF

BUT, say they, the wise man will wage just wars. As if he
would not all the rather lament the necessity of just wars,
if he remembers that he is a man ; for if they were not just
he would not wage them, and would therefore be delivered
from all wars. For it is the wrong-doing of the opposing
party which compels the wise man to wage just wars ; this
wrong-doing, even if it gave rise to no wars, would still be
matter of grief to man because it is man's wrong-doing. Let
every one, then, who thinks with pain on all these great
evils, so horrible, so ruthless, acknowledge this is misery.
And if any one either endures or thinks of them without
mental pain, this is a more miserable plight still, for he
thinks himself happy because he has lost human feeling.

> *Ibid.*

"We may find pacifist sentiments in men like Origen and Tertullian,
who had no experience of the barbarians, but we shall look for them in
vain in St. Ambrose, and St. Augustine and our father St. Gregory, who
knew what they were talking about."—The Rev. H. L. Goudge, D.D.,
Canon of Christ Church, in a sermon preached before the University of
Oxford, Sunday morning, January 30, 1938.

"The relations of Christianity to the sentiment of patriotism were
from the first very unfortunate. They regarded the lawfulness of taking
arms as very questionable, and all those proud and aspiring qualities
that constitute the distinctive beauty of the soldier's character as
emphatically un-Christian."—W. E. H. Lecky, *History of European Morals,*
1869.

SMITTEN FROM ABOVE

Lo, all the things of this world, which we used to hear from the sacred page were doomed to perish, we see already ruined. Cities are overthrown, camps uprooted, churches destroyed ; and no tiller of the ground inhabits our land. Among ourselves who are left, very few in number, the sword of man incessantly rages along with calamities wherewith we are smitten from above.

St. Gregory the Great. *Epistle xxix. c. 593.*

FOREWARNINGS

HERE dire forewarnings were come over the land of the Northumbrians and miserably terrified the folk ; there were excessive whirlwinds and lightnings, and fiery dragons were seen flying in the air.[1] To these tokens followed a great famine ; and a little after that in the same year on vi id. Jan. (Jan. 8th) the harrying of heathen men lamentably destroyed God's church in Lindisfarne by means of plunder and slaughter.

Anglo-Saxon Chronicle, 793. Tr. E. E. C. Gomme.

[1] The condition of war is favourable to the appearance of such phenomena. A wonderful spectacle is recorded in the year 1914 (see p. 383), and the well-authenticated story of the Angels at Mons will be recalled.

Cf. also Spengler, *Der Untergang des Abendlandes Welthistorische Perspektiven*, 1932: "In a small but noteworthy book, R. Mewes, Die Kriegs und Geistesperioden im Völkerleben und Verkündigung des nächsten Weltkrieges (1896), the relation of those war periods and weather periods, sun-spot cycles, and certain conjunctures of the planets is established, and a great war foretold for the period 1910-20. But these and numerous similar connections that come within the reach of our senses ... veil a secret that we have to respect and not to infringe with casual expositions or mystical brainwaves."

A TRUCE OF GOD

WHEREAS in our times the holy church has been afflicted beyond measure by tribulations through having to join in suffering so many oppressions and dangers, we have so striven to aid it, with God's help, that the peace which we could not make lasting by reason of our sins, we should to some extent make binding by at least exempting certain days. In the year of the Lord's incarnation, 1085, in the 8th indiction, it was decreed by God's meditation, the clergy and people unanimously agreeing ; that from the 1st day of the Advent of our Lord until the end of the day of the Epiphany, and from the beginning of Septuagesima until the 8th day after Pentecost, and throughout the whole day, and on every Thursday, Friday, Saturday and Sunday, until sunrise on Monday, and on the day of the fast of the four seasons, and on the eve and the day canonically set apart, or in future to be set apart, for fasting or for celebrating,—this decree of peace shall be observed. . . . No one, no matter on account of what wrong he shall be at feud, shall . . . presume to bear as weapons a shield, sword or lance—or, in fact, the burden of any armour. . . . If it shall happen that a castle is being besieged, the besiegers shall cease from the attack during the days included in the peace, unless they are attacked by the besieged, and are obliged to beat them back. . . .[1]

The Emperor Henry V. *Decree Concerning a Truce of God,*[2] *1085.*

[1] "Pope Nicholas, in his answer to the Bulgarians, forbids them to make war in Lent, unless, he prudently adds, there be an urgent necessity." —Isaac D'Israeli, *Curiosities of Literature.*

[2] *Select Historical Documents of the Middle Ages,* translated and edited by Ernest F. Henderson.

A WHOLESOME APPREHENSION

HE (Henry II.) was a prince of such admirable religious sense that whenever he conquered in battle it was only to be overcome in turn by his gratitude to Heaven. Though

strenuous in war, he prudently tried to avoid it when at
peace ; for during hostilities he always had a wholesome
apprehension of the uncertainty of the issue, and from his
extreme caution he would, in the words of the comic poet,[1]
" try all means rather than resort to arms."

> Gerald de Barri (*Giraldus Cam-
> brensis*). *Expugnatio Hibernica,
> 1189.*

"In Normandy, a few days before the death of Henry II., the fish
of a certain pool near Seez, five miles from the castle of Exme, fought
during the night so furiously with each other, both in the water and
out of it, that the neighbouring people were attracted by the noise to
the spot; and so desperate was the conflict, that scarcely a fish was found
alive in the morning; thus, by a wonderful and unheard-of prognostication, foretelling the death of one by that of many."—*Itinerarium
Kambriae.*

[1] Ter. *Eun.*, iv, 7, 19.

HOW WAR BEGAN

ERE long the unhappy human race
Corrupted grew, and every trace
Of simple living lost, they came
To be false tricksters, void of shame ;
The land they set about to share
In seigniories, and here and there
Fixed lines and limitations, but
Thereout full many a man was shut.
And next they fell to war thereon,
And each man kept whate'er he won
By force or fraud, and thus the strong
Beat back the weak—if right or wrong.

> Jean de Meun, *fl. 1230-1270.
> The Romance of the Rose. Tr. F. S.
> Ellis, 1900.*

INCREASE OF WOES

NOUGHT knew they more of soft-eyed peace,
For growth of wealth but brought increase

Of woes, and things that late were free
As sun and wind and unchained sea,
Through avarice of wealth were set
Apart, each strove good share to get.
Oft one man more than twenty had,
Which doth but shadow forth a bad
And selfish heart. Such cruel gluttons
I count not worth a deuce of buttons.

Ibid.

HERETIC

AFTER this the heretic draws a comparison between the
circumstances of the Romish Church and those of his sect ;
saying thus, " The Doctors of the Romish Church are
proud in their dress and carriage. . . . They love the chief
seats, and seek to be called of men Rabbi,—but such Rabbis
we do not desire to have. . . . Also, they fight, and make
wars, and command the poor to be killed and burned, to
whom it is said, ' He that taketh the sword shall perish by
the sword '; we, however, suffer from them persecution
for righteousness."

Reinerius Saccho.[1] *Of the Sects
of Modern Heretics, 1254. (Bib.
Pat. Tom. IV.). Tr. S. R.
Maitland.*

[1] Reinerius was once a leader of the Cathari, who believed "that it is
a mortal sin to eat flesh, or eggs, or cheese, even in case of urgent necessity.
. . . Also it is a common opinion of all the Cathari, that whosoever kills
a bird, from the least to the greatest, or quadrupeds, from the weasel
to the elephant, commits a great sin; but they do not extend this to
other animals."—S. R. Maitland, *Facts and Documents illustrative of the
History, Doctrine and Rites of the Ancient Albigenses and Waldenses,* 1832.

SACRED TRUMPETERS

PRELATES and clerics may, by the authority of their
superiors, take part in wars, not indeed by taking up arms
themselves, but by affording spiritual help to those who

fight by exhorting and absolving them, and by other like
spiritual helps. Thus in the Old Testament (Jos. vi. 4.)
the priests were commanded to sound the sacred trumpets
in the battle. It was for this purpose that bishops or clerics
were first allowed to go to the front ; and it is an abuse
of this permission if any of them take up arms themselves. . . .

Every power, art or virtue that regards the end, has to
dispose that which is directed to the end. Now, among the
faithful, carnal wars should be considered as having for
their end the Divine spiritual good to which clerics are
deputed. Wherefore it is the duty of clerics to dispose and
counsel other men to engage in just wars. For they are
forbidden to take up arms, not as though it were a sin, but
because such an example is unbecoming their personality.

Although it is meritorious to wage a just war, nevertheless
it is rendered unlawful for clerics, by reason of their being
deputed to works more meritorious still. Thus the marriage
act may be meritorious ; and yet it becomes reprehensible
in those who have vowed virginity, because they are bound
to a yet greater good.

> St. Thomas Aquinas. *Summa
> Theologica*, (*Pt. II, Q. 40, Art. 2*).
> *1265. Tr. by the Fathers of the
> English Dominican Province.*

The Angelic Doctor had two soldier brothers, who once goaded him
into active self-defence. Alban Butler says: "They secretly introduced
into his chamber one of the most beautiful and most insinuating
strumpets in the country. . . . The saint, alarmed and affrighted at the
danger, profoundly humbled himself, and cried out to God most earnestly
for his protection; then snatching up a firebrand, struck her with it
and drove her out of his chamber."

TROOPS RETURNING

IF you could see, fair brother, how dead beat
   The fellows look who come through Rome to-day,—
   Black yellow smoke-dried visages,—you'd say
They thought their haste at going all too fleet.
Their empty victual-waggons up the street

Over the bridge, dreadfully sound and sway ;
  Their eyes, as hanged men's, turning the wrong way ;
And nothing on their backs, or heads, or feet.
One sees the ribs and all the skeletons
  Of their gaunt horses ; and a sorry sight
Are the torn saddles, crammed with straw and stones.
  They are ashamed, and march throughout the night ;
Stumbling, for hunger, on their marrowbones ;
  Like barrels rolling, jolting, in this plight.
Their arms all gone, not even their swords are saved ;
And each as silent as a man being shaved.[1]

Niccolo Degli Albizzi, *1300*.
Tr. D. G. Rossetti.

[1] "Je trouve, à la gare du chemin de fer de Saint-Lazare, un groupe d'un vingtaine de zouaves, débris d'un bataillon qui a donné sous Mac-Mahon. Rien n'est beau, rien n'a du style, rien n'est sculptural, rien n'est pictural comme ces éreintés d'une bataille. Ils portent sur eux une lassitude en rien comparable à aucune lassitude, et leurs uniformes sont usés, déteints, délavés, ainsi que s'ils avaient bu le soleil et la pluie d'années entières."—Edmond de Goncourt, *Journal*, August 23, 1870.

      Now let not Nature's hand
Keep the wild flood confin'd ! let order die !
And let this world no longer be a stage
To feed contention in a lingering act ;
But let one spirit of the first-born Cain
Reign in all bosoms, that, each heart being set
On bloody courses, the rude scene may end,
And darkness be the burier of the dead !

       Shakespeare. *Henry IV., Pt. 2.*

Now let not Nature's hand
Keep the wild flood confin'd! let order die!
And let this world no longer be a stage
To feed contention in a lingering act;
But let one spirit of the first-born Cain
Reign in all bosoms, that, each heart being set
On bloody courses, the rude scene may end,
And darkness be the burier of the dead!

Shakespeare. *Henry IV.*, Pt 2.

IN SEDENTARY QUIETNESS

It has been sufficiently shown that the proper work of the human race, taken as a whole, is to keep the whole capacity of the possible intellect constantly actualised ; primarily for speculation, and secondarily (by extension, and for the sake of the other), for action.

And since it is in the whole as it is in the part ; and in fact, it is in sedentary quietness that the individual man is perfected in knowledge and wisdom ; it is evident that the human race can most freely and easily approach to its proper work (which is almost divine, even as it is said " thou hast made him a little lower than the angels"), in the quiet or tranquillity of peace. Wherefore it is manifest that universal peace is the blest of all those things which are ordained for our blessedness. Hence it is, that there sounded to the shepherds from on high, not riches, not pleasures, not honours, not length of life, but peace. For the celestial soldiery says—" Glory to God in the highest ; and, on earth, peace to men of good will." Hence also, " peace be with you ! " was the salutation of Him who was the salvation of men.

Dante Alighieri. *De Monarchia. c.*
1310. Tr. P. H. Wickstead, 1896.

ARBITRATION ORDERED

Desist from war ; and if you believe yourselves to have a just cause, pursue it by the way of justice before a competent judge or else consent to submit it to the arbitration of mutual friends.

Urban V., *Bull, 1369.*

WYCLIFFE ON WAR

In the old law men fought with God's enemies, to avenge God's injuries, and by no other cause, and neither will men now if their fighting be lawful. . . . " Men shall break their swords into ploughshares, and learn war no more "— yet Antichrist argues to keep men fighting, though humanity teaches that men should not fight. Their saying is—Since an adder by his nature stings a man that treads on him, why should not we fight against our enemies, for else they will destroy us ? What man that hath wit cannot see this fallacy ? Well I know that angels withstood fiends, and many men with right of law withstand their enemies, and yet they kill them not, neither fight with them ; and wise men of the world hold it well thus to vanquish their enemies without striking ; and wise men of the Gospel vanquish by patience, and come to rest and peace by suffering death. Well I know that worldly men will scorn this sentence, but men who would be martyrs for the law of God will hold with it. . . .

Lord ! what honour falls to a knight that he kills many men ?—the hangman killeth more, and with a better title.

John Wycliffe. *Of the Seven Deadly Sins. c. 1383.*

"The argument of Wycliffe seems to involve, to the full, the Quaker principle on the subject of war. He admits that God ' has approved that knights should defend His law by strength,' but insists that He has not granted them permission to ' kill any man.' . . . Wycliffe, it is plain, was not insensible to the difficulties attendant on the principle which he thus advocates, but he appears to have been prepared to abide by the worst supposable consequences of it, rather than consent to see the substitution of the war principle, in any shape, in its room. What is called the right of conquest, he treats as only so much robbery on a larger scale. If the Almighty should ' bid conquest,' such a title might become valid, not otherwise."—Robert Vaughan, D.D., *Tracts and Treaties of John de Wycliffe, D.D.,* 1845.

MADE IN HEAVEN

As to the . . . question . . . where was battle first founden,—I answer thus, that it was founden in heaven.

. . . And in this manner, first when the great God, father of heaven, made the angels He made one so fair and so glorious that through the great beauty of him he passed all angels and other creatures that ever God made in beauty, and therefore was he called Lucifer. . . .

Our lord God Almighty, which quickly kenned his thought and purpose, ordained the battle against him. . . . Wherefore it should not be great marvel to see great wars and battles in this world, since battle was first made against God himself in heaven.

> Honoré Bonet. *L'Arbre des*
> *Batailles, 1387. Tr. Sir Gilbert*
> *Hay.*[1]

[1] "The Buke of the Laws of Armys," Scottish Texts Society, ed. J. H. Stevenson, 1901. Whole chapters from Honoré Bonet were reproduced by Christine de Pisan in *Le Livre des faits d'armes et de chevalerie.* See extracts on p. 51 *et seq.*

THE LAW AND THE SPIRIT

Confessor :
> The law stood ere we were bore
> How that a king's sword is bore
> In sign that he shall defend
> His true people, and make an end
> Of such as would them devour.
> Lo thus, my son, to succour
> The law, and common right to win,
> A man may slay without sin . . .
> And over this for his country
> In time of war a man is free
> Himself, his house, and eke his land
> Defend with his own hand,
> And slay, if that he may no better,
> After the law which is set.

Amans :
> Now, father, then I you beseech
> Of them that deadly wars seek
> In world's cause, and shed blood,
> If such an homicide is good.

Confessor :

My son, upon thy question
The truth of mine opinion . . .
I will thee tell in evidence
To rule with thy conscience.
The high God of his justice
That ilk foul horrible vice
Of homicide he hath forbade
By Moses as it was bade.
When God's son also was bore
He sent his angels down therefore
Whom the shepherds heard sing,
Peace to the men of wellwilling
In earth be among us here.
So for to speak in this matter
After the law of charity,
There shall no deadly war be :
And eke nature it hath defended
And in his law peace commended.
Which is the chief of man's wealth,
Of man's life, of man's health.
But deadly war hath his covin
Of pestilence and of famine,
Of poverty and of all woe . . .
For all thing which God hath wrought
In Earth, war it brings to nought :
The church is burnt, the priest is slain,
The wife, the maid, is eke forlain,
The law is lore, and God unserved :
I not what mede he hath deserved
That such wars leadeth in.
If that he do it for to win,
First to account his great cost
Forth with the folk that he hath lost,
As to the world's reckoning
There shall he find no winning ;
And if he do it to purchase
The heaven mede, of such a grace
I can nought speak, and natheless

Christ hath commanded love and peace,
And he that worketh the reverse
I trow his mede is full diverse.
And sithen then that we find
That wars in their own kind
Be towards God of no desert,
And eke they bring in poverty
Of world's good, it is marvel
Among the men what it may ail
That they at peace ne can set.
I trow Sin be the let.
And every mede of Sin is death . . .
    Lo now, for what profit
Of war it helpeth for to ride
For covetise and world's pride
To slay the world's men about,
As beasts which go thereout.
For every life which reason can
Ought well to know that a man
Ne should through no tyranny
Like to these other beasts die,
Till kind would for him send.
I not how he it might amend
Which taketh away for evermore
The life that he may nought restore.

      John Gower. *Confessio Amantis,*
      Bk. III. 1390.

CABINET MEETING

Up rose an advocate that was wise, by leave and by counsel of other that were wise, and said : Lordings, the need for the which we ben assembled in this place, is a full heavy thing, and an high matter. . . . But certes for to moven war, ne suddenly for to do vengeance, we must not deem it so little time that it were profitable. Wherefore we axen leisure and space to have deliberation in this case to deem. . . .

Up start then the young folk at once, and the most part

of that company had scorned this wise old man, and begunnen to make noise and saiden : Right so as while that the iron is hot men should smite, right so men shulden do wreaken their wrongs, while that they ben fresh and new ; and with a loud voice they cried war, war. Up rose then one of these old wise, and with his hand made countenance that men should hold them still, and give him audience. Lordings (quod he) there is full many a man that crieth war, war, that wote full little what war amounteth. War at the beginning hath so great an entering and so large, that every wight may enter when him liketh, and lightly find war : but certes what end that shall befall, it is not light to know. For soothly when that war is once begun, there is full many a child unborn of his mother that shall starve young because of this war, other else live in sorrow and dien in wretchedness : and therefore or that any war be begun, men must have great counsel and great deliberation. And when this old man wend to enforcen his tale by reasons, well nigh all at once begun they to rise, for to breaken his tale, and bidden him full oft his words for to abridge.

> Geoffrey Chaucer. *The Tale of Melibeus. c. 1390.*

THE PLAIN AND MANIFEST DOCTRINE

I MARVEL why wise men, leaving the plain and manifest doctrine of Christ, whereby He teacheth patience, do seek corners of their own imagining, to the intent they may approve fightings and wars. . . .

How can a man say they may lawfully make war and kill their brethren for the temporal goods, which peradventure they unjustly occupy, or unjustly intend to occupy ? for he that killeth another to get those goods which another body unjustly occupieth, doth love more the very goods than his own brother ; and then he, falling from charity, doth kill himself spiritually ; if he go forward without charity to make war, then doth he evil, and to his own damnation. Wherefore he doth not lawfully nor justly in proceeding to the damnation of his own self and his brother, whom, though he seem unjustly to occupy the goods, yet he doth intend to kill.

> Walter Brute. *Declaration to John,*
> *Bishop of Hereford, 1391. (Foxe's*
> *Acts and Monuments, 1st Eng. ed. 1563).*

THE LAW OF MERCY

THAT manslaughter in war, or by pretended law of justice for a temporal cause, without spiritual revelation, is expressly contrary to the New Testament, which indeed is the law of grace and full of mercies. This conclusion is openly proved by the examples of Christ's preaching here on earth, for He specially taught a man to love his enemies, and to show them pity, and not to slay them. The reason is this, that for the most part, when men fight, after the first blow, charity is broken. And whoever dies without charity goes the straight road to hell. And beyond this we know well that no clergyman can by Scripture or lawful reason remit the punishment of death for one mortal sin and not for another; but the law of mercy, which is the New Testament, prohibits all manner of manslaughter, for in the Gospel : " It was said unto them of old time, Thou shalt not kill." The corollary is that it is indeed robbery of poor folk when lords get indulgences from punishment and guilt for those who aid their army to kill a Christian people in distant lands for temporal gain, just as we too have seen soldiers who run into heathendom to get them a name for the slaughter of men ; much more do they deserve ill thanks from the King of Peace, for by our humility and patience was the faith multiplied, and Christ Jesus hates and threatens men who fight and kill, when He says: " He who smites with the sword shall perish by the sword."

> *The Lollard Conclusions, No. 10.*
> *1394.*

"These Conclusions are said to have been presented in full Parliament by the Lollards in a little book about the year 1394; they are printed in the *Fasciculi Zizaniorum*, in the Rolls Series."—R. Trevor Davies, *Mediæval Documents.*

ADVICE TO A KING

SUSTAIN peace ought every man alive,
First for to set his liege lord in rest,
And eke those other men that they no strive ;
For so this world may stand at best.
What king that would be the worthiest,
The more he might our deadly war cease,
The more he should his worthiness increase.

Peace is the chief of all the world's wealth,
And to the heaven it leadeth eke the way ;
Peace is of soul and life the man's health . . .
My liege lord, take heed of that I say,
If war may be left, take peace on hand,
Which may nought be without God's send. . . .

For vain honour or for the world's good
They that whilom the strong wars made,
Where be they now ? Bethink well in thy mood.
The day is gone, the night is dark and fade,
Their cruelty, which made them then glad,
They sorrow now, and yet have nought the more ;
Their blood is shed, which no man may restore.

The war is mother of the wrongs all ;
It slayeth the priest in holy church at mass,
Forlieth the maid and doeth her flower to fall . . .
There is no thing whereof mischief may grow
Which is not caused of the war, I trow.

The war bringeth in poverty at his heels,
Whereof the common people is sore grieved ;
The war hath set his cart on those wheels
Where that fortune may not be believed.
For when men ween best to have achieved,
Full ofte it is all new to begin :
The war hath no thing siker, though he win. . . .

Ha, well is him that shed never blood,
But if it were in cause of righteousness :
For if a king the peril understood,
What is to slay the people, then I guess
The deadly wars and the heaviness
Whereof the peace disturbed is full oft
Should at some time cease and wax soft.

> John Gower. *To King Henry the
> Fourth in Praise of Peace. 1399.*

A WOMAN ON WAR

To the end that this present work by some envious might be reproached saying that it is but idleness and loss of time as to treat of things not lawful, first it is to wit if wars and battles, chivalry and feats of arms, of which thing we hope to speak, it is or not a thing just, for as in exercising of arms ben done many great evils, extortions and griefs, like as occasions ravin by forces, to burn by fire and infinite harms may seem to some that wars and battles should be accursed thing and not due. And therefore to answer this question, it is to wit that it appeareth manifestly that wars emprised by just cause be permitted and suffered of god, like as we have founden in the holy scripture in many places, how our lord himself ordained to captains of hosts that which they should do against their enemies. . . . Also the holy escripture saith of god that he is fierce and governor of hosts and battles. And war and battle which is made by just quarrels is none other thing but right execution of justice. . . . And as touching the harms and evils that ben done above the right and droit of war, like as other authors sayen, that cometh nothing of the right of war but by evilness of the people that usen it. . . .

> Christine de Pisan.[1] *Le Livre des
> Faits d'Armes et de Chevalerie.
> c. 1408-9. Tr. William Caxton,
> 1489.*[2]

[1] She also wrote of Peace: "Commencé de 1er septembre 1412, le *Livre de la Paix* fut achevé en 1414 et dédié à Louis, duc de Guyenne, dauphin

... ' *Le Livre de la Paix*, dit Thomassy, est l'ouvrage où Christine porte
au plus haut degré l'autorité que donnent le talent et l'amour du bien
public ... Elle donne des leçons de prudence pour le maintien de la
pacification d'Auxerre; elle parle des vertus de justice, de magnanimité
et de force pour les chevaliers; elle parle du gouvernement du peuple
conformément aux trois vertus de clémence, libéralité et justice. ...'
Dans l'ouvrage figurent des citations latines de Sénèque, de Salluste, de
Cassiodore et d'autres auteurs, citations qui sont accompagnées d'une
traduction en français."—Ernest Nys, *Christine de Pisan, et ses Principales
Oeuvres*, Brussels, 1914.

[2] *The Book of Fayttes of Armes and of Chyualrye*, ed. A. T. P. Byles,
E.E.T.S., Or. Ser. 189, 1937.

SOME EXEMPLARS

Scipio Africanus answered to one that wited him that
little he did of his hands in a battle, " My mother," said
he, " childed me as an emperor, and not as a fighter."
. . . Gaius Marius answered to an Almayne that called
him to fight with him body against body, " If my life
were noxious unto me I should have found the means long
syne for to have been slain." . . . And to me it seemeth
that to the purpose of these things may well serve that
that the wise Charles the fifth king of France said when
men said unto him that a great shame it was that with
money he recovered his fortresses that some of his enemies
held and kept from him wrongfully, seeing that he was of
might great enough for to have recovered them by strength,
" It seemeth me," said he, " that which may be bought
ought not to be bought with men's blood."

Ibid.

THE CIVIL POPULATION

I ask thee[1] when a king or a prince hath war against
another though that it be just, whether he may by right
over run the country of his enemy taking all manner of
folk prisoners, that is to wit them of the common poor
people as ben labourers, shepherds and such folk, and it

should seem that nay. For what reason ought they to bear the penance of that that they meddle not themselves, whereas they can not the craft or arms, nor is it not their office, nor they be not called for to judge of wars, and also wars comen not by such poor folk, but they be full sorry for it, as they that full fain would always live in good peace, nor they ask no more. So ought they then as me seemeth to be free thereof, like that of right ben priests religieuse and all folk of the church, by cause that their estate is not to intermit themselves of war. And with this what worship may this be nor what price of arms for to slay and run upon them that never bear harness nor could not help themselves withal, and that have none other office, but poor innocents to go to plough and labour the land and to keep the beasts.

To this I answer thee, supposing in this manner. We put case that the people of England would make no manner of help to their king for to grieve the king of France, and that the Frenchmen went upon them, without fail by right and reason and after the law they ought not to hurt nor misdo neither in body nor in goods of the people nor of them that they should know that had not meddled them self in nothing to help, neither by their goods nor by their counsel their king.

Ibid.

[1] Honoré de Bonet.

GIVE THEM EXAMPLE

How pleasant to god is of peace the mirth !
    What delight eke in peace and union
The prince of peace hath shewed in his birth,
    By angels' delightable song and soun ;
    Also, after his resurrection,
        He peace bade ; and when unto heaven he stigh,
        He left peace in earth truly. . . .

Alas ! also the great dissension,
    The piteous harm, the hateful discord,

That hath endured twixt this region
  And other lands christian ! he, that lord
Of realms all is, the author of concord
    And peace, sore is moved therewith ; but we
    Naught dreaden for to offend his majesty.

Of france and england, O christian princes,
  Syn that your style of worthiness is rung
Throughout the world, in all the provinces,
  If that of you might be read or sung
  That ye were one in heart, there nis no tongue
    That might express how profitable and good
    Unto all people it were of christian blood.

Give them ensamplen ! ye be their mirrors ;
  They follow you : what sorrow lamentable
Is caused of your wars' sharp showers
  There wot no wight, it is irreparable !
  O noble christian princes honourable,
    For him that for you suffered passion,
    Of christian blood, haveth compassion !

Alas ! what people hath your wars slain !
  What corns waste, and downtrod and shent !
How many a wife and maid hath been by lain !
  Castles down beat, and timbered houses brent,
  And drawen down, and all to-torn and rent !
    The harm ne may not reckoned be, ne told ;
    This war waxeth all to hoar and old. . . .

                    Thomas Occleve. *The Regement
                  of Princes, 1412.*

THIS VIRTUE CALLED PEACE

Peace is a princess, daughter to Charity,
  Keeping in rest cities and royal towns ;
  Folk that be froward setting in tranquillity ;
  Monarchies and famous regions

Peace preserveth them from divisions.
As saith the philosopher called Socrates,
Among all virtues making a description,
He most commendeth this virtue called peace.

Peace is a virtue patient and treatable,
Setting in quiet discord of neighbours ;
Froward faces peace maketh amiable,
Of thorny rosiers peace gathereth out the flowers,
Maketh the sword to rust of conquerors.
Provided by poets, not slow nor reckless,
And mediation of wise embassadors ;
The spear made blunt, brought in love and peace.

John Lydgate. *A Praise of Peace.*
c. *1430.*

IN NO WISE AND IN NO CASE

SOME of the lay party holden that no man should be slain
by any other man for any trespass ; but all slaughter upon
man is reserved to God. And also they holden that in
no wise and in no case battle is lawful, betwixt Christian
and Christian, neither betwixt Christian and heathen.

Reginald Pecock, D.D. *The
Represser of over myche blamyng
the Clergie.* c. *1449.*

MAN OF PEACE

CONRADUS PRIMUS reigned 20 years. He loved peace above
all things ; and therefore he made a law that who that
breaketh peace betwixt any princes he should lose his head.

John Capgrave. *Chronicle of
England.*[1] c. *1460.*

[1] Published in the Rolls Series, 1858. It begins at the beginning: "The
first man Adam was mad on a Friday, withoute modir, withoute fader,
in the feld of Damask."

CHILD OF WRATH

In the birth of this Edmund [1402] fell many wonder tokens ; for out of the floor of his father's stable came blood, and welled up so high that it covered the horses' feet ; and all the sheaths of swords and of daggers in the house were full of blood, and all the axes with red of blood. And when the said Edmund lay in his cradle he might not sleep, nor cease of crying, till he saw a sword ; and when he sat in his nurse's lap he would not be still till he had some instrument of war to play with.

> Anon. *A Chronicle of the Reigns of Richard II., Henry IV., and Henry V. c. 1461-1471.*

A LETTER FROM HOME

For God's love, if your brothers go overseas, advise them as ye think best for their safeguard. For some of them be young soldiers, and wote full little what it meaneth to be as a soldier and for to endure as a soldier should do. God save you all, and send me good tidings of you all. And send ye me word in haste how ye do, for I think long to hear of you.

> Margaret Paston. *To her son, Sir John, at Calais, May 23, 1475.*

AN ENGLISH TRAIT DURING WAR

They have a very high reputation in arms ; and from the great fear the French entertain of them, one must believe it to be justly acquired. But I have it on the best information, that when the war is raging most furiously, they will seek for good eating, and all their other comforts, without thinking of what harm might befall them.

> Anon. *Venetian Relation. c. 1500. Tr. C. A. Sneyd, Cam. Soc., 1857.*

INSTRUCTIONS TO A PAINTER

MAKE the beaten and conquered pallid, with brows raised and knit together, and let the skin above the brows be all full of lines of pain ; at the sides of the nose show the furrows going in an arch from the nostrils, and ending where the eye begins, and show the dilation of the nostrils which is the cause of these lines ; and let the lips be arched displaying the upper row of teeth, and let the teeth be parted after the manner of such as cry in lamentation. Show some one using his hand as a shield for his terrified eyes, turning the palm of it towards the enemy, and having the other resting on the ground to support his body ; let others be crying out with their mouths wide open, and fleeing away. Put all sorts of arms lying between the feet of the combatants, such as broken shields, lances, broken swords, and other things like these. Make the dead, some half-buried in dust, others with the dust all mingled with the oozing blood and changing into crimson mud ; and let the line of the blood be discerned by its colour, flowing in a sinuous stream from the corpse to the dust. Show others in the death agony, grinding their teeth and rolling their eyes, with clenched fists grinding against their bodies, and with legs distorted.

> Leonardo da Vinci. *Note-books,*
> *c. 1508.   Tr. Edward McCurdy,*
> *1906.*

ADVICE TO A PRINCE

A PRINCE then is to have no other design, nor thought, nor study, but War, and the Arts and Disciplines of it ; for indeed that is the only profession worthy of a Prince, and is of so much importance that it not only preserves those who are born Princes in their patrimonies, but advances men of private condition to that honourable degree. On the other side, it is frequently seen when

Princes have addicted themselves more to delicacy and softness than to Arms, they have lost all, and been driven out of their States, for the principal thing which deprives or gains a man authority is the neglect or profession of that Art. . . . Among other evils and inconveniences which attend when you are ignorant in war, it makes you contemptible, which is a scandal a Prince ought with all diligence to avoid. . . . He never therefore ought to relax his thoughts from the exercises of war, not so much as in time of peace, and indeed then he should employ his thoughts more studiously therein than in war itself. . . .

Niccolò Machiavelli. *Il Principe*, *1513*.

DIFFERENT ADVICE TO A PRINCE

The Prince who is truly Christian will first weigh the difference between men, born for peace and good will, and beasts, born to prey upon one another ; then the difference between man and Christian men. Let him further reflect how desirable, how beautiful, how wholesome is peace ; how calamitous and accursed, war : remembering what a host of sufferings even the most just war (if any war can be called just) brings in its train. Lastly, let him set aside impulse, calling reason to council long enough to compute accurately what the war will cost and whether—even if victory be certain, not always the case even with the best cause—its object is worth so much. Weigh the anxiety, the expense, the danger, the long and laborious preparation. You must assemble the barbarous and abandoned dregs of mankind, and, to appear more generous than your enemy, bribe and coax that most abject and execrable class of humanity, mercenaries ! The good Prince's fondest wish is to have subjects of the highest worth. But where is there so thorough and instantaneous a corrupter of manners as war ? He would see his people secure and prosperous. But while he learns to campaign, he is compelled to expose his young men to every danger, and often in one hour makes multitudes of orphans, widows, childless old men, beggars and mourners.

Erasmus. *Institutio Principis Christiani, 1516. Tr. Percy Ellwood Corbett, M.C., Grotius Society, 1921.*

A THING VERY BEASTLY

WAR or battle as a thing very beastly, and yet to no kind of beasts in so much use as to man, they do detest and abhor. And contrary to the custom almost of all other nations, they count nothing so much against glory as glory gotten in war. . . . They rejoice and avaunt themselves if they vanquish and oppress their enemies by craft and deceit. And for that act they make a general triumph, and as if the matter were manfully handled, they set up a pillar of stone in the place where they so vanquished their enemies, in token of the victory. For then they glorify, then they boast, and crack that they have played the men indeed, when they have so overcome as no other living creature but only man could : that is to say, by might and puissance of wit. For with bodily strength (say they) bears, lions, boars, wolves, dogs, and other wild beasts do fight.

Sir Thomas More. *Utopia, 1516. Tr. Ralph Robinson, 1551.*

PEACE SPEAKS

THOUGH I certainly deserve no ill-treatment from mortals, yet if the insults and repulses I receive were attended with any advantage to them, I would content myself with lamenting in silence my own unmerited indignities and man's injustice. But since, in forcing me away from them, they remove the source of all human blessings, and let in

a deluge of calamities on themselves, I am more inclined to
bewail their misfortune than complain of ill-usage to
myself ; and I am reduced to the necessity of weeping over
and commiserating those whom I wished to view rather
as objects of indignation than of pity.

For though rudely to reject one who loves them as I do
may appear to be savage cruelty ; to feel an aversion for
one who has deserved so well of them, base ingratitude ; to
trample on one who has nursed and fostered them with all
a parent's care, an unnatural want of filial affection ; yet
voluntarily to renounce so many and so great advantages
as I always bring in my train, to go in search of evils
infinite in number and shocking in nature, how can I
account for such perverse conduct but by attributing it to
downright madness ? We may be angry with the wicked,
but we can only pity the insane. What can I do but weep
over them ? And I weep over them the more bitterly
because they weep not for themselves. No part of
their misfortune is more deplorable than their insensibility
to it.

Erasmus. *Querela Pacis, 1517.*
Tr. Vicesimus Knox, D.D., 1802.

FIRST DESIRE IT

Upon the whole it must be said that the first and most
important step towards peace is sincerely to desire it.
They who once love peace in their hearts will eagerly
seize every opportunity of establishing or recovering it.
All obstacles to it they will despise or remove, all hardships
and difficulties they will bear with patience, so long as they
keep this one great blessing (including as it does so many
others) whole and entire. On the contrary, men, in our
times, go out of their way to seek occasions of war ; and
what makes for peace they run down in their sophistical
speeches, or even basely conceal from the public ; but
whatever tends to promote their favourite war system they

industriously exaggerate and inflame, not scrupling to propagate lies of the most mischievous kind, false or garbled intelligence, and the grossest misrepresentation of the enemy. I am ashamed to relate what real and dreadful tragedies in real life they found on these vile, despicable trifles ; from how small an ember they blow up a flame and set the world on fire. Then they summon before them the whole catalogue of supposed injuries received ; and each party views its own grievance with a glass that magnifies beyond all bounds ; but as for benefits received, they all fall into the profoundest oblivion as soon as received ; so that upon the whole an impartial observer would swear that great men love war for its own sake, with all their hearts and souls, provided their own persons are safe.

Ibid.

CIVILIAN INTO SOLDIER

MANY have been, and are still of opinion, that in the whole world no two things are more incongruous and dissimilar than a Civil and a Military life ; insomuch that many times when a man designs himself for a soldier he not only takes upon himself a new habit, but he changes his customs, his company, his manner of discourse, and leaves off all ways of civil conversation ; for he who would be light and nimble and ready for the execution of all sort of violence, looks upon a civil habit as improper and cumbersome ; civil customs are unsuitable to him who thinks them soft and effeminate and inconsistent with the life he proposes ; and indeed it would be undecent 'if a man whose business it is to look big, and hector, and fright the whole world with his oaths and his blasphemies, should carry himself demurely and behave himself with the usual gentleness and complacency of other men. . . .

Niccolò Machiavelli. *Arte della guerra, 1520. Tr. 1675.*

A GENERAL RULE

It is better to conquer an enemy by hunger than fighting, in which last victory fortune has more share than virtue or courage.[1]

Ibid.

[1] "The British blockade won the war; but the wonder is that the British blockhead did not lose it."—George Bernard Shaw, Preface to *O'Flaherty, V.C.*

A BUSINESS DIVINE IN ITSELF

It is very true that men write and say often what a curse war is. But they ought to consider how much greater is that curse which is averted by war. Briefly, in the business of war men must not regard the massacres, the burnings, the battles, and the marches, etc.—that is what the petty and simple do who only look with the eyes of children at the surgeon, how he cuts off the hand or saws off the leg, but do not see or notice that he does it in order to save the whole body. Thus we must look at the business of war or the sword with the eyes of men, saying, Why these murders and horrors? It will be shown that it is a business, divine in itself, and as needful and necessary to the world as eating or drinking, or any other work.

Martin Luther. *Whether soldiers can be in a state of salvation, 1526.*

"Luther created as a Nordic. Through a new fusion of Christian and German he created a new German culture. The first German culture. No longer Germanic, Western: German!"—Erich Czech-Jochberg, *Deutsche Geschichte, National-Sozialistisch gesehen,* 1933.

WHAT SPIRIT ARE YE OF?

Lord, wilt thou that we command that fire from heaven fall and consume them, as Elijah did. But Jesus turned to them and rebuked them, and said, Ye know not what spirit ye are of. The Son of Man is come not to destroy men's lives, but to save them.— Luke ix. 54, 55.

Here my brothers[1] make a great outcry, as if the devil were there, and say, " Now you see, Balthasar, that Christ did not wish to punish with fire. And so we ought not to do it, nor should we use fire, water, sword or gallows." *Answer*. Look further, dear brother, where Christ comes to the end, [and see] what was the authority and command given him by God. Do that and you shall already have an answer. Christ is come as He himself says, not to judge men, condemn them with fire, water or the sword. He did not become man for that. . . . The power and authority of the magistrate is given by God, that he should protect and guard the pious and punish the wicked ; therefore has he hung the sword at their side, and since it is at their side they must use it. . . . But the government has a special sympathy with all those who have transgressed ; it wishes from the heart that it had not happened ; while the devil and his followers wish that all men were unfortunate. Do you see then, brothers, how far separated from one another are these two kinds of servants, the devil and orderly governments? How also Christ wished to exercise His power on earth ?

Balthasar Hübmaier. On the Sword, 1527.

[1] "It was a curious feature of the teaching of these fanatical Anabaptists, that while they denied the right of the sword to magistrates and denounced all war as ' carnal,' they believed that when Christ should begin His millennial reign it would be not merely the right but the duty of his subjects to take up the sword and put the ungodly to slaughter." —Henry C. Vedder, *Balthasar Hübmaier*, 1905.

See also *The Unfortunate Traveller*, 1594, Thomas Nashe: "Verie devout Asses they were . . . and such as thought they knew as much of God's minde as richer men . . . and they count it flat hel fire for anie man to weare a dagger; nay, so grounded and gravelled were they in this opinion, that now when they should come to Battell, theres never a one of them would bringe a blade (no, not an onion blade) about him to die for it."

WHEN WAR IS PROCLAIMED

THE day that you princes proclaim war against your enemies, you set at liberty all vices to your subjects : yet you say your meaning is not they should be evil. I say it is true : yet all this joined together, ye give them occasion that they be not good. Let us know what thing war is, and then we shall see whether it be good or evil to follow it. In wars, they do naught else but kill men, rob the temples, spoil the people, destroy the innocents, give liberty to thieves, separate friends, and raise strife : all the which things cannot be done without great hurt of justice and scrupulosity of conscience. The seditious man himself cannot deny us, that if two princes take upon them wars between them, and that both of them seem to have right, yet the one of them only hath reason. So that the prince which shall fight against justice, or defend the unjust cause, shall not escape out of that war justified : not issuing out justified, he shall remain condemned : and the condemnation shall be that all the losses, murders, burnings, hangings, and robberies which were done in the one or other commonwealth, shall remain upon the account of him which took upon him the unjust war. Although he doth not find another prince that will demand an account of him here in this life, yet he shall have a just judge that will, in another place, lay it to his charge.

> Antonio de Guevara. *Lo Relox de Principes, 1520. Tr. Sir Thomas North (The Diall of Princes), 1557.*

THE LOSS OF GOOD MEN

THE divine Plato in his fourth book *De Legibus* sayeth that one demanded him why he did exalt the Lydians so much, and so much dispraise the Lacedemonians. Plato answered : " If I commend the Lydians, it is for that they never were occupied but in tilling the field, and if I do reprove here the Lacedemonians, it is because they never knew anything else but to conquer realms. And therefore I say that more happy is that realm where men have their hands with labouring full of blisters, than where their arms in fighting are wounded with swords."

These words which Plato spake are very true, and would to God that in the gates and hearts of princes they were written. Plinius in an epistle sayeth, that it was a proverb much used amongst the Greeks, that he was king which never saw king. The like may we say, that he only may enjoy peace, which never knew what war meant. For simple and innocent though a man be, there is none but will judge him more happy, which occupieth his handkerchief to dry the sweat of his brows ; than he that breaketh it to wipe the blood of his head. . . .

If the war were only with the evil against the evil, little should they feel which presume to be good. But I am sorry the good are persecuted, the good are robbed and the good are slain : for if it were otherwise (as I have said) the evil against the evil, we would take little thought both for the vanquishing of the one, and much less for the destruction of the other.

I ask now what fame, what honour, what glory, what victory, or what riches in that war can be won, wherein so many good, virtuous, and wise men are lost ? There is such a penury of the good in the world, and such need of them in the commonwealth, that if it were in our power, we with tears ought to pluck them out of their graves and give them life, and not lead them into the wars, as to a shambles to be put to death.

Ibid.

NOT ALLOWED

MEN of war are not allowed by the gospel ; the gospel knoweth peace and not war.

Anon. *Sum of Scriptures.*[1] *c. 1530.*

[1] "There came to light in 1530 a number of pieces of anti-Church literature which gathered up in a peculiar way the *message* of the Lollard preachers. These tracts in the reports of the Ecclesiastical Commission bear the titles: ' The Wicked Mammon,' ' The Obedience of a Cristen Man,' ' The Revelation of Anti-Christ,' and most important of all, the ' Sum of Scriptures.' This latter tract bears strong marks of Anabaptist influence, though it may be only the inward development of Lollardy." —Rufus Jones, *Studies in Mystical Religion.*

C

THE READING OF HISTORY

WARS and battles need not be studied closely, for they merely equip the mind with examples for the performance of evil, and show the ways in which we may inflict injuries, one on another. Yet we cannot help noticing briefly, who took up arms, who were the leaders on either side, where the conflict took place, who were beaten, and what happened to them. But whatever is said or read in history, wars should be regarded not otherwise than as cases of theft, as indeed they usually are, excepting perhaps when undertaken against thieves. Let the student give his attention to peaceful affairs, a far more satisfactory and fruitful study. . . .

> Juan Luis Vives.[1] *De Tradendis*
> *Disciplins, 1531. Tr. Foster*
> *Watson, 1913.*

[1] "In 1529 he dedicated his most typical political work to the Emperor Charles V., viz., his book on Concord and Discord amongst Mankind [*De Concordia in humano genere*, Antwerp, 1529.] In sustained eloquence, and with concentrated thought, Vives brings all his powers to bear upon the subject of universal peace amongst Christians. He is full of passion in his desire for the wars of princes to cease. . . . He attempts to induce Charles V. to use his vast power for the good of mankind, to become as it were in his own person the philosopher-prince of Plato, or, shall we say, to surpass the dreams of Sir Thomas More, by the transformation of the *Utopia* from the realms of fiction into an idealistic spirit which should animate the treatment of national and international problems in their practical issues in the whole life of Christian Europe."—Foster Watson, *Vives : on Education*, 1913.

CONSCIENTIOUS OBJECTORS

IT is essential for a just war that an exceedingly careful examination be made of the justice and the causes of the war and that the reasons of those who on grounds of equity oppose it be listened to. . . . For truth and justice in moral questions are hard of attainment, and so any careless treatment of them easily leads to error, an error which will be inexcusable, especially in a concern of great moment, involving danger and calamity to many, and they our neighbours, too, whom we are bound to love as ourselves. . . .

If a subject is convinced of the injustice of a war, he ought not to serve in it, for no one can authorise the killing of an innocent person. . . . Therefore soldiers also are not excused when they fight in bad faith. Again, it is not lawful to kill innocent citizens at the prince's command. Therefore not aliens either. . . .

Hence flows the corollary that subjects whose conscience is against the justice of a war may not engage in it whether they be right or wrong. This is clear, for " what is not of faith is sin." (*Romans*, ch. 14).[1]

> Francisco de Vitoria. *De Jure Belli, c. 1532. Tr. John Pawley Bate*.

[1] From *The Spanish Origin of International Law*, James Brown Scott, 1934.

CONTRARY TO THE GOSPEL

The time is not now as formerly to conquer the kingdoms of our neighbour princes, and to build up our own greatness upon the loss of our nearest Christian brother. This imitation of the ancient Herculeses, Alexanders, Hannibals, Scipios, Cæsars, and other such heroes, is quite contrary to the profession of the gospel of Christ, by which we are commanded to preserve, keep, rule and govern every man his own country and lands, and not in a hostile manner to invade others ; and that which heretofore the Barbarians and Saracens called prowess and valour we now call robbing, thievery, and wickedness.

> François Rabelais. *The Inestimable Life of the Great Gargantua, Bk. II., 1533. Tr. Urquhart and Motteux*.

THE FATHER OF ALL GOOD THINGS

VERY little withholds me from the opinion of good
Heraclitus, which affirmeth war to be the father of all good
things ; and therefore do I believe that war is in Latin
called *bellum*, not by antiphrasis, as some patchers of old
rusty Latin would have us to think, because in war there is
little beauty to be seen ; but absolutely and simply for
that in war appeareth all that is good and graceful, and
that by the wars is purged out all manner of wickedness
and deformity. For proof whereof the wise and pacific
Solomon could no better represent the unspeakable
perfection of the divine wisdom than by comparing it to
the due disposure and ranking of an army in battle array,
well provided and ordered.

> François Rabelais. *The Heroic
> Deeds and Sayings of the Good
> Pantagruel. Prologue to Bk. III.,
> 1546. Tr. Urquhart & Motteux.*

"Remembering the eloquent condemnation of warfare in *Gargantua*,
it is at first a little startling to read in this prologue such a passage. . . .
We should beware of treating this apparent *volte-face* too seriously. . . .
This Third Book has been printed by express permission of the King.
So Rabelais pleasantly pictures himself as unfit for military service but
as doing his little best for his country with his pen."—Francis Watson,
Laughter for Pluto, 1933.

HOLY GHOST DECLARES DEFENSIVE WARS LAWFUL

IT maketh no difference whether he be king or one of the
basest of the commonalty that invadeth another's country
into which he hath no right, and spoileth it like an enemy ;
all are alike to be taken and punished for robbers. This
therefore both natural equity and the rule of duty teacheth,
that Princes are armed not only to restrain private duties
with judicial punishment, but also to defend with war
the dominions committed to their charge, if at any time

they be enemy-like assailed. And such wars the holy
Ghost by many testimonies of scripture declareth to be
lawful. . . .

If we ought to perform much more than that heathen
man[1] required, which would have war to seem a seeking
of peace, truly we ought first to attempt all things ere we
ought to try the matter by war.

> John Calvin. *The Institutes of
> the Christian Religion. c. 1540.
> Tr. Thomas Norton, 1634.*

[1] Cicero.

NO THIRD WAY

WHAT shall the King's Majesty do ? Shall he take these
base and unsure conditions of peace ? I dare not but say,
Nay ; for I fear a miscontentment of the King's Majesty to
follow it. What mean I then ? To continue in war still ?
Herein I say this, that he that would move the King's
Majesty to continue in war alone against France and
Scotland, the Emperor being a doubtful friend, should not
well consider the preservation of the King-Majesty's
honour and estate. And yet, ye will say, either we must
take such a peace as we can get or, of necessity, continue
in war ; for there is no third way. Ye say truth ; and the
other two ways, whereof one must needs be, be so terrible
to advise in as I think no man dare speak on this or that
side, if he have no better stomach than I have. I have
written to you vehemently for peace, and I have noted
the sentence of one that said that the worst peace is
better than the best war ; but the peace the French
now offer is so far under foot in the first appearance, and
hath such a fear of the unsure observation of the
conditions, as I have before said, that I cannot take any
comfort in it.

> Stephen Gardiner. *To Sir
> William Paget. Nov., 1545.*

A CIVIL MEDICINE

A PRINCE in his heart must be full of mercy and peace, a virtue most pleasant to Christ, most agreeable to man's nature, most profitable for rich and poor.

For then the rich man enjoyeth with great pleasure that which he hath : the poor may obtain with his labour that which he lacketh. And although there is nothing worse than war, whereof it taketh his name, through the which great men be in danger, mean men without succour, rich men in fear, because they have somewhat : poor men in care, because they have nothing : and so every man in thought and misery : yet it is a civil medicine, wherewith a prince may from the body of his commonwealth put off that danger which may fall : or else recover again whatsoever it hath lost.

Roger Ascham. Toxophilus, 1545.

O NOBLE PEACE !

O NOBLE peace, what wealth bringest thou in, how do all things flourish in field and town, what forwardness of religion, what increase of learning, what gravity in counsel, what devise of wit, what order of manners, what obedience of laws, what reverence of states, what safeguard of houses, what quietness of life, what honour of countries, what friendship of minds, what honesty of pleasure hast thou always maintained, whose happiness we knew not, while now we feel thy lack, and shall learn by misery to understand plenty, and so to avoid mischief by the hurt that it bringeth, and learn to serve better, where rebellion is once known ; and so to live truly, and keep the king's peace.

Sir John Cheke. The Hurt of Sedition, 1549.

A GUN

VULCAN begat me. Minerva me taught.
Nature, my mother. Craft nourished me year by year.
Three bodies are my food. My strength is in nought.

Anger, Wrath, Waste, and Noise are my children dear.
Guess, friend ! what I am ? and how I am wrought ?
Monster of sea, or of land, or of elsewhere.
    Know me, and use me ; and I may thee defend !
    And if I be thine enemy, I may thy life end !

Sir Thomas Wyatt. Tottell's
Miscellany, 1557.

WHY WE ARE AT WAR

FOR this reason we have thought it necessary to call you to this meeting and tell you about the reasons for this war. Thus you will understand that we hate violence, desire peace and tranquillity, and that our reasons for this warfare not only are just but have been forced upon us unavoidably. Nor shall we tell you dreams and idle trifles such as our enemies delight in and foster. We shall lay before you the honest naked truth whose face, if one could see it, is more radiant than the morning or the evening star, truth who in the end must always prevail. God alone knows the hearts of men ; He looks into our loins and sees and knows that we do not lie. Nothing is dearer to us than peace, nothing more acceptable. Her name, as the orator says, is sweet, and she herself both pleasant and wholesome. In peace laws are observed, subjects protected, God is served, none do wrong with impunity ; virtue enjoys its due rewards and vice pays its due penalties. But war nourishes every kind of evil, and all things human and divine are confounded. We hate any war whose purpose is not peace, we loathe the slaughter of men, nor thirst for human blood. It is not for our See to draw the sword or to sow strife. Our heart has always sought tranquillity and peace among our subjects. But . . .[1]

Pius II. Commentaries, Bk. V.,
1560. Extract tr. by Flora Grierson,
1938.

[1] Ex uno disce omnes.

GLITTERING ARMS

LASTLY stood *War*, in glittering arms yclad,
With visage grim, stern looks, and blackly hued ;
In his right hand a naked sword he had,
That to the hilts was all with blood imbued ;
And in his left (that kings and kingdom rued)
Famine and fire he held, and therewithal
He razed towns, and threw down towers and all.

Cities he sacked, and realms (that whilom flowered
In honour, glory, and rule, above the best)
He overwhelmed, and all their fame devoured,
Consumed, destroyed, wasted and never ceased,
Till he their wealth, their nature, and all oppressed.[1]
His face forhewed with wounds, and by his side
There hung his targe, with gashes deep and wide.

Thomas Sackville, *Earl of Dorset,*
A Mirror for Magistrates, 1563.

[1] "Mankind, it seems, hates nothing so much as its own prosperity.
Menaced with an accession of riches which would lighten its toil, it
makes haste to redouble its labours, and to pour away the perilous stuff,
which might deprive of plausibility the complaint that it is poor. Applied
to the arts of peace, the new resources commanded by Europe during the
first half of the sixteenth century might have done something to exorcise
the spectres of pestilence and famine, and to raise the material fabric of
civilisation to undreamed-of heights. Its rulers, secular and ecclesiastical
alike, thought otherwise. . . . The sluice which they opened to drain
away each new accession of superfluous wealth was war." — R. H. Tawney,
Religion and the Rise of Capitalism, Holland Memorial Lectures, 1922.

ONE OF THE GREATEST PUNISHMENTS

I BELIEVE not that our posterity shall enjoy peace. God
turn His anger graciously from us, for War is one of the
greatest punishments, as that which devastateth and taketh
away Religion, temporal and domestic government ; it
layeth all in the dust. Dearth and Pestilence are fox-tails,

yea nothing in the compare of war. Pestilence is the most gracious and easiest punishment ; therefore David among three punishments made choice of Pestilence.

Martin Luther. *Table Talk.*
Ed. *John Aurifaber, 1569.* Tr.
Henry Bell, 1646.

THE STANDARD QUESTION[1]

A CHRISTIAN carrieth two kinds of persons, namely a believing or a spiritual person, the other a civil or temporal person. The believing or spiritual person ought to suffer and endure all things ; he neither eateth nor drinketh ; he begetteth no children, nor hath share and part in and about such doings and actions. But the temporal and civil person is subject to temporal rights and laws and is tied to obedience : he must maintain and defend himself and his according as the laws and rights do command. Now if in my presence and sight a wicked wretch should presume to force my wife or maid, as then truly I would lay aside the spiritual person and would make use of the temporal ; I would slay him in the act or call for help.[1]

Ibid.

[1] "Another favourite question asked by militarists is the following: ' What would you do if you saw a stranger break into your house and try to violate your wife?' This question might be answered as follows: ' Whatever else I might do—and it is quite evident that I should become very angry and try to knock the intruder down or even to kill him— I should certainly not send my brother to go and poison the man's grandfather and disembowel his infant son.' And that precisely is what war consists of—murdering, either personally or (more often) through the instrumentality of others, all kinds of people who have never done one any sort of injury."—Aldous Huxley, *An Encyclopædia of Pacifism,* 1937.

SUGGESTION OF THE DEVIL

CANNONS and firearms are cruel and damnable machines ; I believe them to have been the direct suggestion of the devil. Against the flying ball no valour avails ; the soldier

is dead ere he sees the means of destruction. If Adam had
seen in a vision the horrible instruments his children were
to invent he would have died of grief.[1]

Martin Luther. *Table Talk*,
1569. Ed. Hazlitt (Bohn).

[1] "Modern civilisation began with the invention of gunpowder. As
these black grains were scattered about, not other than as tiny acorns
over the earth, there sprang up oaks of national strength in the form of
armaments under which, protected from the vicissitudes and storms that
previously assailed national life as well as individual existence, the arts
and sciences of mankind flourished."—Homer Lea, *The Valor of Ignorance*,
1909.

WHAT THING IS WAR

THE Poets old in their fond fables feign
That mighty Mars is god of War and Strife,
These Astronomers think, where Mars doth reign,
That all debate and discord must be rife,
Some think Bellona goddess of that life :
So that some one, and some another judge
To be the cause of every grievous grudge. . . .

Well then, let see what saith the common voice,
These old said saws, of war what can they say ?
Who list to hearken to their whispering noise,
May hear them talk and tattle day by day,
The prince's pride is cause of war alway :
Plenty brings pride, pride plea, plea pine, pine peace,
Peace plenty, and so (say they) they never cease. . . .[1]

[1] This rigmarole is said to have been invented by the Welsh saint,
Cadoc. A version of it is given by Puttenham (Arte of English Poesie,
1589) as an example of "Clymax or the Marching Figure":

> Peace makes plenty, plenty makes pride,
> Pride breeds quarrel, and quarrel brings war.
> War brings spoil, and spoil poverty,
> Poverty patience, and patience peace:
> So peace brings war, and war brings peace.

Puttenham attributes it to "Jhean de Mehune, the French Poet." There
is another version in *Quodlibets*, Robert Hayman, 1630.

Then what is war? define it right at last,
And let us set all old said saws aside,
Let Poets lie, let Painters feign as fast,
Astronomers let mark how stars do glide,
And let these Travellers tell wonders wide :
But let us tell by trusty proof of truth,
What thing is war which raiseth all this ruth.

And for my part my fancy for to write,
I say that war is even the scourge of God,
Tormenting such as dwell in princely plight,
Yet not regard the reaching of his rod,
Whose deeds and duties oftentimes are odd,
Who range at random jesting at the just,
As though they reigned to do even what they lust.

Whom neither plague can pull into remorse,
Nor dearth can draw to mend what is amiss,
Within whose hearts no pity findeth force,
Nor right can rule to judge what reason is.
Whom sickness salveth not, nor bale brings bliss :
Yet can high Jove by waste of bloody war
Send schoolmasters to teach them what they are.

Then since the case so plain by proof doth stand,
That war is such, and such always it was,
How chanceth then that many take in hand
To joy in war, whiles greater pleasure pass ?
Who count the quiet burgher but an ass,
That lives at ease contented with his own,
Whiles they seek more and yet are overthrown. . . .

If pride make war (as common people prate)
Then is it good (no doubt) as good may be,
For pride is root of evil in every state,
The source of sin, the very fiend his fee,
The head of hell, the bough, the branch, the tree,
From which do spring and sprout such fleshy seeds,
As nothing else but moan and mischief breed.

But if war be (as I have said before)
God's scourge, which doth both Prince and people tame,
Then warn the wiser sort by learned lore,
To flee from that which bringeth naught but blame,
And let men count it grief and not a game,
To feel the burden of God's mighty hand,
When he concludes in judgment for to stand.

> George Gascoigne. *The Fruites
> of Warre : The Posies, 1575.*

"Among the lesser late poets, George Gascoigne's works may be endured."—Edmund Bolton, *Hypercritica.*

AUTHOR'S APOLOGY

I DOUBT not but a great number will think I have taken pain more than enough to write of wars, or of warlike disciplines, first because wars have ever been accounted a most grievous plague, and of itself is reputed so evil, so strange, and so pernicious that it comprehendeth and surmounteth all other kinds of evils : for it afflicteth as well the poor and innocents as those that be wicked and evil disposed ; for by it good laws are decayed, humanity is defaced, equity is suppressed, holy places are profaned, murders are committed, virgins are deflowered, chaste matrons are defiled, kingdoms be subdued, cities be ruinated. . . .

War, pestilence and famine are the three darts which the Almighty God is wont to shoot against the earth when He is displeased; and is holden so irksome amongst us that in our Litany we daily use the prayer, From plague, pestilence, famine, battle and murder, good Lord deliver us.

> Barnaby Rich. *Allarme to
> England,*[1] *1578.*

---

[1] *Foreshewing what perilles are procured, where the people live without regarde of Martiall lawe.*

IN ONE WORD

A SECOND reason why I should be condemned is this : because as the war of itself is an evil, and that so loathsomely detested, even so, to be professors, followers, and ministers in the same, is esteemed a thing more fit for ruffians, rioters, blasphemers, and people of the vilest condition, rather than an exercise for honest men, in whom there is any fear of God, or any love towards their neighbours : in so much that Cornelius Agrippa saith, that if you would call a tyrant, a blasphemer, a murderer, a robber, a spoiler, a deflowerer, an oppressor, with many other such like ; if you would (saith he) include all these into one short name, you may call him by the name of a soldier. . . .

Ibid.

FOR THE SCRUPULOUS

THEN first to speak of war, because I know there be many whose conscience be so scrupulous that they think no wars may be lawfully attempted, allowed of by God's word, or agreeing with true christianity, for the number of outrages which by it are committed.

I think it therefore convenient to see what proofs may be alleged in the defence of war, although not in general, yet in the holy scriptures where they have been allowed of, and many times commanded by the almighty God himself. . . .[1]

Ibid.

[1] Rich repeats most of these "proofs" in his *Fruites of Long Experience*. See extracts on p. 99.

A GENTLE RECOMPENSE

THAT noble gentleman, Sir William Drury, a paragon of arms at this day, was wont (I remember) to say that the soldiers of England had always one of three ends to look for : to be slain, to beg, or to be hanged. No doubt a gentle recompense for such merit. Yet want there not some that dare affirm it a vain burden to a commonwealth to maintain soldiers, as the common disturbers and hinderers of public peace. Such a one was sometime Sir Thomas More who having more skill in sealing of a writ than surveying of a Cape, was not ashamed most unwisely to write (if I may so speak of so wise a man) that the common labourer of England, taken from the plough, was he that when it came to the matter, did the deed.

> Barnaby Googe. *Letter to Barn-
> aby Rich in the latter's Allarme to
> England, 1578.*

FOR MARTIAL MINDS

THE wars for martial minds, and peace for Venus' men.
The sword and soldier best agrees, the lawyer for the pen.
The wars call courage up, and peace breeds cowards still,
Makes people proud, destroys great hearts, and pampers
    wanton will.
Peace prowls about for pence, and wars the muck will spend
That greedy gain hoards up in holes, God knows to little
    end.
The wealth that peace doth bring makes many a mischief
    rife,
And peace runs headlong into vice, and wars reform lewd
    life . . .
The naughty natured wight by wars is brought to frame,
The baddest puts on better mind, the wildest waxeth tame.
Peace fills the land with pomp that gives a privy wound,
Feeds folly fat, makes virtue lean, and floods of vice abound.
Dame Lust her pleasure takes, in peace and banquets sweet,
And wars doth quench our hot desires, and daunts the
    dallying sprite.
In wars we honour win, on peace reproach doth grow,
And war contents our noblest friends, and peace doth please
    our foe . . .

Not many hold with peace, though war is called a shrew,
Nor many are by peace made rich, for wealth but falls to
    few . . .
If any win by wars (as divers do indeed)
They lose the same again by peace ; thus peace mislike
    doth breed. . . .

> Thomas Churchyard. *Commendatory Verses prefixed to Barnaby Rich's Allarme to England, 1578.*

IDLE BELLIES

THE nature and due honour of military profession being such, what meaneth the vulgar multitude of the English nation so maliciously to contemn soldiership, and so bravely to despise the profession of arms, as a vile, and damnable occupation ? Surely because they are of servile and unnoble hearts, foolish in discretion, idle bellies, careless of the common wealth of their country, little friendship to mankind in general, and less zealous towards the glory and preservation of their sovereign Prince and government. . . .

If then I say the rural man, by bribes, by a livery coat, by frank laboured friendship, by counterfeit sickness, or by starting from his house under colour of far business, doth shift himself from under the ordinances of the prince, in so high and provident discretion, he is not only to be counted a contemner of Arms, but is also (whether he be gentleman or yeoman) to be rebuked with discredit either as a slothful coward, or else to be punished with stripes, as a traitorous contemner of his sovereign prince and country.

If the citizen or townsman do in like wise put forth his apprentice, his servant, or poor hireling, to supply his place, and so withdraweth his own person from the royal ordinances (being himself of commendable sufficiency in

body had it an honest heart) he is to be noted either a
fearful coward, and dare not deal with Arms, or else a
slothful beast. . . .

> Geffrey Gates. *The Defence of
> Militarie Profession, 1579.*

ARMS AND LETTERS

I FIND Rome to have been most valiant when it was least
learned. The most warlike nations of our days are the
rudest and most ignorant. The Scythians, the Parthians,
and Tamburlane serve to verify my saying. When the
Goths overran and ravaged Greece that which saved all
their libraries from the fire was that one amongst them
scattered this opinion, that such trash of books and papers
must be left untouched and whole for their enemies, as the
only mean and proper instrument to divert them from all
military exercises, and amuse them to idle, secure and
sedentary occupations.

> Michael de Montaigne. *Essays,
> I., xxv., 1580. Tr. John Florio,
> 1603.*

ALL THIS HURLY-BURLY

THIS horror-causing array of so many thousands of armed
men, so great fury, earnest fervour, and undaunted courage
—it would make a man laugh to see by how many vain
occasions it is raised and set on fire, and by what light
means it is again suppressed and extinguished. . . .

The hatred of one man, a spite, a pleasure, a familiar
suspect, or a jealousy—causes which ought not to move
two scolding fish-wives to scratch one another—is the soul
and motive of all this hurly-burly.

> *Ibid, Bk. II., xii.*

GLORY OR IMBECILITY

As for war, which is the greatest and most glorious of all human actions, I would fain know if we will use it for an argument of some prerogative, or otherwise for a testimonial of our imbecility and imperfection, as in truth the science we use to defeat and kill one another, to spoil and utterly to overthrow our own kind, it seemeth it hath not much to make itself to be wished for in beasts that have it not.

Ibid, Bk. II., xii.

PANICAL TERRORS

SUNDRY are the casualties of this present world, the trials many and fearful which we are subject unto. But in the midst of all, this must be the chiefest anchor unto our souls. " The just shall live." Wherefore this God setteth before the eyes of his poor afflicted people as having in it force sufficient to countervail whatsoever misery they either did or might sustain. Those dreadful names of troubles, wars, invasions, the very mention whereof doth so much terrify ; weigh them with hearts resolved in this, that " the just shall live," and what are they but panical terrors ?

Richard Hooker. *Sermon on the Nature of Pride, c. 1586.*

PEACE ! PEACE !

I SEE we shall starve on every side. . . . It is no marvel our men run fast away. I am ashamed to write it, but there was 500 ran away in two days, and a great many to the enemy, of which sort I have taken six. . . . There is of our runagates 200 brought again from the coast-side. Divers I hanged before the rest, and I assure you they could have been content all to have been hanged rather than tarry. Our old ragged rogues here hath so discouraged

our new men as, I protest to you, they look like dead men.
God once deliver me well of this charge, and I will hang
too if I take charge of men and not be sure of better pay
aforehand. I assure you it will fret me to death ere long
to see my soldiers in this case, and cannot help them. I
cry now, " Peace, peace ! " For never was there such a
war and a cause so slenderly countenanced ; but God will
help us I trust.

> Robert Dudley, *Earl of Leycester*.
> *To Mr. Secretary Walsingham,*
> *July 8, 1586.*

ZEAL

THE commonwealth requireth some to betray, some to
lie, and some to massacre : leave we that commission to
people more obedient and more pliable. . . .
But we ought not to term duty (as nowadays we do) a
sour rigour and intestine crabbedness, proceeding of
private interest and passion : nor courage a treacherous
and malicious proceeding. Their disposition to frowardness
and mischief they entitle zeal. That's not the cause doth
heat them—'tis their own interest. They kindle a war, not
because it is just, but because it is war.

> Michael de Montaigne. *Essays,*
> *Bk. III., i., 1588. Tr. John Florio.*

PEARLS AND PEPPER

So many goodly cities ransacked and razed ; so many
nations destroyed and made desolate ; so infinite millions
of harmless people of all sexes, states and ages, massacred,
ravaged and put to the sword : and the richest, the fairest
and the best part of the world topsiturvied, ruined and
defaced for the traffic of pearls and pepper ! O, mechanical
victories, O base conquest !

> *Ibid, Bk. III., vi.*

YOU HAVE BEEN WARNED

A GIFT divine, than pearl more worth
Is blessed peace, to discord deadly foe ;
Most plenteous fruits this blooming tree brings forth,
When war and strife yield crops of care and woe ;
Rash rancour's rage procures fond furious fights ;
Peace makes men swim in seas of pure delights. . . .

If England would perpend the bloody broils
And slaughters huge that foreign realms have tried,
It should meseems be warned by their turmoils
In perfect love and concord to abide ;
But out, alas ! my heart doth rue to tell
Small fear of God amongst us now doth dwell.

Humphrey Gifford. A Posie of
Gilloflowers, 1589.

TAMBURLAINE

THE first day when he pitcheth down his tents,
White is their hue, and on his silver crest,
A snowy feather spangled white he bears,
To signify the mildness of his mind,
That, satiate with spoil, refuseth blood.
But when Aurora mounts the second time
As red as scarlet is his furniture ;
Then must his kindled wrath be quenched with blood,
Not sparing any that can manage arms ;
But if these threats move not submission,
Black are his colours, black pavilion ;
His spear, his shield, his horse, his armour, plumes,
And jetty feathers, menace death and hell !
Without respect of sex, degree, or age,
He razeth all his foes with fire and sword.

Christopher Marlowe. Tam-
burlaine the Great,[1] Pt. I., 1590.

[1] Elsewhere in the same play Marlowe presented the unromantic side
of war:

Mycetes: Accursed be he that first invented war!
　　They knew not, ah they knew not, simple men,
　　How those were hit by pelting cannon shot
　　Stand staggering like a quivering aspen leaf. . . .
cf. also *Hero and Leander*:
　　And as in fury of a dreadful fight,
　　Their fellows being slain or put to flight,
　　Poor soldiers stand with fear of death dead strooken.

CONSCIENTIOUS OBJECTOR

Amyras :
　　What, dar'st thou then be absent from the fight,
　　Knowing my father hates thy cowardice,
　　And oft hath warned thee to be still in field
　　When he himself amidst the thickest troops
　　Beats down our foes to flesh our taintless swords ?
Caliphus :
　　I know, sir, what it is to kill a man,
　　It works remorse of conscience in me.
　　I take no pleasure to be murderous,
　　Nor care for blood when wine will quench my thirst.
　　　　　　　　　　　　　　　　　Ibid. Pt. II.

PEACE OBSCURED

THE husband's scythe was changed to a sword,
　　The cobbler's awl into a sturdy lance ;
Peace was obscured, of war was every word ;
　　All prayed to fortune for successful chance,
　　　　That sits enthroned on her inconstant seat,
　　　　And helps them most who least her help entreat.

As when to purge excessive moist descending,
　　From Saturn's sphere, or else superfluous heat,
Jove stirred up by Mars (common good intending)
　　Sends lightning-flash to lay their angry threat,
　　　　So wiser heads that knew the scourge of war
　　　　Sought soothfast means to mitigate the jar.

But as a troop of fierce incensed bulls
  The herdsman's strokes and threats do set at naught,
So those whose rancorous rage their judgment dulls
  Had little thought to peace or peaceful thought.
     " Who fights for crowns, set life, set all to light.
     Who aim so high will die or hit the white."

Thomas Lodge. *The Complaint of Elstred, 1593.*

SONG FOR BETA

Range all thy swans, fair Thames, together on a rank,
And place them duly one by one, upon thy stately bank ;
    Then set together all a-good,
    Recording to the silver flood,
And crave the tuneful nightingale to help you with her lay,
The ousel and the throstlecock, chief music of our May.

O ! see what troops of nymphs been sporting on the strands,
And they been blessed nymphs of peace, with olives in their
    hands.
    Now merrily the Muses sing,
    That all the flowery meadows ring,
And Beta sits upon the bank, in purple and in pall,
And she the Queen of Muses is, and wears the coronal.

Trim up her golden tresses with Apollo's sacred tree.
O happy sight unto all those that love and honour thee,
    The blessed angels have prepared
    A glorious crown for thy reward,
Not such a golden crown as haughty Cæsar wears,
But such a glittering starry crown as Ariadne bears. . . .

See how the day stands still, admiring of her face,
And Time, lo ! stretcheth forth her arms, thy Beta to
    embrace ;
    The sirens sing sweet lays,
    The tritons sound her praise.

Go pass on, Thames, and hie thee fast unto the ocean
    sea,
And let thy billows there proclaim thy Beta's holiday :

And water thou the blessed root of that green olive
    tree,
With whose sweet shadow all thy banks with peace preserved
    be,
        Laurel for poets and conquerors,
        And myrtle for love's paramours,
That fame may be thy fruit, the boughs preserved by
    peace ;
And let the mournful cypress die, now storms and tempest
    cease.

> Michael Drayton. *The Shep-
> herd's Garland, 1593.*

TIMBRELS OF DELIGHT

Friar Bacon :
    I find by deep prescience of mine art,
    Which once I tempered in my secret cell,
    That here where Brute did built his Troynovant,
    From forth the royal garden of a king
    Shall flourish out so rich and fair a bud,
    Whose brightness shall deface proud Phœbus' flower,
    And over-shadow Albion with her leaves.
    Till then Mars shall be master of the field,
    But then the stormy threats of wars shall cease :
    The horse shall stamp as careless of the pike,
    Drums shall be turned to timbrels of delight ;
    With wealthy favours plenty shall enrich
    The strand that gladded wandering Brute to see,
    And peace from heaven shall harbour in these leaves
    That gorgeous beautify this matchless flower :
    Apollo's heliotropion then shall stoop,
    And Venus' hyacinth shall vail her top ;

Juno shall shut her gilliflowers up,
And Pallas' bay shall 'bash her brightest green ;
Ceres' carnation, in consort with those,
Shall stoop and wonder at Diana's rose.

King Henry :
This prophecy is mystical. . . .[1]

Robert Greene. *Friar Bacon
and Friar Bungay, 1594.*

[1] He could not be expected to know that the prophecy was a piece of
flattery offered to the monarch of the playwright, Queen Elizabeth.

THE OPINION OF SOCINUS

I AM of opinion that it is not allowable for a private
Christian, even in order to keep off war, to kill any one, or
to mutilate him in any limb, though the supreme magistrate
command him to do it : otherwise it appears to me lawful
for a Christian to be armed and to march with others, to
suppress, without the murder of any one, the attack of
assailing enemies, when he has first tried every measure
that he may not be compelled to march forth, but may be
allowed to purchase with money a leave of absence from
personal service of this kind, which if he cannot obtain, it
is better, in my judgment, to run some danger of giving
offence to the weak in the faith than to draw most certain
ruin on himself and his connections.

Faustus Socinus. *To Elias Arcis-
sevius, Feb. 15, 1595. (Memoirs of
Socinus, Joshua Toulmin, 1777.)*

"The Socinian religion cannot suit a whole nation nor the greatest
number; it is only adapted to some persons of a particular temper. And
if it be true that a Pope, hearing that Protestants punished adulterers
and fornicators, cried out that their religion would be of no long continuance, it may be affirmed that his prognostication would have been
more just if he had applied it to a sect of men who will neither bear
arms nor exercise any office."—Bayle, *Dict.* Art. *Socinus.*

MORE DIGNIFIED

DELIVORUS

By arms, realms, empires, monarchies are won,
To arms, laws, justice magistrates submit,
Art, sciences before their triumphs sit
And beg their grace, and sing what they have done,
Amazed to see the race which they have run.

FELICIUS

Delivorus, war honour doth deserve,
Yet counsel in all kingdoms policied
Is far more worthy and more dignified ;
For arms but in extremes do never serve
To reconcile, and punish such as swerve. . . .

Say military virtue doth require
A valiant heart, great strength and constancy ;
The selflike gifts in civil policy
Are requisite for such as do aspire
To gain renown by counsel for their hire :

In brief, for what is war ordained but for peace ?
And perfect peace is end of bloody war :
And sith the ends 'fore means is prized far,
Let war his boast of dignity surcease,
And yield to wisdom which doth peace increase.

Peace doth depend on Reason, war on Force ;
The one is humane, honest and upright,
The other brutish, fostered by despite ;
The one extreme, concluded with remorse,
The other all injustice doth divorce.

                              Thomas Lodge. *A Fig for Momus,*
                              Eclogue 4, 1595.

BRAVE BE HER WARS

SAD be the sights and bitter fruits of war,
And thousand furies wait on wrathful sword :
Ne aught the praise of prowess more doth mar
Than foul revenging rage and base contentious jar.

But lovely concord and most sacred peace
Doth nourish virtue, and fast friendship breeds ;
Weak she makes strong, and strong thing does increase
Till it the pitch of highest praise exceeds :
Brave be her wars and honourable deeds,
By which she triumphs over ire and pride,
And wins an olive garland for her meeds.

> Edmund Spenser.   *The Faerie
> Queene, II., ii, 30-31.   1596.*

HAPPY PLOUGHMAN

THE sturdy ploughman doth the soldier see
All scarfed with pied colours to the knee,
Whom Indian pillage hath made fortunate.
And now he gins to loathe his former state :
Now doth he inly scorn his Kendal-green,
And his patch'd cockers now despised been.
Nor list he now go whistling to the car,
But sells his team and settleth to the war.
O War ! to them that never tried thee, sweet !
When his dead mate falls grovelling at his feet,
And angry bullets whistlen at his ear,
And his dim eyes see nought but death and drere—
Oh, happy ploughman ![1]

> Joseph Hall.   *Satire vi, Bk. IV.
> 1597.*

[1] O fortunatos nimium, sua si bona nôrint,
Agricolas, quibus ipsa procul discordibus armis,
Fundit humo facilem victum justissima tellus.
—Virgil.

NATURE NOT WANTING

To give you a view of the equity of this action [War] you shall find it to be just in reason, in religion, and in the practice of the church. It is just in reason Thomas 1. p. q. 76 a.s. disputing how fit a receptacle is the body of man for the soul of man, shows that Natura non deest in necessarius, Nature is not wanting in things necessary. But as nature hath given to brute beasts, horns and hooves, teeth and talents, for defence and offence, so having given unto man none of these, she hath given him reason and hands instead of these. Man naturally consists of a body and a soul ; but his soul is comprehensive of universalities ; and hath Virtutem ad infinita, it is able to devise and contrive infinite things : nature hath set no bounds to the covering of the body, but as the soul is able to devise a covering for the body of such a temper as shall hold out the dint of sword, and smaller shot, and to devise engines of war for battery and assault, so hath she given hands to the body which are organa organum, instruments of instruments to frame these when they are devised. Nature not being wanting in things necessary, there may be a time wherein it shall be just and necessary for the soul of man to contrive weapons and engines of offence, for the hands to work them, the body and arms to wear and wield them, and to put them in execution : such is the time of war. . . .

Stephen Gosson. *The Trumpet
of Warre,*[1] *1598.*

[1] A sermon preached at Paules Crosse, the seventh of Maie, 1598, by M. Stephen Gosson, parson of Great Wigborrow, in Essex.

PROGRESS

THE first and riper world of men and skill
Yields to our later world for three inventions ;
Miraculously we write, we sail, we kill,
As neither ancient scroll nor story mentions.

The first hath opened learnings old concealed,
And obscure arts restored to the light ;
The second hidden countries hath revealed,
And sent Christ's Gospel to each living wight.
These we commend, but oh, what needeth more
To teach Death more skill than he had before.[1]

> Thomas Bastard. *Chrestoleros.*
> *Liber Quartus, Epigr. 33, 1598.*

[1] "By the benefit of this light of reason they have found out artillery, by which wars come to quicker ends than heretofore, and the great expense of blood is avoided: for the numbers of men slain now, since the invention of artillery, are much less than before when the sword was the executioner."—John Donne, sermon on Xmas Day, 1621.

GROUNDS FOR WAR

WE find that princes always allege some plausible reason for beginning their wars ; although frequently they have no reason at all.

You notice how Moses sought for pretexts, although he had the most legitimate reason of all, the command of God. . . . Hercules too (as Apollonius says) sought for a pretext for war against the Dryopes, although they were wicked men.

Therefore there should be grounds for war, and they should not be trivial ; for too little hardly differs from nothing at all.

> Alberico Gentili. *De Iure Belli
> Libri Tres,*[1] *1598.*

[1] Tr. from 1612 ed. (The Three Books on the Law of War) by John C. Rolfe, 1933. Classics of International Law, No. 16. Carnegie Endowment for International Peace.

PUT AN END TO WARS

Now may the Great and Good God lead princes to put an end once for all to war and piously keep the terms of peace and treaties. " Peace is a work full of virtue, peace is the reward for a completed war, and the price of peril endured. In peace the stars are strong and earth's creatures are at rest. Nothing without peace is dear to God." [1]

Again and again I beseech thee, O God, put an end to wars ; do Thou give us peace, pardoning our sins, and made propitious to us through Thy Son our Saviour Jesus Christ.

Ibid.

[1] Prudentius, *Psychomachia.*

THAT DELIGHTSOME PATH

FIGHT, lords and captains, that your sovereign's face
May shine in honour brighter than the sun ;
And with the virtue of my beauteous rays
Make this fair land as fruitful as the fields
That with sweet milk and honey overflow'd.
God, in the whizzing of a pleasant wind,
Shall march upon the tops of mulberry-trees,
To cool all breasts that burn with any griefs,
As whilom he was good to Moses' men.
By day the Lord shall sit within a cloud,
To guide your footsteps to the field of joy ;
And in the night a pillar, bright as fire,
Shall go before you, like a second sun,
Wherein the essence of his godhead is ;
That day and night you may be brought to peace,
And never swerve from that delightsome path
That leads our souls to perfect happiness.
This shall he do for joy when I am king.
Then fight, brave captains, that these joys may fly
Into your bosoms with sweet victory.

George Peele. *David and
Bethsabe, 1599.*

GODDESS OF GRACES

THE daughter of the Highest,
Whose beauty builds the towers of Israel,
She that in chains of pearl and unicorn
Leads at her train the ancient golden world,
The world that Adam held in paradise,
Whose breath refineth all infectious airs,
And makes the meadows smile at her repair,—
She, she, my dearest Bethsabe,
Fair Peace, the goddess of our graces here,
Is fled the streets of fair Jerusalem,
The fields of Israel and the heart of David.

Ibid.

DIVINITY IN WAR

When thou goest out with the host against thine enemies, keep thee then from all wickedness. Deuteronomy xxiii. 9.—To entitle this time to this text, or to shew it pertinent to the present occasion, will ask no long preface. " When thou goest forth," etc. This " when " is now. There be enemies, and we have an host ; it is going forth.[1] . . . Moses doth here out of his own experience bestow an advice upon us. And Moses could skill what belonged to war, as one that forty years was never out of camp. Which advice is, that among our military points we would reckon the abatement of sin for one ; that now this time of our going forth we would go forth against sin too, and keep us from it as we would keep us from our enemy. . . .

And this is an use of Divinity in war. And as this an use of Divinity in war, so have we withal an use of war in Divinity. For Moses telling us, that " when our forces go forth against the enemy,"—that we then, at that time, are in any wise " to keep us from wickedness ; " by sorting these thus together doth plainly intimate that when the time of war is, then is a fit time, a very good opportunity, to draw from sin and to return to God. . . .

This is the sum. These the double use, 1. of war in divinity ; that our going forth might procure the giving over sin. 2. Of Divinity in war ; that our giving over sin might procure good speed to our going forth, even an honourable and happy return.

Lancelot Andrewes.[2]   *Sermon*
preached before Queen Elizabeth at
Richmond, Feb. 21, 1599.

[1] To deal with Hugh O'Neal, Earl of Tyrone. The enterprise was not attended with the success which the bishop expected.

[2] "It was a shrewd and severe animadversion of a Scotish lord, who, when K. James asked him how he liked Bp. A.'s sermon, sayd, that he was learned, but he did play with his text, as a Jack-an-apes does, who takes up a thing and tosses and playes with it—Here's a pretty thing, and there's a pretty thing!"—Aubrey.

NO TIME TO SIN

FROM war in respect of God I know not what we reckon of war ; peace is His blessing we are sure, and a special favour it is from Him as the Prophets account it, for a land to spend more iron in scythes and plough-shares than in sword-blades or spear-heads.[1] And if peace be a blessing and a chief of His blessings, we may reduce from thence what war is. To make no otherwise of it than it is, " the rod of God's wrath," as Esay[2] termeth it ; His " iron flail," as Amos ;[3] " the hammer of the earth," as Jeremy,[4] whereby He dasheth two nations together—one of them must in pieces, both the worse for it. War is no matter of sport. Indeed I see Abner esteem of it as of a sport : " let the young men rise," saith he to Joab, " and shew us some sport."[5] But I see the same Abner before the end of the same chapter weary of his sport, and treating with Joab for an end of it ; " How long shall the sword devour," saith he, " shall it not be bitterness in the end ? "[6] So it may be " sport " in the beginning ; it will be " bitterness in the end," if it hold long. " Do we provoke the Lord to

anger, are we stronger than He ? "[7]   Then since war is
God's rod, choose some other time ;   under the rod sin
not, then forbear it.   Certainly that time is no time to sin.

Ibid.

[1] Isa. 2, 4. Mic. 4, 3.   [2] Isa. 10, 5.   [3] Amos 1, 3.   [4] Jer. 50, 23.
[5] 2 Sam. 2, 14.   [6] 2 Sam. 2, 26.   [7] 1 Cor. 10, 22.

WISE SAYINGS OF BURLEIGH

HE ever said of danger that our enemies shall do no more
than God will suffer them ;   that war is soon kindled, but
peace very hardly procured ;   that war is the curse and
peace the blessing of God upon a nation ;   that a realm
gaineth more by one year's peace than ten years war.

Anon. The Compleat Statesman, c.
1600. (Peck's Desiderata Curiosa.)

FATHER TO SON

SUFFER not thy sons to pass the Alps, for they shall learn
nothing there but pride, blasphemy and atheism.   And if by
travel they get a few broken languages, that shall profit
them nothing more than to have one meat served in divers
dishes.   Neither, by my consent, shalt thou train them up
in wars ;   for he that sets up his rest to live by that profession can hardly be an honest man or a good Christian.
Besides it is a science no longer in request than use ;   for
soldiers in peace are like chimneys in summer.

Ibid.

"War being a profession by which men cannot live honourably at
all times, it is not to be taken up as a trade . . . for he will never be
thought a good man who takes upon him an employment by which, if
he would reap any profit at any time, he is obliged to be false, and
rapacious, and cruel, and to entertain several other qualities that are
not consistent in a good man; nor can any man (great or small) who
makes war his profession, be otherwise than vicious; because that that
trade being not to be followed in time of peace, they are necessitated
either to prevent or obstruct peace; and neither of those two ways are
practicable to an honest man."—Niccolò Machiavelli, Arte della guerra,
1520.

SONG

Time's eldest son, Old Age, the heir of Ease,
  Strength's foe, Love's woe, and foster to Devotion,
Bids gallant youths in martial prowess please,
  As for himself he hath no earthly motion,
But thinks sighs, tears, vows, prayers, and sacrifices
As good as shows, masks, jousts, or tilt devises.

Then sit thee down and say thy *Nunc dimittis*,
  With *De profundis, Credo,* and *Te Deum,*
Chant *Miserere* ; for what now so fit is
  As that, or this : *Paratum est cor meum* ?
O that thy saint would take in worth thy heart,
Thou canst not please her with a better part.

When others sing *Venite exultemus,*
  Stand by and turn to *Noli æmulare* ;
For *Quare fremuerunt* use *Oremus,*
  Vivat Eliza for an *Ave Mary* ;
And teach those swains that live about thy cell
To say *Amen* when thou dost pray so well.

Anon. *John Dowland's Book of
Songs, 1600.*

Follow thy drum ;
With man's blood paint the ground gules, gules :
Religious canons, civil laws are cruel ;
Then what should war be ?

Shakespeare. *Timon of Athens.*

D

REJOICE! REJOICE!

HEAVEN's sacred Imp, fair goddess that renewest
Th' old golden age, and brightly now re-bluest
Our cloudy sky, making our fields to smile :
Hope of the virtuous, horror of the vile,
Virgin unseen in France this many a year,
O blessed peace, we bid thee welcome here . . .
Lo, how the shops with busy craftsmen swarm,
How sheep and cattle cover every farm :
Behold the bonfires waving to the skies ;
Hark, hark the cheerful and re-chanting cries
Of old and young, singing this joyful ditty,
Iô, rejoice, rejoice, through town and city. . . .

> Joshua Sylvester. *The Handie-*
> *Crafts, c. 1602.*

CAPTAIN PILL AND CAPTAIN SKILL

Captain Pill : I will first begin with war itself, that I think cannot be managed but with disorder, whose best fruits are so enormous that it hath been had in question, and many times disputed on, whether war may be approved to be either good or lawful before the seat and majesty of God.

Captain Skill : I think those men that will move such doubts to be utterly ignorant as well in the history of the Scriptures as in the state of a happy commonwealth, for he that taught David to sing, Blessed to the Lord my strength which teacheth my hands to make war, and my fingers to fight, had likewise willed Moses long before to make war upon the Midianites, and that by an express command-ment, and Abraham the father of the faithful, made no scruple to enter into armies himself and his household to recover his brother Lot. . . .

Captain Pill : But what excuse for the great effusion of blood, or is it not a horror to think of the murders and slaughters made by men upon men in the fury and heat of war ?

Captain Skill : I will refer this to the noble Joshua, who being in pursuit of his enemies, and fearing that the day had been too short, commanded the sun to neglect his accustomed course, and to stay herself in the middle of the heavens, till he had performed his slaughter to the full.

Captain Pill : Why then to spoil and kill an enemy we see the warrant is good ; but there be some that will make difficulties, and then they will distinguish between ambitious war, and war that is but defensive, and almost they admit of no war at all to be lawful.

Captain Skill : War is to be undertaken but to the end to have peace, and for matters in claim, in defence of liberty, and such other like, as well the laws of nature as the laws of nations doth admit it.

For these distinctions I will leave them to the Divines, but war is evermore attended on by sword, fire, famine, and murder : the sins of the people is it that giveth the first alarm, and unsheatheth the soldier's sword, and war having once displayed his banner, it is the justice of the cause that approveth it either to be good or bad.

But yet the obtaining of a victory is not a sure confirmation of this right and equity, for when the children of Israel were gathered in Silo, to punish the shameful sodometry of the tribe of Benjamin, they lost in two several battles 40,000 men : notwithstanding they had a just cause, and fought both the times by the appointment and commandment of God.

> Barnaby Rich. *The Fruites of Long Experience,*[1] *1604.*

[1] "*A pleasing view for Peace, A Looking-Glasse for Warre, Or Call it what you list, Discoursed between two Captaines.*"

OUR PEACE-MONGERS

Captain Skill : When is the storm more rather to be provided for but whilst the weather is fair ; neither is there a more dangerous thing than in the time of peace to neglect the knowledge of arms, for when that care is set aside, both prince and people are left as a prey for every oppressor, and is an inducement for him to attempt that otherwise would be glad to combine.

Captain Pill : I can tell you Captain Skill this doctrine will be reputed flat heresy : what in the time of peace to provide for war, to spend money when they see no danger ? I can tell you our peace mongers cannot abide it, nay, they will not hear the name of war so much as spoken of, till they have news that the beacons be on fire about their ears.

Captain Skill : I might be a long time in delivering precedents, how many inconveniences have been incurred where they have neglected this preparation, and omitting all the rest, let Solomon give us light, who though he were promised a peaceable government by God himself, and had this addition to be called *Rex pacificus*, yet he furnished his garrisons with more warlike provisions than even his father David had done before him, notwithstanding he was still turmoiled and every day busied in the wars, for if preparation be neglected till the wars begin, either it cometh too late and out of season, or it heapeth together such confusion with making haste, as it proveth unprofitable, and the proceedings will be slow, the execution slender, and the wants intolerable.

Ibid.

THE HEALTH OF A KINGDOM

As he can give best rules to preserve the health of a body natural that by observing the divers honours, accidents and dispositions thereof, findeth at length the cause from whence it is or well or ill-affected, and so by mixture of art

or observation sets to his patient rules of exercise and diet :
so it is in a kingdom or commonwealth. If then out of the
registers of record and story, the true remembrancers of
art and error in passages of State, it shall appear that those
times which have been glorified with the mightiest princes
and wisest councils, would ever acknowledge that *Pax una
triumphis Innumeris potior* ; one Peace outgoes for worth
innumerable triumphs : that combustions at home were
like meteors, ever kindled in another region, but spent
themselves there ; that our men instead of laurel and olive
garlands to adorn with victory and peace our gates and
temples, have ever brought home fire-balls to burn our
cities ; that foreign spoils have been summed up with taxes
and penury ; that this addition of revenue hath tied us
to a perpetual issue of our own treasure ; that by these
titles of honour we have bought slavery, and by extenture
of territories, dangers ; and that difficulty either to undertake or pursue any foreign enterprise now is much more
than in any age before ; I think that no Englishman will
either love his own error so much, or his country so little,
as to advise a course so far estranged either from judgment
or security.

Sir Robert Bruce Cotton. *Wars
with Foreign Princes,*[1] *c. 1604.*

[1] "Warrs with Forreign Princes Dangerous to our Common-Wealth:
or Reasons for Forreign Wars answered, with a List of all the Confederates from Henry the first's Reign to the end of Queen Elizabeth:
proving that the Kings of England alwayes preferred Unjust Peace
before the Justest Warre."—Title page to 1657 ed.

THE GREAT ILLUSION

THE profits gained by foreign expeditions cannot be any
ways so truly esteemed as by setting down the expense of
money, men and munition by which we have made
purchase of them. I will therefore deliver as they fall in
sequence all the impositions, taxes and loans, whether by
general grant or prerogative power levied of the people ;

summing up as I go along the times of our Princes, the
number of men, ships, and vast provisions of victuals raised
to supply the necessity and expense of war.

[Here follows, occupying 32 pages, " a summary of all
the exactions upon this State from the Conquest to the
end of the late Queen."]

It now resteth by some few particulars to observe with
what wealth we have returned home, loaden with the spoils
of our enemies ; since no motives are so powerful to the
common greedy peoples as the hopes of gain, which will
easily enforce them

> *Ire super gladios, superque cadavera patrum,*
> *Et cæsos calcare Duces,—*
> Tread upon swords, and on their fathers' graves,
> And spurn their slaughtered captains—

As for the imaginary profit grown by the many rich
spoils at sea and attempts in Spain, it may be well cast up
by two examples of our best fortunes. The journey of
Calais defrayed not the charge to her Majesty by £64,000.
And our times of most advantage by prizes between anno
30 and 34 of the Queen, wherein we received but £64,044
defrayed not the charge of the Navy, arising in the same
years to £275,761. As to the greatest loss, expense of
Christian blood, it may well suffice to bemoan with
Horace. . . .

> Is there as yet so little Latin blood
> Spilt on the fields and floods ?
> Nor wolves nor lions do we ever find
> So cruel to their kind.

Ibid.

A GOODLY CREATURE

MOST happy, prince. . . . I presume to interrupt your
royal passage . . . being a messenger sent from the lady
Eirene, my mistress. . . . Many kingdoms hath the lady

sought out to abide in, but from them all hath she been
most churlishly banished ; not that her beauty did deserve
such unkindness, but that (like the eye of Heaven) hers was
too bright, and there were no eagles breeding in those nests
that could truly behold them.

At last here she arrived, *Destiny* subscribing to this
warrant, that none but this land should be her inheritance.
In contempt of which happiness, Envy shoots his em-
poisoned stings at her heart, but his adders (being charmed)
turn their dangerous heads upon his own bosom.   Those
that dwell far off, pine away with vexing to see her prosper,
because all the acquaintance which they have of her, is
this, that they know there is such a goodly creature as
Eirene in the world, yet her face they know not : whilst all
those that here sleep under the warmth of her wings, adore
her by the sacred and celestial name of Peace, for number
being (as her blessings are) infinite.

> Thomas Dekker. *The Magnificent
> Entertainment,*[1] *1604.*

[1] Given to King James, Queene Anne his wife, and Henry Frederick
the Prince, upon the day of his Majesties' Tryumphant Passage (from
the Tower) through his Honourable Citie (and Chamber) of London,
being the 15. of March, 1603."

PEACE AND HER DAUGHTER PLENTY

PEACE was richly attired, her upper garment of carnation,
hanging loose, a robe of white under it, powdered with
stars, and girt to her : her hair of a bright colour, long,
and hanging at her back, but interwoven with white
ribbands and jewels ; her brows were encompassed with a
wreath of the olive, the laurel and the date tree. In one
hand she held a Caduceus (or Mercury's rod, the god of
eloquence) : in the other, ripe ears of corn gilded : on
her lap sate a dove—all these being ensigns and furnitures
of *Peace. Plenty*, her daughter, sate of the left hand, in
changeable colours, a rich mantle of gold traversing her
body : her hair large and loosely spreading over her

shoulders : on her head a crown of poppy and mustard seed—the antique badges of Fertility and Abundance. In her right hand a cornucopia, filled with flowers, fruits, etc.

Ibid.

ALL HAIL

FAIR fruitful Daughter of th' Omnipotent,
Great Umpire that dost either world sustain,
Without whose help all would return again
(Like hideous Chaos) to confusion bent.
O Mother of the living, second Nature
Of th' elements, fire, water, earth and air :
The grace whereby men climb the heavenly chair,
Whence void, this world harbours no happy creature.
Pillar of laws, religion's pedestal,
Hope of the glory, glory of the immortal.
Honour of cities, pearl of kingdoms all,
The Nurse of virtues, Muses' chief supportal,
Patron of Arts, of good the special spring,
All hail (dear Peace) which us all heal doth bring.

Joshua Sylvester. *The Miracle of Peace, c. 1605.*

THE FIRST GOOD NEWS

THE first good news that ever the world had or men received were those which the angels brought on that night which was our day, when they sang in the skies, " Glory be in the heights, and peace on earth to men of good minds." And the salutation which the best Master that ever was on earth or in heaven taught to His disciples and favourites was, that when they entered into any house they would say, " Peace be to this house "; and many other times He said, " I give unto you My peace ; I leave My peace unto you ; peace be amongst you." It is a good, as precious as a jewel, and a gift given, and left by such a hand ; a jewel without which neither on earth nor in heaven can there be any perfect good. This peace is the true end of war.

Miguel de Cervantes. *Don Quixote*, *1605*. *Tr. Thomas Shelton, 1612*.

ORDNANCE AND KNIGHTS

THOSE blessed ages were fortunate which wanted the dreadful fury of the devilish and murdering pieces of ordnance, to whose inventor[1] I am verily persuaded that they render in hell an eternal guerdon for his diabolical invention, by which he hath given power to an infamous, base, vile, and dastardly arm to bereave the most valorous knights of life ; and that, without knowing how or from whence; in the midst of the stomach and courage that inflames and animates valorous minds, there arrives a wandering bullet (shot off, perhaps, by him that was afraid, and fled at the very blaze of the powder, as he discharged the accursed engine), and cuts off and finisheth in a moment the thoughts and life of him who merited to enjoy it many ages.

Ibid.

[1] I am far from controverting, continued my uncle Toby, what historians agree in, that in the year of our Lord 1380, under the reign of Wenceslaus, son of Charles the Fourth, a certain priest, whose name was Schwartz, showed the use of powder to the Venetians; but 'tis certain he was not the first; because if we are to believe Don Pedro, the bishop of Leon—How came priests and bishops, an' please your honour, to trouble their heads about gunpowder?—God knows, said my uncle Toby—His providence brings good out of everything."—Laurence Sterne, *Tristram Shandy*.

A VOICE FROM HEAVEN

THEY that are redeemed of the Lord do change their fleshly weapons, namely their swords, into shares, and their spears into scythes, do lift up no sword, neither have nor consent to battle. . . .

Yea, rather they are called of Him (who they are commanded to obey by a voice heard from heaven) to the following of His unarmed and unweaponed life, and His cross-bearing footsteps.[1]

> John Smyth. *The Differences of the Church of the Separation, 1608.*

[1] Quoted by Rufus Jones, *Studies in Mystical Religion*, p. 411.

SONG

Th' Assyrian pomp, the Persian pride,
Greeks' glory, and the Romans' died :
    And who yet imitate
Their noises tarry the same fate.
Force greatness all the glorious ways
    You can, it soon decays ;
But so good Fame shall never :
Her triumphs, as their causes, are for ever.

> Ben Jonson. *The Masque of Queens. Presented at Whitehall, Feb. 2, 1609.*

BETTER DAYS ARE COMING

SOLDIERS, and to a name more full of ancient honour, or of more honourable worth, I cannot speak : you have for a long time scarce made saving voyages into the field ; so far as the Red Sea (of blood) have you ventured ; and yet instead of purchasing glory, have you brought home nothing but contempt and beggary, or at least little or no money. The Hollander and the Spaniard have been (and I think still are) your best lords and masters : if ever captains did pray, they have prayed for them only. Cutlers and Armourers have got more by them within these few years than by any four nations (beside them) in Christendom all their whole lives. But for this beyond-sea quarrel, the people of this utmost end of the world (if all the fence schools had been put down too) had (I think) forgotten how to handle their weapon. The Low Countries therefore have (in renown) gone beyond kingdoms of higher fame, only for thus repairing and keeping open those old and ruinated temples of Bellona, which had been shut up in these latter ages, and stood despised because defaced.

Yet even those Dutch Wars have been unto you that served in them but as wars in these dead times are to merchants or tradesmen : you were richer for having them in your hands, but you had not such hot doings as you desired. You came often to the cracking of crowns, but never to the true cutting of throats : your commanders had too much of the martial theorick, you soldiers too little of the practick. But be of good courage, the wind shifts his point, better days are coming up, this sick world lies on the mending hand : for this present year of 1609 drums will be struck up and colours spread, under which you may all fight and have good pay.

Thomas Dekker. Worke for
Armorours,[1] 1609.

[1] "*Or The Peace is Broken. Open Warres likely to happin this year* 1609. *God helpe the Poore, The rich can shift.*"

VICE VERSA

Peace is a great evil, war a great boon ; peace is our death, war our life ; peace scatters us, war brings us together ; peace kills the good, war is their mainstay ; peace is for the wicked, war for the true christian. To him therefore who desires sweet rest, and the recovery of his true liberty, war is necessary, peace worthless.

L'Abbé de la Frenade. Les
Triomphes du Roy,[1] 1609.

[1] Qt. Bayle, *Oeuvres Diverses*, 1737.

SPEECH OF THE CAPTAINS

What have we won when we in grave are dead,
Though we have spoiled and filled the world with dread ?
When all our days we lived have like fools
We must at last ev'n tumble down our tools,

Our spears and swords must all at last give place
To those who by their wisdom do make peace.
O happy king who spare men's blood and bones,
With blunted sword who sit on Mercy's thrones ;
When we were young we smiled with *Ha Ha*,
We smelled the battle and did cry *Sa, Sa*[1];
But waxed old we think it now a grace
That far from trumpets we may live in peace.

> Joshua Sylvester (?) *Nebuchadnez-*
> *zars Fierie Furnace,*[2] *c. 1612.*

[1] "A French word of war."—Marginal note.
[2] Harl. MS. 7578, tentatively attributed to Sylvester by Margarete Rösler, *Materials for the Study of the Old English Drama, New Series, No. 12,* 1936. (This series is a continuation by Henry de Vocht, Professor of English Philology in the University of Louvain, of the *Materialien zur Kunde des Älteren Englischen Dramas* founded by Professor W. Bang, the first 44 volumes of which, together with manuscripts, documents and finished sheets of nine volumes in printing, were mostly destroyed at Louvain in August, 1914.)

THE BASIS OF INTERNATIONAL LAW

THE rational basis of this branch of law, indeed, consists in the fact that the human race, however many the various peoples and kingdoms into which it may be divided, always preserves a certain unity, not only as a species, but also, as it were, a moral and political unity called for by the natural precept of mutual love and mercy, which applies to all, even to strangers of any nation.

> Francisco Suárez. *de Legibus,*
> *1612.*

Qt. James Brown Scott, *The Spanish Conception of International Law and of Sanctions,* Pt. II., 1934.

FOR A QUIET LIFE

LET others watch in guilty arms, and stand
The fury of a rash command,
Go enter breaches, meet the cannon's rage,
That they may sleep with scars in age,

And show their feathers shot, and colours torn,
And brag that they were therefore born . . .
Thy peace is made ; and, when man's state is well,
'Tis better, if he there can dwell.
God wishest none should wreck on a strange shelf :
To Him man's dearer than t'himself,
And, howsoever we may think things sweet,
He always gives what He knows meet ;
Which who can use is happy : such be thou.
Thy morning's and thy evening's vow
Be thanks to him, and earnest-prayer, to find
A body sound, with sounder mind ;
To do thy country service, thyself right ;
That neither want do thee affright,
Nor death ; but when thy latest sand is spent,
Thou may'st think life a thing but lent.

Ben Jonson. To Sir Robert Wroth, 1616.

THE SHEDDING OF BLOOD

THE blood that is shed in battle, and in times of lawful
war, you all suppose as lawfully shed ; yet notwithstanding,
Moses in xvi. of *Numbers*, gives charge, that the soldiers
returning from battle, should stay a while without the
camp, even seven days, until they were cleansed. Again,
when David advised with himself about the building of an
house unto God, He sends him word to lay by all thought of
that, he was no fit person to do it ; and He gives the reason
of it. . . . *For thou art a man who hast shed much blood, and
fought many battles.* Beloved, the battles which David fought
were called the Lord's battles, and therefore whatsoever
he did in that kind, he had doubtless very good warrant
to do ; and yet you see, that it is an imputation to him,
that he shed blood, though lawfully. . . . So it seems
blood cannot be justly shed, but that it brings with it some
stain and spot of injustice.

John Hales. Sermon preached at
the Hague, 1617. (Golden Remains,
1673.)

CHRISTMAS SERMON

*And this shall be a sign unto you ; ye shall find the Child swaddled,
  and laid in a cratch.*

*And straightway there was with the Angel a multitude of Heavenly
  soldiers, praising God, and saying,*

*Glory be to God on high, and peace upon earth, and towards men
  good-will. . . .*

These personages were Angels. It is said expressly ver. 15,[1]
yet they are here said to be soldiers. What, shall we have
war then ? for they are in the habit of war. True, of war ;
but it is war, not that now is or hereafter should be, but
of war that had been before even to the day of this birth,
but now to cease—witness *pax in terris*. There had been no
peace with Heaven, but plain hostility between earth and
it. . . . Their habit shows what was before, their song
what now should be. By virtue of Christ's Nativity, " peace
to earth " from Heaven, " good-will to men " from God.
So now upon His birth they were to disarm ; but before
they put their armour off, yet being in it they would have
a pæan, and sing of the new world that was now to ensue.
A sign this and a strange one, this conjunction, *species
præliantium*, and *voces cantantium*, " the habit of war," and
" the song of peace." Soldiers make a camp, come to
fight ; these make a choir, come to sing. They are not in
the habit of choirmen, yet they sing ; they are in the habit
of men of war, yet sing of peace.

> Lancelot Andrewes. *Sermon
> preached before James I. at White-
> hall, Christmas Day, 1618.*

[1] Luke 2.

A HEAVENLY THING

Let " earth " be content with " peace "; peace is her
portion, and a blessed portion if she may well hold it ; a
fair portion, a rich wish. For I would fain know, what

could be said more to the praise of this portion, than is here in this song ? First, that in general it reacheth to the whole earth ; not to men alone, though they have their share too in whatsoever good cometh to the earth, but it reacheth to all on earth ; *omni animantium generi*, " to all the beasts, all the green things on the earth ; " all are the better for it.

Secondly, what more for the credit of peace than that it is *votum militare*, " it comes from the mouths of soldiers" that were there in their military habit. Even they sing of peace, and praise it, and wish it, where they wish any good ; and know not what better thing to wish to the earth than it. It is the earth's happiness, peace ; it flourisheth by it. " Before was the earth as the garden of Paradise," said the Prophet,[1] " behind it was a waste and barren wilderness, all spoiled and burnt up."

Thirdly, that it is *votum Angelicum*, " an Angel's wish," peace. They being Heavenly Spirits, wish not any thing at any time but Heavenly ; so that a Heavenly thing is peace. And so it is, as Nazianzen[2] here well observed, *pugnas et dissidia nescire Deum et Angelos*, " no broils, no brabbles in Heaven, nothing but peace there." And a kind of Heaven there is upon earth, when there is peace upon earth ; and justly are they blessed, and rightly are they " called the children of God,"[3] the most blessed that are, or shall be at any time, that are the procurers of it.

Ibid.

[1] Joel 2, 3.   [2] S. Greg. Nazianz. Orat. 12. circ. med.   [3] Mat. 5, 9.

A GOSHEN

FOR the first temporal blessing of peace we may consider the loveliness, the amiableness of that, if we look upon the horror and ghastliness of war, either in effigy, in that picture of war which is drawn in every leaf of our own chronicles, in the blood of so many princes and noble families, or if we look upon war itself at that distance where it cannot hurt us, as God had formerly kindled it amongst our neighbours, and as he hath transferred it now to remoter nations, whilst we enjoy yet a Goshen in the midst of all those Egypts.

In all cities, disorderly and facinorous men, covet to draw themselves into the skirts and suburbs of those cities, that so they may be nearer the spoil, which they make upon passengers. In all kingdoms that border upon other kingdoms, and in islands which have no other border but the sea, particular men, who by dwelling in these skirts and borders may make their profit of spoil, delight in hostility, and have an adverseness and detestation of peace : but it is not so within : they who till the earth and breed up cattle and employ their industry upon God's creatures, according to God's ordinance, feel the benefit and apprehend the sweetness and pray for the continuance of peace.

> John Donne. *Sermon at White-hall, April 30, 1620.*

Cowley, too, commends the peace-loving countryman. "They are, without dispute, of all men, the most quiet and least apt to be inflamed to the disturbance of the commonwealth: their manner of life inclines them, and interest binds them, to live in peace: in our late mad and miserable civil wars, all other trades, even to the meanest, set forth whole troops, and raised up some great commanders, who became famous and mighty for the mischiefs they had done: but I do not remember the name of any one husbandman, who had so considerable a share in the twenty years' ruin of his country, as to deserve the curses of his countrymen."—*Of Agriculture*. Cowley proceeds to translate Virgil [Georg. Lib. 11, 458] and Horace [Epod. Ode 11], testifying to the same effect.

THOSE RELIGIOUS GENERALS

As a boy in Italy, a young man in Belgium, and a grown-up man in France, I have seen the dying slaughtered in cold blood, and have myself tasted the torments of siege and starvation. I will not say anything about the many crimes or iniquities which I have either beheld committed with my own eyes, or have heard of from others, by men who died shortly after in battle and found themselves in Hell before they had begun to think of preparing for their judgment. It is such happenings as these that made me respect and venerate those religious generals and commanders who teach their men by word and example how to shed the blood of the enemy without offence to God, and who inspire them to lay down their own lives for the cause of justice and religion.

> Robert Francis, Cardinal Bellar-
> mine, *to Duke Maximilian, Nov.,*
> *1620.*[1]

[1] From *The Life and Work of Blessed Robert Francis, Cardinal Bellarmine, S. J.*, by James Brodrick, S.J., 1928.

A PURGE AND BLOOD-LETTING

AFTER a long scene of peace, war ever enters the stage, and indeed is so much of the world's physic as it is both a purge[1] and blood-letting. Peace, fulness, pride and war are the four felloes that being let into one another make the wheel that the times turn on. As we see in bees, when the hive multiplies and fills, nature hath always taught it a way of ease by swarms : so the world and nations, when they grow over-populous, they discharge themselves by troops and bands. It is but the distemper of the body politic which (like the natural) rest and a full diet hath burdened with repletion, and that heightens humours either to sickness or evacuation. When it is eased of these, it subsides again to a quiet rest and temper. So war is begotten out of peace graduately, and ends in peace immediately. Between peace and war are two stages— luxury, ambition : between war and peace, none at all.

> Owen Feltham. *Resolves, 1620.*

[1] If nations sent their trash, instead of their treasure, to fight their battles, then indeed war might be defended as a dreadful purgative of nations."—Dr. C. W. Saleeby, *Contem. Rev.*, April, 1915.

HARE-BRAINS

LOOK into our histories, and you shall almost meet with no other subject but what a company of hare-brains[1] have done in their rage. We may do well therefore to put this in our procession amongst the rest : " From all blindness of heart, from pride, vain-glory, and hypocrisy, from envy, hatred and malice, anger, and all such pestiferous per-turbations, good Lord deliver us."

Robert Burton. *The Anatomy of Melancholy, 1621.*

[1] "When we consider that the destinies of nations are commonly in the hands of elderly gentlemen whose blood-pressures tend to be too high owing to their fierce political activities, it is not too much to say that arterio-sclerosis is one of the greatest tragedies that afflict the human race. Every politician should have his blood-pressure tested and his urine examined about once a quarter, and if it should show signs of rising he should undoubtedly take a long rest until it falls again; it is not fair that the lives of millions should depend upon the judgment of a man whose mind is warped by arterio-sclerosis."—C. MacLaurin, *Post Mortem,* 1923.

"Any megalomaniac who is not openly certifiable, but whose eccen-tricity and ego-centricity have left a trail of destruction from the nursery floor to the hustings may, for all we know to the countrary, be firmly established as Secretary for the Admiralty, at a time when graver heads are at their wits' end to tackle some international complication."— Edward Glover, *War, Sadism and Peace,* 1933.

NATURE EXPOSTULATES

What plague, what fury brought so devilish, so brutish a thing as war first into men's minds ? Who made so soft and peaceable a creature, born to love, mercy, meekness, so to rave, rage like beasts, and run on to their own destruction ? How may Nature expostulate with mankind. . . . I made thee an harmless, quiet, a divine creature, and all good men, yet . . . these are the brave spirits, the gallants of the world, these admired alone, triumph alone, have statues, crowns, pyramids, obelisks to their eternal fame, that immortal genius attends on them.

Ibid.

THE TOUCHSTONE

Pray for the peace of Jerusalem ; but let them prosper that love thee. Peace be within thy walls, and prosperity within thy palaces. Psalm cxxii. 6, 7.

Peace is one of the greatest temporal blessings which a State or a Church can receive : for where God Himself describes the excellency of government, he describes it by " peace." " The work of justice shall be peace ; and My people shall dwell in the tabernacle of peace." I will not load you with a long discourse of " peace," and the benefits it brings. It hath the same fate that some other of God's blessings have ; it is better known by want than use ; and thought most worth the having by them that have it not. Look, therefore, not upon yourselves in peace, but upon a State in blood, upon a Church in persecution ; ask them which are divided by the sword, which are roasting at the flame, conceive your case theirs,—that is the touch-stone which deceives not,—then tell me whether it be not good counsel, *rogare pacem*, to " pray for the peace " of both. And I do ill to call it barely " peace ; " our prophet calls it the " blessing of peace." And doubtless it is to teach the world that all earthly benefits are, as it were, unblessed, till " peace " be upon them : for, till then, no enjoying of any. . . .

William Laud. *Sermon preached before James I. at Wanstead on his birthday, June 19, 1621.*

Laud was at this time Dean of Gloucester, and one of His Majesty's Chaplains in Ordinary. The following passages from Laud's Diary are relevant: "Anno 1621 – The King's gracious speech unto me, June 3, concerning my long service. He was pleased to say: He had given me nothing but Gloucester, which he well knew was a shell without a kernel." "June 29 – His Majesty gave me the grant of the Bishopric of St. David's, being St. Peter's day."

TAKE THIS WITH YOU

HOWBEIT, take this with you :—they bear not the best minds, cases of necessity and honourable safety always excepted, that desire the waters either of the Church or the Commonwealth should run troubled that they may have the better fishing. And the Historian sets his brand upon them. Who are they whom peace cannot please ?

Who? Why? *Quibus pessima est, et immodica cupiditas*,[1]—
they whose desires are worse than naught in their object,
and void of all moderation in their pursuit.

Ibid.

[1] "Tentavit [Sulla] justis legibus et aequis conditionibus bellum com-
ponere: sed iis, quibus et pessima et immodica cupiditas erat, non poterat
pax placere."—Vell. Paterc. Hist. Roman. lib. ii. c. xxv. p. 226. Ed.
Burmann.

WHAT TO DO WITH MILITARISTS

THE Germans exercised their young men in brigandage
in order to fill their time. What then will so many valiant
men do to-day, who can smell nothing but gunpowder,
nor place their hands anywhere but on their sword-hilts,
nor their feet anywhere but on a battlefield or a breach?
. . . The answer to this question is very brief. The world
is not made for those people who only know how to do
harm. . . . They should all be sent to the cannibals and
savages. . . . Cursed nature which seeks repose in disturbance, honour in infamy, and pastime in inhumanity!
. . . What can one hope from those who only breathe
blood and carnage?

Émeric Crucé. *Le Nouveau
Cynee*,[1] *1623.*

[1] The reference is to the Cineas mentioned on p. 24 *ante*.

ABOLISH FRONTIERS

WHAT a pleasure it would be to see men go freely from
place to place and communicate together without any
barriers of country, formalities, or other such differences,
as if the earth were, as it truly is, a city common to all.
There are only the savages and thieves that can prevent so
great a good : but it is quite possible that, seeing themselves alone, they will think of their conscience ; or that,
if they wish to continue their brutal way of life, they will

not be enough to resist the consensus of so many people, who will fall on them and will block, attack and kill them like poor beasts in their lairs.

Ibid.

INTERNATIONAL ASSEMBLY

It would be necessary to choose a town where all sovereigns should keep perpetual ambassadors, so that the differences which might arise should be settled by the judgment of the whole assembly. . . . If any one rebelled against the decision of so notable a company, he would encounter the disapproval of all the other princes, who would have good means of bringing him to reason. . . . Now the most convenient place for such an assembly would be Venice. . . .

They try in vain in their present state. Let them fortify themselves with alliances as much as they wish, let them build citadels and arm on every side, they will always have something to fear if they do not agree unanimously on a general concord. . . .

Ibid.

THE OIL OF PEACE

It is no longer time to dream of trophies. One must leave these barbarous manners, and show the people the way of humanity and true honour, so that they shall live no longer in a brutal way. Reason and justice must reign, and not violence, which is only fit for beasts. . . . Let us replace the sword in the scabbard. . . . We have raised enough storms. It is time to calm this great ocean, by throwing on it the oil of perfect reconciliation. . . . We seek a peace which is not patched up, nor to last three days, but which is voluntary, just, and permanent : a peace which gives to each that which belongs to him.

Ibid.

A USELESS PROTEST

We shall put back the sword into the scabbard when we shall have reflected on the vanity of the opinions that make us take up arms. Let us leave the Scythians to adore the sword : rather let us imitate the Essenes, who had among them no armourer ; or those ancient people of Cathay, who did not know what it was to kill or to do evil. As for me, I can only bring wishes and humble protests, which will perhaps be useless. I have wished, nevertheless, to leave this testimony to posterity. If it proves useless, patience. It is a small thing to lose paper and words. I shall protest in that case like Solon, that I have said and done what was possible to me for the public good.

Ibid.

THE SECRET WAR

Clinias the Candian (in Plato) speaks desperately and wildly, as if there were no such thing as peace between nations ; but that every nation expects but his advantage to war upon another. But yet in that excess of speech there is thus much that may have a civil construction ; namely, that every state ought to stand upon his guard, and rather prevent than be prevented. His words are : Quam rem fere vocant pacem, nudum et inane nomen est ; revera autem omnibus adversus omnes civitates bellum sempiternum perdurat. " That which men for the most part call peace is but a naked and empty name ; but the truth is that there is ever between all estates a secret war." I know well this speech is the objection and not the decision, and that it is after refuted ; but yet (as I said before) it bears thus much of truth, that if that general malignity and predisposition to war (which he untruly figureth to be in all nations) be produced and extended to a just fear of being oppressed, then it is no more a true peace, but a name of a peace.

As for the opinion of Iphicrates the Athenian, it demands
not so much towards a war as a just fear, but rather cometh
near the opinion of Clinias ; as if there were ever amongst
nations a brooding of war, and that there is no sure league
but impuissance to do hurt.

> Francis Bacon. *Considerations
> touching a war with Spain, 1624.*

THE TRUE EXERCISE

No body can be healthful without exercise, neither natural
nor politic ; and certainly to a kingdom or estate a just
and honourable war is the true exercise. A civil war,
indeed, is like the heat of a fever, but a foreign war is like
the heat of exercise, and serveth to keep the body in health.
For in a slothful peace both courages will effeminate and
manners corrupt. But howsoever it be for happiness,
without all question for greatness it maketh, to be still, for
the most part, in arms.

> Francis Bacon. *Essays : On the
> True Greatness of Kingdoms and
> Estates. 3rd ed., 1625.*

THIS MONSTROUS BARBARITY

I OBSERVED everywhere in Christendom a lawlessness in
warfare of which even barbarous nations would be ashamed.
Nations would rush to arms on the slightest pretext or even
without cause at all. And arms once taken up, there would
be an end to all respect for law, whether human or divine,
as though a fury had been let loose with general licence for
all manner of crime.

And the spectacle of this monstrous barbarity has led
many men—in no wise extremists—to the opinion that all
arms should be forbidden a Christian, whose rule of life is
mainly the loving of all men. Those ardent lovers of peace,
both ecclesiastical and civil, John Ferus and our countryman Erasmus, seem sometimes to incline to this opinion,

though I believe that they do so on the principle that to straighten a bent stick one must bend it strongly the other way.

Hugo Grotius. *De Jure Belli ac Pacis, 1625. Tr. W. S. M. Knight, 1922.*

CONSCIENTIOUS OBJECTION

THOUGH the justice of the war cannot be in doubt, yet, nevertheless, it does not seem at all right that Christians should be forced, against their will, into military service. And this is so because abstention from military service, even when such service is permissible, is conduct of that greater holiness which for a long time has been required of the clergy and penitents and is strongly approved in many ways, for other Christians. . . .

Ibid.

ONE BLEST ISLE

Now War is all the world about,
And everywhere Erynnis reigns,
Or else the Torch so late put out,
The stench remains. . . .
Only the Island which we sow,
(A world without the world) so far
From present wounds, it cannot show
An ancient scar.
White Peace (the beautifull'st of things)
Seems here her everlasting rest
To fix, and spreads her downy wings
Over the nest :
As when great Jove, usurping reign,
From the plagu'd world did her exile,

> And tied her with a golden chain
> To one blest Isle :
> Which in a sea of plenty swam
> And turtles sang on ev'ry bough,
> A safe retreat to all that came
> As ours is now.

Sir Richard Fanshawe. Ode, 1630.

THIS HACKING AND HEWING

IF Democritus were alive now . . . what would he have said to see, hear, and read so many bloody battles, so many thousands slain at once, such streams of blood able to turn mills . . . or to make sport for princes, without any just cause, "for vain titles," (saith Austin)[1] "precedency, some wench, or such-like toy, or out of desire of domineering, vainglory, malice, revenge, folly, madness" (goodly causes all), while statesmen themselves in the meantime are secure at home, pampered with all delights and pleasures, take their ease, and follow their lusts, not considering what intolerable misery poor soldiers endure, their often wounds, hunger, thirst, etc., the lamentable cares, torments, calamities, and oppressions that accompany such proceedings, they feel not, take no notice of it. . . . *Flos hominum,* proper men, well proportioned, carefully brought up, able both in body and mind, sound, led like so many beasts to the slaughter in the flower of their years, pride, and full strength, without all remorse and pity, sacrificed to Pluto, killed up as so many sheep, for devils' food, 40,000 at once. At once, said I, that were tolerable, but these wars last always, and for ages ; nothing so familiar as this hacking and hewing, massacres, murders, desolations.

Robert Burton. The Anatomy of
Melancholy, 1632.[2]

[1] St. Augustine.

[2] A comparison of *Democritus to the Reader* in the three earlier editions will show the intensification of Burton's dislike of war.

FALSE HONOUR

" THEY commonly call the most hair-brain bloodsuckers, strongest thieves, the most desperate villains, treacherous rogues, inhuman murderers, rash, cruel, and dissolute caitiffs ; courageous and generous spirits, heroical and worthy captains, brave men-at-arms, valiant and renowned soldiers, possessed with a brute persuasion of false honour," as Pontus Heuter in his Burgundian History complains. By means of which it comes to pass that daily so many voluntaries offer themselves, leaving their sweet wives, children, friends, for sixpence (if they can get it) a day, prostitute their lives and limbs, desire to enter upon breaches, lie sentinel, perdu, give the first onset, stand in the fore-front of the battle, marching bravely on, with a cheerful noise of drums and trumpets, such vigour and alacrity, so many banners streaming in the air, glittering armours, motions of plumes, woods of pikes and swords, variety of colours, cost and magnificence, as if they went in triumph, now victors to the Capitol, and with such pomp as when Darius' army marched to meet Alexander at Issus. . . . Of fifteen thousand proletaries slain in a battle, scarce fifteen are recorded in history, or one alone, the general perhaps, and after a while his and their names are likewise blotted out, the whole battle itself is forgotten.

Ibid.

WHAT AN ANSWER !

O WHEN our Clergy, at the dreadful Day,
Shall make their audit ; when the judge shall say,
Give your accompts : What, have my Lambs been fed ?
Say, do they all stand sound ? Is there none dead
By your defaults ? Come, Shepherds, bring them forth
That I may crown your labours in their worth.
O what an answer will be given by some !
We have been silenced : Cannons struck us dumb.

Francis Quarles. *Divine Fancies, 1632.*

HE MUST EXCUSE US

                THE league proclaim'd between us
Bound neither of us further than to aid
Each other, if by foreign power invaded ;
And so far in my honour I was tied.
But since, without our consent, or allowance,
He hath ta'en arms ; with his good leave, he must
Excuse us if we steer not on a rock
We see and may avoid. Let other monarchs
Contend to be made glorious by proud war,
And, with the blood of their poor subjects, purchase
Increase of empire, and augment their cares
In keeping that which was by wrongs extorted,
Gilding unjust invasions with the trim
Of glorious conquests ; we, that would be known
The father of our people, in our study
And vigilance for their safety, must not change
Their ploughshares into swords, and force them from
The secure shade of their own vines, to be
Scorch'd with the flames of war : or, for our sport,
Expose their lives to ruin.

                Philip Massinger. *The Maid of
Honour, 1632.*

ARMAMENTS AND EDUCATION

To you, in particular, do I direct my prayers, ye rulers
and magistrates, who, in God's name, preside over human
affairs. . . . For Christ's sake, for the sake of our children's
salvation, I beseech you to listen unto me. This is a
weighty question, and concerns the glory of God and the
salvation of mankind. Well do I know how much you love
your country. If a man came to you and promised to tell
you how all your towns might be fortified at a slight cost,
how all your youths might be instructed in the art of
warfare, how your rivers might be made navigable and be
filled with merchant vessels, in short, how your state might

be brought to a better pitch of prosperity and security, you would give, not only your careful attention, but your heartiest thanks as well, to him who showed such solicitude for your welfare. . . . With truth did the sainted Luther write, when exhorting the cities of Germany to found schools : " Where one ducat is expended in building cities, fortresses, monuments, and arsenals, one hundred should be spent in educating our youth aright. . . ."

> John Amos Comenius. *Didactica Magna, written c. 1632. Tr. M. W. Keatinge, 1896.*

" The teachers of the future . . . must be trained to be men capable of bearing arms and ready to carry them, ready and able to evoke in the children in their care the same military spirit, the same military will. The National-Socialist type of teacher is the soldier type."—Reichsminister Rust, 1933.

CALM SECURITY

WHAT though the German drum
Bellow for freedom and revenge, the noise
Concerns us not, nor should divert our joys ;
Nor ought the thunder of the carabines
Drown the sweet airs of our tuned violins.
Believe me, friend, if their prevailing powers
Gain them a calm security like ours,
They'll hang their arms upon the olive bough,
And dance and revel then, as we do now.

> Thomas Carew. *In an answer of an elegiacal letter from Aurelian Townsend, c. 1632.*

BEASTLY REIGN

PEACE is the harvest of man's rich creation,
Where wit and pain have scope to sow and reap
The mind, by arts to work her elevation ;
Care is sold dear, and sloth is never cheap,
Beyond the intent of Nature it proves
The Earth, and fruitful industry it loves. . . .

If Peace be such, what must we think of War
But horror from above, below confusion,
Where the unhappy happy only are,
As making mischief ever her conclusion ;
 Scourges of God, figures of Hell to come,
 Of vanity a vain, infamous tomb,

Where neither throne nor crown have reverence,
Sentence nor writ nor sergeant be in fashion,
All terror scorned, of guiltiness no sense ;
A discipline whereof the rule is passion :
 And as men's vices beasts' chief virtues are,
 So be the shames of peace the pride of war.

Here Northern bodies vanquish Southern wit,
Greek sciences obey the Roman pride,
Order serves both to save and kill with it,
Wisdom to ruin only is applied :
 Fame, worth, religion, all do but assure
 Vain man which way to give wounds and
 endure.

And when the reins of human hope and fear
Are thus laid on our necks, and order changed,
Pride will no more the yoke of heaven bear,
Nor our desires in any bounds be ranged ;
 The world must take new forms of wrong and
 right,
 For war did never love things definite.

Here books are burnt, fair monuments of mind,
Here ignorance doth on all arts tyrannise ;
Virtue no other mould but courage finds,
All other beings in her being dies ;
 Wisdom ofttimes grows infancy again ;
 Beasts rule in men, and men do beastly reign. . . .

      Fulke Greville, Lord Brooke.
      A Treatise of Warres, 1633.

COSTUME PIECE

THE Antimasques being past, there appears in the highest and foremost part of the heaven by little and little to break forth a whitish cloud bearing a chariot feigned of goldsmith's work, in it sate *Irene*, or Peace, in a flowery vesture like the Spring, a garland of olives on her head, a branch of palm in her hand, buskins of green taffeta, great puffs about her neck and shoulders.

James Shirley. *The Triumph of Peace, 1633.*

GIVE ME LUTES

LET soldiers beg and starve, or steal and hang.
Would I had here ten thousand soldiers' heads,
Their skulls set all in silver, to drink healths
To his confusion who first invented war,
And the health drunk to drown the bowls in the sea.
That very name of soldier makes me shrug,
And think I crawl with vermin. Give me lutes,
Mischief on drums, for soldiers ; fetch me whores. . . .

Thomas Dekker. *The Wonder of a Kingdom, 1636.*

THE GRAND DESIGN OF HENRY IV.

BY this he would have convinced all his neighbours that his whole design was to save, both himself and them, those immense sums which the maintenance of so many thousand soldiers, so many fortified places, and so many military expenses requires ; to free them for ever from the fear of those bloody catastrophes so common in Europe ; to procure them an uninterrupted repose ; and, finally, to unite them all in an indissoluble bond of security and friendship. . . .

Does it not indeed reflect shame and reproach on a
people who affect to be so polished and refined in their
manners that all their pretended improvements have not
yet guarded them from these barbarities which they
detest in nations the most savage and uncultivated ? To
destroy these pernicious seeds of confusion and disorder, and
prevent the barbarities of which they are the cause, could
any scheme have been more happily and perfectly contrived
than that of Henry the Great ?[1]

> Maximilien de Béthune duc de
> Sully.   *Mémoires, 1638-1662.*
> *English translation, 1778.*

[1] For an excellent account of the scheme see *Grotius Society Publications
No.* 2, ed. David Ogg, 1921.

PERPLEXED

I HATE the country's dirt and manners, yet
I love the silence ; I embrace the wit
And courtship, flowing here in a full tide,
But loathe the expense, the vanity, and pride.
No place each way is happy. Here I hold
Commerce with some, who to my ear unfold
(After a due oath ministered) the height
And greatness of each star shine in the state :
The brightness, the eclipse, the influence.
With others I commune, who tell me whence
The torrent doth of foreign discord flow :
Relate each skirmish, battle, overthrow,
Soon as they happen ; and by rote can tell
Those German towns even puzzle me to spell.
The cross or prosperous fate of Princes they
Ascribe to rashness, cunning, or delay :
And on each action comment, with more skill
Than upon Livy did old Machavill.
O busy folly ! Why do I my brain
Perplex with the dull policies of Spain,
Or quick designs of France ? Why not repair

To the pure innocence o' th' country air :
And neighbour thee, dear friend ? . . .
              Do but in thine own shade
(Thy head upon some flowry pillow laid,
King Nature's huswifery) contemplate all
His stratagems who labours to inthrall
The world to his great Master ; and you'll find
Ambition mocks itself, and grasps the wind.
Not conquest makes us great. Blood is too dear
A price for glory : Honour doth appear
To statesmen like a vision in the night,
And juggler-like works o' th' deluded sight. . . .

                        William Habington. *Castara,*
                        The Second Part, 1639.

DISARMAMENT

THE helmet now a hive for bees becomes,
And hilts of swords may serve for spiders' looms ;
              Sharp pikes may make
              Teeth for a rake ;
And the keen blade, th' arch enemy of life,
Shall be degraded to a pruning knife.
              The rustic spade
              Which first was made
For honest agriculture, shall retake
Its primitive employment, and forsake
              The rampire's steep
              And trenches deep.
Tame conies in our brazen guns shall breed,
Or gentle doves their young ones there shall feed.
              In musket barrels
              Mice shall raise quarrels
For their quarters. The ventriloquious drum
Like lawyers in vacation shall be dumb.
              Now all recruits
              (But those of fruits)

E

Shall be forgot ; and th' unarmed soldier
Shall only boast of what he did whilere,
In chimneys' ends
Among his friends.

Ralph Knevet. *Add. MS. B.M.*
27447, c. 1640.[1]

[1] Printed in *Rare Poems of the Seventeenth Century*, ed. L. Birkett Marshall, 1936.

A THANKSGIVING FOR PEACE

So cause us, Lord ! to think upon
The blessing we possess,
That we may praise what Thou hast done,
And Thy great love confess.
For we whose fields in ages past
With bloodshed were distained,
Whilst fire and sword laid others waste,
In safety have remained.

No armed bands the ploughman fears,
No towers are overturned ;
No temple shakes about our ears,
No townships now are burned.
No father hears his little child
In vain for succour cry :
No husband sees his wife defiled,
Whilst he doth wounded lie. . . .

George Wither. *Hallelujah :*
Hymn LXXIV. 1641.

A CONSTANT TRUTH

In those days there shall come Wars and rumours of Wars, to me seems no prophecy, but a constant truth, in all times verified since it was pronounced.

Sir Thomas Browne. *Religio Medici, 1642.*

TONGUES AND PENS

SCHOLARS are men of Peace, they bear no arms, but their tongues are sharper than Actius his razor ; their pens carry farther, and give a louder report than thunder.

Ibid.

"Contemplative and bookish men must of necessity be more quarrelsome than others, because they contend not about matter of fact, nor can determine their controversies by any certain witnesses nor judges. But as long as they go towards peace, that is truth, it is no matter which way."—John Donne, *Biathanatos*, 1608.

UPON A PIECE OF CLOTH

MY heart has been in no rest since you went. I confess I was never so full of sorrow. I fear the provision of corn and malt will not hold out, if this continue ; and they say they will burn my barns ; and my fear is that they will place soldiers so near me that there will be no going out. My comfort is that you are not with me, lest they should take you : but I do most dearly miss you. I wish, if it pleased God, that I were with your father. I would have writ to him, but I durst not write upon paper. Dear Ned, write to me, though you write upon a piece of cloth, as this is. I pray God bless you, as I desire my own soul should be blessed. There's a thousand dragoneers came into Hertford five hours after my Lord Hertford.

Lady Brilliana Harley. *To her son Edward, Dec. 13, 1642.*

A BEAUTIFUL BLESSING

Blessed are the Peace-makers. Matt. 5, 9.

OBSERVE in the words the best work and the best wages : the best work, *Peace-makers* ; the best wages, *They are blessed.*

I begin with the work, which shall employ my pains and

your attention this day. Now the goodness of peace will
the better appear if we consider the misery of war. It
is said, Gen. 12, 11, *And it came to pass when Abraham was
come near to enter into Egypt, that he said unto Sara his wife,
Behold now I know that thou art a fair woman to look upon.*
Why *Now I know thou art a beautiful woman?* Did Abraham
live thus long in ignorance of his wife's beauty? Did he
now first begin to know her handsomeness? Learned
Tremelius[1] on the place starts and answers the objection :
Now, that is, when Abraham came into Egypt ; as if he
had said, When I see the tawny faces and swarthy com-
plexions of the sun-burnt Egyptians, thy face seemeth the
fairer, and thy beauty the brighter in mine eyes.

I must confess I ever prized Peace for a pearl ; but we
never did or could set the true estimate and value upon
it till this interruption and suspension of it. *Now* we know,
being taught by dear experience, that peace is a beautiful
blessing. . . .

> Thomas Fuller, D.D. *Sermon
> preached at the Savoy Chapel,*[2]
> *Dec. 28, 1642.*

[1] Tremellii et Junii *Test. Veteris Bib.*, ed. 1607, p. 16.
[2] In *Truth Maintained*, 1643, Fuller has an address to "My Deare Parish
Saint Mary Savoy," in which he says: "You know how I in all my
sermons unto you, by leave of my text, would have a passage in the
praise of peace. Still I am of the same opinion. The longer I see this
war, the less I like it— and the more I loathe it."

WIFE TO HUSBAND

I PRAISE God we in this family and all the rest of friends
are in good health ; we in the same condition you left us,
or better, nothing wanting but thyself, which is more
prized than all the rest, and I hope ere long to enjoy. Tom
is at the Dungre, my sister Ellen at Geaton, Brereton's army
within 3 miles of Chester. . . . I long much to hear of thy
resolution, which I hope will be to go no further nor to
alter thy condition any way. I hope there will be no cause
for it. However, as thou tender the life of thy poor desolate

wife, go no further from her. Thou knowest the condition
thou left me in, and if thou go any further I shall despair
of ever seeing thee. Therefore desire, love, let me hear
that thy resolution is to stay where thou art. I hope it will
be but a short time. Do not think I doubt of God's all-
sufficience, for I have daily experience of his delivering
and forbearing mercies unto me all my life through, and
especially of late days, but if you go further you must pass
a great deal of danger, so must I, before we can meet again.

K. Lloyd. *To her husband, Luke*
Lloyd, Feb. 3, 1643-4.

DEATHBED THOUGHT

It's our duty to sympathise in all mercies, that we praise
the Lord together in chastisements or trials, that so we may
sorrow together. Truly England and the Church of God
hath had a great favour from the Lord in this great victory
given unto us, such as the like never was since the war began.
It had all the evidences of an absolute victory obtained by
the Lord's blessing upon the godly party principally. We
never charged but we routed the enemy. The left wing
which I commanded, being our own horse, beat all the
Prince's horse. God made them as stubble to our swords.
We charged their regiments of foot with our horse, and
routed all we charged. The particulars I cannot relate
now ; but I believe of twenty thousand the Prince hath not
four thousand left. Give glory, all the glory, to God.

Sir, God hath taken away your eldest son by a cannon
shot. It brake his leg. We were necessitated to have it cut
off, whereof he died.

Sir, you know my trials this way, but the Lord supported
me with this, that the Lord took him into the happiness we
all pant after and live for. There is your precious child, full
of glory, to know sin nor sorrow any more. He was a gallant
young man, exceeding gracious. God give you His comfort.
Before his death he was so full of comfort that to Frank
Russell and myself he could not express it, it was so great

above his pain. This he said to us. A little after he said one thing lay upon his spirit ; I asked him what that was ; he told me that it was that God had not suffered him to be no more the executioner of his enemies.

> Oliver Cromwell. *To Colonel Valentine Walton, his brother-in-law, July 5, 1644.*

Marvell was not prophetically inspired when he wrote:
Thee, many ages hence, in martial verse
Shall the English soldier, ere he charge, rehearse;
Singing of thee, inflame himself to fight,
And, with the name of Cromwell, armies fright.

OUR CURSE

No more, no more,
We are already pin'd ;
And sore, and poor,
In body and in mind :
And yet our sufferings have been
Less than our sin.
Come long-desired peace, we thee implore,
And let our pains be less, or power more. . . .

Since 'tis our curse,
To fight we know not why ;
'Tis worse and worse
The longer thus we lie :
For War itself is but a Nurse
To make us worse.
Come blessed peace, we once again implore,
And let our pains be less, or power more.

> Alexander Brome. *The Riddle, 1644.*

ENGLAND'S TEARS

Sweet Peace, most benign and amiable Goddess, how comes it to pass that thou hast so abandoned Earth, and, taking thy flight to heaven, as once Astrea did, dost reject the sighs and sacrifices of poor mortals ? Was that flaming Usher of God's Vengeance, which appeared six and twenty years since in the heavens, the herald that fetched thee away ? For ever since poor Europe hath been harassed, and pitifully rent up and down with wars, and now I am become the last scene. Gentle Peace, thou which goest always attended on by plenty and pleasure ; thou which fillest the husband-man's barns, the grafter's folds, the tradesman's shop, the vintner's cellars, the lawyer's desk, the merchant's magazines, the prince's treasury, how comes it to pass that thou hast given up thy throne to Bellona, that all-destroying Fury ? Behold how my plundering yeoman wants hinds and horses to plow up my fertile soil ; the poor labourer, who useth to mingle the morning dew with his anheled sweat, shakes at his work for fear of pressing ; the trades-man shuts up his shop, and keeps more holidays than willingly he would ; the merchant walks to the Exchange, only to learn news, not to negotiate. Sweet Peace, thou which wast used to make princes' courts triumph with tilt and tournaments, and other gallantries, to make them receive lustre by foreign ambassadors ; to make the arts and sciences flourish ; to make cities and suburbs shine with goodly structures ; to make the country ring with the huntsman's horn, and the shepherd's pipe : how comes it to pass that blood-thirsty discord now usurps thy place, and flings her snakes in every corner ? Behold my prince's court is now full of nothing but buff-coats, spanners, and musket-rests ; the country echoes with nothing but the sound of drums and trumpets. Hark how pitifully my lions roar, how dejectedly my roses and flowers-de-luces hang down their heads, what doleful strains my harp gives.

James Howell. *England's Tears for the Present Wars, 1644.*

LOOKING WESTWARD

And will remove thy Candlestick out of his place except thou repent. Revel. 2, 5. . . . . From Jerusalem (whence the gospel first started) this Candlestick is observed to have a favourable inclination to verge more and more westward. This putteth us in some hopes of America, in God's due time ; God knows what good effects to them our sad war may produce : some may be frighted therewith over into those parts (being more willing to endure American than English savages) ; or out of curiosity to see, necessity to live, frugality to gain, may carry religion over with them into this barbarous country.

Thomas Fuller, D.D. *Sermon preached at Exeter,*[1] *1646.*

[1] Fuller was present at the siege of Exeter, and was witness of a remarkable instance of Divine Providence. "When the city of Exeter was besieged by the Parliamentary forces, so that only the south side thereof, towards the sea, was open unto it, incredible numbers of larks were found in that quarter, for multitude like quails in the wilderness, though (blessed be God!) unlike them both in cause and effect—as not desired with man's destruction, nor sent with God's anger—as appeared by their digestion into wholesome nourishment: hereof I was an eye and mouth witness. I will save my credit, in not conjecturing any number, knowing that therein, though I should stop beneath the truth, I should mount above belief. They were as fat as plentiful; so that, being sold for twopence a dozen and under, the poor—who could have no cheaper, as the rich no better, meat—used to make pottage of them, boiling them down therein. Several natural causes were assigned thereof. However, the cause of causes was Divine Providence."

FAREWELL FROST

FLED are the frosts, and now the fields appear
Re-clothed in fresh and verdant diaper.
Thawed are the snows, and now the lusty Spring
Gives to each mead a neat enamelling.
The Palms put forth their gems, and every tree
Now swaggers in her leavy gallantry.
The while the Daulian minstrel sweetly sings
With warbling notes her Tyrrean sufferings.
What gentle winds perspire ? As if here
Never had been the Northern Plunderer
To strip the trees and fields, to their distress,
Leaving them to a pitied nakedness.

And look how when a frantic storm doth tear
A stubborn oak or holm (long growing there)
But lulled to calmness, then succeeds a breeze
That scarcely stirs the nodding leaves of trees :
So when this war (which tempest-like doth spoil
Our salt, our corn, our honey, wine and oil)
Falls to a temper, and doth mildly cast
His inconsiderate frenzy off at last,
The gentle Dove may, when these turmoils cease,
Bring in her bill once more the Branch of Peace.

Robert Herrick. Hesperides, 1647.

IN RETREAT

HERE is no other case in law
But what the sun-burnt hat of straw
With crooked sickle reaps and binds
Up into sheaves to help the hinds ;
Whose arguing alone's in this,
Which cop lies well, and which amiss,
How the hock-cart with all its gear
Should be tricked up, and what good cheer
Bacon with cook's reports express,
And how to make the tenth go less.

There are no other wars or strifes'
Encouragers, shrill trumpets, fifes,
Or horrid drums, but what excels
All music, Nature's minstrels
Piping and chirping, as they sit
Embower'd in branches, dance to it ;
And, if at all those do contest,
It is in this, but which sings best ;
And when they have contended long,
I, though unseen, must judge the song.

Thus out of fears or noise of war,
Crowds and the clamourings at bar,

The merchant's dread, th' unconstant tides,
With all vexations besides,
I hug my Quiet, and alone
Take thee for my companion,
And deem in doing so, I've all
I can true conversation call ;
For so my thoughts by this retreat
Grow stronger, like contracted heat.

Mildmay Fane. *Otia Sacra, 1648.*

STRANGE GIDDINESS

STRANGE giddiness of war ; some men must groan
To further others' mirth. What fury rules
O'er human sense, that we should struggle to
Destroy in wounds, and rage, our life, that heaven
Decreed so short ? It is a mystery
Too sad to be remembered by the wise,
That half mankind consume their noble blood
In causes not beloved or understood.

Sir William Davenant.[1] *Love
and Honour, 1649.*

[1] "His private opinion was, that Religion at last—e.g. a hundred years
hence—would come to a settlement, and that in a kind of ingeniose
Quakerisme."—Aubrey.

WHEN RELIGION PUTS ON ARMOUR

I HAVE lived to see religion painted upon banners, and
thrust out of churches, and the temple burned into a
tabernacle, and that tabernacle made ambulatory, and
covered with skins of beasts and torn curtains, and God to
be worshipped not as He is the Father of our Lord Jesus
(an afflicted Prince, the King of sufferings,) nor as the God
of Peace (which two appellatives God newly took upon
Him in the New Testament, and glories in for ever :) but
He is owned now rather as the Lord of Hosts, which title

He was pleased to lay aside when the kingdom of the Gospel was preached by the Prince of Peace. But when religion puts on armour, and God is not acknowledged by His New Testament titles, religion may have in it the power of the sword, but not the power of godliness ; and we may claim of this to God, and amongst them that are afflicted, but we have no remedy, but what we must expect from the fellowship of Christ's sufferings, and the returns of the God of peace.

Jeremy Taylor.   *Dedication to Richard, Lord Vaughan, of Holy Living, 1650.*

COMMISSION DECLINED

So Worcester fight came on and my time being out of being committed six months to the house of correction ; and then they filled the house of correction with persons that they had taken up to be soldiers : and they would have had me to be captain of them to go forth to Worcester to fight, and the soldiers cried they would have none but me : so the keeper of the house of correction was commanded to bring me up before the commissioners and soldiers in the market place : and there they proffered me that preferment because of my virtue, as they said, with many other compliments : and asked me if I would not take up arms for the commonwealth against the king. But I told them I lived in the virtue of that life and power that took away the occasion of all wars : and I knew from whence all wars did rise, from the lust, according to James his doctrine : and still they courted me to accept of their offer : and thought that I did but compliment with them, but I told them I was come into the covenant of peace which was before wars and strifes was : and they said they offered it in love and kindness to me because of my virtue, and such like : and I told them if that were their love and kindness I trampled it under my feet.

Then said they, Take him away, gaoler, and cast him

into the dungeon amongst the rogues and felons : which they then did put me into the dungeon amongst 30 felons in a lousy stinking place without any bed : where they kept me almost half a year : unless it were at times : and some times they would let me walk in the garden for they had a belief of me that I would not go away.

George Fox. *Journal, 1650.*

PREACHING AND FIGHTING

I was not satisfied with your last speech to me about Empson, that he was a better preacher than a fighter or soldier or words to that effect. Truly I think he that prays and preaches best will fight best.[1] I know nothing will give like courage and confidence as the knowledge of God in Christ will, and I bless God to see any in this Army able and willing to impart the knowledge they have for the good of others. And I expect it be encouraged by all chief officers in this army especially : and I hope you will do so.

Oliver Cromwell. *To Colonel Hacker, Dec. 25, 1650.*

[1] Nehemiah Wallington's testimony is of interest: "The enemy discharged three times their two pieces of ordnance upon the very body of our army, but not a man hurt by God's great mercy. Nay, God's wonderful mark was observed in the guidance of the adverse party's bullets. For one went over the Lord Brooks, his head, as also another bullet went close to the Lord Grey; some went on one side, and some flew clean over their heads, both horse and foot, touching no man, nor doing any harm at all. And some bullets grazed along, and some bullets fell down flat upon the ground before them, and struck or spattered dirt in some of their faces; but not a man hurt, which shows the protection of God is over them that trust in Him. Which, after command given on our side to discharge one of our pieces or ordnance, which was charged with musket bullets, which with the scattering many of the adverse party were dangerously wounded, a drummer, with two others, was slain, and supposed many others; and five very good horses found dead."

A NEW SHUFFLE

COMPETITION of riches, honour, command, or other power, inclineth to contention, enmity, and war ; because the way of one competitor, to the attaining of his desire, is to kill, subdue, supplant, or repel the other. . . . Desire of ease, and sensual delight, disposeth men to obey a common power, because by such desires a man doth abandon the protection that might be hoped for from his own industry and labour. Fear of death, and wounds, disposeth to the same, and for the same reason. On the contrary, needy men, and hardy, not contented with their present condition, as also all men that are ambitious of military command, are inclined to continue the causes of war ; and to stir up trouble and sedition, for there is no honour military but by war, nor any such hope to mend an ill game, as by causing a new shuffle.

Thomas Hobbes. *Leviathan, 1651.*

THE POSTURE OF WAR

BUT though there had never been any time, wherein particular men were in a condition of war one against another ; yet in all times, kings, and persons of sovereign authority, because of their independency, are in continual jealousies, and in the state and posture of gladiators ; having their weapons pointing, and their eyes fixed on one another ; that is, their forts, garrisons, and guns upon the frontiers of their kingdoms ; and continual spies upon their neighbours ; which is a posture of war. But because they uphold thereby the industry of their subjects ; there does not follow from it that misery which accompanies the liberty of particular men.

Ibid.

RIDICULOUS MISERY

COME then ! and while the slow icicle hangs
At the stiff latch, and Winter's frosty pangs
Benumb the year, blithe (as of old) lets us
'Midst noise and war, of peace and mirth discuss.
This portion thou wert born for : why should we

Vex at the times' ridiculous misery?
An age that thus hath fooled itself, and will
(Spite of thy teeth and mine) persist so still.

Henry Vaughan. Olor Iscanus, 1651.

PARADISE LOST

OH thou, that dear and happy isle,
The garden of the world erewhile,
Thou paradise of the four seas,
Which Heaven planted us to please,
But, to exclude the world, did guard
With watery, if not flaming sword—
What luckless apple did we taste
To make us mortal, and thee waste?
Unhappy! shall we never more
That sweet militia restore,
When gardens only had their towers
And all the garrisons were flowers;
When roses only arms might bear,
And men did rosy garlands wear?
Tulips, in several colours barred,
Were then the Switzers of our guard;
The gardener had the soldier's place,
And his more gentle forts did trace;
The nursery of all things green
Was then the only magazine;
The winter quarters were the stoves,
Where he the tender plants removes.
But war all this doth overgrow:
We ordnance plant, and powder sow.

Andrew Marvell. Upon Appleton
House, 1651-2.

ABEL'S BLOOD

SAD, purple well! whose bubbling eye
Did first against a murd'rer cry;
Whose streams, still vocal, still complain

Of bloody Cain ;
And now at evening are as red
As in the morning when first shed.
If single thou
—Though single voices are but low,—
Couldst such a shrill and long cry rear
As speaks still in thy Maker's ear,
What thunders shall those men arraign
Who cannot count those they have slain,
Who bathe not in a shallow flood,
But in a deep, wide sea of blood ?
A sea, whose loud waves cannot sleep,
But deep still calleth upon deep :
Whose urgent sound, like unto that
Of many waters, beateth at
The everlasting doors above,
Where souls behind the altar move,
And with one strong, incessant cry
Inquire " How long ? " of the Most High.

Henry Vaughan. *Silex
Scintillans, Pt. II., 1655.*

THAT INHUMANE INCLINATION

In all times and places a wise Christian will abhor war.
It is the very empire of the devil, and in nothing so much
doth he show himself the Prince of this World. It is the
discipline of robbery and murder. It is the deep gulf of all
misery. It is the sink of all wickedness and villainy. Yet
the best men are often engaged in it even out of conscience
and duty, for every one oweth his life to the defence of his
country. But for one to love the trade of man-butcher, and
delight in the hunting of man his own kind, as others do
in the hunting of the wolf or wild boar, is an unnatural
barbarousness, not valour. Who so will keep the integrity
and serenity of his conscience, and hopeth for the salvation
of his soul, must keep himself free from that inhumane
inclination, the true image of satan, who was a murderer

from the beginning. God's children are children of peace, which they entertain in their mind and advance by their prayers and counsels.

> Peter du Moulin, the son. *Of Peace and Contentment of Mind,* *1657.*

THE BASILISK

PLINY in his Natural History writeth that the nature of the basilisk is to kill all trees and shrubs it breathes upon, and to scorch and burn all herbs and grass it passeth over. Such are the dismal effects of War ; for the title never so clear, the cause never so just, yet the means are not without fire and sword nor the end without horror and bloodshed. Peace therefore is to be preferred to it.

> John Spencer. *Things New and Old, 1658.*

RECRUITER

Mattemores :
> Methinks there is no nobler thing on earth
> Than to see hills of bodies, lakes of blood—
> No braver music than the martial drum,
> Nor diapasons sweeter to the ear
> Than unto it the warlike trumpets make.
> When I but hear this harmony, I could,
> Full of delight, venture my single person
> Against an armed troop. Away with peace !
> It is the canker and the bane of minds ;
> 'Tis that which makes us to forget ourselves,
> And spend our lives in sensuality.
> Then glorious war, advance thy armed arm,
> That soldiers may have ways to show themselves ! . . .
> Hast thou a mind to become now a soldier ?

Trappolin : Indeed, Seignior Captain, I cannot resolve you as yet. I am about a wife ; I'll ask her if she will turn soldier too, and then, if I like it, there's an end. But I pray you, Captain, what is a soldier ?

Mattemores :

A soldier, Trappolin, is he that does
Venture his life a hundred times a day—
Would in his country's and his prince's cause
Stand cannon shot, and wood of steeled pikes—
Would, when his body's full of wounds, all night
Lie in the field, and sleep upon his helm.

Trappolin : Good Captain, pardon me, neither I nor Flametta will be soldiers. Heavens defend ! Venture my life so many times a day ? there is more safety and gain in turning thief ! I love my country and my prince well, but myself better. 'Tis good sleeping in a whole skin ; 'tis better lying with Flametta in a warm bed ! Marry, I had thought a soldier had not been such a fool ! How many of them might there be in Florence, sir Captain?

Mattemores : Thou coward, many hundreds.

Trappolin : The gods send them more wit, that's e'en all that I can say.

Sir Aston Cokain. *Trappolin, 1658.*

A TESTIMONY

WE confess to him alone who is the Lord of Glory and the Prince of Peace, who unto peace hath called us and in peace to rest, that in peace we may conquer the nations, and in quietness overcome the people that delight in war . . . and we have not used either sword or spear, or looked unto the arm of flesh to be a defence unto us. . . .

Reports have been spread in the nation of the Quakers rising and cutting throats, which are bad reports, yet we have gone through them in patience. . . . And thus have we experienced His everlasting loving kindness, and His wonderful Works we are made to declare amongst the Children of Men, that all may know there is no God like unto our God, unto whom alone we look, and our eye is towards Him, and we cannot join with weapons of war, nor with any party who is striving with them.

> William Smith. *A Short Testi-mony, 1660. (Balm from Gilead, 1675.)*

[1] "About seven years I was his wife. . . . I have known him in many trials and afflictions, yet I never knew a hasty word to come forth of his mouth. . . . He had six children by a former wife. . . . He was a daily labourer in the work of God, as in writing many serviceable books, several of which he did in times of his imprisonment."—Elizabeth Smith.

BEFORE THE WAR

AH, happy isle, how art thou changed and cursed
    Since I was born and knew thee first !
When Peace, which had forsook the world around
(Frighted with noise and the shrill trumpet's sound)
        Thee for a private place of rest,
        And a secure retirement chose
    Wherein to build her Halcyon nest ;
No wind durst stir abroad the air to discompose.

When all the riches of the globe beside
    Flowed in thee with every tide ;
When all that Nature did thy soil deny
The growth was of thy fruitful industry ;
        When all the proud and dreadful sea,
        And all his tributary streams,
    A constant tribute paid to thee ;
When all the liquid world was one extended Thames. . . .

> Abraham Cowley. *A Vision, 1661.*

FROM THE STAGE

O MONEY ! money ! if the wits would dress
With ornaments the present face of peace,
And to our poet half that treasure spare

Which faction gets from fools to nourish war,
Then his contracted scenes should wider be,
And move by greater engines. . . .

> Sir William Davenant. *The Siege
> of Rhodes (Prologue to Second Part),
> 1663.*

VIRTUE OR MADNESS?

In honour's orb the Christians shine ;
  Their light in war does still increase,
Though oft misled by mists of wine
  Or blinder love, the crime of peace.
Bold in adult'ry's frequent change
  And ev'ry loud expensive vice,
Ebbing out wealth by ways as strange
  As it flowed in by avarice—
Thus vilely they dare live, and yet dare die.
  If courage be a virtue, 'tis allowed
But to those few on whom our crowns rely,
  And is condemned as madness in the crowd.

> *Ibid.*

CHORUS OF WOMEN

Let us live, live ! for being dead
    The pretty spots,
    Ribbands and knots,
And the fine French dress for the head,
    No lady wears upon her
    In the cold, cold bed of honour.
Beat down our grottos, and hew down our bowers,
Dig up our arbours, and root up our flowers !
Our gardens are bulwarks and bastions become :
Then hang up our lutes, we must sing to the drum.
    Our patches and our curls,
    So exact in each station,
    Our powders and our purls
    Are now out of fashion.

Hence with our needles, and give us your spades ;
We, that were ladies, grow coarse as our maids.
Our coaches have drove us to balls at the Court,
We now must drive barrows to earth up the port.

Ibid.

In *The Soldier going to the Field* (*Works*, 1673), Davenant has a familiar phrase:

For I must go where lazy Peace
Will hide her drowsy head,
And, for the sport of kings, increase
The number of the dead.

STRANGE SPORT

AFTER dinner, having nothing else to do till flood, I went and saw Mrs. Daniel, to whom I did not tell that the fleets were engaged, because of her husband, who is in the *Royal Charles*. Very pleasant with her half an hour, and so away and down to Blackwall, and there saw the soldiers (who were by this time gotten most of them drunk) shipped off. But, Lord ! to see how the poor fellows kissed their wives and sweethearts in that simple manner at their going off, and shouted, and let off their guns, was strange sport.

Samuel Pepys. *Diary, June 2, 1666.*

PRESSED MEN

AFTER dinner to the office again, where busy, and then down to Deptford to the yard, thinking to have seen Bagwell's wife, whose husband is gone yesterday to the fleet, but I did not see her, so missed what I went for, and so back to the Tower several times, about the business of the pressed men, and late at it till twelve at night, shipping of them. But, Lord ! how some poor women did cry ; and in my life I never did see such natural expression of passion as I did here in some women's bewailing themselves and running to every parcel of men that were brought, one after another, to look for their husbands, and wept over every vessel that went off, thinking they might be there, and looking after the ship as far as ever they could by moonlight, that it grieved me to the heart to hear them. Besides, to see the poor patient labouring men and house-keepers, leaving poor wives and families, taking up on a sudden by strangers, was very hard, and that without press-money, but forced against all law to be gone. It is a great tyranny.

Ibid, July 1, 1666.

ADAM'S VISION

HE looked and saw wide territory spread
Before him, towns, and rural works between,
Cities of men with lofty gates and towers,
Concourse in arms, fierce faces threat'ning war,
Giants of mighty bone, and bold emprise ;
Part wield their arms, part curb the foaming steed,
Single or in array of battle rang'd
Both horse and foot, nor idly must'ring stood ;
One way a band select from forage drives
A herd of beeves, fair oxen and fair kine
From a fat meadow ground ; or fleecy flock.
Ewes and their bleating lambs over the plain,
Their booty ; scarce with life the shepherds fly,
But call in aid, which tacks a bloody fray ;
With cruel tournament the squadrons' join
Where cattle pastured late, now scatterd lies;
With carcasses and arms th' ensanguined field
Deserted : Others to a city strong
Lay siege, encamp'd ; by battery, scale, and mine,
Assaulting ; others from the wall defend
With dart and jav'lin, stones and sulphurous fire ;
On each hand slaughter and gigantic deeds.
The other part the scepter'd heralds call
To Council in the city gates : anon
Grey-headed men and grave, with warriors mix'd,

Assemble, and harangues are heard, but soon
In factious opposition, till at last
Of middle age one rising, eminent
In wise deport, spake much of Right and Wrong,
Of Justice, of Religion, Truth and Peace,
And Judgment from above : him old and young
Exploded, and had seiz'd with violent hands,
Had not a cloud descending snatch'd him thence
    Unseen amid the throng : so violence
Proceeded, and Oppression, and Sword-Law
Through all the plain, and refuge none was found.
Adam was all in tears, and to his guide
Lamenting turn'd full sad ; O what are these,
Death's ministers, not men, who thus deal death
Inhumanly to men, and multiply
Then thousandfold the sin of him who slew
His brother ; for of whom such massacre
Make they but of their brethren, men of men ?

> John Milton. *Paradise Lost,*
> *Bk. XI., 1667.*

Milton, it has been suggested, was not in favour of conscription:

> For life
> To noble and ignoble is more sweet
> Untrained in Arms, where rashness leads not on.
>
> *Paradise Lost,* Bk. XII.

THE WAR WORTH FIGHTING

AND now how blessed a thing were it, if we could once
thus follow the things that make for Peace, that the
numberless mutual enmities that are now among us may
all be reduced into one, that we may fight not against
single adversaries, but against War itself, and contend
against nothing but contention. And sure our victory here
were worth millions of those petty conquests wherewith
men please themselves, and which acquire them so little
of real advantage, that the same account which was given
to Otho and Vitellius, that the *war* would swallow up the
one, and the *victory* the other, is too applicable to our com-

batants who are like to be equally unhappy in *defeat* or *success*. The Spartans had an order, that when any of their generals had compassed his design by policy or treaty, he should sacrifice an *ox*, but when by force and bloodshed, a *cock* only. From the distant values of which oblations, Plutarch observes how much they preferred the achievements of calm and sober counsels, before those of strength and power. . . .

'Twas Abner's admonition to Joab, when he was in a hot pursuit of the Israelites, 2 Sam. 2, 26, *Shall the sword devour for ever ? knowest thou not that it will be bitterness in the latter end ?* And sure 'tis more than time for our Leaders to make the same reflection, and, as Joab did there, call back the people from following their brethren. Nay indeed, would they but attend, they might hear themselves called back, the great Captain of their Salvation sounding a retreat from these fatal skirmishes. . . .

And now if after all that hath or can be said of the *obligation, necessity,* or *advantages* of Peace, we are put to the Psalmist's complaint, *That there are still those that will make them ready to battle,* if men are of so untreatable a temper that nothing can be obtained of them, what remains for those that are peaceable and faithful in Israel, but to bewail those mischiefs that they cannot redress ?

Richard Allestree (?) *Causes of
the Decay of Christian Piety, 1667.*

OBJECTIONS TO MARRIED SOLDIERS

No less importance I judge to put under your Majesty's consideration, of what prejudice can be to your Majesty to suffer that your ordinary soldiers and inferior officers marry at their pleasure ; because after they are married, and have children and make a family, they are not ready to your service ; they are out of love of their officers and regiment, and, in occasion to serve in civil wars, they have their families in the towns that are to be taken, and are drawn by the affections of their wives and children to serve and adhere more to the people than to the King ; and, for my part, a married man in this country I do not reckon a soldier fit for your Majesty's service.

Sir Bernard Gascoigne. *To Charles II., c. 1668.*

BLASPHEMING IN THE ARMY

AND because the respect and honour that we are obliged to give to God Almighty should not be despised with that cursed custom of blaspheming His holy name (error too much common in the armies) and which in other countries is punished by boring the tongue of the blasphemers, let be infallible law in this Christian army that all those soldiers who shall be so profane as to blaspheme God shall be for the first time corrected by their officers, and, not leaving their infamous fault for it, shall be cashiered as the most dangerous plague that can be in one army.

Ibid.

It is odd that so often the soldier is begrudged the use of strong language. See pp. 211, 230, 391.

AN INFERIOR DAY OF JUDGMENT

WAR is a cessation of humanity, a demurrer to all civil justice, an appeal to the sentence of the sword, a trial by ballotting of guns, and the supreme Court of Judicature in the whole world, to which all nations equally submit, and put themselves upon God and their country. It is a kind of inferior Day of Judgment, only the proceedings are different ; for as the trumpets sound and the dead rise in the one, so the trumpets sound and the living fall in the other—so contrary are the ways of divine and human justice, for God's judgments commonly hang half and save half without any appearing consideration of particulars, which among men is the most unequal way in the world, though the justest to him that understands all things. . . .

It is a disease contracted by the surfeits and disorders of Peace, a burning fever and running gout which the world always has in some part or other : an evil spirit that possesses it, and removes from one limb to another, makes it mad and raving, and is not to be cast out but by fasting, that is, until it has destroyed and consumed all that which went to maintain it. For as all creatures are nourished by the dam that bred them, so is war supported by the disorders that brought it forth, and does not degenerate from the breed it came of, for it puts all things out of order wherever it comes. It is a monster in a labyrinth that feeds upon man's flesh, for when it is once engaged it is a matter of exceeding difficulty to get out of it again. It destroys all the productions of peace that bred it . . . and plants nothing but barbarousness wherever it prevails. . . .

It is said to be the last reason of kings, because it should be kept as a reserve when all others fail. It is a storm raised by statesmen, the conjurors of the world, that bears down all before it like a hurricane, and is not so easily allayed as raised. It is never so barbarous as when it is civil, for in civil wars parties are inflamed with particular animosities, and provocations given and received in the quarrel, which never happens in foreign wars.

Samuel Butler. *Inconsistent Opinions, c. 1669.*

A LICENCE TO KILL

WAR is a licence to kill and slay all those who inhabit that land which is therefore called the enemy's, because he who makes the war hath a mind to possess it. And must there not many of the laws of God, as well as of man, be cancelled and abolished before a man can honestly execute or take such a licence ? What have the poor inhabitants of that land done that they must be destroyed for cultivating their own land in the country where they were born ? And can any king believe that the names of those are left out of the records of God's creation, and that the injuries done to them shall not be considered? War is a de-population, defaces all that art and industry hath produced, destroys all plantations, burns churches and palaces, and mingles them in the same ashes with the cottages of the peasant and the labourer ; it distinguishes not of age, or sex, or dignity, but exposes all things and persons, sacred and profane, to the same contempt and confusion, and reduces all that blessed order and harmony, which hath been the product of peace and religion, into the chaos it was first in ; as if it would contend with the Almighty in uncreating what he so wonderfully created and since polished.

Edward Hyde, Earl of Clarendon. *Essay on War, 1670.*

EFFECTS LONG AFTER

In war the confidence and courage which a victorious army contracts by notable successes, and the dejection of spirit and the consternation which a subdued party under-goes by frequent defeats, is not at an end when the war is determined, but hath its effects very long after ; and the tenderness of nature, and the integrity of manners, which are driven away, or powerfully discountenanced by the corruption of war, are not quickly recovered, but instead thereof a roughness, jealousy, and distrust introduced that makes conversation unpleasant and uneasy ; and the weeds which grow up in the shortest war can hardly be pulled up and extirpated without a long and unsuspected peace.

Ibid.

THE GREATEST COMFORT AND ORNAMENT

Peace is that harmony in the state that health is in the body. No honour, no profit, no plenty can make him happy who is sick with a fever in his blood, and with defluxions and aches in his joints and bones ; but health restored gives a relish to the other blessings, and is very merry without them. No kingdom can flourish and be at ease in which there is no peace, which only makes men dwell at home, and enjoy the labour of their own hands, and improve all the advantages which the air and the climate and the soil administers to them ; and all which yield no comfort where there is no peace. God himself reckons health the greatest blessing he can bestow upon mankind, and peace the greatest comfort and ornament he can confer upon states. . . . There is nothing of real and substantial comfort in the world but what is the product of peace ; and whatsoever we may lawfully and innocently take delight in is the fruit and effect of peace.

Idem.   Essay on Peace, 1670.

HELL AND HEAVEN

WE cannot make a more lively representation and emblem to ourselves of Hell than by the view of a kingdom in war, where there is nothing to be seen but destruction and fire, and the discord itself is a great part of the torment ; nor a more sensible reflection upon the joys of Heaven than as it is all quiet and peace, and where nothing is to be discerned but consent and harmony, and what is amiable in all the circumstances of it. And as far as we may warrantly judge the inhabitants of either climate, they who love and cherish discord among men, and take delight in war, have large mansions provided for them in that region of faction and disagreement ; as we may presume that they who set their hearts upon peace in this world, and labour and promote it in their several stations amongst all men, and who are instruments to prevent the breach of it amongst Princes and States, or to renew it when it is broken, have infallible title to a place and mansions in Heaven, where there is only peace in that perfection that all other blessings are comprehended in it and a part of it.

Ibid.

FROM ONE THING ONLY

I HAVE discovered that all the misfortunes of men arise
from one thing only, that they are unable to stay quietly
in their own chamber. . . . Hence it comes that play and
the society of women, war, and offices of state are so
sought after.

> Blaise Pascal. *Pensées, 1670. Tr.*
> *C. Kegan Paul.*

THEY ERR

THEY err who count it glorious to subdue
By Conquest far and wide, to over-run
Large Countries, and in field Great Battles win,
Great Cities by assault : what do these Worthies,
But rob and spoil, burn, slaughter, and enslave,
Peaceable Nations, neighbouring, or remote,
Made Captive, yet deserving freedom more
Than those their Conquerors, who leave behind
Nothing but ruin wheresoe'er they rove,
And all the flourishing works of peace destroy,
Then swell with pride, and must be titled Gods,
Great Benefactors of mankind, Deliverers,
Worshipped with Temple, Priest and Sacrifice ;
One is the Son of Jove, of Mars the other,
Till Conqueror Death discover them scarce men,
Rolling in brutish vices, and deformed,
Violent or shameful death their due reward.

> John Milton. *Paradise Regained,*
> *Bk. III., 1671.*

In his Commonplace Book Milton has a précis of Lactantius (vi. 6)
expressing similar sentiments.

A PECULIAR DISTINCTION

ALTHOUGH nothing is more agreeable to the laws of nature than the mutual peace of men with one another, preserved by the voluntary application of each person to his duty—living together in a state of peace being a peculiar distinction of men from brutes—yet it is sometimes both lawful and necessary to go to war, when by means of another's injustice we cannot without use of force preserve what is our own, nor enjoy those rights which are properly ours. But here common prudence and humanity do admonish us to forbear our arms there, where the prosecution of the injuries we resent is likely to return more hurt upon us and ours than it can do good. . . .

The liberty that is in war of killing, plundering, and laying all things waste, extends itself to so very large a compass that though a man carries his rage beyond the uttermost bounds of humanity, yet in the opinion of nations he is not to be accounted infamous, or one that ought to be avoided by persons of worth. Excepting that, among the more civilised world, they look upon some particular methods of doing hurt to enemies to be base, as poisoning fountains, or corrupting soldiers or subjects to kill their masters, etc.

Samuel Pufendorf. *De Jure Naturæ Gentium,*[1] *1672.* Tr. *Andrew Tooke, 1716.*

[1] The copy from which this extract was taken (by the courtesy of Mr. F. Norman, Bookseller) once belonged to Christopher Smart, who refers to peace in a charming context:

> Now labour his reward receives,
> For ADORATION counts his sheaves
> To peace, her bounteous prince;
> The nectarine his strong tint imbibes,
> And apples of ten thousand tribes,
> And quick peculiar quince.
> *A Song to David.*

THROUGH CONTEMPT OF CHRIST'S LAW

The last thing to be considered is Revenge and War, an evil so opposite and contrary to the spirit and doctrine of Christ as light to darkness. For, as is manifest by what is said, through contempt of Christ's law, the whole world is filled with various oaths, cursings, blasphemous profanations, and horrid perjuries ; so likewise through contempt of the same law the world is filled with violence, oppression, murders, ravishing of women and virgins, spoilings, depredations, burnings, devastations, and all manner of laciviousness and cruelty : so that it is strange that men, made after the image of God, should have so much degenerated, that they rather bear the image and nature of roaring lions, tearing tigers, devouring wolves, and raging boars, than rational creatures endued with reason. And is it not yet much more admirable that this horrid monster should find place and be fomented among those men that profess themselves disciples of our peaceable Lord and Master Jesus Christ, who by excellency is called the Prince of Peace, and hath expressly prohibited His children all violence ; and on the contrary commanded them that according to His example they should follow patience, charity, forbearance, and other virtues worthy of a Christian ?

> Robert Barclay. *An Apology for the True Christian Divinity, as the same is held forth, and preached, by the people, called in scorn, Quakers, 1676.*

THE QUAKER'S VIEW

If to revenge ourselves, or to render injury, evil for evil, wound for wound, to take eye for eye, tooth for tooth ; if to fight for outward and perishing things, to go a-warring one against another, whom we never saw, nor with whom we never had any contest, nor anything to do ; being, moreover, altogether ignorant of the cause of the war, but only that the magistrates of the nations foment quarrels one against another, the causes whereof are, for the most part, unknown to the soldiers that fight, as well as upon those whose side the right or wrong is ; and yet to be so furious and rage one against another, to destroy and spoil all, that this or the other worship may be received or abolished ; if to do this, and much more of this kind, be to fulfil the law of Christ, then are our adversaries indeed true Christians, and we miserable heretics, that suffer ourselves to be spoiled, taken, imprisoned, banished, beaten, and evilly treated, without any resistance, placing our trust only in God, that He may defend us, and lead us by the way of the cross into His kingdom.

Ibid.

AN ERRONEOUS OPINION

THAT Christians ought not to maintain religion by the sword, nor to fight for their lives and liberties, nor to fight at all, nor to kill any thing, nay not a chicken for our use.[1]

Alexander Ross. *A View of all Religions, 1675.*

[1] This is No. 78 in a list of 106 "erroneous opinions in religion . . . lately revived, or hatched since the fall of our Church Government."

ABOVE THESE STORMS

PEACE, wayward soul ! let not those various storms
Which hourly fill the world with fresh alarms
Invade thy Peace, nor discompose that rest
Which thou mayest keep untouched within thy breast
Amidst those whirlwinds, if thou keep but free
The intercourse between thy God and thee.
Thy region lies above these storms :
Thy thoughts are earthly, and they creep too low
If these can reach thee, or access can find
To bring or raise like tempest in thy mind.

Sir Matthew Hale. *Contemplations Moral and Divine, 1676.*

SLENDER PRETEXTS

UPON every slender pretext such as their own small discontents, or that they judge the present peace they have with their neighbours cannot suit with their own worldly glory, they sheathe their swords in one another's bowels ; ruin, waste, and destroy whole countries ; expose to the greatest misery many thousand families ; make thousands of widows and ten thousands of orphans ; cause the banks to overflow with the blood of those for whom the Lord Jesus shed His precious blood ; and spend and destroy many of the good creatures of God, and all this while they pretend to be followers of the lamb-like Jesus, who came not to destroy men's lives but to save them, the song of whose appearance to the world was, " Glory to God in the highest, and goodwill and peace to all men " ; not to kill, murder, and destroy men ; not to hire and force poor men to run upon and murder one another, merely to satisfy the lust and ambition of great men ; they being often times ignorant of the ground of the quarrel, and not having the least occasion of evil or prejudice against those their fellow Christians whom they thus kill ; amongst whom not one of a thousand perhaps ever saw one another before.

Robert Barclay. *An Epistle to the Ambassadors at Nimeguen, 1678.*

IF ALL MEN WERE CHRISTIANS

ALTHOUGH the Christian religion doth lay the greatest obligations on mankind to Peace and Unity, by the strictest commands, the highest examples, and the most prevailing arguments ; yet so much have the passions and interests of men overweighed the sense of their duty, that so nothing ought to be more in our *wishes*, so nothing seems more remote from our *hopes*, than the Universal

Peace of the Christian World. Not that there is any impossibility in the thing, or any considerably difficulty, if all men were such Christians as they ought to be.

> Edward Stillingfleet, D.D.,
> *Dean of St. Paul's. Sermon at the*
> *Guildhall Chapel, May 11, 1680.*

THE ENORMITIES OF THE PRESS

What truths, politics or news suffer by the Press is weekly experienced. It is nothing to kill a man this week and, with ink instead of aqua vitae, fetch him alive the next ; to drown two admirals in one week, and to buoy them up again next . . .

Nor fareth it better with Peace than Truth ; the feathers and plume seconding the quarrel of the quill, from inveighings to invading, declarations to defiance, remonstrances to resistance, and that to blood.

The press rippeth up the faults and differences of a nation, and then the sword the bowels of it. What printing beginneth by way of challenge, its contemporary invention, guns, answers in destruction-accents.

And the enormities of the press are caused partly by writers, and partly by readers.

> Anon. *The Tears of the Press, 1681.*

A SAVAGE WILDERNESS

How like a paradise the world would be, flourishing in joy and rest, if men would cheerfully conspire in affection, and helpfully contribute to each other's content : and how like a savage wilderness now it is, when, like wild beasts, they vex and persecute, worry and devour each other.

> Isaac Barrow, D.D. *Sermon : Of*
> *a Peaceable Temper and Carriage.*
> *Works, 1683.*

F

OUT OF THE ROAD

WELL, I have thought on't, and I find
This busy world is nonsense all ;
I here despair to please my mind,
Her sweetest honey is so mixt with gall.
Come then, I'll try how 'tis to be alone,
Live to myself awhile, and be my own . . .

Let plots and news embroil the State,
Pray what's that to my books and me ?
Whatever be the kingdom's fate,
Here I am sure t' enjoy a monarchy.
Lord of myself, accountable to none,
Like the first man in Paradise, alone . . .

Th' uneasy pageantry of State,
And all the plagues of thought and sense
Are far removed ; I'm placed by Fate
Out of the road of all impertinence.
Thus, though my fleeting life runs swiftly on,
'Twill not be short, because 'tis all my own.

John Norris. *The Retirement :
Poems, 1684.*

A LIVING MONUMENT

MAY not every soldier that comes alive out of the battle,
pass for a living monument of a benign chance, and a happy
providence ? For was he not in the nearest neighbourhood
to death ? And might not the bullet, that perhaps razed
his cheek, have as easily gone into his head ? And the
sword that glanced upon his arm, with a little diversion
have found the way to his heart ? But the workings o

Providence are marvellous, and the methods secret and untraceable, by which it disposes of the lives of men.[1]

> Robert South, D.D. *Sermon at*
> *Westminster Abbey, Feb. 22, 1684-5*

[1] The invidious distinctions made by Providence on the battlefield are celebrated in verse by John Pomfret:

> Did not th' Almighty, with immediate care,
> Direct and govern this capacious all,
> How soon would things into confusion fall ! . . .
> Let the brave speak, who oft has been
> In dreadful sieges, and fierce battles seen,
> How he's preserved, when bombs and bullets fly
> So thick, that scarce one inch of air is free;
> And though he does ten thousand see
> Fall at his feet, and in a moment die,
> Unhurt retreats, or gains unhurt the victory.

> —Upon the Divine Attributes: *Poems, 1699.*

TRUE GLORY

EARTH praises conquerors for shedding blood :
Heav'n, those that love their foes, and do them good.
It is terrestrial honour to be crown'd
For strowing men, like rushes, on the ground.
True glory 'tis to rise above them all,
Without th' advantage taken by their fall.
He that in fight diminishes mankind
Does no addition to his stature find :
But he that does a noble nature show,
Obliging others, still does higher grow.
For virtue practis'd such an habit gives,
That among men he like an Angel lives. . . .
The humble man, when he receives a wrong,
Refers revenge to whom it doth belong.
Nor sees he reason why he should engage,
Or vex his spirit, for another's rage.

> Edmund Waller. *Of the fear of*
> *God, 1685.*

THE PREROGATIVE OF HUMAN KIND

'Tis less to conquer than to make war cease,
And, without fighting, awe the world to peace ;
For proudest triumphs from contempt arise ;
The vanquish'd first the conqueror's arms despise :
Won ensigns are the gaudy marks of scorn ;
They brave the victor first and then adorn.
But peaceful monarchs reign like gods : while none
Dispute, all love, bless, reverence their throne.
Tigers and bears, with all the savage host,
May boldness, strength, and daring conquest boast ;
But the sweet passions of a generous mind
Are the prerogative of human kind. . . .

> Charles Montague, Earl of
> Halifax. *On the death of
> Charles II., 1685.*

LANGUISHING PEACE

I should tremble to sound a trumpet to war (which is always accompanied with fearful circumstances) did I not from my soul believe that a supreme peace, like an incurable gangrene, would create greater calamities, and introduce both a certain war, and the hazard of a total subversion. . . .

And, although we must not expect a cheap war, yet certainly it cannot be dearer than a watchful, suspected, and languishing peace, in which we must consume the treasure of our nation, by upholding great armaments by sea and land, to watch a *seeming Friend*, that he become not a *real Enemy*, and yet not be able to prevent it at last.

> Thomas Manly. *The present state
> of Europe, 1689.*

PENN'S PROPOSAL

Now if the sovereign princes of Europe, who represent that society or independent state of men that was previous to the obligations of society, would for the same reason that engaged men first into society, *viz.* love of peace and order, agree to meet by their stated deputies in a general diet, estate, or parliament, and there establish rules of justice for sovereign princes to observe one to another ; and thus to meet yearly, or once in two or three years at farthest, or as they shall see cause, and to be stiled, the sovereign assembly or imperial diet, parliament, or state of Europe ; before which sovereign assembly should be brought all differences depending between one sovereign and another, that cannot be made up by private embassies, before the session begins ; and that if any of the sovereignties that constitute these imperial states shall refuse to submit their claims or pretensions to them, or to abide and perform the judgment thereof, and seek their remedy by arms, or delay their complaints beyond the time prefixed in their resolutions, all the other sovereignties, united as one strength, shall compel the submission and performance of the sentence with damages to the suffering party, and charges to the sovereignties, that obliged their submission : to be sure Europe would quietly obtain the so much desired and needed peace to her harassed inhabitants ; no sovereignty in Europe having the power, and therefore cannot show the will to dispute the conclusion ; and consequently peace would be procured and continued in Europe.

William Penn. *An Essay Towards the Present and Future Peace of Europe, 1693.*

PURE OR STRICT RIGHT

THE law of pure *strict right* is, *No one is to be injured,* so that in the state no cause for action be given him, out of the state no right of war. . . .

The highest degree of right I have called by the name of probity, or rather piety. . . . Pure or strict right springs from the principle of preserving peace.

Gottfried Wilhelm Leibnitz.[1]
Preface to Codex Diplomaticus Juris Gentium, 1693.

[1] He wrote to Saint-Pierre (see p. 191): "I have read it with attention, and am persuaded that such a project for perpetual peace on the whole is feasible, and that its execution would be one of the most useful things in the world. Although my suffrage cannot be of any weight, I have nevertheless thought that gratitude obliged me not to withhold it, and to join to it some remarks for the satisfaction of a meritorious author, who ought to have much reputation and firmness to have dared and been able to oppose with such success the prejudiced crowd, and the unbridled tongue of mockers."

PEACE WITH ALL ITS INCONVENIENCES PREFERABLE

NOT fighting, but suffering, is another testimony peculiar to this people : they affirm that Christianity teacheth people to beat their swords into ploughshares, and their spears into pruning hooks, and to learn war no more, that so the wolf may lie down with the lamb, and the lion with the calf, and nothing that destroys be entertained in the hearts of people : exhorting them to employ their zeal against sin, and turn their anger against Satan, and no longer war one against another ; because all wars and fightings come of men's own hearts' lusts, according to the apostle James, and not of the meek spirit of Christ Jesus, who is captain of another warfare, and which is carried on with other weapons. Thus as truth-speaking succeeded swearing, so faith and patience succeeded fighting in the doctrine and practice of this people. Nor ought they for this to be obnoxious to civil government, since if they cannot fight for it neither can they fight against it ; which is no mean security to any state. And, Christianity set aside, if the costs and fruits of war were well considered, peace with all its inconveniences is generally preferable.

William Penn. *Rise and Progress of the People called Quakers, 1694.*

PERSISTING TYPES

Spy : We are a couple o' pure rogues. We sell arms to the Romans, to cut the throats of our own countrymen, the Carthaginians.

Batto : Ay, but we sell our arms so dear, we cut the throats o' the Romans too. . . . In what condition did you find the Roman army ?

Spy : A very good one.

Batto : I am very glad of it. Then the blockade will continue, and so corn must rise. 'Tis true, thanks to the gods, there is a pretty good convenient famine amongst us, which makes corn a good commodity ; and I have a large stock. But I'll keep my corn a while longer, and make the best o' the famine.

Spy : Oh ! you inhuman rogue ! your corn already grinds all the town. Hast thou no conscience ?

Batto : I don't see anybody has any conscience after they come to years of discretion. Most people have it when they are young, as they have the small-pox ; but when they are once cured of it, they are seldom troubled with it any more.

Spy : If thou hast no regard to the gods, thou mayst have a little to the Commonwealth.

Batto : Hang the Commonwealth ! Does not everybody cheat the Commonwealth as much as he can ! Why should I be honest all alone by myself ?

John Crowne. Regulus, 1694.

THE REPROACH OF MAN

WHAT is the race of man but one family widely scattered upon the earth ? All men by nature are brothers, and should be mutually endeared by a brother's love ; accursed

be those impious barbarians who seek for glory in the
kindred blood, which differs but in name from their own !
War, indeed, is sometimes necessary ; but the necessity of
war is the reproach of man. . . . He ought to be lightly
esteemed of men by whom men are so lightly esteemed that,
to gratify a brutal vanity, he will deluge the earth with their
blood. Happy is the prince who loves his people and is
beloved by them ; who have confidence in all his neighbours ; who is so far from making war against them, that
he prevents their making war against each other ; and who
can excite envy in foreign states only by the happiness which
he diffuses through his own.

> François Salignac de la Mothe-
> Fénelon. *Télémaque, 1699. Tr.*
> *John Hawkesworth, 1768.*

MARS AND MOMUS

Mars

INSPIRE the vocal brass, inspire ;
The world is past its infant age :
      Arms and honour,
      Arms and honour,
Set the martial mind on fire,
And kindle manly rage.
Mars has looked the sky to red,
And Peace, the lazy good, is fled.
Plenty, Peace and Pleasure fly ;
      The sprightly green
In woodland walks no more is seen ;
The sprightly green has drunk the Tyrian dye . . .
   Sound the trumpet, beat the drum ;
   Through all the world around,
Sound a reveille, sound, sound,
      The warrior God is come. . . .

Momus

Thy sword within the scabbard keep,
  And let mankind agree ;
Better the world were fast asleep
  Than kept awake by thee.
The fools are only thinner,
  With all our cost and care ;
But neither side a winner,
  For things are as they were. . . .

          John Dryden. *The Secular*
          Masque, 1700.

1701—1800

Now for the bare-pick'd bone of majesty
Doth dogged war bristle his angry crest,
And snarleth in the gentle eyes of peace.

                    Shakespeare. *King John.*

BRITAIN'S CARE

'Tis Britain's care to watch o'er Europe's fate ;
And hold in balance each contending state ;
To threaten bold presumptuous Kings with war ;
And answer her afflicted neighbour's prayer !
The Dane and Swede, roused up by fierce alarms,
Bless the wise conduct of her pious Arms !
Soon as her Fleets appear, their terrors cease ;
And all the Northern World lies hushed in peace !

Th' ambitious Gaul beholds, with secret dread,
Her thunder aimed at his aspiring head ;
And fain her Godlike sons would disunite
By foreign gold, or by domestic spite :
But strives in vain to conquer, or divide ;
Whom Nassau's Arms defend, and counsels guide.

Joseph Addison. *A Letter from
Italy, 1701.*

MEDICINE

You see then that the evil of war is to be thought of as the
bitterness of a medicine. A private individual who is very
careful of his health takes remedies not only when he is ill
but when he is extremely well. He purges himself, he has
himself bled as a precaution : he is like those who drink
to quench a thirst to come. As yet he feels no attack of
illness ; he wishes only to ward off an indisposition which
might perhaps take him unawares.

States behave in the same way. They engage in a war
not only when they are attacked, but also when it is
probable that they will be attacked some day. They will
have none of the peace that is offered ; they see in it only
a trap, and feel that the peaceful sentiments of others are

due only to their weak position and their desire to strengthen it. They believe that one should profit by the occasion, take advantage of the moment ; and they think the public good is so precious that one must anticipate long in advance anything which might disturb it.

> Pierre Bayle.   *Réponse aux Questions d'un Provincial, 1703.*

FROM FEAR TO FEAR

WHICH is the basest Creature, Man, or Beast ?
Birds feed on Birds, Beasts on each other prey :
But savage Man alone, does Man betray.
Press'd by Necessity, *They* kill for Food ;
Man undoes Man, to do himself no good . . .
For Hunger, or for Love *They* bite or tear,
Whilst wretched Man is still in Arms for Fear :
For Fear he arms, and is of Arms afraid ;
From Fear, to Fear, successively betray'd.

> John Wilmot, Earl of Rochester.
> *A Satyr against Mankind. Poems on Several Occasions, 1705.*

MARLBOROUGH

       THAT sword great Anne
Fix'd not in vain on thy puissant side,
When thee sh' enrolled her gartered knights among,
Illustrating the noble list ; her hand
Assures good omen, and Saint George's worth
Enkindles like desire of high exploits.
Immediate sieges, and the tire of war,
Roll in thy eager mind ; thy plumy crest
Nods horrible ; with most terrific port
Thou walk'st and seem'st already in the fight.

> John Philips. *Blenheim,*[1] *1705.*

[1] This poem should be compared with Addison's *The Campaign.* John Philips is not content, like Addison, to permit Marlborough, calm and

serene as an angel, to ride in the whirlwind and direct the storm: he represents him as winning the Battle of Blenheim almost single-handed:

In Gallic Blood
He dyes his reeking sword, and strews the ground
With headless ranks. What can they do? Or how
Withstand his wide-destroying sword?

INSTRUMENTS OF DEATH

                    Now from each
The brazen instruments of Death discharge
Horrific flames, and turbid streaming clouds
Of smoke sulphureous ; intermixt with these
Large globous irons fly, of dreadful hiss,
Singeing the air, and from long distance bring
Surprising slaughter ; on each side they fly
By chains connext, and with destructive sweep
Behead whole troops at once ; the hairy scalps
Are whirl'd aloof, while numerous trunks bestrew
Th' ensanguined field : with latent mischief stored
Showers of granadoes rain, by sudden burst
Disploding murderous bowels, fragments of steel,
And stones and glass, and nitrous grains adust ;
A thousand ways at once the shivered orbs
Fly diverse, working torment, and foul rout
With deadly bruise, and gashes furrowed deep. . . .
Thus through each army Death in various shapes
Prevailed ; here mangled limbs, here brains and
    gore
Lie clotted ; lifeless some : with anguish these
Gnashing, and loud laments invoking aid,
Unpitied, and unheard. . . .

                                        Ibid.

Now who says Poets don't in blood delight?
'Tis true the varlets care not much to fight;
But, faith, they claw it off whene'er they write. . . .
                    Epilogue to Otway's *Alcibiades.*

THE HARDY SOLDIER

" O, why is Man so thoughtless grown ?
  Why, guilty souls in haste to die ?
Vent'ring the leap to the worlds unknown ;
  Heedless, to Arms and blood they fly !

" Are lives but worth a soldier's pay ?
  Why will ye join such wide extremes,
And stake immortal souls, in play
  At desperate Chance, and bloody games ?

" Valour's a nobler turn of thought,
  Whose pardoned guilt forbids her fears :
Calmly she meets the deadly shot,
  Secure of life beyond the stars :

" But Frenzy dares eternal Fate ;
  And, spurred with Honour's airy dreams,
Flies to attack th' Infernal Gate,
  And force a passage to the flames."

Thus, hov'ring o'er Namuria's plains,
  Sang Heavenly Love, in Gabriel's form.
Your Thraso felt the moving strains ;
  And vowed to pray, before the storm.

Anon, the thundering trumpet calls.
  " Vows are but wind ! " the Hero cries,
Then swears by Heaven, and scales the walls :
  Drops in the ditch, despairs, and dies.

Isaac Watts, D.D. *To the Rt.*
Hon. John Lord Cutts. *At the*
Siege of Namur. Horæ Lyricæ, 1706

PEACE AND THE PRESS

THERE is another sort of gentleman whom I am much more concerned for, and that is the ingenious fraternity of which I have the honour to be an unworthy member ; I mean the News-Writers of Great Britain, whether Post Men or Post Boys, or by what other name or title soever dignified or distinguished. The case of these gentlemen is, I think, more hard than that of the soldiers, considering that they have taken more towns, and fought more battles. They have been upon parties and skirmishes, when our Armies have lain still, and given the general assault to many a place, when the besiegers were quiet in their trenches. They have made us masters of several strong towns many weeks before our generals could do it ; and completed victories, when our greatest captains have been glad to come off with a drawn battle. . . . It is impossible for this ingenious sort of men to subsist after a Peace ; every one remembers the shifts they were driven to in the Reign of King Charles the Second, when they could not furnish out a single Paper of News, without lighting up a comet in Germany, or a Fire in Moscow. There scarce appeared a letter without a paragraph on an Earthquake. . . . I remember Mr. Dyer, who is justly looked upon by all Fox-Hunters in the nation as the greatest statesman our country has produced, was particularly famous for dealing in Whales ; insomuch that in five months time (for I had the curiosity to examine his letters on that occasion) he brought three into the mouth of the river Thames, besides two porpusses and a sturgeon.

Richard Steele. *The Tatler,*
No. 17, May 20, 1709.

TO THE LORDS AND COMMONS OF GREAT BRITAIN, IN PARLIAMENT ASSEMBLED

THE deluge of Christian blood and the vast treasure which have been spent to procure the expected Peace, is a most powerful argument of the necessity when made, that it may be perpetual if possible.

Who can be more sensible the happiness of it than yourselves, whilst you have borne so much of the burthen of the war ?

If there should be many sessions of parliament spent to find out such an acceptable expedient as would fix the peace to perpetuity, as there have been to procure it, it would be time well spent ; tho', I hope, much fewer will do it.

A guarantee among the present Confederation, as in the Address of your august assembly to the Queen, is highly necessary ; yet a general one through all Europe will make it much more effectual, whilst every Prince and State having the benefit of it, they will all account it their interest to have it inviolably kept, with such additional articles of agreement as may make it more lasting than guarantees usually are. . . .

For which reason I humbly propose as an expedient that by sufficient Articles of Agreement among the present Confederates they provide some Supreme Court to decide their future disputes without blood ; such a jurisdiction seeming as needful as any barrier against the most public enemy ; it being unity among themselves that will keep them strong and steady to support their outworks or barriers.

> John Bellers. *Some Reasons for an European State, 1710.*

FUTURE TIMes

RAPT into future times, the bard begun :
" A Virgin shall conceive, A virgin bear a Son !
From Jesse's root behold a branch arise,
Whose sacred flower with fragrance fills the skies :
The ethereal Spirit o'er its leaves shall move,
And on its top descend the mystic dove.
Ye heavens ! from high the dewy nectar pour,
And in soft silence shed the kindly shower !
The sick and weak the healing plant shall aid,
From storms a shelter and from heat a shade.
All crimes shall cease, and ancient fraud shall fail ;
Returning Justice lift aloft her scale ;
Peace o'er the world her olive wand extend,
And white-robed Innocence from heaven descend. . . .
No more shall nation against nation rise,
Nor ardent warriors meet with hateful eyes,
Nor fields with gleaming steel be cover'd o'er,
The brazen trumpets kindle rage no more ;
But useless lances into scythes shall bend.
And the broad falchion in a ploughshare end. . . ."

Alexander Pope. *Messiah*,[1] *first
printed in Spectator, May 14, 1712.*

[1] The sub-title of Pope's poem is: "A Sacred Eclogue. In Imitation of Virgil's Pollio." He says: "In reading several passages of the prophet Isaiah, which foretell the coming of Christ, and the felicities attending it, I could not but observe a remarkable parity between many of the thoughts and those in the Pollio of Virgil. This will not seem surprising when we reflect that the eclogue was taken from a sibylline prophecy on the same subject."

NOT WITHOUT UNEASY IMAGES

OUR whig is a decided enemy to all wars, if they are not absolutely necessary. Though he honours a soldier as he does a physician, yet he prays God that he may never have occasion for either. Arbitrary courts abroad are, for the most part, composed of officers of the Army ; and our whig has so great a weakness about him that he cannot, without very uneasy images, see a glare of scarlet where he would least wish it. He would not have the men of the sword grow familiar to the eyes of the people, nor become the equipage of our British kings.

Military men are a proper equipage for those princes who are fathers of their people against their will ; who lay the foundations of justice in fear and blood, and use the sword as the most natural means to support those foundations. . . .

We do not at present see in Great Britain more forces than are necessary to the civil list ; and I hope in proper time there will not be one more.

> Thomas Gordon. *The Character of an Independent Whig, 1719. (Reprinted in A Cordial for Low Spirits,*[1] *a Collection of Curious Tracts, Vol. I. 3rd. imp., 1763.)*

[1] "Porson would often carry in his pocket a volume of *A Cordial for Low Spirits.*"—*Porsoniana,* 1856. The tracts are mostly by Gordon, and are not very "curious."

MILITARY FUNERAL

TRAIL all your pikes, dispirit every drum,
March in a slow procession from afar,
Be silent, ye dejected Men of War !
Be still the hautboys, and the flute be dumb !
Display no more, in vain, the lofty banner ;
For see ! where on the bier before ye lies
The pale, the fall'n, the untimely Sacrifice
To your mistaken Shrine, to your false Idol Honour.

> Anne Finch, Countess of Winch-ilsea. *Miscellany Poems, 1713.*

WISE AND POOR

THANK heaven ! at last our wars are o'er ;
We're very wise, and very poor ;
All our campaigns at once are done ;
We've ended where we just begun
In perfect peace. Long may it last !
And pay for all the taxes past,
Refill th' Exchequer, chase our fears,
And dry up all our ladies' tears. . . .

Abel Evans. *Vertumnus, 1713.*

BY ANNA'S ORDERS

AT length great Anna said, " Let discord cease ! "
She said ! the world obeyed, and all was peace !
  In that blest moment from his oozy bed
Old father Thames advanced his reverend head. . . .
High in the midst, upon his urn reclined
(His sea-green mantle waving with the wind),
The god appeared : he turned his azure eyes
Where Windsor domes and pompous turrets rise ;
Then bowed and spoke ; the winds forgot to roar,
And the hushed waves glide softly to the shore.
  " Hail, sacred peace ! hail, long-expected days,
That Thames's glory to the stars shall raise. . . .
Let Volga's banks with iron squadrons shine,
And groves of lances glitter on the Rhine ;
Let barbarous Ganges arm a servile train,
Be mine the blessings of a peaceful reign.
No more my sons shall dye with British blood
Red Iber's sands, or Ister's foaming flood :
Safe on my shore each unmolested swain
Shall tend the flocks, or reap the bearded grain ;
The shady empire shall retain no trace
Of war or blood, but in the sylvan chase ;

The trumpet sleep while cheerful horns are blown,
And arms employed on birds and beasts alone.
Behold, th' ascending villas on my side
   Project long shadows o'er the crystal tide ;
Behold ! Augusta's glittering spires increase,
And temples rise, the beauteous works of Peace.
I see, I see, where two fair cities bend
Their ample bow, a new Whitehall ascend !
There mighty nations shall inquire their doom,
The world's great oracle in times to come. . . ."

Alexander Pope. *Windsor Forest, 1713.*

WOULD IT NOT BE BETTER ?

THE direct or indirect destruction of a German soldier costs us 20,000 francs, without counting the loss to our population, which is only repaired at the end of twenty-five years. Would it not be better to save the expense of this costly, inconvenient and dangerous apparatus of a permanent army, and instead to buy the enemy army when the opportunity presents itself ? An Englishman put the value of a man at 480 pounds sterling. That is the highest valuation, and they are not all as dear, as one knows ; but even so there would still be a great deal to be gained in finance and everything in population, since we should have a new man for our money, whereas under the present system we lose the one we have, without profiting by the one we have so expensively destroyed.[1]

John Law. *Written c. 1714. Œuvres, 1790.*

[1] Qt. Denis de Rougemont, *Nouvelle Revue Francaise*, Jan., 1937. Extract tr. Enid McLeod, 1938.

A MAN WOULD BE LAUGHED AT

THE good effects of charity may be considered either with respect to public communities of men, or with respect to private persons. As to the first, the advantages of an amiable correspondence between different nations are plainly to be seen in traffic and commerce, whereby the product of each particular soil is communicated to distant countries, useful inventions are made common and flourish, and men mutually supply the wants of each other. But when the spirit of ambition or revenge begins to operate, when jealousy of each other's wealth and power divides nations and breaks the bonds of charity, then all those advantages are interrupted, and men, instead of promoting each other's benefit, are employed in destroying one another. Whole provinces are laid waste ; cities, palaces, and churches, the work of many ages, are in an instant demolished and burnt to the ground ; thousands of widows and orphans are made in one day ; and he who makes the greatest havoc of his fellow-Christians is esteemed worthy of renown and honour. After an infinity of rapes, murders, rapines, sacrileges, when fire and sword have spent their rage, and are glutted with human blood, the dreadful scene often ends in plague or famine, as the natural consequences of war. The commands of God are on all sides forgotten, and when two armies are on the point of engaging, a man would be laughed at who should put them in mind of our Saviour's precept, " By this shall all men know that ye are My disciples, if ye have love one to another."

George Berkeley, D.D. *Sermon preached at Leghorn, 1714.*

GOOD GOVERNMENT

IT is possible by good government to keep a society always quiet in itself, but nobody can ensure peace from without for ever. The society may have occasion to extend their limits further, and enlarge their territories, or others may invade theirs, or something else will happen that man must be brought to fight ; for how civilised soever men may be, they never forget that force goes beyond reason. The politician now must alter his measures, and take off some of man's fears ; he must strive to persuade him, that all that was told him before of the barbarity of killing men ceases as soon as these men are enemies to the public, and that their adversaries are neither so good nor so strong as themselves. . . .

If therefore a law-giver or politician they have a great veneration for, should tell them, that the generality of men had within them a principle of valour distinct from anger, or any other passion, that made them to despise danger and face death itself with intrepidity, and that they who had most of it were the most valuable of their kind, it is very likely, considering what has been said, that most of them, though they felt nothing of this principle, would swallow it for truth, and that the proudest feeling themselves moved at this piece of flattery, and not well versed in distinguishing the passions, might imagine that they felt it heaving in their breasts, by mistaking pride for courage.

> Bernard Mandeville. *The Fable of the Bees, 1714.*

HONOUR AND SHAME

As soon as the notions of honour and shame are received among a society, it is not difficult to make men fight. First, take care they are persuaded of the justice of their cause ; for no man fights heartily that thinks himself in the wrong ; then show them that their altars, their possessions, wives, children, and everything that is near and dear to them is concerned in the present quarrel, or at least may be influenced by it hereafter ; then put feathers in their caps, and distinguish them from others, talk of public-spiritedness, the love of their country, facing an enemy with intrepidity, despising death, the bed of honour, and such like high-sounding words, and every proud man will take up arms and fight himself to death before he will turn tail, if it be by daylight. One man in an army is a check upon another, and a hundred of them that, single and without witness, would be all cowards, are for fear of incurring one another's contempt made valiant by being together. To continue and heighten this artificial courage, all that run away ought to be punished with ignominy ; those that fought well, whether they did beat or were beaten, must be flattered and solemnly commended ; those that lost their limbs rewarded, and those that were killed ought, above all, to be taken notice of, artfully lamented, and to have extraordinary encomiums bestowed upon them ; for to pay honours to the dead, will ever be a sure method to make bubbles of the living.

Ibid.

PEACE AND CAROLINA

THOU fairest, sweetest daughter of the skies,
    Indulgent, gentle life-restoring Peace !
With what auspicious beauties dost thou rise,
    And Britain's new-revolving Janus bless ! . . .

      Awake the golden lyre,
      Ye Heliconian choir,
      Swell every note still higher,
      And melody inspire
      At Heaven and Earth's desire.

      Hark, how the sounds agree,
      With due complacency !
      Sweet Peace, 'tis all by thee,
      For thou art harmony.

Who, by Nature's fairest Creatures,
Can describe her heavenly features ?
What comparison can fit her ?
Sweet are roses, she is sweeter ;

Light is good, but Peace is better.
Would you see her such as Jove,
Formed for universal love,
Blessed by man and gods above ?
Would you every feature trace,
Every sweetly smiling grace ?
Seek our Carolina's face.

Peace and she are Britain's treasures,
Fruitful in eternal pleasures. . . .

Chorus

Hail, ye celestial pair,
Still let Britannia be your care,
And Peace and Carolina crown the Year.

Nicholas Rowe.[1]   *Ode to Peace
for the year 1718.*

[1] He sometimes got beyond himself in his patriotic fervour:

"Beyond or love or friendship's sacred band,
Beyond myself I prize my native land;
Think England's peace bought cheaply with my blood,
And die with pleasure for my country's good."

WHITE ELEPHANTS

His Grace, Villiers first duke of Buckingham, engaged his
country in two mad wars at once with the two greatest
powers in Europe, because his honour had suffered a rebuff
in his attempts to debauch two great foreign ladies. Europe
was to be embroiled, lives, treasure, and the safety of
kingdoms to be risked and thrown away to vindicate,
forsooth, his Grace's debauched honour.

Cambyses, to revenge an affront put upon his father many
years before, by an Egyptian king in the business of
sending him a wife, involved the world in a flame of war,
and at the expense perhaps of a million of lives, and the

destruction of kingdoms, did at last heroically vindicate his father's honour and his own upon the bones of a dead king, whom he caused to be dug up, and after many indignities cast into the fire.

White elephants are rare in nature, and so greatly valued in the Indies that the King of Pegu, hearing that the King of Siam had got two, sent an embassy in form, to desire one of them of his royal brother at any price : but being refused, he thought his honour concerned to wage war for so great an affront. So he engaged Siam with a vast army, and with the loss of five hundred thousand of his own men, and the destruction of as many of the Siamese, he made himself master of the elephant and retrieved his honour.

Darius (I think it was Darius the Mede) found his honour concerned to chastise the Scythians for having invaded Asia a hundred and thirty years before, and lost a great army to vindicate his honour, which yet was not vindicated ; that is, he missed the white elephant.

For in short, honour and victory are generally no more than white elephants ; and for white elephants the most destructive wars have been often made. What man, free either by birth or spirit, could, without pity and contempt, behold, as in a late French reign he frequently might behold, a swarm of slavish Frenchmen, in wooden shoes, with hungry bellies, and no clothes, dancing round a may-pole, because their *grand monarque*, at the expense of a million of their money, and thirty or forty thousand lives, had acquired a white elephant, or in other words, gained a town or a victory ?

Thomas Gordon. *Cato's Letters,*
No. 57, Dec. 16, 1721. 4th ed., 1737

WAR'S GLORIOUS ART

WHILE I survey the blessings of our isle,
Her arts triumphant in the royal smile,
Her public wounds bound up, her credit high,
Her commerce spreading sails in every sky,
The pleasing scene recalls my theme agen,
And shews the madness of ambitious men,
Who, fond of bloodshed, draw the murd'ring sword,
And burn to give mankind a single lord. . . .
One to destroy is murder by the law,
And gibbets keep the lifted hand in awe ;
To murder thousands takes a specious name,
War's glorious art, and gives immortal fame.
When after battle I the field have seen
Spread o'er with ghastly shapes which once were men,
A nation crush'd, a nation of the brave !
A realm of death ! and on this side the grave !
Are there, said I, who from this sad survey,
This human chaos, carry smiles away ?
How did my heart with indignation rise !
How honest Nature swell'd into my eyes !
How was I shock'd to think the hero's trade
Of such materials, fame and triumph, made !

Dr. Edward Young. *Love of*
Fame : Satire VII. 1725.

MISERABLE EFFECTS OF A CONFINED EDUCATION

To confirm what I have now said, and further to shew the
miserable effects of a confined education ; I shall here
insert a passage which will hardly obtain belief. In hopes
to ingratiate myself farther into his Majesty's favour, I told
him of an invention discovered between three and four
hundred years ago, to make a certain powder ; into a heap
of which the smallest spark of fire falling, would kindle the

whole in a moment, although it were as big as a mountain ; and make it all fly up in the air together, with a noise and agitation greater than thunder. That, a proper quantity of this powder rammed into an hollow tube of brass or iron, according to its bigness, would drive a ball of iron or lead with such violence and speed, as nothing was able to sustain its force. That, the largest balls thus discharged, would not only destroy whole ranks of an army at once ; but batter the strongest walls to the ground ; sink down ships with a thousand men in each, to the bottom of the sea ; and when linked together by a chain, would cut through masts and rigging ; divide hundreds of bodies in the middle, and lay all waste before them. That we often put this powder into large hollow balls of iron, and discharged them by an engine into some city we were besieging ; which would rip up the pavement, tear the houses to pieces, burst and throw splinters on every side, dashing out the brains of all who came near. That I knew the ingredients very well, which were cheap, and common ; I understood the manner of compounding them, and could direct his workmen how to make those tubes of a size proportionable to all other things in his Majesty's kingdom.

The King was struck with horror at the description I had given of those terrible engines, and the proposal I had made. He was amazed how so impotent and grovelling an insect as I (these were his expressions) could entertain such inhuman ideas, and in so familiar a manner as to appear wholly unmoved at all the scenes of blood and desolation, which I had painted as the common effects of those destructive machines ; whereof he said, some evil genius, enemy to mankind, must have been the first contriver. As for himself, he protested, that although few things delighted him so much as new discoveries in art or in nature ; yet he would rather lose half his kingdom than be privy to such a secret ; which he commanded me, as I valued my life, never to mention any more.

Jonathan Swift. *Voyage to Brobdingnag, 1726.*

CREATURES PRETENDING TO REASON

WHAT you have told me (said my Master), upon the subject of War, doth indeed discover most admirably the effects of that reason you pretend to : however, it is happy that the shame is greater than the danger ; and that Nature hath left you utterly incapable of doing much mischief : for your mouths lying flat with your faces, you can hardly bite each other to any purpose, unless by consent. Then, as to the claws upon your feet before and behind, they are so short and tender, that one of our Yahoos could drive a dozen of yours before him. And therefore in recounting the numbers of those who have been killed in battle, I cannot but think that you have said the thing which is not.

I could not forbear shaking my head and smiling a little at his ignorance. And, being no stranger to the art of war, I gave him a description of cannons, culverins, muskets, carabines, pistols, bullets, powder, swords, bayonets, battles, sieges, retreats, attacks, undermines, countermines, bombardments, sea-fights ; ships sunk with a thousand men ; twenty thousand killed on each side ; dying groans, limbs flying in the air ; smoke, noise, confusion, trampling to death under horses' feet ; flight, pursuit, victory ; fields strewed with carcases left for food to dogs, and wolves, and birds of prey ; plundering, stripping, ravishing, burning and destroying. And, to set forth the valour of our own dear countrymen, I assured him, that I had seen them blow up a hundred enemies at once in a siege, and as many in a ship ; and beheld the dead bodies drop down in pieces from the clouds, to the great diversion of all the spectators.

I was going on to more particulars, when my Master commanded me to silence. He said, whoever understood the nature of Yahoos might easily believe it possible for so vile an animal, to be capable of every action I had named, if their strength and cunning equalled their malice. But, as my discourse had increased his abhorrence of the whole species, so he found it gave him a disturbance in his mind, to which he was wholly a stranger before. He thought his ears being used to such abominable words, might by degrees admit them with less detestation. That, although he hated the Yahoos of this country, yet he no more blamed them for their odious qualities, than he did a Gnnayh (a bird of prey) for its cruelty, or a sharp stone for cutting his hoof. But, when a creature pretending to reason, could be capable of such enormities, he dreaded lest the corruption of that faculty might be worse than brutality itself. He seemed therefore confident, that instead of reason, we were possessed of some quality fitted to increase our natural vices ; as the reflection from a troubled stream returns the image of an ill-shapen body, not only larger, but more distorted.

Jonathan Swift. *Voyage to the Houyhnhnms, 1726.*

DOES NOT THE PAST TEACH US ?

THE bulk of the cessions and promises made under previous treaties have only been made, by those who yielded them in spite of themselves and for fear of losing still more by the continuation of the war than by the treaties. Thus those who yielded have only yielded in appearance and until the first occasion when they shall with impunity be able to recover what they have yielded or some equivalent. Thus, in the present situation of Europe there is no complete security for the duration of peace.

There must be no mistake. Such is the temper of him who makes a surrender that there is no surrender which can prevent him from a war which he can conduct with advantage. The allies, it is true, can promise the guarantee of these cessions. But what is to prevent the Allies themselves from falling out, and from forming party alliances against one another ? Does not the past teach us to divine the future ? And will not, then, the promise of a guarantee become an empty promise, and the security against war a mere chimera ? . . .

As the causes of war in the past continue to subsist without any new and sufficient preventive, it would be very unwise to think that they will not produce similar effects. The wood is dry, the fire is near, the wind blows the fire upon the wood, why should not the wood kindle ? So that, so long as the Sovereigns do not sign certain new articles, there is no security for the duration of peace.

> Charles François Irénée Castel de Saint-Pierre. *Abrégé du Projet de Paix Perpétuelle.*[1]   *1729*
> *Selections : Grotius Society, 1927.*

[1] His "Projet pour rendre la paix perpétuelle en Europe" was published 1713..

"Among the most sanguine, and the most singular of modern philosophers, is the worthy Abbé de Saint-Pierre. The honesty of his heart exceeded the rectitude of his understanding. His project of ' An Universal Peace,' by the infelicity of his style, could find no readers; a philanthropist as singular, but more eloquent, the celebrated Rousseau (see p. 203), embellished the neglected labour, enabled us to read the performance, and perceive its humane imbecility. . . . Our good Abbé had a notion that an age was not far distant, when such would be the progress of that mass of light, which was daily gathering, that it would influence every species of knowledge, and penetrate to the lowest orders of society. This future generation is to be remarkable for the force of its reason, and the severity of its truth."—Isaac D'Israeli, *Literary Miscellanies.*

FIRST OF HUMAN BLESSINGS

Oh, first of human blessings ! and supreme !
Fair Peace ! how lovely, how delightful thou !
By whose wide tie the kindred sons of men
Like brothers live, in amity combined
And unsuspicious faith ; whose honest toil
Gives every joy, and to those joys a right,
Which idle, barbarous rapine usurps.
Pure is thy reign ; when, unaccursed by blood,
Nought, save the sweetness of indulgent showers,
Trickling distils into the verdant glebe ;
Instead of mangled carcasses, sad-seen,
When the blithe sheaves lie scatter'd o'er the field ;
When only shining shares, the crooked knife,
And hooks imprint the vegetable wound ;
When the land blushes with the rose alone,

The falling fruitage, and the bleeding vine.
O Peace, thou source and soul of social life,
Beneath whose calm, inspiring influence,
Science his views enlarges, Art refines,
And swelling Commerce opens all her ports ;
Bless'd be the man divine who gives us thee !
Who bids the trumpet hush its horrid clang,
Nor blow the giddy nations into rage ;
Who sheathes the murderous blade ; the deadly gun
Into the well-piled armoury returns ;
And every vigour, from the work of death
To grateful industry converting, makes
The country flourish, and the city smile.
Unviolated, him the virgin sings ;
And him the smiling mother to her train ;
Of him the shepherd, in the peaceful dale,
Chants ; and, the treasures of his labour sure,
The husbandman of him, as at the plough,
Or team, he toils ; with him the sailor soothes,
Beneath the trembling moon, the midnight wave ;
And the full city, warm, from street to street,
And shop to shop, responsive, rings of him.
Nor joys one land alone : his praise extends
Far as the sun rolls the diffusive day ;
Far as the breeze can bear the gifts of peace,
Till all the happy nations catch the song.

James Thomson. Britannia, 1729.

THE BRITISH LION

WHENCE this unwonted transport in my breast ?
Why glow my thoughts, and whither would the Muse
Aspire with rapid wing ? Her country's cause
Demands her efforts ; at that sacred call
She summons all her ardour, throws aside
The trembling lyre, and with the warrior's trump
She means to thunder in each British ear ;
And if one spark of honour or of fame,

G

Disdain of insult, dread of infamy,
One thought of public virtue yet survive,
She means to wake it, rouse the gen'rous flame,
With patriot zeal inspirit ev'ry breast,
And fire each British heart with British wrongs. . . .
                    [136 lines omitted]
                    Yet, Britons, are ye cold ?
Yet deaf to glory, virtue, and the call
Of your poor injur'd countrymen ? Ah ! no,
I see ye are not ; ev'ry bosom glows
With native greatness, and in all its state
The British spirit rises : glorious change !
Fame, Virtue, Freedom, welcome ! Oh ! forgive
The Muse, that ardent in her sacred cause
Your glory question'd : she beholds with joy,
She owns, she triumphs in her wish'd mistake.

  See ! from her sea-beat throne in awful march
Britannia tow'rs : upon her laurel crest
The plumes majestic nod ; behold she heaves
Her guardian shields, and terrible in arms
For battle shakes her adamantine spear :
Loud at her foot the British lion roars,
Frighting the nations. . . .

                    Mark Akenside. *A British
                    Philippic, 1738.*

SUCH-LIKE TRIFLES

THE Abbé de Saint-Pierre, who distinguishes me so far as
to honour me with his correspondence, has sent me a most
excellent treatise on the means of restoring peace to all
Europe and on the manner of preserving it continually.
The thing is exceedingly practicable nor is anything, except
the consent of all Europe and some other such-like trifles,
wanting for its accomplishment.

                    Frederick the Great.[1] *To
                    Voltaire, April 12, 1742.*

[1] "One of his Royal Highness's performances was a refutation of
Machiavelli. . . . It was entitled the Anti-Machiavel, and was an edifying

homily against rapacity, perfidy, arbitrary government, unjust war, in short against almost every thing for which its author is now remembered among men."—Lord Macaulay.

In L'ODE DE LA GUERRE he wrote of "this brazen-headed monster, the war demon, athirst for blood and destruction. . . . Bellona, that woful, wild woman, beloved of ancient Chaos." There is a translation in the *Gentleman's Magazine*, January, 1780.

THESE DELIGHTS

HENCE, dull lethargic Peace,
 Born in some hoary beadsman's cell obscure ;
 Or in Circæan bower,
Where Manhood dies, and Reason's vigils cease ;
 Hie to congenial climes,
Where some seraglio's downy tyrant reigns ;
 Or where Italian swains,
'Midst wavy shades, and myrtle-blooming bowers,
 Lull their ambrosial hours,
And deck with languid trills their tinkling rhymes.
 But rouse, thou God by Furies drest,
 In helm with Terror's plumed crest,
 In adamantine steel bedight,
 Glistening formidably bright,
 With step unfix'd and aspect wild. . . .

 Come then, Genius of the war,
 Roll me in thy iron car ;
 And while thy coursers pierce the sky,
 Breathing fury as they fly,
 Let Courage hurry swift before,
 All stain'd around with purple gore,
 And Victory follow close behind,
 With wreath of palm and laurel join'd,
 While high above, fair Fame assumes
 Her place, and waves her eagle plumes. . . .

 Hurry me to Gallic plain,
 Just when each patriot Talbot bleeds,

Or when heaven-prosper'd Harry leads
His troops with seven-fold courage steel'd,
To Agincourt's immortal field.
But when th' embattled troops advance,
O Mars, my every thought entrance :
Guide me, thundering, martial god,
Guide thro' Glory's arduous road !
While hailing bullets round me fly,
And human thunders shake the sky,
While crowds of heroes heap the ground,
And dying groans are heard around,
With armour clanking, clarions sounding,
Cannons bellowing, shouts rebounding ;
Guide me, thundering martial god,
Guide thro' Glory's arduous road.
But should on land thy triumphs cease,
Still lead me far from hated Peace ;
Me bear, dread Power, for warlike sport,
To some wave-encircled fort ;
Or (if it yield more open fight)
To some hoar promontory's height,
Whose high-arch'd brow o'erlooks the scene,
Where Tritons blue and Naiads green,
Sportive from their coral cave,
Through the fluid crystal lave ;
There eagerly I ken from far
All the waste of naval war,
And catch a sympathetic rage,
While the numerous fleets engage,
And every distant shore rebounds
To the cannons' rattling sounds. . . .
   And when at length cold creeping Age
Freezes the torrent of my rage,
Let me live amongst a crew
Of invalids, of kindred hue !
Of some main limb bereft by War,
Or blest with some deep glorious scar ;
Scar that endless glory draws
From Liberty and Albion's cause :

Then oft well pleas'd with them retire
To circle round a sea-coal fire,
And all our past campaigns recite,
Of Vigo's sack, and Blenheim's fight ;
How valiant Rooke majestic trod,
How Marlbro' thunder'd, half a god !
And then with sage prophetic eye,
In future battles to descry
That Britain shall not fail to yield
Equal generals for the field ;
That France again should pour her blood,
And Danube roll a purpled flood.
And when my children round me throng,
The same grand theme shall grace my tongue ;
To teach them, should fair England need
Their blood, 'tis theirs to wish to bleed ;
And, as I speak, to mark with joy
New courage start in every boy ;
And gladsome read in all their eyes,
Each will a future hero rise,
These delights if Mars afford,
Mars, with thee I whet my sword.

William Mason. *Il Bellicoso, 1744.*

REFLECTION

THE essence of a peace is to be eternal, and yet we never
see one that lasts a man's lifetime, nor hardly through a
reign without being renewed several times. But ought one
to be astonished that those who need laws in order to be
just should be capable of violating them ?

Luc de Clapiers, Marquis de
Vauvenargues.   *Réflexions et
Maximes, 1746.*

ODE TO PEACE

1

O Thou, who bad'st thy turtles bear
Swift from his grasp thy golden hair,
    And sought'st thy native skies:
When *War*, by vultures drawn from far,
To *Britain* bent his iron car,
    And bad his storms arise !

2

Tir'd of his rude tyrannic sway,
Our Youth shall fix some festive day,
    His sullen shrines to burn :
But Thou who hear'st the turning spheres,
What sounds may charm thy partial ears,
    And gain thy blest return !

3

O *Peace*, thy injur'd robes up-bind,
O rise, and leave not one behind
    Of all thy beamy train :
The *British* Lion, Goddess sweet,
Lies stretch'd on earth to kiss thy feet,
    And own thy holier reign.

4

Let others court thy transient smile,
But come to grace thy western isle,
    By warlike *Honour* led !
And, while around her ports rejoice,
While all her sons adore thy choice,
    With Him for ever wed !

William Collins. *Odes, 1747.*

WHERE THEY WERE BEFORE

But what most showed the vanity of life
Was to behold the nations all on fire,
In cruel broils engaged, and deadly strife ;
Most Christian kings, inflamed by black desire,
With honourable ruffians in their hire,
Cause war to rage, and blood around to pour ;
Of this sad work when each begins to tire,
They sit them down just where they were before,
Till, for new scenes of woe, peace shall their force restore.

James Thomson. *The Castle of Indolence, 1748.*

HEROES AND CONQUERORS

I am far from intending to vindicate the sanguinary projects of heroes and conquerors, and would wish rather to diminish the reputation of their success, than the infamy of their miscarriages : for I cannot conceive, why he that has burnt cities, wasted nations, and filled the world with horror and desolation, should be more kindly regarded by mankind, than he that died in the rudiments of wickedness ; why he that accomplished mischief should be glorious, and he that only endeavoured it should be criminal. I would wish Cæsar and Catiline, Xerxes and Alexander, Charles and Peter, huddled together in obscurity or detestation.

Samuel Johnson. *The Adventurer No. 99, Oct. 16, 1753.*

THREE OPINIONS

Can a ruler who has only a probable opinion of justice on his side declare war on another who holds a kingdom in good faith ?

The first opinion says he can. The reason is that a ruler ought not to be in a worse position than a private person. . . .

The second opinion says that to declare war, the ruler not in possession must have at least a more probable opinion on his side. . . .

The third opinion, which seems to me more probable, says that a ruler cannot declare war on another who possesses in good faith unless he is *certain* of his right. . . .

There is no doubt that since war generally brings in its train so many evils and so much harm to religion, to innocent people, and to the honour of women, etc., in practice it is hardly ever just if declared on probable reasons of justice alone and not certain reasons.

> St. Alphonsus de Liguori. *In-stitutiones Theologicæ, 1753.*

SOLDIERS AND POETS

A SOLDIER is the least master of his own life of any man in the community. . . .

Of what violences, murders, depredations, have not the epic poets, from all antiquity, been the occasion by propagating false honour, false glory, and false religion !

> Samuel Richardson.[1] *Sir Charles Grandison, 1753.*

[1] "Il est cruel, pour un homme aussi vif que je le suis, de lire neuf volumes entiers dans lesquels on ne trouve rien du tout."—Voltaire to Mme du Deffand, who had recommended him to read Richardson.

MEN OF LETTERS AND MEN OF ARMS

MEN of letters are tried at a severer tribunal than men of arms ; their claim to merit is fixed on more established principles, and a better foundation ; and yet, such is the event, the eclat of fire and sword, ruined nations, kings enslaved, and slaughtered millions, are more the admiration of mankind than the man of study who advances arts and sciences, happiness and health, a public blessing.

There is scarce a more depreciating consideration to human nature than that the mild arts of peace should meet such little success, and the professors of slaughter and destruction find applause and honourable reception everywhere : this disposition seems to be inherent in the nature of man.

For myself I confess, when I behold the monuments and tombs of those ravagers, with pompous panegyrics of their military actions, I conceive the greatest abhorrence of their names and characters ;[1] I can never esteem that being whose malicious heart prompts his understanding and his arm by the worst of passions, to the destruction of his own species ; he is to my eyes only a robber, more illustrious and pernicious than the common highwayman ; and tho' the world have agreed to honour such men with all that is to be given in it, yet to me every monument which preserves the memory of these kind of beings is but a standing satire against the persons who performed the actions they recount, those who have bestowed on them these superb acknowledgments, all who look on, read and applaud, and perhaps human nature itself.

What is a long list of victories but a keen invective on human nature ? What are the histories of thousands slain but a demonstration of our delight in bloodshed ? Cities ruined, nations plundered, temples and deities profaned, are the glories of that being which boasts of humanity and calls itself lord of the creation.

Batista Angeloni (John Shebbeare).
Letters on the English Nation, 1756.

[1] Men of letters (except for a consideration, which Shebbeare himself would not have been above accepting) do not as a rule admire conquering heroes. Landor makes Fulke Greville say: "Shame upon those light ones who carol at the feat of blood! and worse upon those graver ones who nail upon their escutcheons the name of great! Ambition is but Avarice on stilts and masked. God sometimes sends a famine, sometimes a pestilence, and sometimes a hero, for the chastisement of mankind: none of them surely for our admiration." — *Imaginary Conversations*: *Lord Brooke and Sir Philip Sidney.*

SO BLOODY A PROSPECT

THE first accounts we have of mankind are but so many
accounts of their butcheries. All empires have been
cemented in blood ; and in those early periods when the
race of mankind began first to form themselves into parties
and combinations, the first effect of the combination, and
indeed the end for which it seems purposely formed and
best calculated, is their mutual destruction. All ancient
history is dark and uncertain. There were Conquerors
and Conquests in those days ; and consequently all that
devastation, by which they are formed, and all that
oppression by which they are maintained. . . .

I intended to have proceeded in a sort of method, in
estimating the numbers of mankind cut off in these wars
which we have on record. But I am obliged to alter my
design. Such a tragical uniformity of havoc and murder
would disgust ; and I confess I already feel my eyes ache
by keeping them so long intent on so bloody a prospect. . . .

The numbers I particularised are about thirty-six
millions. Besides those killed in battles I have said something, not half what the matter would have justified, but
something I have said, concerning the consequences of
war even more dreadful than that monstrous carnage
itself which shocks our humanity, and almost staggers
our belief. . . .

In a state of nature, it had been impossible to find a
number of men sufficient for such slaughters, agreed in
the same bloody purpose ; or allowing that they might
have come to such an agreement (an impossible supposi-
tion) yet the means that simple nature has supplied them
with are by no means adequate to such an end ; many
scratches, many bruises, undoubtedly would be received
on all hands ; but only a few, a very few deaths. . . .

From the earliest dawnings of policy to this day, the
invention of men has been sharpening and improving the
mystery of murder, from the first rude essays of clubs and
staves, to the present perfection of gunnery, cannoneering,

bombarding, mining, and all these species of artificial, learned, and refined cruelty, which make a principal part of what politicians have taught us to believe is our principal glory.

Edmund Burke. *Vindication of Natural Society, 1756.*

A PROJECT OF PERPETUAL PEACE

I SEE, as in a vision, men living together in unity and goodwill. I conjure up a sweet and peaceful society of brothers, living in eternal concord, all guided by the same principles, all happy in a common happiness, and as my imagination realises a picture so touching, an image of the unattained, I enjoy a momentary taste of true happiness.

I could not help writing these opening words in response to the feelings which filled my heart. Now let us try to reason coolly. Being determined to assert nothing that I cannot prove, I have the right to ask the reader in his turn to deny nothing he cannot refute ; for it is not the logicians I fear so much as those who, though refusing to accept my proofs, are unwilling to formulate their objections thereto.

No long reflection on the means of perfecting any government is needed to bring into view the embarrassments and hindrances which spring less from its internal constitution than from its foreign relations ; so that the greater part of that attention which ought to be given to administration must needs be devoted to defence, and more care spent to enable it to resist other powers than to perfect its own institutions. If the social order were, as is pretended, the work of reason rather than of the passions, should we have been so long in seeing that either too much or too little has been done for our happiness ; that, as we are each of us in the civil state with our fellow-citizens, and in the state of nature with the rest of the world, we have prevented private feuds only to fan the

flames of public wars which are a thousand times more
terrible ;   in short, mankind, by gathering itself into
groups, has become its own enemy.

> Jean Jacques Rousseau. *Extrait
> du Projet de Paix Perpétuelle de
> M. L'Abbé de Saint-Pierre,*[1] *1756.
> Tr. Edith Nuttall, 1927.*

[1] In the *Projét de Paix Perpétuelle*, Rousseau has treated his materials
with the freest hand. The long introduction . . . itself a brilliant historical
essay, is all his own. . . . In a word, except as regards the mere kernel of
the Project, there is much more of Rousseau than of Saint-Pierre in the
whole statement."—C. E. Vaughan, *Political Writings of Jean Jacques
Rousseau*, 1915, Vol. I.

EUROPE

EUROPE has special advantages over the other continents.
It is more equally populated, more evenly fertile, and
more compact in all its parts. The continual blending of
interests, which the ties of blood and the business of
commerce, of the arts and of colonisation have formed
between sovereigns ; the large number of rivers the variety
of whose courses makes all communications easy ; the
restlessness of the inhabitants ceaselessly moving about
and frequently travelling beyond their own frontiers ; the
invention of printing and general taste for letters, which
has given them a common stock of studies and knowledge ;
and finally the large number and small size of the states,
combined with the craving for luxury and the diversities
of climate, make every part of Europe necessary to every
other. All these causes combined, form out of Europe no
mere fanciful collection of peoples with only a name in
common as in Asia and Africa, but a real society which
has its religion, its manners, its customs and even its laws,
from which none of the people who compose it can withdraw without at once causing trouble.

To see on the other hand the perpetual dissensions, the
brigandage, the usurpations, the rebellions, the wars, the

murders which daily distress this venerable abode of sages, this resplendent sanctuary of science and art, and to think of our fine talk and then of our horrible actions, so much humanity in principle, so much cruelty in deed, a religion so gentle and an intolerance so bloodthirsty, a political system so wise on paper, so harsh in practice, rulers so benevolent and people so miserable, governments so moderate and wars so cruel, one hardly knows how to make these strange contradictions agree ; and this pretended brotherhood of the nations of Europe seems nothing but a term of derision to express ironically their mutual animosity.

Ibid.

TRUCES RATHER THAN TRUE PEACE

LET us agree, then, that in relation to one another the European powers are properly speaking in a state of war, and that all the partial treaties between particular powers represent passing truces rather than true peace, either because these treaties have generally no other guarantee than that of the contracting parties, or because the rights of the two parties are never thoroughly settled, and that these unextinguished rights, or, it may be, the claims of the powers who recognise no superior, will infallibly become sources of new wars, as soon as a change of circumstances gives new strength to the claimants.

Ibid.

THIS DEGENERATE AGE

EVEN war is pusillanimously carried out in this degenerate age ; quarter is given ; towns are taken and the people are spared : even in a storm a woman can hardly hope for the benefit of a rape.

Philip Dormer Stanhope, Earl
of Chesterfield. *Letter to his son,*
Jan. 12, 1757.

BRITAIN'S DELIGHT

Rejoice, ye nations, vindicate the sway
Ordained for common happiness. Wide, o'er
The globe terraqueous, let Britannia pour
The fruits of plenty from her copious horn.
What can avail to her, whose fertile earth
By ocean's briny waves are circumscribed,
The armed host, and murd'ring sword of war,
And conquest o'er her neighbours ? She ne'er breaks
Her solemn compacts, in the lust of rule :
Studious of arts and trade, she ne'er disturbs
The holy peace of states. 'Tis her delight
To fold the world with harmony, and spread,
Among the habitations of mankind,
The various wealth of toil, and what her fleece,
To clothe the naked, and her skilful looms,
Peculiar give.

> John Dyer. *The Fleece, 1757.*

PEACE AND POETRY

POETRY demands something huge, barbaric, savage. It
is when the fury of civil war or fanaticism arms men with
daggers, and blood flows on the earth in great streams,
that Apollo's laurel quivers and grows green. It needs
blood to water it. It withers in times of peace and leisure.
The golden age might perhaps have produced a song or
an elegy. Epic and dramatic poetry call for a different
way of life.

> Denis Diderot. *De la poésie
> dramatique, 1758.*

A VERY CELEBRATED QUESTION

HERE a very celebrated question, and of the highest
importance, presents itself. It is asked, whether the
aggrandisement of a neighbouring power, by whom a

nation fears she may one day be crushed, be a sufficient reason for making war against him—whether she be justifiable in taking up arms to oppose his aggrandisement, or to weaken him, with the sole view of securing herself from those dangers which the weaker states have almost always reason to apprehend from an overgrown power. To the majority of politicians the question is no problem : it is more difficult of solution to those who wish to see justice and prudence ever inseparably united. . . .

Suppose that powerful state, by the justice and circumspection of her conduct, affords us no room to take exception to her proceedings, are we to view her progress with an eye of indifference ? . . . But force of arms is not the only expedient by which we may guard against a formidable power. There are other means of a gentler nature, and which are at all times lawful. The most effectual is a confederacy of the less powerful sovereigns, who, by this coalition of strength, become able to hold the balance against that potentate whose power excites their alarms.

They may also mutually favour each other, to the exclusion of him whom they fear ; and by reciprocally allowing various advantages to the subjects of the allies, especially in trade, and refusing them to those of the dangerous potentate, they will augment their own strength, and diminish his, without affording him any just cause of complaint. . . .

Emmerich Vattel. *The Law of Nations, 1758. Ed. Chitty, 1833.*

WHAT A BURDEN

IF a sovereign continues to keep up a powerful army in profound peace, his neighbours must not suffer their vigilance to be entirely lulled to sleep by his bare word ; and prudence requires that they should keep themselves on their guard. However certain they may be of the good faith of that prince, unforeseen differences may intervene ; and shall they leave him the advantage of being provided,

at that juncture, with a numerous and well-disciplined
army, while they themselves will have only new levies to
oppose it ? Unquestionably no. This would be leaving
themselves almost wholly at his discretion. They are
therefore under the necessity of following his example,
and keeping, as he does, a numerous army on foot : and
what a burden is this to a state ! Formerly, and without
going any further back than the last century, it was pretty
generally made an article in every treaty of peace, that
the belligerent powers should disarm on both sides—that
they should disband their troops. If, in a time of profound
peace, a prince was disposed to keep up a considerable
number of forces, his neighbours took their measures
accordingly, formed leagues against him, and obliged him
to disarm. Why has not that salutary custom been preserved ?

Ibid.

" *I SMILE BUT I TREMBLE* "

IF you grow wise and ask me with a political face, whether
St. Maloes is an object worth risking fourteen thousand of
our best troops, an expense of fifty thousand pounds, and
half the purplest blood of England, I shall toss up my
head with an air of heroism and contempt, and only tell
you—*There ! there is a Duke of Marlborough in the heart of
France* (for in the heroic dictionary the heart and the coast
signify the same thing) ; *what would you have ? Did Harry V.
or Edward III. mind whether it was a rich town or a fishing town,
provided they did but take a town in France ? We are as great as
ever we were in the most barbarous ages, and you are asking
mercantile questions with all the littleness of soul that attends the
improvements in modern politics !* Well ! my dear child, I
smile, but I tremble ; and though it is pleasanter to
tremble when one invades than when one is invaded, I
don't like to be at the eve even of an Agincourt.

Horace Walpole. *To Sir Horace
Mann, June 11, 1758.*

UNEMPLOYED SOLDIERS AND SCRIBBLERS

AMONG the calamities of war may be justly numbered the diminution of the love of truth, by the falsehoods which interest dictates, and credulity encourages. A peace will equally leave the warrior and relator of wars destitute of employment ; and I know not whether more is to be dreaded from streets filled with soldiers accustomed to plunder, or from garrets filled with scribblers accustomed to lie.

Samuel Johnson. *Idler, No. 30, 1758.*

PEACE KEEPS BREAKING OUT

MEN cannot always live in a state of war. After some time it becomes necessary to lay down their arms, and put an end to hostilities. The first treaty of peace was owing to this mutual imbecility of two contending nations. Necessity made them both think of the means of procuring tranquillity. They agreed at last to terminate their dispute by a solemn treaty, which might regulate their mutual pretensions, restore union and concord, and secure the peace of both nations. We have examples in Scripture of such treaties of peace made in the most ancient time. We even see that in those ages they knew how to take measures for preventing future animosities and disputes.

Antoine Yves Goguet. *De l'Origine des lois, 1758.*

NEW REFINEMENTS, FIERCER WEAPONS

THOU, heedless Albion, what, alas, the while
Dost thou presume ? O inexpert in arms,
Yet vain of freedom, how dost thou beguile
With dreams of hope, these near and loud alarms ?

Thy splendid home, thy plan of laws renowned,
Thy praise and envy of the nations round,
What care hast thou to guard from fortune's sway ?
Amid the storms of war, how soon may all
The lofty pile from its foundations fall,
Of ages the proud toil, the ruin of a day ! . . .

But what hath force or war to do with thee ?
Girt by the azure tide and throned sublime
Amid thy floating bulwarks, thou canst see,
With scorn, the fury of each hostile clime
Dashed ere it reach thee. Sacred from the foe
Are thy fair fields : athwart thy guardian prow
No bold invader's foot shall tempt the strand—
Yet say, my country, will the waves and wind
Obey thee ? Hast thou all thy hopes resigned
To the sky's fickle faith ? the pilot's wavering hand ? . . .

Nor yet be awed, nor yet your task disown,
Though war's proud votaries look on severe ;
Though secrets, taught erewhile to them alone,
They deem profaned by your intruding ear.
Let them in vain, your martial hope to quell,
Of new refinements, fiercer weapons tell,
And mock the old simplicity, in vain :
To the time's warfare, simple or refined,
The time itself adapts the warrior's mind ;
And equal prowess still shall equal palms obtain.

> Mark Akenside. *An Ode to the
> Country Gentlemen of England,
> 1758.*

WITH WOLFE BEFORE QUEBEC

I HOPE Mr. Perceval will arrive safe and bring you these
two letters from me. The happiness of writing to you is
beyond all I know. My concern for your sufferings, my
affection for you and your dear little ones, convince me
how unfit I am for this scene, which another month will,

thank God, give a conclusion to. The captive women and children which I see every day brought in here, often tell me what I am and who belong to me, but above all, the melancholy news I received the day before yesterday upon my arrival from the cursed camp of Montmorenoi of my poor brother's death has reproved me for not consulting my own nature more, when I asked you to return to the Army. It had then pleaded for you, when you did not plead for yourself, and I had not been now in a scene of ambition, confusion, misery ; and you oppressed, as I know you must be, with terrors and affliction. I dare say poor Lady Townshend too now starts at every knock at the door. Let us look up with hopes, my Charlotte, to the Disposer of all things, and trust He will in His mercy and goodness do all for the best. I have wrote a line to poor Lady Townshend to comfort her by convincing her of my own health and safety. One month more will put an end to our troubles. I never served so disagreeable a campaign as this. Our unequal force has reduced our operations to a scene of skirmishing cruelty and devastation. It is war of the worst shape. A scene I ought not to be in ; for the future, believe me, my dear Charlotte, I will seek the reverse of it.

General George Townsend.
To his wife, Sept., 1759.

THE GIVER OF VICTORY

IT is not impossible that we may be so vain and arrogant as to *sacrifice to our own net, and burn incense to our own drag* ; to imagine that our extraordinary success is the reward of our extraordinary piety, and that it is because we have more religon and virtue than the rest of the world, that we have been so greatly and signally prospered. If indeed we sink into a forgetfulness what manner of persons we are, we may thus imagine. . . . Was love of professing Christians ever more cold and frozen ? Was the Name of the Lord our God ever more commonly blasphemed ? Did ever profane swearing and cursing more abound in our Navy and Army ? . . .

But I ought not to make this a day of reproach which is devoted to congratulation and joy. Surely we had little reason to expect that God should have been on our side.

Samuel Lavington. *Sermon preached at Bideford, Nov. 29, 1759. (Being the 'day appointed for a General Thanksgiving.)*

HUMAN POLICY AND CHRISTIAN BENEVOLENCE

A GREAT general once said, when he was congratulated on his success in a very obstinate and bloody engagement, " Such another victory would ruin me." But when in consequence of our success, our dominions are like to be enlarged, our riches increased, our trade improved, and our enemies are greatly weakened and distressed, it is a proportionately convincing argument that herein God *had a favour unto us*. I own myself not enough versed in mercantile affairs to determine how many profitable branches of trade will be opened in Africa by the conquest of Senegal and Goree ; what greater quantities of sugar, coffee, cotton and indigo will be imported by our being in possession of Marygalante and Guadelupe ; how greatly our fishery will be enlarged and secured by the acquisition of Cape Breton and the Isle of St. John's ; and above all, what an almost universal trade will be opened by the reduction of Canada. . . .

But the happiest consequence of all would be the opportunity it might open to us of introducing the gospel amongst the Indian nations ; which it is hoped, should we extend our territories on the Continent of America, and be settled in peaceable possession of them, our Governors will readily and seriously encourage. Human policy suggests it, and Christian benevolence strongly recommends it. Nothing will more familiarise and endear their conquerors, nothing will more attach them to our interest, nothing will more effectually annex them to our Crown, and be a firmer tie upon their allegiance, than gratitude for the Gospel. Who can help anticipating the joyous (and God grant it may not be far distant) time when amongst other valuable exports from this country to our colonies there shall be a large demand for the Bible ?

Ibid.

The following is said to have been "written on a church-door on a Day of Thanksgiving during the American War":

> Vain-glorious man, are these thy pranks,
> First murder men, then give God thanks?
> Vile hypocrite, proceed no further,
> For God receives no thanks for murder.

ARTIFICERS OF DEATH

First envy, eldest born of hell, embrued
Her hands in blood, and taught the sons of men
To make a death which nature never made,
And God abhorr'd ; with violence rude to break
The thread of life ere half its length was run,
And rob a wretched brother of his being.
With joy ambition saw, and soon improv'd
The execrable deed. 'Twas not enough
By subtle fraud to snatch a single life,
Puny impiety ! whose kingdoms fell
To sate the list of power : more horrid still,
The foulest stain and scandal of our nature
Became its boast. *One* murderer makes a villain,
Millions a hero. Princes were privileged
To kill, and numbers sanctified the crime.
Ah ! why will kings forget that they are men ?
And men that they are brethren ? Why delight
In human sacrifice ? Why burst the ties
Of nature that should knit their souls together
In one soft bond of amity and love ?
Yet still they breathe destruction, still go on,
Inhumanly ingenious, to find out
New pains for death, new terrors for the grave,

Artificers of death ! still monarchs dream
Of universal empire growing up
Of universal ruin. Blast the design,
Great God of hosts, nor let thy creatures fall
Unpitied victims at ambition's shrine.

> Beilby Porteis, D.D., *Bishop of*
> *London. Poem on Death, 1759.*

MY UNCLE TOBY'S APOLOGETICAL ORATION

I AM not insensible, brother Shandy, that when a man
whose profession is arms, wishes, as I have done, for war,
—it has an ill aspect to the world ;—and that, how just
and right soever his motives and intentions may be,—he
stands in an uneasy posture in vindicating himself from
private views in doing it. . . .

If, when I was a schoolboy, I could not hear a drum
beat, but my heart beat with it—was it my fault ?—Did
I plant the propensity ?—Did I sound the alarm within,
or Nature ? . . .

O brother ! 'tis one thing for a soldier to gather laurels,
—and 'tis another to scatter cypress. [Who told thee, my
dear Toby, that cypress was used by the ancients on
mournful occasions ?]

'Tis one thing, brother Shandy, for a soldier to hazard
his own life—to leap first down into the trench, where he
is sure to be cut to pieces :—'Tis one thing, from public
spirit and a thirst of glory, to enter the breach the first
man,—To stand in the foremost rank, and march bravely
on with drums and trumpets, and colours flying about his
ears :—'Tis one thing, I say, brother Shandy, to do this,
—and 'tis another thing to reflect on the miseries of war ;
—to view the desolations of whole countries, and consider
the intolerable fatigues and hardships which the soldier
himself, the instrument who works them is forced (for
sixpence a day, if he can get it) to undergo. . . .

For what is war ? what is it, Yorick, when fought as

ours has been, upon principles of liberty, and upon principles of honour—what is it, but getting together of quiet and harmless people, with their swords in their hands, to keep the ambitious and the turbulent within bounds ?

Laurence Sterne. *Tristram Shandy, 1759-67.*

THOUGHTS IN A GARDEN

IF national reflections are unjust, because there are good men in all nations, are not national wars upon much the same footing ?

There ought, no doubt, to be heroes in society as well as butchers ; and who knows but the necessity of butchers (inflaming and stimulating the passions with animal food) might at first occasion the necessity of heroes. Butchers, I believe, were prior.

How ready have all nations been, after having allowed a proper portion of laud and praise to their own abilities, to attribute their success in war to the peculiar favour of a just Providence. Perhaps, this construction, as it is often applied, argues more of presumption than gratitude. In the first place, such is the partiality of the human heart, that, perhaps, two hostile nations may alike rely upon the justice of their cause ; and which of the two has the better claim to it, none but Providence can itself discover. In the next, it should be observed, that success by no means demonstrates justice. Again, we must not wholly forget to consider, that success may be no more than a means of destruction. And lastly, supposing success to be really and absolutely good, do we find that individuals are always favoured with it in proportion to their desert ; and if not individuals, why must we then suppose it to be the uniform recompense of society ?

William Shenstone. *Men and Manners, c. 1760.*

BLASPHEMOUS ABSURDITY

Now fancy to yourself Christ, the Lamb of God, after His divine Sermon on the Mount, putting Himself at the head of a bloodthirsty army, or St. Paul going forth with a squadron of fire and brimstone to make more havoc in human lives than a devouring earthquake.

But if this be too blasphemous an absurdity to be supposed, what follows but that the Christian who acts in the destroying fury of war acts in full contrariety to the whole nature and spirit of Christ, and can no more be said to be led by His spirit, or be one with Him, than those His enemies who " came forth with swords and staves to take Him."

> William Law. *An humble, earnest and affectionate Address to the Clergy, April, 1761.*

A FORM OF PRAYER

For the Glory of His Majesty's Arms, said once a Most Christian King. Now if at that time his Catholic Church had called a solemn assembly to unite hearts and voices in this pious prayer, " O blessed Jesus, dear redeeming Lamb of God, who camest down from Heaven to save men's lives, and not to destroy them, go along, we humbly pray Thee, with our bomb-vessels and fire-ships, suffer not our thundering cannon to roar in vain, but let Thy tender hand of love and mercy direct their balls to more heads and hearts of Thine own redeemed creatures than the poor skill of man is able of itself to do "—had not such prayers had more of the Man of Earth, more of the Son of Perdition in them, than the Most Christian King's glorying in his arms.[1]

> *Ibid.*

[1] cf. Mark Twain's *War Prayer*: " O Lord our God, help us to tear their soldiers to bloody shreds with our shells; help us to cover their smiling fields with the pale forms of their patriot dead. . . . We ask of one who is the Spirit of Love and who is the ever-faithful refuge and friend of all that are sore beset, and seek His aid with humble and contrite hearts. . . ."

" *THE SPIRIT OF THE TROOPS IS EXCELLENT* "

CONSIDERING the immense force we are opposed to—though our troops are in excellent order and good spirits—every one with whom I have conversed wishes the war concluded by a good peace.

The Marquess of Granby. *To the Duke of Newcastle, July 6, 1761.*

ALL WARS AVOIDABLE

EVERYTHING is now swayed more by superiority of force than by circumstances ; and the sword, which was formerly called the last argument of kings, *ultima ratio regum*, is now become the beginning of disputes. A manifesto, that no one gives any credit to, and which is published only in compliance with an old-established custom,[1] is sent to all foreign courts. Hostilities follow next ; and this is a manner of proceeding of those whom a superiority of strength makes unfaithful to their engagements.

To the shame of most crowned heads, it is a certain fact that of all wars that have been waged since this dreadful scourge was first known among men, there has not been one which might not have been avoided, if the parties concerned would have sincerely endeavoured after an accommodation.

Suppose, for instance, two sovereigns have a dispute with each other, which tends to a rupture : in such a conjuncture, the means of reconciliation should first be tried. If these fail, through the obstinacy of one of the parties, those powers who were willing to have concurred in the accommodation should unite together against the oppressor, in favour of the oppressed. How glorious would it be to see princes act in this wise and prudent manner !

Charles Louis Auguste Fouquet,
Duc de Belle-Isle. *Testament Politique,*[2] *1761.*

[1] This old-established custom has since gone by the board.
[2] Qt. *The Warrior's Looking-Glass,* 1808.

WITH DECORUM

IF the Spaniards land in Ireland, shall you make the campaign ? No, no, come back to England ; you and I will not be Patriots, till the Gauls are in the city, and we must take our great chairs and our fasces, and be knocked on the head with decorum in St. James's Market. Good-night !

Horace Walpole. *To George
Montagu, Dec. 30, 1761.*

PEACE TREATIES

WERE an Asiatic politician to read the treaties of peace and friendship that have been annually making for more than a hundred years among the inhabitants of Europe, he would probably be surprised how it should ever happen that Christian princes should quarrel among each other. Their compacts for peace are drawn up with the utmost precision, and ratified with the greatest solemnity : to these each party promises a sincere and inviolable obedience, and all wears the appearance of open friendship and unre-served reconciliation. Yet, notwithstanding those treaties, the people of Europe are almost continually at war. There is nothing more easy than to break a treaty ratified in all the usual forms, and yet neither party be the aggressor. One side, for instance, breaks a trifling article by mistake ; the opposite party, upon this, makes a small but premeditated reprisal ; this brings on a return of greater from the other ; both sides complain of injuries and infractions ; war is declared ; they beat—are beaten ; some two or three hundred thousand men are killed ; they grow tired ; leave off just where they began ; and so sit coolly down to make new treaties.

Oliver Goldsmith. *Citizen of
the World, 1762.*

"Quelque amour qu'on ait pour les grandes affaires, il y a peu de lectures si ennuyeuses et si fatigantes que celles d'un traité entre les princes."—Vauvenargues.

THE SOFTER LUTE

O curst Ambition, foe to human good,
Pregnant with woe and prodigal of blood !
Thou fruitful source whence streams of sorrow flow,
What devastation to thy guilt we owe ! . . .
Where Ceres flourished and gay Flora smiled,
Behold a barren, solitary wild ! . . .
But come, fair Peace, and be the nation's pride,
And let thy sister Plenty grace thy side,
O come ! and with thy placid presence cheer
Our drooping hearts, and stay for ever here.
Now be the shrill, strife-stirring trumpet mute,
Now let us listen to the softer lute.

> Francis Fawkes. *On Occasion of
> the Peace, Dec., 1762.*

VERSES FOR NEWSMEN

The peace is made at last—Heigh ho !
The folks above would have it so !
Sure they were mov'd with strange vagaries
To sign so soon preliminaries.
'Tis mighty odd the Parliament
Should not petition our consent.
We were in hopes, since Keppel's thunder
Had got the haughty Spaniards under,
That some new conquest would arrive
To make us hungry Newsmen thrive ;
And that another siege would come,
To clothe our squalling brats at home.

But since upon our columns four
We grave new victories no more ;
Since now blockades, capitulations,
Fleets, countermarches, camps, invasions,

By sea, by land, with many a drub,
Amuse no more the weekly club,
We must attempt to entertain
Your fancies in another strain :
Our troops at Portsmouth safely landed,
And every regiment disbanded ;
Those sons of Mars on Hounslow's plain
Will make, I trust, a new campaign :
Hence we new paragraphs shall fetch,
And show you that great general, Ketch,
Leading his heroes on to die
Without one shrug, or feature wry. . . .

> Thomas Warton. *Verses . . .*
> *for the year, 1763.*

OSTENTATIOUS EXCUSE

You may imagine that I am anxious to have the Peace,
and to see Mr. Conway safe in England. I wish it privately
and publicly—I pray for an end to the woes of mankind ;
in one word, I have no public spirit, and don't care a
farthing for the interests of the merchants. Soldiers and
sailors who are knocked on the head, and peasants plundered
or butchered, are to my eyes as valuable as a lazy luxurious
set of men who hire others to acquire riches for them ;
who would embroil all the earth, that they may heap or
squander ; and I *dare* to say this, for I am no minister.
Beckford is a patriot, because he will clamour if Guada-
loupe or Martinico is given up, and the price of sugars
falls. I am a bad Englishman, because I think the advantages of commerce are dearly bought for some by the
lives of many more. This wise age counts its merchants,
and reckons its armies ciphers. But why do I talk of this
age ? Every age has some ostentatious excuse for the havoc
it commits. Conquest, honour, chivalry, religion, balance
of power, commerce, no matter what, mankind must bleed,
and take a term for a reason. 'Tis shocking ! Good-night.

> Horace Walpole. *To Sir Horace*
> *Mann, May 26, 1762.*

THREE FAMOUS INGREDIENTS

FAMINE, the plague, and war, are the three most famous
ingredients in this lower world. Under famine may be
classed all the noxious foods which want obliges us to have
recourse to ; thus shortening our life while we hope to
support it.

In the plague are included all contagious distempers ;
and there are not less than two or three thousand. These
two gifts we hold from Providence ; but war, in which all
those gifts are concentrated, we owe to the fancy of three
or four hundred persons scattered over the surface of this
globe, under the name of princes and ministers ; and on
this account it may be that in several dedications they are
called living images of the Deity.

The most hardened flatterer will allow that war is ever
attended with plague and famine, especially if he has seen
the military hospitals in Germany, or passed through some
villages where some notable feat of arms has been performed.

It is unquestionably a very noble art to ravage countries,
destroy dwellings, and communibus annis out of a hundred
thousand men to cut off forty thousand. . . .

An odd circumstance in this infernal enterprise is that
every chief of these ruffians has his colours consecrated ;
and solemnly prays to God before he goes to destroy his
neighbour. If the slain in a battle do not exceed two or
three thousand, the fortunate commander does not think
it worth thanking God for ; but if, besides killing ten or
twelve thousand men, he has been so far favoured by
heaven, as totally to destroy some remarkable place, then
a verbose hymn is sung in four parts, composed in a
language unknown to all the combatants. . . .

All countries pay a certain number of orators to celebrate
these sanguinary actions ; some in a long black coat, and
over it a short docked cloak ; others in a gown with a
kind of shirt over it. . . . They are all very long-winded in
their harangues, and to illustrate a battle fought in

Weteravia, bring up what passed thousands of years ago in Palestine.

> Voltaire. *Dictionnaire
> Philosophique,*[1] *1764.*

[1] The Philosophical Dictionary for the Pocket, written in French by a Society of Men of Letters, and translated into English from the last Geneva edition, corrected by the authors. London, 1765.

A SPLENDID GAME

It is wonderful with what coolness and indifference the greater part of mankind see war commenced. Those that hear of it at a distance or read of it in books, but have never presented its evils to their minds, consider it as little more than a splendid game, a proclamation, an army, a battle, and a triumph. Some indeed must perish in the most successful field, but they die upon the bed of honour, *resign their lives amidst the joys of conquest, and filled with* England's *glory, smile in death.*[1]

> Samuel Johnson.   *Falkland's
> Islands, 1771.*

[1] The quotation is from Addison's *Blenheim.*

ILL-REPRESENTED BY HEROIC FICTION

The life of a modern soldier is ill-represented by heroic fiction. War has means of destruction more formidable than the cannon and the sword. Of the thousands and ten thousands that perished in our late contests with France and Spain, a very small part ever felt the stroke of an enemy ; the rest languished in tents and ships, amidst damps and putrefaction, pale, torpid, spiritless and helpless ; gasping and groaning, unpitied among men made obdurate by long continuance of hopeless misery ; and were at last whelmed in pits or heaved into the ocean, without notice and without remembrance. By incommodious encampments and unwholesome stations, where courage is useless and enterprise impracticable, fleets are silently dispeopled and armies sluggishly melted away.

> *Ibid.*

THE FORTUNES OF WAR

THE wars of civilised nations make very slow changes in the system of empire. The public perceive scarcely any alteration but an increase of debt ; and the few individuals who are benefited are not supposed to have the clearest right to their advantages. If he that shared the danger enjoyed the profit, and after bleeding in the battle grew rich by the victory, he might shew his gains without envy. But at the conclusion of a ten-years' war, how are we recompensed for the death of multitudes and the expense of millions, but by contemplating the sudden glories of paymasters and agents, contractors and commissaries, whose equipages shine like meteors, and whose palaces rise like exhalations.

These are the men who, without virtue, labour or hazard, are growing rich as their country is impoverished ; they rejoice when obstinacy or ambition adds another year to the slaughter and devastation ; and laugh from their desks at bravery and science, while they are adding figure to figure, and cypher to cypher, hoping for a new contract from a new armament, and computing the profits of a siege or tempest.[1]

Ibid.

[1] War is the harvest, sir, of all ill men,
In war they may be brutes with reputation.
John Crowne, *Ambitious Statesman*, 1679.

VERSES FOR NEWSMEN

Delicious news—a war with Spain ;
New raptures fire our Christmas strain,
Behold, to strike each Briton's eyes,
What bright victorious scenes arise !
What paragraphs of English glory
Will master Jackson set before ye !
The governor of Buenos Ayres
Shall dearly pay for his vagaries ;

For whether North, or whether Chatham,
Shall rule the roast, we must have at 'em . . .
After a dreary season past,
Our turn to live is come at last :
Gen'rals, and admirals, and Jews,
Contractors, printers, *men of news*,
All thrive by war, and line their pockets,
And leave the works of peace to blockheads.
But stay, my muse, this hasty fit—
The war is not declar'd as yet :
And we, though now so blithe we sing,
May all be *press'd* to serve the king ! . . .

Thomas Warton (?)   *Verses for
the year 1771.*

STRAINED ARGUMENTS

HE this day again defended duelling, and put his argument
upon what I have ever thought the most solid bases ;
that if public war be allowed to be consistent with morality,
private war must be equally so. Indeed we may observe
what strained arguments are used to reconcile war with
the Christian religion. But, in my opinion, it is exceedingly clear that duelling having better reasons for its barbarous violence, is more justifiable than war in which
thousands go forth without any cause of personal quarrel,
and massacre each other.

James Boswell.   *Life of Johnson.
April 19, 1773.*

THE PAMPHLETEER

THE province of this creature is to be a kind of jackal to
the patriot-lion ; for he beats the forest and first starts
the game ; he explores the reigning humour and whim of
the populace, and by frequent trials discovers the part
where the ministry are most vulnerable. But above all,

he never fails to put the mob in mind of what indeed they believed before, that politics is a subject which every one understands—except the ministry ; and that nothing is so easy as to bring the King of France to sue for peace on his knees at the bar of a British House of Commons, were such and such at the helm as honest and uncorrupt as they ought to be. " But alas ! what shall we say ? French gold will find an admission everywhere ; and what can we expect when the very persons who ought to have saved us have sold their country ? " This is delightful ; and this, with the old stories of Agincourt and Cressy regales, nay intoxicates, the mob, and inspires them with an enthusiasm bordering upon madness. The same ideas return; the former battles are fought over again ; and we have already taken possession of the gates of Paris in the warmth of a frantic imagination.

> Josiah Tucker, D.D.,[1] Dean of
> Gloucester. *The Case of Going to
> War, 1774.*

[1] Dean Tucker (of whom Warburton said that religion was his trade, and trade his religion) remarked: "To fight for the sake of procuring trade is a species of madness reserved only for Britons."

TRADING IN BLOOD

THESE people may be truly said to *trade in blood* ; for a war is their harvest, and a gazette extraordinary produces a crop of an hundredfold. How then can it be supposed that any ministers can be their favourites but the ministers of war ? Yet these are the men who may be truly said to govern the minds of the good people of England, and to turn their affections whithersoever they please ; who can render any scheme unpopular which they dislike, and whose approbation, or disapprobation, are regarded by thousands, and almost by millions, as the standard of right and wrong, of truth or falsehood : for it is a fact, an indisputable fact, that this country is as much news-mad, and news-ridden now, as ever it was Popery-mad and Priest-ridden, in the days of our forefathers.

> *Ibid.*

PEACEFUL BANNERS

IT is to the cultivation of the arts and sciences that we must in a great measure ascribe the existence of that party which is now opposed to war : it has received its birth amid the occupations and pleasures furnished by the fine arts. These arts, so to speak, have enrolled under their peaceful banners that army of idlers which would have otherwise possessed no amusement but in the hazardous and bloody game of war.

Jeremy Bentham. *The Rationale of Reward, Bk. III. Written c. 1775. Published 1825.*[1]

[1] Originally published in French by Etienne Dumont in 1811 under the title of *Théorie des Peines et des Récompenses.*

PULPIT CASUISTRY

THE doctrine of non-resistance has been fully exploded among every virtuous people. The free-born soul revolts against it, and must have been long debased and have drank in the last dregs of corruption before it can brook the idea " that a whole people injured may, in no case, recognise their trampled majesty." But to draw the line, and say where submission ends and resistance begins, is not the province of the ministers of Christ, who has given no rule in this matter, but left it to the feelings and conscience of the injured. . . . Pulpit casuistry is too feeble to direct or control here.[1]

William Smith, D.D. *Sermon at Philadelphia, June 23, 1775.*

[1] "In this connection we may observe that Jesus Himself did not anticipate the speedy cessation of war, nor denounce war as such; indeed, in His comment on the Sixth Commandment He virtually draws the distinction which our conscience feels to exist between war and murder; it is not the act of slaying, but the spirit of murder, hatred, and revenge, which He condemns. The distinction is for us a matter of very delicate casuistry in practice, and can easily be attacked in theory *ratione ruentis acervi*; but it exists."—The Rev. James H. F. Peile, M.A., Bampton Lectures, 1907.

FOR LIBERTY AND PEACE

IF, notwithstanding all this, Britain, or rather some degenerate sons of Britain, and enemies to our common liberty, still persist in embracing a delusion and believing a lie—if the sword is still unsheathed against us, and *submit or perish* is the sanguinary decree—why then—I cannot close the sentence—Indulge a minister of Jesus !— My soul shrinks back with horror from the tragic scene of fraternal slaughter—and the free spirit of the citizen is arrested by the tenderness of the Gospel love. Gracious God ! stop the precious effusion of British and American blood—too precious to be spilt in any other cause than the joint interest of both against a common foe !

Pained as I am at this melancholy prospect, I mean not, however, to decline addressing you in your military capacity, and suggesting such a conduct for the preservation of your temporal rights, as by the blessing of heaven will be most likely to ensure your success. . . .

If to spread undistinguishing ruin and devastation through a country ; if with more than Gothic rage to break into the sweet retreats of domestic felicity, and drive the aged and helpless from their once quiet habitations— O my God ! if this be heroism, if this be military virtue— suffer not our people to learn the destructive art. Let them rather continue to be injured and oppressed themselves, than taught thus wantonly to injure and oppress others. This caution, however, is unnecessary to you. Permit me, then, only to observe, that in our present circumstances we contend not for victory but for Liberty and Peace.

Jacob Duché. *Sermon at Philadelphia before the 1st Batt. of the City and Liberties of Philadelphia. July 7, 1775.*

THE STRAINS OF THE PROPHET

LET us examine the causes and motives from which war
in general arises. Let us behold the dreadful effects it produces. Let us anticipate the probable consequences which
await the prosecution of the civil war in which we are now
engaged with the once indulged and protected colonies.
These enquiries will pain our hearts, will call forth our
tears, especially when every light in which the subject is
placed will show the propriety of regarding war as one of
those means divine Providence uses to correct or to inflict
deserved ruin on a sinful nation.

At the mention of these things we are ready to adopt
the expressive strains of the prophet—*My bowels, my bowels* :
*I am pained at my very heart ; my heart maketh a noise in me ;
because thou hast heard, O my soul, the sound of the trumpet, the
alarm of war.*[1]

Joshua Toulmin.   *Sermon at
Taunton.   Feb. 18, 1776.*

[1] Jeremiah iv, 19.

FAVOURABLE TO CIVILISATION

IN modern war the great expense of fire-arms gives an
evident advantage to the nation which can best afford
that expense ;   and consequently to an opulent and
civilised, over a poor and barbarous nation. In ancient
times the opulent and civilised found it difficult to defend
themselves against the poor and barbarous nations. In
modern times the poor and barbarous find it difficult to
defend themselves against the opulent and civilised. The
invention of fire-arms, an invention which at first sight
appears to be so pernicious, is certainly favourable both
to the permanency and to the extension of civilisation.

Adam Smith.   *The Wealth of
Nations, 1776.*

FEAR AND HOPE

How little the fear of misfortune is . . . capable of balancing the hope of good luck, appears still more evidently in the readiness of the common people to enlist as soldiers, or to go to sea. . . .

What a common soldier may lose is obvious enough. Without regarding the danger, however, young volunteers never enlist so readily as at the beginning of a new war ; and though they have scarce any chance of preferment, they figure to themselves, in their youthful fancies, a thousand occasions of acquiring honour and distinction which never occur. These romantic hopes make the whole price of their blood.

Ibid.

UNIVERSAL, YET STRANGE

WE talked of war. Johnson : " Every man thinks meanly of himself for not having been a soldier,[1] or not having been at sea." Boswell : " Lord Mansfield does not." Johnson : " Sir, if Lord Mansfield were in a company of general officers and admirals who have been in service, he would shrink ; he'd wish to creep under the table." Boswell : " No ; he'd think he could *try* them all." Johnson : " Yes, if he could catch them : but they'd try him much sooner. No, sir ; were Socrates and Charles the Twelfth both present in any company, and Socrates to say, ' Follow me, and hear a lecture on philosophy ' ; and Charles, laying his hand on his sword, to say, ' Follow me, and dethrone the Czar ' ; a man would be ashamed to follow Socrates. Sir, the impression is universal ; yet it is strange." . . .

In conversation he always exalted the profession of a soldier. And yet I have, in my large and various collection of his writings, a letter to an eminent friend, in which he expresses himself thus : " My godson called on me lately.

He is weary, and rationally weary of a military life. If you can place him in some other state, I think you may increase his happiness, and secure his virtue. A soldier's time is passed in distress and danger, or in idleness and corruption." Such was his cool reflection in his study ; but whenever he was warmed and animated by the presence of company, he, like other philosophers, whose minds are impregnated with poetical fancy, caught the common enthusiasm for splendid renown.

James Boswell. Life of Johnson, 1791.

[1] "None is so poore of sence or eyne
To whom a souldier doth not shine."
George Chapman, The Contention of Phillis and Flora, 1595.

DISGRACEFUL PRIVILEGE

It is a notion as impolitic as it is vicious, that religion is not to be looked for in a British soldier ; in him, who of all others ought to have the most, because he would have the best ; because what he would learn of it in this enlightened land would do him the most honour, surround his heart with the most generous cheerfulness, and lift him to the noblest deeds. . . .

For is it forsooth the privilege of a soldier to be set above his God ? of him more than others to be turned loose from the duties of religion ? of him with a singular impunity to blaspheme the name, and sport with the terrors of the great King of Kings ? Disgraceful privilege !

Anon. The Duty and Character of a National Soldier. Sermon preached at the High Church, Hull, Jan. 2, 1779.

PECULIAR TO OUR KIND

To a speculative mind warmed by a general philanthropy, humanised by philosophy, or enlightened by Christianity, there can be but few justifiable occasions for commencing offensive war. The acquisition of food for the support of life, is one of the chief. But to this primary cause (which the plenty God has poured upon the earth seldom suffers to take place) the sad passions of mankind have added a thousand others. Revenge for fancied injuries has, at times, in every country reared its relentless standard ; avarice has slain its millions ; a lust of domination has deluged every region of the globe with human blood ; every mean, debasing propensity of our nature has become the occasion of exciting or extending the calamities of war.

This ferocity so peculiar and so disgraceful to our kind might be subdued by the power of natural reason. Were all men dispassionate and just, as reason tells them they ought to be, there would be an end of contention by force : the state of Nature is a state of Peace. But the history of the world does not authorise us to expect such a desirable event from the prevalence of reason alone. We think it may be expected from the universal prevalence of genuine Christianity ; *the Messiah will cut off the chariot from Ephraim, and the horse from Jerusalem, and speak peace unto the heathen.*

Richard Watson, D.D. *Sermon preached before the University of Cambridge, Feb. 4, 1780.*

THE DRUM

I hate that drum's discordant sound,
Parading round, and round, and round :
To thoughtless youth it pleasure yields,
And lures from cities and from fields,
To sell their liberty for charms
Of tawdry lace, and glittering arms ;
And when Ambition's voice commands,
To march, and fight, and fall, in foreign lands.

I hate that drum's discordant sound,
Parading round, and round, and round :

To me it talks of ravaged plains,
And burning towns, and ruined swains,
And mangled limbs, and dying groans,
And widows' tears, and orphans' moans ;
And all that Misery's hand bestows,
To fill the catalogue of human woes.

John Scott (of Amwell). *Poetical
Works :* [1] *Ode XIII, 1782.*

[1] The volume is embellished with engravings in the eighteenth century classical style, which led a writer in the *Critical Review* to remark: "There is a profusion of ornaments and finery about this book, not quite suitable to the plainness and simplicity of the Barclean system; but Mr. Scott is fond of the Muses, and wishes, we suppose, to see his ladies well dressed." Whereat the Quaker poet took umbrage.

THE SCOURGE

O war ! what art thou !
At once the proof and scourge of man's fall'n state.
After the brightest conquest, what appears
Of all thy glories ! for the vanquish'd, chains !
For the proud victor, what ? Alas ! to reign
O'er desolated nations ! a drear waste,
By one man's crime, by one man's lust of power,
Unpeopled ! Ravaged fields assume the place
Of smiling harvests, and uncultur'd plains
Succeed the fertile vineyard : barren waste
Deforms the spot once rich with luscious fig
And the fat olive—Devastation reigns.
Here, rifled temples are the cavern'd dens
Of savage beast, or haunt of birds obscene :
There, pop'lous cities blacken in the sun,
And, in the gen'ral wreck, proud palaces
Lie undistinguish'd, save by the dun smoke
Of recent conflagration. When the song
Of dear-bought joy, with many a triumph swell'd,
Salutes the victor's ear, and soothes his pride,
How is the grateful harmony profan'd
With the sad dissonance of virgins' cries,

Who mourn their brothers slain ! of matrons hoar,
Who clasp their wither'd hands, and fondly ask,
With iteration shrill, their slaughter'd sons !
How is the laurel's verdure stain'd with blood ;
And soil'd with widows' tears !

Hannah More.   *David and
Goliath, 1782.*

THE VOLUNTEER

Oh why the deuce should I repine,
   And be an ill foreboder ?
I'm twenty-three, and five feet nine—
   I'll go and be a sodger.[1]

I gat some gear wi' meikle care,
   I held it weel thegither ;
But now it's gane, and something mair—
   I'll go and be a sodger.

Robert Burns, *April, 1782.*

[1] These four lines were used as a recruiting poster with the caption,
WHAT BURNS SAID, 1782, HOLDS GOOD IN 1915. TAKE HIS TIP. Burns
has another poem, not so suitable for recruiting purposes:

I murder hate by field or flood,
Though glory's name may screen us;
In wars at hame I'll spend my blood,
Life-giving wars of Venus.
The deities that I adore
Are social Peace and Plenty;
I'm better pleased to make one more
Than be the death of twenty.

WHAT IDIOTS !

I DOUBT we must wade through more destruction to peace.
What idiots are mankind to sacrifice themselves to the
frantic passions of a few ! The slain only pass for rubbish
of which the use is destroyed : who thinks on them ?

Horace Walpole. *To Sir Horace
Mann, May 18, 1782.*

THANK GOD !

THE day that I little expected to see is arrived ! Peace came this morning, thank God ! That is the first thought : the effusion of human blood is stopped, nor are there to be more widows and orphans out of the common course of things.

Ibid. Dec. 2, 1782.

TRAGEDY AND FARCE

THE capital point, the Peace, is attained. . . . War is a tragedy ; other politics but a farce. It is plain mankind think so.

Ibid. Feb. 10, 1783.

NEVER A GOOD WAR OR A BAD PEACE

I JOIN with you most cordially in rejoicing at the return of Peace. I hope it will be lasting, and that mankind will at length, as they call themselves reasonable creatures, have reason and sense enough to settle their differences without cutting throats. For in my opinion, *there never was a good war, or a bad peace.*

What vast additions to the conveniences and comforts of living might mankind have acquired, if the money spent in wars had been employed in works of public utility ; what an extension of agriculture even to the tops of our mountains ; what rivers rendered navigable, or joined by canals ; what bridges, aqueducts, new roads, and other public works, edifices, and improvements, rendering England a complete paradise, might not have been obtained by spending those millions in doing good, which in the last war have been spent in doing mischief ; in bringing misery into thousands of families, and destroying

the lives of so many thousands of working people who
might have performed the useful labour.[1]

Benjamin Franklin. *To Sir
Joseph Banks, July 27, 1783.*

[1] "The more I am acquainted with agricultural affairs, the better I
am pleased with them, insomuch that I can no where find so great satisfaction as in those innocent and useful pursuits. In indulging these
feelings, I am led to reflect how much more delightful to an unde-
bauched mind is the task of making improvements on the earth than
the vain glory which can be acquired from ravaging it by the most
uninterrupted career of conquest." — George Washington to Arthur
Young.

PEACE, NOT WAR, THE NATURAL STATE

PEACE, not war, is the natural state of mankind when at
liberty : war is the offspring of necessity, not the legitimate
child of enjoyment. In the hand of Nature it is never an
end, cannibalism itself even included, but here and there
a severe and melancholy mean, with which even the
mother of all things could not entirely dispense, but
which, as a compensation, she has employed for various,
higher, and more valuable purposes.

Before we proceed to the afflicting consideration of
enmity, let us therefore examine delightful love : love,
which extends its sway over all the earth, though everywhere appearing in different forms. . . .

Johann Gottfried von Herder. *Outlines
of a Philosophy of the History of Man, 1784.
Tr. T. Churchill, 1800.*

EARTH UNWORTHY OF THE NAME

THUS has our old earth been a prey to violence ; and its
history forms a melancholy picture of man-hunting and
conquests : almost every little variation of a boundary,
every new epoch, is delineated in the book of Time with
the blood of human victims, and the tears of the oppressed.
The most celebrated names are those of murderers of

mankind, crowned or crown-seeking executioners ; and
what is still more to be lamented, the worthiest men have
often been compelled to appear on the dark scaffold where
the chains of their brethren were forged. Whence comes
it that the histories of kingdoms display so few rational
purposes ? Because the greatest and most of their events
originated not from any rational views : for the passions,
not humanity, have overpowered the earth, and urged
its people like wild beasts against each other. Had it
pleased Providence to permit us to be governed by superior
beings, how different would the history of man have
appeared ! But instead of this they have been for the
most part *heroes*, that is to say ambitious men, possessed of
power, or artful and enterprising, who have spun the
thread of events under the guidance of passion, and
woven it as it pleased Fate. If nothing else in the history
of the world indicated the inferiority of the human species,
the history of governments would demonstrate it ; according to which the greater part of our earth merits not such
a name, but that of Mars or child-devouring Saturn.

Ibid.

MAN'S OBDURATE HEART

Oh for a lodge in some vast wilderness,
Some boundless contiguity of shade,
Where rumour of oppression and deceit,
    Of unsuccessful or successful war
Might never reach me more ! My ear is pain'd,
My soul is sick with every day's report
Of wrong and outrage with which earth is fill'd.
There is no flesh in man's obdurate heart,
It does not feel for man. The natural bond
Of brotherhood is sever'd as the flax
That falls asunder at the touch of fire. . . .
Lands intersected by a narrow frith
Abhor each other. Mountains interposed,
Make enemies of nations who had else

> Like kindred drops been mingled into one. . . .
>   Sure there is need of social intercourse,
> Benevolence and peace and mutual aid
> Between the nations, in a world that seems
> To toll the death-bell of its own decease.

William Cowper. The Task,
Bk. I. 1785.

BABY MINDS

>   Nations would do well
> To extort their truncheons from the puny hands
> Of heroes, whose infirm and baby minds
> Are gratified with mischief, and who spoil
> Because men suffer it, their toy the world.

Ibid. Bk. V.

IN A LARGER SENSE

BECAUSE the Christian Scriptures describe wars as what they are, as crimes or judgments, some have been led to believe that it is unlawful for a Christian to bear arms. But it should be remembered that it may be necessary for individuals to unite their force, and for this end to resign themselves to the direction of a common will ; and yet it may be true that that will is often actuated by criminal motives, and often determined to destructive purposes. Hence, although the origin of wars be ascribed, in Scripture, to the operation of lawless and malignant passions, and though war itself be enumerated among the sorest calamities with which a land can be visited, the profession of the soldier is nowhere forbidden or condemned. . . .

The *justifying* causes of war are deliberate invasions of right and the necessity of maintaining such a balance of power amongst neighbouring nations as that no single state, or confederacy of states, be strong enough to overwhelm the rest. The objects of just war are precaution, defence or reparation. In a larger sense, every just war is a *defensive* war, inasmuch as every just war supposes an injury perpetrated, attempted or feared.

William Paley, D.D. *The Principles of Moral and Political Philosophy, 1785.*

IN STRICT PHILOSOPHY

IN strict philosophy, a limitation of the rights of war seems to imply nonsense and contradiction. Grotius himself is lost in an idle distinction between the *jus naturae* and the *jus gentium*, between poison and infection. . . . Yet I can understand the benefit and validity of an agreement, tacit or express, mutually to abstain from certain modes of hostility.[1]

Edward Gibbon. *Decline and Fall of the Roman Empire, 1788.*

[1] Professor J. Husband, president of the Institution of Structural Engineers, speaking at the annual dinner of the institute in London last night, said: "The first and most important step towards the establishment of peaceful security is the universal abolition of aircraft, both military and civil. You cannot abolish the one and retain the other. Despite the important benefits of civil aviation, its advantages are trivial when weighed in the balance against the world-wide suffering and material loss caused by aerial warfare."—*Daily Telegraph,* April 9, 1938.

A NECESSARY, THOUGH PERNICIOUS, SCIENCE

THE single combats of the heroes of history or fable amuse our fancy and engage our affections : the skilful evolutions of war may inform the mind, and improve a necessary, though pernicious, science. But in the uniform and odious pictures of a general assault, all is blood and horror and confusion ; nor shall I strive, at the distance of three centuries and a thousand miles, to delineate a scene at which there could be no spectators, and of which the actors themselves were incapable of forming any just or adequate idea.[1]

Ibid.

[1] *Hanno*: How went the battle? Who got the better on't?

Thrasymachus: What with the noise and clamour of drums, trumpets, horses, and arms, I was so far from knowing what became of others that I could hardly tell where I was myself.

Hanno: But I have seen those that after a fought field would paint yet every circumstance so to the life, as if they had only looked on. Such an officer said this, and t'other did that; every word and action to a tittle.

Thrasymachus: I am of opinion that these men lied most confoundedly.

—Erasmus, *Colloquies* tr. L'Estrange.

HISTORY TO A FEELING MIND

THE melancholy retrospect that history affords of the calamities of past ages has been augmented through the depraved taste of men, who have, in all ages since the practice of war was introduced upon earth, unhappily lavished the bewitching reward of praise on the destroyers of men ; and the eager desire for false glory, which has stimulated poor mortals to their mutual destruction, and necessarily swelled the historic page with rueful feats of arms, seems to have almost precluded from the records of antiquity any account of the sweet fruits of peace : nations have seldom desired to be accounted an inglorious people, living in quietness and ease, while their exploits in battle have been extravagantly delineated. The pious philosopher, spending his time and himself for the good of mankind, the husbandman, mechanic and physician, with all their useful labours, cut but a poor figure in the annals of time ; while the hero, the man of war, rises glaringly in view, mounted on trophies, the wreck of nations ; hence history, to a feeling mind, will appear little more than a catalogue of human woes. In one page we often see thousands devoted to the sword, and the victor's triumph, raised at an expense of blood, which a remote nation mourns with floods of tears ; while the sweet intervals of peace, which all nations have probably enjoyed a greater share of than a mere superficial view of history would encourage us to believe, have often been passed over in silence and buried in oblivion.

> John Walker. *Elements
> of Geography, 1788.*

VISIONARY AND RIDICULOUS

THE object of the present essay is to submit to the world a plan for an universal and perpetual peace. The globe is the field of dominion to which the author aspires,—the press the engine, and the only one he employs,—the cabinet of mankind the theatre of his intrigue. . . .

As to the utility of such an universal and lasting peace, supposing a plan for that purpose practicable, and likely to be adopted, there can be but one voice. The objection, and the only objection to it, is the apparent impracticability of it ;—that it is not only hopeless, but that to such a degree that any proposal to that effect deserves the name of visionary and ridiculous. This objection I shall endeavour in the first place to remove ; for the removal of this prejudice may be necessary to procure for the plan a hearing.

What can be better suited to the preparing of men's minds for the reception of such a proposal than the proposal itself ?

Let it not be objected that the age is not ripe for such a proposal : the more it wants of being ripe, the sooner we should begin to do what can be done to ripen it ; the more we should do to ripen it. A proposal of this sort is one of those things that can never come too early or too late.

> Jeremy Bentham. *A Plan for an
> Universal and Perpetual Peace.
> Written 1789.*[1]

[1] First published 1843, Works, Vol. 2. Principles of International Law, Essay IV. Bentham's plan included the emancipation of all colonial dependencies, the reduction of armed forces, an International Court of Judicature, and the suppression of secret diplomacy.

FOREIGN RELATIONS

FOREIGN nations are not yet considered as objects susceptible of an injury. For the citizens of other civilised nations, we have not so much feeling as for our negroes. There are instances in which ministers have been punished for making peace—there are none where they have been so much as questioned for bringing the nation into war ; and if punishment had been ever applied on such an occasion, it would be not for the mischief done to the foreign nation, but purely for the mischief brought upon their own ; not for the injustice, but purely for the imprudence.[1]

It has never been laid down as a rule that you should pay any regard to foreign nations : it has never been laid down that you should stick at anything which would give you an advantage in your dealings with foreign nations. On what ground could a minister be punished for a war, even the most unsuccessful, brought on by any such means ? I did my best to serve you, he would say—the worse the measure was for the foreign nations, the more I took upon me : the greater therefore the zeal I showed for your cause : the event has proved unfavourable. Are zeal and misfortune to be represented as crimes ?

Ibid.

[1] Towards the end of 1918 the Inter-Allied Supreme Council proposed to put the German Emperor on trial; he was to be held "personally responsible for his crimes against international law." The proposal was popular, and in England "Hang the Kaiser!" became, with "Make Germany Pay!" a very useful electioneering cry. The Kaiser was not brought to judgment, the Dutch Government refusing to consent to his extradition; but an execution order was obtained against Germany for the purpose of making her pay.

HOW GLORIOUS THE PROSPECT !

How glorious, then, is the prospect, the reverse of all the past, which is now opening upon us, and upon the world. . . .

Together with the general prevalence of the true principles of civil government, we may expect to see the extinction of all *national prejudice* and enmity, and the establishment of *universal peace* and goodwill among all nations. When the affairs of the various societies of mankind shall be conducted by those who shall truly represent them, who shall feel as they feel, and think as they think, who shall really understand, and consult their interests, they will no more engage in those mutually offensive *wars*, which the experience of many centuries has shown to be constantly expensive and ruinous. They will no longer covet what belongs to others, and which they have found to be of no real service to them, but will content themselves with making the most of their own. . . .

If *time* be allowed for the discussion of differences, so great a majority will form one opinion, that the minority will see the necessity of giving way. Thus will *reason* be the umpire in all disputes, and extinguish civil wars as well as foreign ones. The empire of reason will ever be the reign of peace.

Joseph Priestley. *Letters to the Right Honourable Edmund Burke. No. xiv. 1791.*

GOOD NEWS

" Good news ! Great news ! Glorious news ! " cried young Oswald, as he entered his father's house. " We have got a complete victory and killed I don't know how many of the enemy ; and we are to have bonfires and illuminations ! "

" And so," said his father, " you think that killing a great many thousands of human creatures is a thing to be very glad about ? "

Oswald : No—I do not think quite so, neither ; but surely it is right to be glad that our country has gained a great advantage.

Father : No doubt, it is right to wish well to our own

country, as far as its prosperity can be promoted without
injuring the rest of mankind. But wars are very seldom to
the real advantage of any nation ; and when they are
deemed ever so useful or necessary, so many dreadful evils
attend them, that a humane man will scarce rejoice in
them, if he considers at all on the subject.

Oswald : But if our enemies would do us a great deal
of mischief, and we prevent it by beating them, have not
we a right to be glad of it ?

Father : Alas ! we are in general very little judges
which of the parties has the most mischievous intention.
Commonly they are both in the wrong, and success will
make both of them unjust and unreasonable. But putting
that out of the question, he who rejoices in the event of a
battle, rejoices in the misery of many thousands of his
species, and the thought of that should make him pause a
little. Suppose a surgeon were to come with a smiling
countenance, and tell us triumphantly that he had cut off
half a dozen legs to-day—what would you think of him ?

Oswald : I should think him very hard-hearted.

Father : And yet these operations are done for the
benefit of the sufferers, and by their own desire. But in
a battle the probability is, that none of those engaged on
either side have any interest at all in the cause they are
fighting for, but many of them come there because they
cannot help it. In this battle that you are so rejoiced
about, there have been ten thousand men killed upon the
spot, and nearly as many wounded.

Oswald : On both sides !

Father : Yes—but they are men on both sides. Consider
now, that the ten thousand sent out of the world in this
morning's work, though they are past feeling themselves,
have left probably two persons each on an average to
lament their loss, either parents, wives, or children. Here
are then twenty thousand people made unhappy at one
stroke on their account. This, however, is hardly so
dreadful to think of as the condition of the wounded. At
the moment we are talking eight or ten thousand more
are lying in agony, torn with shot, or gashed with cuts,

their wounds all festering, some hourly to die a most excruciating death, others to linger in torture weeks and months, and many doomed to drag on a miserable existence for the rest of their lives, with diseased and mutilated bodies.

Oswald : This is shocking to think of indeed !

Father : When you light your candles, then, this evening, think what they cost !

Oswald : But everybody else is glad, and seem to think nothing of these things.

Father : True they do *not* think of them. If they did, I cannot suppose they would be so void of feeling as to enjoy themselves in merriment when so many of their fellow creatures are made miserable. Do you not remember when poor Dickens had his leg broken by a loaded wagon, how all the town pitied him ?

Oswald : Yes, very well. I could not sleep the night after for thinking of him.

Father : But here are thousands suffering as much as he, and we scarce bestow a single thought upon them. If any one of these poor creatures were before our eyes, we should probably feel much more than we now do for all together.

Mrs. Barbauld and J. Aiken.
Evenings at Home, 1792.

THE BITTER CUP

If the stroke of war
Fell certainly on the guilty head, none else,
If they that made the cause might taste th' effect,
And drink, themselves, the bitter cup they mix,
Then might the bard (though child of peace) delight
To twine fresh wreaths around the conqueror's brow ;
Or haply strike his high-toned harp, to swell
The trumpet's martial sound, and bid them on
Whom Justice arms for vengeance ; but, alas !
That undistinguishing and deathful storm

Beats heaviest on th' exposed innocent,
And they that stir its fury, while it raves,
Stand at safe distance, send their mandate forth
Unto the mortal ministers that wait
To do their bidding.—Ah, who then regards
The widow's tears, the friendless orphan's cry,
And Famine, and the ghastly train of woes
That follow at the dogged heels of War ?
They, in the pomp and pride of victory
Rejoicing, o'er the desolated earth,
As at an altar wet with human blood,
And flaming with the fire of cities burnt,
Sing their mad hymns of triumph ; hymns to God,
O'er the destruction of His gracious works !
Hymns to the Father, o'er His slaughtered sons !

> William Crowe. *Verses intended to have been spoken in the theatre to the Duke of Portland at his installation as Chancellor of the University of Oxford, in the year 1793.*

William Crowe's son was killed at the Battle of Waterloo, 1815. In the 1827 edition of *Lewesdon Hill* is a Latin monody by the father on his loss. The D.N.B. is wrong in stating that the monody was not printed before it appeared in *N. & Q.*, 1853.

THE CRISIS

IT is wonderful with what indifference and unconcern a crisis, so serious as the present, is beheld. But our wonder will be diminished, when we enumerate the mean and despicable artifices which governments ever employ to produce this infatuation, and to make war (the curse of the whole human race) a subject popular to the people. They keep them in profound ignorance of its effects ; they inflame their passions, flatter their pride, and deceive them by all the empty and disgusting pageantries which march in the train of military preparation. Armaments, reviews, drums, flags, crowds and acclamations, are the hackneyed stage-tricks employed to cover a measure which will not bear a cool examination.

But war is neither the innocent, amusing, nor honourable pastime, which Ministers and their adherents often represent it to be. It is at no time, and under no circumstances, a very desirable measure. It is an evil to be endured when unavoidable, rather than coveted when unnecessary. Religion condemns the practice of war ; reason forbids it ; true policy is averse to it ; and experience declares it to be the scourge of mankind. It destroys commerce, suspends agriculture, ruins manufactures ; and makes the poorest man much poorer, by augmenting the taxes, and by rendering every article of his own consumption, every article he buys for the use of his little household, twice as dear as it was before.

Considered in a moral view, war will be found to pervert the social affections, to corrupt the useful virtues, to banish the idea of justice, and to give opportunity to the most flagitious and destructive propensities. It inflames anger, ambition, avarice, cruelty, rapine, revenge. War, then, is the greatest of all evils that can befall a flourishing nation.

Anon. Pamphlet, The Crisis Stated.
Jan., 1793.

WAR PREFERABLE TO PEACE WITHOUT HONOUR

As to the time, as to the moment when war is to commence, if there is yet any possibility of satisfactory explanation and security for the future, it is not to the last moment precluded. But I should disguise my sentiments to the House, if I stated, that I thought it in any degree probable. This country has always been desirous of peace. We desire it still, but such as may be real and solid, and consistent with the interests and dignity of Britain, and with the general security of Europe. War, whenever it comes, will be preferable to peace without honour, without security, and which is incompatible either with the external safety or the internal happiness of this country.

William Pitt. *In the House of Commons, Feb. 1, 1793.*

UNEXPECTED OCCURRENCES OF A WAR

BUT there is another object to be attended to. Whatever degree of exertion may be made in the present contest, which involves the dearest and most sacred objects, still we must now allow ourselves to neglect what likewise involves it in the permanent interests of ourselves and our posterity. . . .

If the situation of this country lead us, as I hope it will, to take an efficient part along with our numerous allies, in carrying on offensive operations against the enemy, a considerable increase of expense in our military establishment will be necessary. Hitherto, we have hired none but the Hanoverian troops ; but, in this case, we may have occasion to employ a considerable body of other foreign troops, in order to press on all sides the common enemy. . . . A loss may perhaps accrue in the lottery, on account of certain regulations which it has been found necessary to make. It is, therefore, my opinion, that a considerable sum should be set apart to enable His Majesty to provide for the unexpected occurrences of a war, and defray its exigencies as they arise.

William Pitt. *In the House of Commons, March 11, 1793.*

SPLENDID ISOLATION

HAPPY Americans ! while the whirlwind spreads desolation over one quarter of the globe, you remain protected from its baneful effects by your own virtues and the wisdom of your government ! Separated from Europe by an immense ocean, you feel not the effect of those prejudices and passions which convert the boasted seats of civilisation into scenes of horror and bloodshed ! You profit by the folly and madness of contending nations, and afford in your more congenial clime an asylum to those blessings and virtues which they wantonly contemn, or wickedly exclude from the bosom ! Cultivating the arts of peace under the influence of freedom, you advance by rapid strides to opulence and distinction ; and if by accident you should be compelled to take part in the present unhappy contest, if you should find it necessary to avenge insult or repel injury, the world will bear witness to the equity of your sentiments and the moderation of your views, and the success of your arms will, no doubt, be proportioned to the justice of your cause !

> Charles James Fox. *Speech in House of Commons, 1794.*

"*THE EVERLASTING PEACE*"

WHETHER this satirical inscription, placed by a Dutch landlord upon the signboard of his inn underneath the picture of a churchyard, was intended for men in general, and more especially for rulers of States, who can never be weary of warfare ; or merely for philosophers who indulge in the sweet dreams there indicated—all this we may set aside. The Author of this present treatise merely reserves for himself one condition, which he will now explain. The practical politician, it is well known, stands in relation to the theoretical one upon such a footing, that in his own self-complacency he merely looks down upon him as a scholastic pedant, who can bring no danger to the State in ventilating his empty ideas, and that for the simple reason that the State can only act upon the maxims of human experience. To such a theoriser, accordingly, the worldly-wise Statesman is willing to allow the full play of his arguments, without considering himself obliged to take any notice of them. In case, therefore, of a dispute arising between them, the Statesman is bound to act consistently with his professed belief, and not pretend to scent out any danger to the State, from opinions intended only for good, and made public with this sole idea. Under the shelter of this Safety Clause (*Clausula Salvatoria*) the Author now desires expressly to guard himself, in best form, against any malignant interpretation.

> Immanuel Kant. *Zum Ewigen Frieden,* *1795.* Tr. J. D. Morell : *A Philosophical Treatise on Perpetual Peace.*[1]

[1] "It is not written in the form of a philanthropic appeal, nor of a moral and philosophical disquisition. It is really a quiet and often a sarcastic manifesto against the proceedings and the value of modern diplomacy, couched in the form of a protocol, and even imitating to a considerable extent the confused and intricate style by which such documents were often characterised."—J. D. Morell.

THE TERM RIGHT

CONSIDERING the perversity of human nature which shows itself unblushingly in the free relations of nations with each other (when not kept from sight by the coercion of respective governments), it is a matter of surprise that the word *Right* has not been banished from their vocabulary as being altogether pedantic, so far as war is concerned, and that no State has been bold enough to side openly with this view of the question. . . . Nevertheless, this homage, which every State pays to the idea of right (in words at least) clearly proves that a superior moral principle, though for the time quiescent, still exists in the human mind, which is always impelling it to rise above the undeniable principle of evil within, and to hope for the same in respect of others. Were this not the case the term Right would never be employed by different States in their mutual quarrels ; unless indeed it were used in mockery, as it was by the French prince when he said that " the preference which nature has given to the strong over the weak was seen in the fact that the latter is bound to obey the former."

But now the only mode in which States can defend the right is not by entering into a legal process, but simply by means of war. The *Right*, however, in the true sense of that word, is not really decided by the result of war (that is by a victory) ; for although hostilities are brought to an end by a treaty of peace, the state of war still remains, always ready to find a new pretext for fresh outbreaks ; all which cannot be pronounced *unjust*, so long as each State is sole judge of its own affairs.

Ibid.

THE CHRISTIAN SOLDIER

A CONSCIENTIOUS officer, while he courageously discharges his duty to his country in the camp and the field, will rejoice in every opportunity which presents itself of mitigating the horror and alleviating the miseries of war. He will spare, whenever it is practicable, the blood of his enemies. He will remember that those who fall in the field of battle, to whatever nation or party they belong, are men like himself ; and that the life of every single unit in the long sum of slaughtered thousands was of the utmost possible consequence at least to one person, if not to more. He will contain his troops within the strict bounds of discipline ; he will inculcate on them constant regard to moderation and humanity ; and will chastise with exemplary vigour every act of barbarity and unauthorised rapine whenever and by whomever it may be perpetrated. He will never forget the common ties of human nature, by which he is inseparably united to his enemy ; an enemy whom he is shortly to meet before the throne of their common judge.[1]

Thomas Gisborne. *An Enquiry into the Duties of Men in the Higher and Middle Classes, 1795.*

[1] "I never knew nor heard of an army all of saints, save the holy Army of Martyrs; and those, you know, were dead first."—Thomas Fuller, Sermon, 1642.

A MORE SERIOUS EVIL

THE depravation of private morals is a more serious and less transient evil. All our happiness and the greater part of our virtues depend on social confidence. This beautiful fabric of Love the system of spies and informers has shaken to the very foundation. There have been multiplied among us " Men who carry tales to shed blood ! " Men who resemble the familiar spirits described by Isaiah, as " dark ones, that peep and that mutter ! " Men, who may seem to have been typically shadowed out in the frogs that formed the second plague of Egypt : little low animals with chilly blood and staring eyes, that " come up into our houses and our bed-chambers ! " These men are plenteously scattered among us : our very looks are deciphered into disaffection, and we cannot move without treading on some political spring-gun. Nor here has the evil stopped. We have breathed so long the atmosphere of panic, that many honest minds have caught an aguish disorder ; in their cold fits they shiver at Freedom, in their hot fits they turn savage against its advocates ; and sacrifice to party rage what they would have scornfully refused to Corruption.

Samuel Taylor Coleridge.
Conciones ad Populum, 1795.

Coleridge's military career in 1794 as Trooper Silas Tomkyn Comberbacke of the 15th Dragoons was brief and inglorious, but many a temporary soldier since his day has been cheered by remembering incidents recorded of it. "Whose rusty gun is this ?" asked the inspecting officer. "Is it very rusty ?" said Coleridge, "because if it is I think it must be mine." He considered that a horse ought to "rub himself down and so shine in all his native beauty." And once, overhearing an officer quote two lines in Greek and ascribe them to Euripides, he said, "I hope your honour will excuse me, but the lines you have repeated are not quite accurately cited; moreover, instead of being in Euripides they will be found in the second antistrophe of the Œdipus of Sophocles."

SILLY OBJECTS

THE truth is, *national glory*, the trappings of a court, the parade of armies, the finery of external appearance, have been the silly objects of *state* solicitude ; while MAN was left to bewail, in the recesses of want and obscurity, that his mother had brought him into a world of woe, without means of comfort or support, with little other prospect than to labour without ceasing, to fight those who never injured him, and to die prematurely, unknown, and unlamented.

Vicesimus Knox,[1] D.D. *The Spirit of Despotism, 1795.*

[1] "The Reverend Dr. Knox, master of Tunbridge School, appears to have the *imitari aveo* of Johnson's style perpetually in his mind."— Boswell.

PAGEANTRY

PAGEANTRY has contributed perhaps more than any other cause to the prevalence of war, the bane of happiness, the disgrace of human nature. The grand operations of war, the splendour of arms, the finery of military dress, have been the amusements which despots have chiefly delighted in, whenever they could behold them in perfect consistence with their own personal safety. The pageantry of war dazzles young minds, and supplies both armies and navies with willing victims. The ugliness of slaughter, the desolation of fertile plains, the burning of peaceful villages, have all been unnoticed, amid the pride, pomp, and circumstances of glorious war. The taste for false glare and deceitful appearances of happiness and glory, has been one of the most prolific parents of human calamity. It has palliated robbery, and covered foul murder with a glittering veil of tinsel.

Ibid.

NOTHING CAN BANISH IT

As to war, if it be the means of wrong and violence, it is the sole means of justice amongst nations. Nothing can banish it from the world. They who say otherwise, intending to impose upon us, do not impose upon themselves.

Edmund Burke. *Letters on a Regicide Peace, 1796.*

SECURITY

THE observation with which the honourable gentleman[1] concluded his speech, appears to me one of the strangest I ever heard advanced, and first challenges my attention. He defies me to state, in one sentence, what is the object of the war. I know not whether I can do it in one sentence ; but in one word I can tell him that it is *security* : security against a danger, the greatest that ever threatened the world. It is security against a danger which never existed in any past period of society. It is security against a danger which in degree and extent was never equalled ; against a danger which threatened all the nations of the earth ; against a danger which has been resisted by all the nations of Europe, and resisted by none with so much success as by this nation, because by none has it been resisted so uniformly and with so much energy.

William Pitt. *In the House of Commons, Feb. 17, 1800.*

[1] Tierney, who had challenged Pitt to define the real object of the war. "It is not the destruction of Jacobin principles; it may be the restoration of the House of Bourbon; but I would wish the right honourable gentleman in one sentence to state, if he can, without his *ifs* and *buts* and special pleading and ambiguity, what this object is. I am persuaded he cannot, and that he calls us to prosecute a war, and to lavish our treasure and blood in its support, when no one plain satisfactory reason can be given for its continuance."

IN THE SPIRIT OF PEACE

IF we seek for peace, it must be done in the spirit of peace. We are not to make it a question who was the first aggressor, or endeavour to throw the blame that may attach to us on our enemy. Such circumstances should be consigned to oblivion, as tending to no one useful purpose.

Richard Brinsley Sheridan. *In the House of Commons, Feb. 17, 1800.*

SECURITY

The observation with which the honourable gentleman[1] concluded his speech, appears to me one of the strangest I ever heard advanced, and that challenges my attention. He defies me to state, in one sentence, what is the object of the war. I know not whether I can do it in one sentence; but in one word I can tell him that it is security: security against a danger, the greatest that ever threatened the world. It is security against a danger which never existed in any past period of society. It is security against a danger which in degree and extent was never equalled; against a danger which threatened all the nations of the earth; against a danger which has been resisted by all the nations of Europe, and resisted by none with so much success as by this nation, because by none has it been resisted so uniformly and with so much energy.

> William Pitt. In the House of
> Commons, Feb. 17, 1800.

[1] Tierney, who had challenged Pitt to define the real object of the war.
"It is not the destruction of Jacobin principles; it may be the restoration of the House of Bourbon; but I would wish the right honourable gentleman in one sentence to state, if he can, without his ifs and buts and special pleading and ambiguity, what this object is; I am persuaded he cannot, and that he calls us to prosecute a war, and to lavish our treasure and blood in its support, when no one plain satisfactory reason can be given for its continuance."

IN THE SPIRIT OF PEACE

If we seek for peace, it must be done in the spirit of peace. We are not to make it a question who was the first aggressor, or endeavour to throw the blame that may attach to us on our enemy. Such circumstances should be consigned to oblivion, as tending to no one useful purpose.

> Richard Brinsley Sheridan. In the
> House of Commons, Feb. 17, 1800.

2nd Servant : Why, then we shall have a stirring world again. This peace is good for nothing but to rust iron, increase tailors, and breed ballad-makers.

1st Servant : Let me have war, say I ; it exceeds peace as far as day does night ; it's spritely, waking, audible, and full of vent. Peace is a very apoplexy, lethargy; mulled, deaf, sleepy, insensible ; a getter of more bastard children than wars a destroyer of men.

2nd Servant : 'Tis so : and as wars, in some sort, may be said to be a ravisher, so it cannot be denied but peace is a great maker of cuckolds.

1st Servant : Ay, and it makes men hate one another.

3rd Servant : Reason ; because they then less need one another. The wars for my money.

Shakespeare. *Coriolanus.*

2nd Servant : Why, then we shall have a stirring world again. This peace is good for nothing but to rust iron, increase tailors, and breed ballad-makers.

1st Servant : Let me have war, say I ; it exceeds peace as far as day does night ; it's spritely, waking, audible, and full of vent. Peace is a very apoplexy, lethargy ; mulled, deaf, sleepy, insensible ; a getter of more bastard children than wars a destroyer of men.

2nd Servant : 'Tis so : and as wars, in some sort, may be said to be a ravisher, so it cannot be denied but peace is a great maker of cuckolds.

1st Servant : Ay, and it makes men hate one another.

3rd Servant : Reason ; because they then less need one another. The wars for my money.

Shakespeare, Coriolanus.

AN ENTHUSIAST

In these days of fashionable despair of the final amendment of human manners I am not ashamed to own myself of the number of those reputed enthusiasts who look forward to fairer times. I am free to confess that my hopes, as well as wishes, point to a state of peace far other than any which has yet borne that beautiful name, which has indeed been little more than an inactive war ; an armed, although a quiet scene ; a season of calm in a system of society containing all the materials of tempest and principles of storm ; a motley picture at variance with itself, of national civility and jealousy, rest and insecurity, amity and rivalship ; of steel wiped from its slaughterous stain but retaining its slaughterous shape ; of arms put off by their wearers only to be reposited in arsenals ; of forts whose thunder is hushed but that still threaten in silence with frowning battlements ; of fleets and armies ceasing from murderous action but maintained in proud existence, and bearing the venerable name of *Establishments* ; and of garments, though no longer " rolled in blood," continuing to be worn, with undiminished ornament, as the gay badge of barbarous occupation.

Joseph Fawcett.[1] *War Elegies :
Introduction. 1801.*

[1] " He [the Rev. Joseph Fawcett] was the friend of my early youth. He was the first person of literary eminence whom I had then known; and the conversations I had with him on the subjects of taste and philosophy (for his taste was as refined as his powers of reasoning were profound and subtle) gave me a delight such as I can never feel again."—Hazlitt, note in *Memoirs of Thomas Holcroft.*

NIGHT PIECE

Figuring the raven vest that robes the sky,
  Gay lines of light in lofty arches glow !
Ruin, like Iris, learns to please the eye,
  And proudly sets in heaven his gaudy bow.

Lit by his fires, broad conflagration's flame,
  Burns but to point his distant war its way :
Tremendous lamp, that guides each engine's aim,
  And lends the dark assailant dreadful day !

Ye stars, whose innocent and milky light
  All mildly seems to blame yon crimson blaze,
That with a ravenous splendour fiercely bright
  On useful piles and beauteous structures preys :

If suns ye be that beam on peopled balls,
  The seats of moral Nature's varied powers,
Say, if on scenes like these your daylight falls ?
  Say, rolls there round you one such orb as ours ?

Ibid. The Siege, 1801.

THE SOLDIER

The soldier, armed with rod and gun,
Palsied strikes the summer's sun.
The strongest poison ever known
Came from Cæsar's laurel crown.
Nought can deform the human race
Like to the armour's iron brace.

William Blake. *Auguries of
Innocence. Written c. 1801-3.
Gilchrist's Life, 1863.*

STOUT ENGLISH PEASANTRY, NOBILITY AND GENTRY

I will not, however, stop to inquire into the time which
has been already lost ; but I shall express my earnest hope
that no time will be wasted hereafter—that every instant
will be actively engaged until the country be completely
safe. I think that some arrangements should be made to
connect the different departments of the executive authority,
so that, upon orders issued from Government to the

Lords-Lieutenant of counties, the people might be immediately set in motion ; so that, without interfering with agriculture, which should not by any means be disturbed, the several classes might be disciplined, to attend the drill at least two days in each week, to assemble in particular places throughout the country ; the limitation of distance from the residence of each man to the place of assembly, to be about six miles, the time of attendance to be not less than half a day. The distance I propose is not more than the stout English peasantry are in the habit of going, when led to a cricket match or any rural amusement. . . .

As to the trouble which the nobility and gentry may be called upon to submit to, in this general armament, I cannot do them the injustice of supposing that they would not submit to it with alacrity, or that questions of mere personal convenience would, in such a crisis as the present, have any weight with them.

William Pitt. *In the House of Commons, July 18, 1803.*

MINOR TRAGEDY

THIS war has affected me in every possible shape ; in the *King George* packet I lost a whole cargo of books, for which I had been a year and a half waiting.

Robert Southey. *To Lieut. Southey, Oct. 29, 1803.*

PROFESSOR WILLIAM SMYTH'S SONG

A SOLDIER am I, the world over I range ;
And would not my lot with a Monarch exchange !
How welcome a Soldier, wherever he roves,
Attended, like Venus, by Mars and the Loves !
How dull is the Ball, how cheerless the Fair !
What's a feast, or a frolic ? if we are not there !
Kind, hearty, and gallant, and joyous, we come ;
And the World looks alive at the sound of the Drum ! . . . .

The Veteran, half-dozing, awakes at the news,
Hobbles out, and our column with triumph reviews :
Near his knee, his young grandson, with ecstasy, hears
Of Majors, and Generals, and fierce Brigadiers ;
Of the marches he took, and the hardships he knew ;
Of the battles he fought, and the foes that he slew :
To his heart spirits new in wild revelry come,
And make one rally more at the sound of the Drum !

Who loves not the Soldier ? the generous, the brave,
The heart that can feel, and the arm that can save !
In peace, the gay friend, with manners that charm,
The thought ever liberal, the soul ever warm !
In his mind, nothing selfish or pitiful known ;
'Tis a Temple, which Honour can enter alone !
No titles I boast ; yet, wherever I come,
I can always feel proud at the sound of the Drum !

Professor William Smyth.[1]
English Lyrics, 1806.

[1] Professor of modern history at Cambridge, he devoted his declining
years to a work on the Evidences of Christianity.

EVERY WAR A CIVIL WAR

So little yet does man regard the interests of man. Confined
to his clod of earth, like the insect to its leaf, he does not
perceive that every war on the face of the globe is, in fact,
a civil war ; and a dark sea, in a spiritual sense as truly
as in physical fact, gives, by its concealing cloak, the
appearance of separate enchanting islands to the girdle of
mountains which surrounds the world.

Jean Paul Richter. *Levana, 1806.*

CONSIDER IT, O PRINCE !

How can a young prince ever behold the dark side of
the glittering form of war, that hellish stream which
surrounds the living earth and is peopled with the dead ?

. . . Will you let him hear the chorus of all wise men and poets cursing war, the last ghost and savage army of barbarism ? Will you, before war, preach such a sermon as this on peace to the king who is about to hurl his torch-like missive to kindle the fire of war ? " Consider well : one step beyond your frontiers changes the whole face of two empires ; thine own is consumed behind thee, thine enemy's before thee. That moment an earthquake takes possession of both, and labours to the destruction of both ; all ancient law-courts, all judgment-seats, are overturned ; heights and depths are confounded together. It is a last day, full of rising sinners and falling stars ; it is the tribunal at which the Devil judges the world, where bodies condemn spirits, physical force the power of love. Consider it, O prince ! Every soldier in this empire of lawlessness becomes thy crowned brother in a foreign land, bearing the sword of Justice without her balance, and governing more despotically than thyself. Every meanest drudge in the enemy's ranks is thy king and judge, carrying in his hand an axe and a halter for thee. The arbitrary powers of force and chance only sit upon the double throne of conscience and of knowledge. Two nations are converted, half into slave-dealers, half into slaves, mingled without order among one another. In the eyes of higher beings, the human race has become an assemblage of lawless, conscienceless, stone-blind beasts and machines, which robs, devours, strikes, bleeds, and dies. . . ."

Ibid.

THE FALCON

THERE is a nobler courage, which once, though not long, Sparta, Athens, and Rome possessed—the courage of peace and of freedom, the bravery which showed itself at home. Many a nation, a cowardly slave in its own country, but a bold hero out of it, resembles the falcon (though become tame, unlike it, by sleeping rather than by sleeplessness) which is carried hooded on the wrist of the falconer, until left to its ancient freedom ; a momentary wooer of the air, it boldly and bravely vanquishes some new bird, and then retires with it to the slavish earth. But the truly, because freely, brave people carries on its war of freedom at home, against every hand which would stay its flight or blind its eye ; this, indeed, is the longest and bravest war, and the only one which admits no truce. Just so brave, and in a higher sense, may a monarch be. Let the great ideal of art, to unite dignity with repose, be the ideal of the throne. To extinguish the flames of war is more worthy of a king, as it is more difficult, than to kindle them.

Ibid.

A VISITOR FROM THE NEAREST PLANET

I WONDER what a superior being, living in the nearest planet to our earth, and seeing us of the size of ants, would say if he were enabled to get any insight into the nature of modern wars.

It must certainly strike him, if he were to see a number of such diminutive persons chasing one another in bodies over different parts of the hills and valleys of the earth, and following each other in little nut shells, as it were, upon the ocean, as a very extraordinary sight, and as mysterious and hard to be explained. But when he saw them stop and fight, and destroy one another, and was assured that they were actually engaged in the solemn game of death, and this at such a distance from their own homes, he would wonder at the causes of these movements, and the reason of the destruction ; and, not knowing they possessed rational faculties, he would probably consider them as animals destined by nature to live upon one another.

Thomas Clarkson. *Portraiture of Quakerism, 1806.*

QUESTIONS AND ANSWERS

BUT the superior being would say, "Is it really defined, and is it defined clearly in the great book of the spirit, that if one of them should kill another he is guilty of a crime?" It would be replied,—not only of a crime, but of the greatest of all crimes; and that no dispensation is given to any of them to commit it in any case. And it would be observed, further, that there are other crimes which these fightings generally include, which are equally specified and forbidden in the great book, but which they think it proper to sanction in the present case. . . .

"Strange!" the superior being would reply. "They seem to me to be reversing the order of their nature, and the end of their existence. But how do they justify themselves on these occasions?" It would be answered,—they not only justify themselves, but they even go so far as to call these fightings *honourable*. The greater the treachery, if it succeed, and the greater the number of these beings killed, the more glorious is the action esteemed.

"Still more strange!" the superior being would reply. "And is it possible," he would add, "that they enter into this profession with a belief that they are entering into an honourable employ!" Some of them, it would be replied, consider it as a genteel employ; and hence engage in it. Others, of a lazy disposition, prefer it to any other. Others are decoyed into it by treachery in various ways. There are also strong drinks which they are fond of; and if they are prevailed upon to take these to excess they lose their reason, and they are obliged to submit to it. It must be owned, too, that when these wars begin the trades of many of these little beings are stopped; so that, to get a temporary livelihood, they go out and fight. Nor must it be concealed that many are forced to go, both against their judgment and against their will.

The superior being, hurt at these various accounts, would probably ask, "And what then does the community get by these wars, as a counterbalance for the loss of so much

happiness, and the production of so much evil ? " It would
be replied—NOTHING. The community is generally worse
off at the end of these wars than when it began to contend.
But here the superior being would wish to hear no more of
the system. He would suddenly turn away his face, and
retire into one of the deep valleys of his planet, either with
exclamations against the folly, or with emotions of pity for
the situation, or with expressions of disgust at the wickedness
of these little creatures.

Ibid.

"The conditions that obtain in Mars itself are almost incredibly
ridiculous. The planet is divided into a number of continents, empires
and nations, each of which is ready at a moment's notice to fly at the
throat of its neighbour for reasons that the historians of succeeding
generations try in vain to explain. Some thousands of years ago a great
statesman appeared among them who taught them that war was an evil,
and that the only war worth engaging in was a war to end war. Since
then, it has been a matter of faith with them that every war must be a
war to end war."—Robert Lynd, *The Mad Martian.*

A JUST MEDIUM

IT has lately been the favourite scheme to descant on the
miseries of war, and to magnify the blessings of peace ;
one of the greatest blessings of the latter proceeds from
commerce, but commerce it is said produces luxury, and
luxury corruption. Perhaps it does less harm in England
than in other states ; this may be perhaps owing to the
climate, to our position in the midst of a boisterous ocean ;
perhaps also to our frequent wars, to the habits and
exercises of the people, and also to the form of the government ; all these tend to preserve us from the baneful
influence of luxury ; but commerce increases capital, and
that capital sustains the spirit of enterprise and speculation,
while the frequent wars, in which we are engaged, contribute
their share to the general result. Too long a war may at
length fatigue the people ; too long a peace may weaken
their sentiments, and degrade their principles. A people
which never goes to war, loses its personal energy ; it

becomes selfish and timid ; a warlike state every day produces examples which elevate the individual, and ennoble the sentiments of the heart.

Mankind, accustomed to the dangers of war, cease to make personal safety and convenience the spring of their actions, hence that character of frankness which all warlike nations preserve. Peaceful nations cease to esteem themselves, and form the most unworthy prejudices against foreigners ; they become shut out from the great theatre of politics, and fall a prey to their more enterprising neighbours.

Let us trust that the prudence of our government will be able to strike a just medium, that we shall go to war often enough to prevent degeneracy, and admit such intervals of peace, as to give us leisure to improve our finances and commerce, to repose from our fatigues, and enjoy the fruit of our struggles.

> Gould Francis Leckie. *An Historical Survey, or The Foreign Affairs of Great Britain, 1808.*

DYING FOR ONE'S COUNTRY

BUT if it were commendable for men to die for their country, it ought even then to be confined to those who have a country to die for ; I mean those who possess merchandise or landed property ; for what consummate folly it must be for poor men who have not the breadth of their foot of land in all the world, nor even the value of that, to lose or even risk their lives for any country. If men will fight for this world's goods, it is but reason that they who possess them should fight for them.

But let us, for argument's sake, admit that a man ought to bear arms and fight for his country ; then, of course, the man must abide in his own land, and never cross its boundaries. Now even this principle acted upon would entirely abrogate war. But can an Englishman fight at Seringapatam in Asia, at the Cape of Good Hope in Africa, at Buenos Aires in America, and at Copenhagen in Europe, and yet fight in defence of his country? If so, then the whole world is the Englishman's country and all his countrymen are his enemies.

Rev. George Beaumont. *The Warrior's Looking-Glass,*[1] *1808.*

[1] "*Wherein is shewn from many high authorities the trivial causes, cruel nature, direful effects and anti-Christian spirit and practice of war.*"

FIGHTING FOR WIFE, CHILDREN AND LIBERTY

It is said that the poor man, when a soldier, fights for his wife and children and his liberty. To this I answer, in the first place, that many take up arms who have neither wife nor children, and if they had I think they might render them much more service by working for them than fighting for them : and as to the poor man's liberties, all that he can expect in any nation in Europe which keeps a standing army and is generally in a state of warfare, is hard labour and high taxation, with implicit submission to all the sad variety of privations and burdens. Now this kind of liberty any man may find under the dominion of their serene Majesties, the Dey of Algiers and the Emperor of Morocco !

Ibid.

MINISTERS OF STATE AND MINISTERS OF GOSPEL

Among those whose province it is to attempt the destruction of the destructive practice of war are ministers of state ; these are first in power, and therefore ought to be first in effort. But these are generally gainers by war, they fatten whilst others starve, and grow in wealth and splendour as the nation sinks in indigence and bankruptcy.

The next are ministers of the gospel : these men are by profession Ministers of Peace ; and therefore much, in reason, ought to be expected from them : but some of these are indolent, others selfish, and others again downright vicious. Instead of lifting up their voices in the name of the Lord *against* war, they frequently go forth in their sacerdotals, and, to the disgrace of heaven and earth, consecrate its banners, and in the name of the Prince of Peace bid *God speed* to instruments of destruction, and pray for the *success* of *bloodshed* and *devastation*.

Ibid.

PRESS AND PULPIT

THERE is yet another set of men who, with a few exceptions, ought to rank amongst the vilest of the vile, I mean News-Printers. These men have been accessary to all the blood that has been shed within the last twenty years, to say nothing of former wars ; they have prophesied *lies* for *hire*, and disseminated *deception* for a *reward*. In plain terms, they have sold themselves to be the *tools* of the enemies of all righteousness ; they have rekindled the dying embers of war, when it would have died away ; they have inflamed ambition, fomented pride, and aggravated party rage ; they have made themselves an abomination to all honest men, and have given discerning philanthropists just reason to question whether the Press, with all its boasting, has been a greater curse or blessing to mankind !

I feel no scruple in asserting, as my own opinion, at least, that had all the Pulpits and Presses in Europe been occupied by honest men and delivered nothing but the truth, during the last hundred years, there would have been no wars for at least ninety years back ! And I believe, moreover, that were they even now to make truth their refuge, and abide by principle at the risk of interest, they would soon effect an universal peace. Solomon says, " Life and Death are in the power of the tongue." How much more then are *Peace* and *War* in the power of the Press and the Pulpit, which may be called the two great tongues of the world.

Ibid.

CHEAP AND VULGAR RESOURCES

How easy it is to shed human blood—how easy it is to persuade ourselves that it is our duty to do so—and that the decision has cost us a severe struggle—how much in all ages have wounds and shrieks and tears been the cheap and vulgar resources of the rulers of mankind—how difficult and how noble it is to govern in kindness and to found an empire upon the everlasting basis of justice and affection ! —But what do men call vigour ? To let loose hussars and to bring up artillery, to govern with lighted matches, and to cut, and push, and prime—I call this, not vigour, but the *sloth of cruelty and ignorance*.

The Rev. Sydney Smith.
Peter Plymley Letters, 1808.

BRINGING UP OUR YOUNG ONES

I DARE say it cost you much to part with Charles ; but in the present state of the world, it is better to bring up our young ones to war than to peace. I burn gunpowder every day under the nostrils of my little boy, and talk to him often of fighting, to put him out of conceit of civil sciences, and prepare him for the evil times which are coming.

Idem. To Lady Holland, Sept. 9, 1809.

THE DISPELLER OF ENNUI

MEN delight in war, in spite of the pains and miseries which it entails upon them and their fellows, because it exercises all the talents, and calls out all the energies of their nature—because it holds them out conspicuously as the objects of public sentiment and general sympathy— because it gratifies their pride of art, and gives them a lofty sentiment of their own power, worth, and courage,—but principally because it sets the game of existence upon a higher stake, and dispels, by its powerful interest, those feelings of *ennui* which steal upon every condition from which hazard and anxiety are excluded, and drive us into danger and suffering as a relief. While human nature continues to be distinguished by those attributes, we do not see any chance of war being superseded by the increase of wisdom and morality.[1]

Francis Jeffrey. *Edinburgh Review, Feb., 1813.*

[1] On July 2nd, 1803, he wrote to his brother: "We are all in great horror about the war here. . . . For my part I am often in absolute despair, and wish I were fairly piked, and done with it. . . . I hate the business of war and despise the parade of it."

THIS INFANT ARM

THE child
Ere he can lisp his mother's sacred name
Swells with the unnatural pride of crime, and lifts
His baby-sword even in a hero's mood.
This infant arm becomes the bloodiest scourge
Of devastated earth ; whilst specious names
Learnt in soft childhood's unsuspecting hour
Serve as the sophisms with which manhood dims
Bright reason's ray, and sanctifies the sword
Upraised to shed a brother's innocent blood.

Percy Bysshe Shelley.
Queen Mab, 1813.

"We begin with the child when he is three years old. As soon as he begins to think he gets a little flag put in his hand; then follows the school, the Hitler Youth, the S.A. and military training. We don't let him go; and when adolescence is past, then comes the Arbeitsfront which takes him again and does not let him go till he dies, whether he likes it or not."—Dr. Ley, German Minister for Labour.

GARDENING

OH ! my wish is to be dancing with those I love, or beating them, or anything so as to be living with you, and to pitch my sword where it ought to be—with the devil ! Henry says, if it were so the wish would come to have it back ; but my craving for rest is such that twenty years would hardly serve to satisfy me, and that is probably ten more than I am likely to live—a soldier nowadays is old at forty. I could get on with a duck, a chicken, a turkey, a horse, a pig, a cat, a cow, and a wife, in a very contented way ; why ! gardening has become so interesting to me here, as to force me to give it up lest neglect of business should follow : it is a kind of madness with me. Gardening from morning to night should be my occupation if there was any one to command the regiment, it won't let me think of anything else. So hang the garden, and the sweet red and blue birds that swarm around : and hang Dame Nature for making me love such things, and women's company, more than the sublime pleasure of cutting people's throats, and teaching young men to do so.

Charles Napier.[1] To his mother,
April 20, 1813.

[1] Afterwards Sir Charles, conqueror of Scinde (1843), from which place besides sending the famous despatch, *Peccavi!* he wrote to his brother Richard: "I have had nearly all the Chiefs of Scinde in this room laying their swords at my feet, which would, if taken, make a rich armoury, all having gold scabbards and each worth full £100. Certainly I could have got thirty thousand pounds since coming to Scinde, but my hands do not want washing yet; our dear father's sword which I wore in both battles is unstained, even with blood, for I did not kill any one with my own hand. I rode pistol in hand and might have shot a Belooch, but thought some one else would, and as he did not rush at me let him alone: a 22nd soldier killed him. At Dubba I got them into a better spirit, but at Meeanee, as the soldier said, 'the shambles had it all to themselves.'"

WAR TO END WAR

NONE will regret that the art of robbery (for death in war is only a means of robbing) should utterly cease, for it, more than any other pursuit, destroys sensibility in the best of men, and involves every vice which can debase them to the level of brutes ; nor will any one pretend that it would lead to excessive population, who remembers that there is even in Europe more desert than cultivated land.

Unfortunately this result is rendered less probable by the greater or less strength of the physical boundaries of different states, their less or greater population which modify that strength, the freedom of their governments, the knowledge of the people, and their zeal to defend existing establishments—circumstances all of which must give origin to eternal war.

One circumstance, perhaps, alone could put a period to war, namely, such improvement in the art, that of those who took the field, none could escape destruction.

> Anon. *An address to the British nation for the purpose of still further diffusing the love of military glory, 1814.*

A WINDOW IN BRUSSELS

It is not near the scene of battle that war, even with victory, wears an aspect of felicity,—no, not even in the midst of its highest resplendence of glory. A more terrific or afflicting sojourn than that of Brussels at this period can hardly be imagined. The universal voice declared that so sanguinary a battle as that which we fought almost in its neighbourhood, and quite within its hearing, never yet had spread the plains with slaughter ; and, though exultation cannot ever have been prouder, nor satisfaction more complete, in the brilliancy of success, all my senses were shocked in view of the effects of its attainment. For more than a week from this time I never approached my window but to witness sights of wretchedness. . . . Others of these wretched prisoners had, to me, as I first saw them, the air of the lowest and most disgusting of Jacobins, in dirty, tattered vestments of all sorts and colours, or soiled carters' frocks ; but disgust was soon turned to pity, when I afterwards learnt that these shabby accoutrements had been cast over them by their conquerors after despoiling them of their own.

> Madame D'Arblay (Fanny Burney).
> *June 20, 1815. Diary Letters, 1892.*

A VERY WRONG FEELING

A LETTER that condescends to speak of two housemaids, without talking of battles and Bonaparte, is a very delightful novelty, as I am quite tired of rejoicing and lamenting over this news[1] which, upon the whole, strikes me as very melancholy, though I know that is a very wrong feeling.

> Emily Eden. *To Lady Bucking-*
> *hamshire, June 24, 1815.*

[1] The Battle of Waterloo had been fought on the 18th June.

A SURGEON'S VIEW

Sunday. I was interrupted, and now I perceive I was falling into the mistake of attempting to convey to you the feelings which took possession of me, amidst the miseries of Brussels. After being eight days among the wounded I visited the field of battle. The view of the field, the gallant stories, the charges, the individual instances of enterprise and valour, recalled me to the sense which the world has of victory and Waterloo. But this was transient, a gloomy uncomfortable view of human nature is the inevitable consequence of looking upon the whole as I did—as I was forced to do.

It is a misfortune to have our sentiments so at variance with the universal sentiment. But there must ever be associated with the honours of Waterloo, to my eyes, the most shocking signs of woe ; to my ear, accents of entreaty ; outcry from the manly breast, interrupted forcible expressions of the dying, and *noisome smells*. I must show you my notebooks, for as I took my notes of cases generally by sketching the object of our remarks, it may convey an excuse for this excess of *sentiment*.

> Sir Charles Bell. *To Francis*
> *Horner, July, 1815.*

THE FIELD OF WATERLOO

THE front, upon which the armies engaged, does not exceed a long mile. Our line, indeed, originally extended half a mile farther towards the village of Brain-la-Leude ; but as the French indicated no disposition to attack in that direction, the troops which occupied this space were gradually concentrated by Lord Wellington, and made to advance till they had reached Hougoumont—a sort of chateau, with a garden and wood attached to it, which was powerfully and effectually maintained by the Guards during the action. This place was particularly interesting. It was a quiet-looking gentleman's house, which had been burnt by the French shells. The defenders, burnt out of the house itself, betook themselves to the little garden, where, breaking loop-holes through the brick walls, they kept up a most destructive fire on the assailants. . . . In this spot vast numbers had fallen ; and being hastily buried, the smell is most offensive at this moment. Indeed, I felt the same annoyance in many parts of the field ; and, did I live near the spot, I should be anxious about the diseases which this steaming carnage might occasion.

Sir Walter Scott. *To the Duke of Buccleuch, 1815.*

Sir Walter wrote a poem on Waterloo. Neither good nor popular, it provoked the unfeeling epigram attributed to Erskine:

On Waterloo's ensanguined plain
Full many a gallant man lies slain;
But none, by powder or by shot,
Fell half so flat as Walter Scott.

IN THE NAME OF THE MOST HOLY AND INDIVISIBLE TRINITY

THEIR MAJESTIES the Emperor of Austria, the King of Prussia, and the Emperor of Russia, having, in consequence of the great events which have marked the course of the last three years in Europe, and especially of the blessings which it has pleased Divine Providence to shower down upon those States which place their confidence and their hope on it alone, acquired the intimate conviction of the necessity of settling the steps to be observed by the Powers, in their reciprocal relations, upon the sublime truths which the Holy Religion of our Saviour teaches ; they solemnly declare that the present Act has no other object than to publish, in the face of the whole world, their fixed resolution, both in the administration of their respective States, and in their political relations with every other Government, to take for their sole guide the precepts of that Holy Religion, namely, the precepts of Justice, Christian Charity, and Peace, which, far from being applicable only to private concerns, must have an immediate influence on the councils of Princes, and guide all their steps, as being the only means of consolidating human institutions and remedying their imperfections.

Treaty between Austria, Prussia and
Russia, signed at Paris, Sept. 26, 1815.

ARTICLES OF THE HOLY ALLIANCE

ART. I. Conformably to the words of the Holy Scriptures, which command all men to consider each other as brethren, the Three contracting Monarchs will remain united by the bonds of a true and indissoluble fraternity, and considering each other as fellow countrymen, they will, on all occasions and in all places, lend each other aid and assistance ; and, regarding themselves towards their subjects and armies as fathers of families, they will lead them, in the same spirit of fraternity with which they are animated, to protect Religion, Peace and Justice.

ART. II. In consequence, the sole principle of force, whether between the said Governments or between their Subjects, shall be that of doing each other reciprocal service, and of testifying by unalterable good will the mutual affection with which they ought to be animated, to consider themselves all as members of the same Christian nation ; the three allied Princes looking on themselves as merely delegated by Providence to govern three branches of the one family, namely, Austria, Prussia, and Russia, thus confessing that the Christian world, of which they and their people form a part, has in reality no other sovereign than Him to whom alone power really belongs, because in Him alone are found all the treasures of love, science, and infinite wisdom, that is to say, God, our Divine Saviour, the Word of the Most High, the Word of Life. Their Majesties consequently recommend to their people with the most tender solicitude, as the sole means of enjoying that Peace which arises from a good conscience, and which alone is durable, to strengthen themselves every day more and more in the principles and exercises of the duties which the Divine Saviour has taught to mankind.

ART. III. All the Powers who shall choose solemnly to avow the sacred principles which have dictated the present Act, and shall acknowledge how important it is for the happiness of nations, too long agitated, that these truths shall henceforth exercise over the destinies of mankind all the influence which belongs to them, will be received with equal ardour and affection into this Holy Alliance.

Ibid.

"Castlereagh's judgment upon this rigmarole is well known. 'A piece of sublime mysticism and nonsense.' Metternich was no less contemptuous, though he hoped to make some use of Alexander's plan for solidarity of action. The Sultan of Turkey, who found himself unable to make a solemn profession of Christian principles, might well ask whether behind these lofty sentiments there was any intention of extending the area of Christian sovereignty."—E. L. Woodward, *War and Peace in Europe, 1815-1870.*

THE PRINCE REGENT OF GREAT BRITAIN TO THE SOVEREIGNS OF AUSTRIA, PRUSSIA, AND RUSSIA, RESPECTIVELY

SIR MY BROTHER AND COUSIN,

I have had the honour of receiving your Imperial Majesty's letter, together with the

copy of the Treaty signed by your Majesty and your august
Allies, at Paris, on the 26th of September.

As the forms of the British Constitution, which I am
called upon to administer in the name of and on the behalf
of the King, my father, preclude me from acceding formally
to this Treaty, in the shape in which it has been presented
to me, I adopt this course of conveying to the august
Sovereigns who have signed it, my entire concurrence in the
principles they have laid down, and in the declaration
which they have set forth, of making the Divine Precepts of
the Christian Religion the invariable rule of their conduct,
in all their relations, social and political, and of cementing
the union which ought ever to subsist between all Christian
Nations ; and it will be always my earnest endeavour to
regulate my conduct, in the station in which Divine
Providence has vouchsafed to place me, by these sacred
maxims, and to co-operate with my august Allies in all
measures which may be likely to contribute to the peace
and happiness of mankind.

With the most invariable sentiments of friendship and
affection,

I am,

> Sir, my Brother and Cousin,
> *Your Imperial Majesty's good Brother*
> *George, P.R. Carlton House, Oct. 6,*
> *1815.*

WATERLOO AND THE SOLDIERS

In general I am very averse to bringing forward instances
of misconduct after such a battle as that of Waterloo. Many
a brave man, and I believe even some very great men, have
been found a little terrified by such a battle as that, and
have behaved afterwards extremely well.

> The Duke of Wellington. *To
> Lieut.-General Sir G. Nugent,
> G.C.B., Nov. 11, 1815.*

"I have found," said the Duke, "that raw troops, however inferior
to the old ones in manœuvring, are far superior to them in downright
hard fighting with the enemy: at Waterloo, the young ensigns and

lieutenants, who had never before seen a battle, rushed to meet death as if they had been playing at cricket." — *Recollections of the Table Talk of Samuel Rogers, 1856.*

"Boys in 1917 who expected war to be a horrible business suffered less from shell shock, according to Korzybski, than those suffused with 'glory,' 'patriotism,' and a 'battle for democracy.'" — Stuart Chase, *The Tyranny of Words, 1938.*

WATERLOO AND THE ANGELS

THE Bard—whose soul is meek as dawning day,
Yet trained to judgments righteously severe,
Fervid, yet conversant with holy fear,
As recognising one Almighty sway :
He—whose experienced eye can pierce the array
Of past events ; to whom, in vision clear,
The aspiring heads of future things appear,
Like mountain-tops whose mists have rolled away—
Assoiled from all encumbrance of our time,
He only, if such breathe, in strains devout
Shall comprehend this victory sublime ;
Shall worthily rehearse the hideous rout,
The triumph hail, which from their peaceful clime
Angels might welcome with a choral shout !

> William Wordsworth. *Occasioned by the Battle of Waterloo, Feb., 1816.*

Wordsworth should not be left like this. We may at least remember that he wrote:

> Earth is sick,
> And Heaven weary, of the hollow words
> That States and Kingdoms utter when they talk
> Of truth and justice. — *Excursion, V.*

THE GOD OF PEACE AND LOVE

NOR will the God of peace and love
Such martial service disapprove.
He guides the Pestilence—the cloud
Of locusts travels on his breath ;

The region that in hope was ploughed
His drought consumes, his mildew taints with death ;
He springs the hushed Volcano's mine,
He puts the Earthquake on her still design,
Darkens the sun, hath bade the forest sink,
And, drinking towns and cities, still can drink
Cities and towns—'tis Thou—the work is Thine !—
The fierce Tornado sleeps within Thy courts—
    He hears the word—he flies—
    And navies perish in their ports ;
For Thou art angry with Thine enemies !
    For these, and mourning for our errors,
    And sins, that point their terrors,
We bow our heads before Thee, and we laud
And magnify Thy name, Almighty God !
    But Thy most dreaded instrument,
    In working out a pure intent,
    Is Man—arrayed for mutual slaughter,
    —Yea, Carnage, is thy daughter.

> *Idem. From Ode, 1815. Composed 1816.*

"Most heartily, and with my profoundest sympathy, do I go along with Wordsworth in his grand lyrical proclamation of a truth not less divine than it is mysterious, not less triumphant than it is sorrowful—viz., that amongst God's holiest instruments for the elevation of human nature, is ' mutual slaughter ' amongst men, yes, that ' Carnage is God's Daughter.'"—De Quincey, *Explanatory Notices* to *Miscellanies*, Collective Ed., 1854.

CHORDS OF VICTORY

THOUGH War's high-sounding harp may be
    Most welcome to the hero's ears,
Alas, his chords of victory
    Are wet, all o'er, with human tears.

> Thomas Moore. *Sacred Songs, 1816.*

S.P.P.U.P.

THOSE who have duly appreciated the best interests of mankind have always considered War as one of the greatest scourges to which the human race is liable. . . .

They who are influenced merely by the common feelings of humanity would rejoice if it could be proved to be possible to avoid War ; but it becomes those, in an especial manner, who profess themselves to be the followers of Jesus Christ, the Prince of Peace, to consider whether War in any shape, or upon any account, can be justified upon Christian principles. What is the tendency of the Gospel dispensation ?—To promote peace on earth and good will towards men. What was the farewell legacy of our blessed Saviour to His disciples ?—Peace. What His last command ? —To love one another. What His last prayer ?—For His enemies.

The Society for the Promotion of Permanent and Universal Peace, in announcing themselves to the world, think it their duty to state most distinctly that they are principled against *all War upon any pretence*, and that they have not been led to the work either by political considerations or by party spirit, but by a persuasion that the united efforts of Christians of every denomination in this important cause will greatly tend to promote the happiness of mankind and the extension of the Redeemer's kingdom.

Robert Marsden. (*Chairman of the Committee of the Society for the Promotion of Permanent and Universal Peace.) An Address, 1817.*

IN DREAMS OF POETS OLD

WISDOM ! thy irresistible children rise
To hail thee, and the elements they chain
And their own will to swell the glory of thy train.

O Spirit vast and deep as Night and Heaven !
Mother and soul of all to which is given
The light of life, the loveliness of being,
Lo ! thou dost re-ascend the human heart,
Thy throne of power, almighty as thou wert,
 In dreams of Poets old grown pale by seeing
 The shade of thee :—now, millions start
To feel thy lightnings through them burning :
Nature, or God, or Love, or Pleasure,
Or Sympathy, the sad tears turning
To mutual smiles, a drainless treasure,
Descends amidst us ;—Scorn and Hate,
Revenge and Selfishness, are desolate—
A hundred nations swear that there shall be
Pity and Peace and Love, among the good and free !

      Percy Bysshe Shelley. *The*
      Revolt of Islam, 1817.

ABROAD AS I WAS WALKING

ABROAD as I was walking for my recreation,
 And through the green pastures so carelessly strayed,
I heard a young damsel make sad lamentation,
 Crying " Jemmy is slain in the wars, I'm afraid."

I stood still amazed and round me I gazed ;
 At last in an arbour I saw the fair maid ;
Her cheeks were like roses, in her hand she held posies,
 Crying " Jemmy is slain in the wars, I'm afraid."

The sweet little thrushes sing on the green bushes,
 The warblers all seem to mourn for this maid ;
Her song was concerning young Jemmy, her darling,
 For that he was slain she was sorely afraid.

" Distress on the nation and great tribulation
 This war has brought on us," cried this fair maid ;
" The maidens are wailing, and widows complaining,
 Many thousands are slain in the wars, I'm afraid." . . .

May success attend every friend on the ocean,
   That parents and children may be blest with their own ;
That peace with all nations may soon be concluded,
   And every soldier and sailor may safely return.

Anon. The Vocal Library, 1818.

Most of the popular songs of this period (indeed, of all periods) treat of war in terms of Glory and Gallantry. Dibdin wrote scores of them, but once at least he changed his note:

What art thou, fascinating war,
   Thou trophied, painted pest,
That thus men seek, and yet abhor,
   Pursue, and yet detest?

Are Honour and Remorse the same?
   Does murder laurels bring?
Is Rapine Glory? Carnage Fame?
   Flies Crime on Vict'ry's wing? . . .

Where will Ambition's folly reach?
   Sure Nature ne'er designed
Her noble gifts an art should teach
   To man to thin his kind . . .

UNION OF THE FIVE POWERS

(Great Britain, Austria, France, Prussia, and Russia)

THE object of this Union is as simple as it is great and salutary. It does not tend to any new political combination —to any change in the Relations sanctioned by existing Treaties. Calm and consistent in its proceedings, it has no other object that the maintenance of Peace, and the guarantee of those transactions on which the Peace was founded and consolidated.

The Sovereigns, in forming this august Union, have regarded as its fundamental basis their invariable resolution never to depart, either among themselves, or in their Relations with other States, from the strictest observation of the principles of the Right of Nations ; principles, which, in their application to a state of permanent Peace, can alone effectually guarantee the Independence of each Government, and the stability of the general association. . . .

The repose of the world will be constantly their motive and their end.

It is with these sentiments that the Sovereigns have consummated the work to which they were called. They will not cease to labour for its confirmation and perfection. They solemnly acknowledge that their duties towards God and the people whom they govern make it peremptory on them to give to the world, as far as it is in their power, an example of justice, of concord, and of moderation ; happy in their power of consecrating, from henceforth, all their efforts to protect the arts of peace, to increase the internal prosperity of their States, and to awaken those sentiments of religion and morality, whose influence has been but too much enfeebled by the misfortunes of the times.

Metternich	Hardenberg
Richelieu	Bernstorff
Castlereagh	Nesselrode
Wellington	Capo D'Istria.

Aix-la-Chapelle, Nov. 15, 1818.

VILLAINTON

Oh, Wellington ! (or " Villainton," for Fame
   Sounds the heroic syllables both ways :
France could not even conquer your great name,
   But punn'd it down to this facetious phrase—
Beating or beaten, she will laugh the same),
   You have obtained great pensions and much praise :
Glory like yours should any dare gainsay,
Humanity would rise, and thunder " Nay ! " . . .

Though Britain owes (and pays you too) so much,
   Yet Europe doubtless owes you greatly more :
You have repaired Legitimacy's crutch,
   A prop not quite so certain as before ;
The Spanish and the French, as well as Dutch,
   Have seen, and felt, how strongly you *restore* :
And Waterloo has made the world your debtor
(I wish your bards would sing it rather better).

You are " the best of cut-throats : "—do not start :
   The phrase is Shakespeare's, and not misapplied :—

War's a brain-spattering, windpipe-slitting art,
　Unless her cause by right be sanctified.
If you have acted *once* a generous part,
　The world, not the world's masters, will decide ;
And I shall be delighted to learn who,
Save you and yours, have gain'd by Waterloo.

I am no flatterer—you've supped full of flattery :
　They say you like it too—'tis no great wonder :
He whose whole life has been assault and battery,
　At last may get a little tired of thunder ;
And, swallowing eulogy much more than satire, he
　May like being praised for every lucky blunder ;
Call'd " Saviour of the Nations " not yet saved,
And " Europe's Liberator," still enslaved.

Lord Byron. Don Juan, 1819.

A VERY DIFFICULT QUESTION

I own that as at present advised I do not really think the
Holy Scriptures forbid defensive War, though it cannot be
denied that what really and bona fide is defensive war, and
what is not, may often be a very difficult question. But
blessed be God, we serve a Master who is satisfied with
truth in the inner man, and who will pardon our errors of
judgment and accept the will for the deed. I have not the
time now, however, to enter into a discussion of this
important question. One remark, however, I will make to
you, viz., that even if I were myself of opinion that all Wars
were wrong, I should greatly doubt the propriety of
becoming a member of your Society,[1] because, by having
thus proclaimed myself a condemner of War universally, I
should have put it out of my power to contribute my aid
towards preventing my country engaging in war in any
instance.

William Wilberforce. To John
Clarkson, March 11, 1820. Qt. by
A. T. Milne in Bulletin of Institute
of Historical Research, Feb., 1938.

[1] The Society for the Promotion of Permanent and Universal Peace.

OH, CEASE !

OH, cease ! must hate and death return ?
       Cease ! must men kill and die ?
Cease ! drain not to its dregs the urn
       Of bitter prophecy.
The world is weary of the past,
       Oh, might it die or rest at last !

> Percy Bysshe Shelley. *Hellas, 1822.*

THE CANNIBALS OF EUROPE

To turn to the news of the day, it seems that the cannibals
of Europe are going to eating one another again. A war
between Russia and Turkey is like the battle of the kite
and snake. Whichever destroys the other leaves a destroyer
less for the world. This pugnacious humour of mankind
seems to be the law of his nature, one of the obstacles to too
great multiplication provided in the mechanism of the
universe. The cocks of the hen-yard kill one another.
Bears, bulls, rams, do the same. And the horse, in his
wild state, kills all the young males, until, worn down with
age and war, some vigorous youth kills him, and takes to
himself the harem of the females. I hope we shall prove
how much happier for man the Quaker policy is, and that
the life of the feeder is better than that of the fighter ; and
it is some consolation that the desolation by these maniacs
of one part of the earth is the means of improving it in
other parts.

> Thomas Jefferson. *To John
> Adams, June 1, 1822.*

A SIMPLE PRINCIPLE

WAR must be wholly forbidden, or allowed, without
restriction to defence ; for no definitions of lawful or
unlawful war will be, or can be, attended to. . . . There
is no hope of an eradication of war but by an absolute and
total abandonment of it.

What then is the principle for which we contend—*An unreasoning reliance upon Providence for defence in all those cases in which we should violate His laws by defending ourselves.* The principle can claim a species of merit, which must at least be denied to some systems of morality—that of simplicity, of easiness of apprehension, of adaptation to every understanding, of applicability to every circumstance of life.

Jonathan Dymond. *Observations on the Applicability of the Pacific Principle of the New Testament, 1823.*

PEACE ONLY WAR RETARDED

From all these descriptions of ancient wars, and treaties of peace, no longer applicable or of interest to the present world, or present order of things, historical philosophy can deduce but one, though by no means unimportant, result. It is this—that the internal discord, innate in man and in the human race, may easily and at every moment break out into real and open strife—nay, that peace itself—that immutable object of high political art, when regarded from this point of view, appears to be nothing else than a war retarded or kept under by human dexterity ; for some secret disposition, some diseased political matter, is almost ever at hand to call it into existence.

Frederick von Schlegel. *Philosophy of History, 1828. Tr. James Buchanan Robertson, 2nd ed. 1845.*

WHAT THEY GET

Whene'er contending parties fight,
For private pique, or public right ;
Armies are raised, the fleets are mann'd,
They combat both by sea and land.
When, after many battles past,
Both, tired with blows, make peace at last ;

What is it, after all, they get ?
Why, widows, taxes, wooden legs, and debt !

Francis Moore. *Almanac :*
Monthly Observations for 1829.

BEFORE THE INTRODUCTION OF CHRISTIANITY

WHEN any of the Romans or Saxons, who invaded the
island, fell into the hands of the Britons, before the introduction of Christianity, they were handed over to the
Druids, who sacrificed them, with pious ceremonies, to
their goddess Andraste. These human sacrifices have done
much injury to the Druidical character, amongst us, who
never practise them in the same way. They lacked, it must
be confessed, some of our light . . . to enable them to
perceive that the act of coming, in great multitudes, with
fire and sword, to the remote dwellings of peaceable men,
with the premeditated design of cutting their throats,
ravishing their wives and daughters, killing their children,
and appropriating their worldly goods, belongs, not to the
department of murder and robbery, but to that of legitimate
war, of which all the practitioners are gentlemen, and
entitled to be treated like gentlemen.

Thomas Love Peacock. *The*
Misfortunes of Elphin, 1829.

THE BRITISH ARMY

LET us now consider what the British army is. It is an
exotic in England—unknown to the old constitution of the
country ; required, or supposed to be required, only for the
defence of its foreign possessions ; disliked by the inhabitants, particularly by the higher orders, some of whom
never allow one of their family to serve in it. Even the
common people will make an exertion to find means to
purchase the discharge of a relation who may have enlisted
notwithstanding the advantages of pay, etc., which a soldier
enjoys, compared with a common labourer.

In the moments of the greatest distress in the country, recruits cannot be obtained for the army. Service in the army is an advantage to none. The officers and soldiers of the army are a subject of dislike and suspicion to the inhabitants, while serving with their regiments, and of jealousy afterwards, and they are always ill-treated. . . .

Then the man who enlists into the British army is, in general, the most drunken and probably the worst man of the trade or profession to which he belongs, or of the village or town in which he lives. There is not one in a hundred of them who, when enlisted, ought not to be put in the second or degraded class of any society or body into which they may be introduced ; and they can be brought to be fit for what is to be called the first class, only by discipline, and the precept and example of the old soldiers of the company, who, if not themselves in that same second or degraded class, deserve to be placed there for some action or other twenty times in every week. . . .

I have myself kept whole divisions of the army under arms for days : no crime could then be committed. In the same manner I can have half-hourly or hourly roll calls or parades. I can confine men to barrack-yards ; I can send them out to walk in a town, in squads, in charge of a non-commissioned officer : in short, I may torment them into regularity, but corporal punishment, unlimited, at least to the extent to which it exists at present, must be the foundation of that or any other system established in the British army. . . .

I wish those who consider this subject would read over all the proceedings of Major ——'s case. He was anxious to have his battalion in good order, and no corporal punishment. But he inflicted misery and torture of every other description, and corporal punishment into the bargain ; and the affair ended by the battalion firing their buttons at him when at exercise.

> The Duke of Wellington. *Memorandum on Proposed Plan for altering the Discipline of the Army. April 22, 1829.*

WHO FEARS TO DIE?

Who fears to die? Who fears to die?
Is there any here who fears to die?
He shall find what he fears; and none shall grieve
For the man who fears to die;
But the withering scorn of the many shall cleave
To the man who fears to die.

    Chorus : Shout for England!
          Ho! for England!
          Merry England,
          England for ay!

The hollow at heart shall crouch forlorn,
He shall eat the bread of common scorn;
It shall be steeped in the salt, salt tear,
Shall be steeped in his own salt tear:
Far better, far better he never were born
Than to shame merry England here.

    Chorus : Shout for England! etc.

There standeth our ancient enemy!
Will he dare to battle with the free?
Spur along! spur amain! charge to the fight:
Charge! charge to the fight!
Hold up the Lion of England on high!
Shout for God and our right!

    Chorus : Shout for England! etc.

Alfred, Lord Tennyson.
Poems Chiefly Lyrical, 1830.

WAR-SONGS AND HATRED

" To write military songs, and sit in a room ! That forsooth was my duty ! To have written them in the bivouac,
when the horses at the enemy's outposts are heard neighing
would have been well enough ; however, that was not my
life and not my business, but that of Theodore Körner.
His war-songs suit him perfectly. But to me, who am not
of a war-like nature, and who have no war-like sense,
war-songs would have been a mask fitting my face very
badly. . . . I have only composed love-songs when I have
loved. How could I write songs of hatred without
hating ! . . . Altogether national hatred is something
peculiar. You will find it strongest and most violent when
there is the lowest degree of culture. But there is a degree
where it vanishes altogether, and where a person stands to
a certain extent *above* nations, and feels the weal or woe of a
neighbouring people as if it had happened to his own. This
degree of culture was conformable to my nature, and I had
become strengthened in it long before I had reached my
sixtieth year."

Johann Wolfgang von Goethe.
Conversation with Eckermann, 1830.

THE EXAMPLE OF GENOA

WAR is a game at which all are sure to lose, sooner or
later, play they how they will ; yet every nation has
delighted in war, and none more in their day than the
little republic of Genoa, whose galleys, while she had any,
were always burning and sinking those of the Pisans, the
Venetians, the Greeks, or the Turks ; Christians and
infidels alike to her.

But experience, when dearly bought, is seldom thrown
away altogether. A moment of sober reflection came at
last ; and after a victory, the most splendid and ruinous

K

of any in her annals, she resolved from that day and for
ever to live at peace with all mankind ; having in her
long career acquired nothing but glory and a tax on every
article of life.

> Samuel Rogers. *Italy : Marco
> Griffoni, 1830.*

THE CHERUBS

Two spirits reached this world of ours :
The lightning's locomotive powers
    Were slow in their agility :
In broad daylight they moved incog.,
Enjoying without mist or fog,
    Entire invisibility.

The one, a simple cherub lad,
Much interest in our planet had,
    Its face was so romantic ;
He couldn't persuade himself that man
Was such as heavenly rumours ran,
    A being base and frantic.

The elder spirit, wise and cool,
Brought down the youth as to a school ;
    But strictly on condition,
Whatever they should see or hear,
With mortals not to interfere ;
    'Twas not in their commission.

They reached a sovereign city proud,
Whose emperor prayed to God aloud,
    With all his people kneeling,
And priests performed religious rites :
" Come," said the younger of the sprites,
    " This shows a pious feeling."

Young Spirit :
  " Aren't these a decent godly race ? "
Old Spirit :
  " The dirtiest thieves on Nature's face."
Young Spirit :
  " But hark, what cheers they're giving
    Their emperor !—And is he a thief ? "
Old Spirit :
  " Ay, and a cut-throat too ; in brief,
    The greatest scoundrel living."
Young Spirit :
  " But say, what were they praying for,
    This people and their emperor ? "
Old Spirit :
  " Why, but for God's assistance
    To help their army, late sent out :
    And what that army is about,
        You'll see at no great distance."

On wings outspeeding mail or post,
Our sprites o'ertook the Imperial host,
    In massacres it wallowed :
A noble nation met its hordes,
But broken fell their cause and swords,
    Unfortunate, though hallowed.

They saw a late bombarded town,
Its streets still warm with blood ran down ;
    Still smoked each burning rafter ;
And hideously, 'midst rape and sack,
The murderer's laughter answered back
    His prey's convulsive laughter. . . .

" Fie ! fie ! " the younger heavenly spark
Exclaimed ; " we must have missed our mark,
    And entered hell's own portals :
Earth can't be stained with crimes so black ;
Nay, sure, we've got among the pack
    Of fiends, and not of mortals."

" No," said the elder ; " no such thing :
Fiends are not fools enough to wring
    The necks of one another :
They know their interests too well :
Men fight ; but every devil in hell
    Lives friendly with his brother. . . ."
                    Thomas Campbell. *The Cherubs, 1832.*

THE ENGLISH WARLIKE WITHOUT BEING MILITARY

AND why was all this striving in blood against insur-
mountable difficulties ? Why were men sent thus to
slaughter, when the application of a just science would
have rendered the operation comparatively easy ? Because
the English ministers, so ready to plunge into war, were
quite ignorant of its exigencies ; because the English people
are warlike without being military, and under the pretence
of maintaining a liberty which they do not possess, oppose
in peace all useful martial establishments. Expatiating in
their schools and colleges upon Roman discipline and
Roman valour, they are heedless of Roman institutions ;
they desire, like that ancient republic, to be free at home
and conquerors abroad, but start at perfecting their
military system, as a thing incompatible with a constitution, which they yet suffer to be violated by every
minister who trembles at the exposure of corruption. In
the beginning of each war, England has to seek in blood
for the knowledge necessary to insure success, and like the
fiend's progress towards Eden, her conquering course is
through chaos followed by death !

Sir William Francis Patrick
Napier. *History of Peninsular
War. Vol. IV. 1834.*

THE CONDITION OF THIS WORLD

WAR is the condition of this world. From man to the smallest insect, all are at strife, and the glory of arms, which cannot be obtained without the exercise of honour, fortitude, courage, obedience, modesty and temperance, excites the brave man's patriotism, and is a chastening correction of the rich man's pride.

Ibid.

THE GIRDLE OF BENEFICENCE

As knowledge has, in its progress, gathered families and tribes, once hostile, into the regions of common interest and mutual affection, so it will, in its further triumphs, fling the girdle of beneficence around now-separated nations. As the crimes of violence have diminished under the rebuke of more enlightened opinion—as that opinion, acquiring strength, will not fail to act upon the other departments of improbity, who can doubt that war—the maximiser of every crime, the harvester of every violence, the picture of every horror, the representative of every folly, will at last be overwhelmed and annihilated by the mighty and resistless influence of truth, virtue and felicity.

Jeremy Bentham. *Deontology,*[1] *1834.*

[1] *Deontology: or, The Science of Morality: in which the harmony and coincidence of Duty and Self-Interest, Virtue and Felicity, Prudence and Benevolence, are explained and exemplified. From the MSS. of Jeremy Bentham. Arranged and edited by John Bowring.*

THE FIELD

DEATH for death ! The storm begins ;
Rush the drums in a torrent of dins ;
Crash the muskets, gash the swords ;
Shoes grow red in a thousand fords ;

Now for the flint, and the cartridge bite ;
Darkly gathers the breath of the fight,
Salt to the palate, and stinging to sight ;
Muskets are pointed they scarce know where ;
No matter : Murder is cluttering there.
Reel the hollows : close up ! close up !
Death feeds thick, and his food is his cup.
Down go bodies, snap burst eyes ;
Trod on the ground are tender cries ;
Brains are dashed against plashing ears ;
Hah ! no time has battle for tears ;
Cursing helps better—cursing, that goes
Slipping through friends' blood, athirst for foes.
What have soldiers with tears to do ?—
We, who this mad-house must now go through,
This twenty-fold Bedlam, let loose with knives—
To murder, and stab, and grow liquid with lives—
Gasping, staring, treading red mud,
Till the drunkenness' self makes us steady of blood ?

[Oh ! shrink not thou, reader ! Thy part's in it, too ;
Has not thy praise made the thing they go through
Shocking to read of, but noble to do ?] . . . .

Behold him ! By a ditch he lies
Clutching the wet earth, his eyes
Beginning to be mad. In vain
His tongue still thirsts to lick the rain,
That mocked but now his homeward tears ;
And ever and anon he rears
His legs and knees with all their strength,
    And then as strongly thrusts at length.
Raised or stretched, he cannot bear
The wound that girds him, weltering there :
And " Water " he cries, with a moonward stare.

[" I will not read it ! " with a start,
Burning cries some honest heart ;
" I will not read it ! Why endure
Pangs which horror cannot cure ?

Why—oh why ? and rob the brave,
And the bereaved, of all they crave,
A little hope to gild the grave ? "

Askest thou why, thou honest heart ?
'Tis *because* thou dost ask, and *because* thou dost start.
'Tis because thine own praise and fond outward thought
Have aided the shows which this sorrow has wrought.]

A wound unutterable—O God !
Mingles his being with the sod.

[" I'll read no more." Thou must, thou must :
In thine own pang doth wisdom trust.]

His nails are in earth, his eyes in air,
And " Water ! " he crieth—he may not forbear.
Brave and good was he, yet now he dreams
The moon looks cruel ; and he blasphemes.

[" No more ! no more ! " Nay, this is but one ;
Were the whole tale told, it would not be done
From wonderful setting to rising sun.
But God's good time is at hand—be calm,
Thou reader ! and steep thee in all thy balm
Of tears or patience, of thought or good will,
For the field—the field awaiteth us still.]

J. H. Leigh Hunt. *Captain Sword
and Captain Pen, 1835.*

POSTSCRIPT TO THE FOREGOING POEM

THE object of this poem is to show the horrors of war, the
false ideas of power produced in the minds of its leaders,
and, by inference, the unfitness of those leaders for the
government of the world.

The author intends no more offence to any one than can

be helped : he feels due admiration for that courage and energy, the supposed misdirection of which it deplores ; he heartily acknowledges the probability, that that supposed misdirection has been hitherto no misdirection, but a necessity—but he believes that the time is come when, by encouraging the disposition to question it, its services and its sufferings may be no longer required, and he would fain tear asunder the veil from the sore places of war— would show what has been hitherto kept concealed, or not shown earnestly, and for the purpose—would prove, at all events, that the time has come for putting an end to those phrases in the narratives of warfare, by which a suspicious delicacy is palmed upon the reader, who is told, after everything has been done to excite his admiration of war, that his feelings are " spared " a recital of its miseries— that " a veil " is drawn over them—a " truce " given to descriptions which only " harrow up the soul," etc.

Suppose it be necessary to " harrow up the soul " in order that the soul be no longer harrowed ? Moralists and preachers do not deal after this tender fashion with moral, or even physical consequences, resulting from other evils. Why should they spare these ? Why refuse to look their own effeminacy in the face—their own gaudy and overweening encouragement of what they dare not contemplate in its results ? . . . Does it become us to let others endure what we cannot bear even to think of ?

Ibid.

PROVE IT !

To those who tell us that nations would grow cowardly and effeminate without war, we answer, " Try a reasonable condition of peace, and then prove it. Try a state of things which mankind has never yet attained, because they had no press, and no universal comparison of notes ; and consider, in the meanwhile, whether so cheerful, and intelligent, and just a state, seeing fair play between body and mind, and educated into habits of activity, would be likely to uneducate itself into what was neither respected nor customary. . . .

I firmly believe that war, or the sending thousands of our fellow creatures to cut one another to bits, often for what they have no concern in, nor understand, will one day be reckoned more absurd than if people were to settle an argument over the dinner-table with their knives—a logic indeed which was once fashionable in some places during the " good old times." The world has seen the absurdity of that practice : why should it not come to years of discretion, with respect to violence on a larger scale.

Ibid.

UNOFFICIAL LANGUAGE

WHAT, speaking in quite unofficial language, is the net purport and upshot of war ? To my own knowledge, for example, there dwell and toil, in the British village of Dumdrudge, usually some five hundred souls. From these, by certain " natural enemies " of the French, there are successively selected, during the French war, say thirty able-bodied men : Dumdrudge, at her own expense, has suckled and nursed them : she has, not without difficulty and sorrow, fed them up to manhood, and even trained them to crafts, so that one can weave, another build, another hammer, and the weakest can stand under thirty stone avoirdupois. Nevertheless, amid much weeping and swearing, they are selected ; all dressed in red ; and shipped away, at the public charges, some two thousand miles, or say only to the south of Spain ; and fed there till wanted. And now to that same spot, in the south of Spain, are thirty similar French artisans, from a French Dumdrudge, in like manner wending : till at length, after infinite effort, the two parties come into actual juxta-position ; and Thirty stands fronting Thirty, each with a gun in his hand. Straightway the word " Fire ! " is given : and they blow the souls out of one another ; and in place of sixty brisk useful craftsmen, the world has sixty dead carcases, which it must bury, and anew shed tears for. Had these men any quarrel ? Busy as the Devil is, not the smallest ! They lived far apart enough ; were the entirest strangers ; nay, in so wide a universe, there was even, unconsciously, by commerce, some mutual helpfulness between them. How then ? Simpleton ! Their governors had fallen out ; and, instead of shooting one another, had the cunning to make these poor blockheads shoot.

                     Thomas Carlyle. *Sartor Resartus, 1835.*

AH ! WHEN ?

WAR is it, O grave heads ! that ye
With stern and stately pomp decree ?
Inviting all the gods from far
To join you in the game of war !
Have ye then lived so many years
To find no purer joy than tears ?
And seek ye now the highest good
In strife, in anguish, and in blood ?
Your wisdom may be more than ours,
But you have spent your golden hours,
And have methinks but little right
To make the happier fret and fight.
Ah ! when will come the calmer day
When these dark clouds shall pass away ?
When (should two cities disagree)
The young, the beauteous, and the free,
Rushing with all their force, shall meet
And struggle with embraces sweet,
Till they who may have suffer'd most
Give in, and own the battle lost.

                     Walter Savage Landor.
                     Pericles and Aspasia, 1836.

NOT MATTERS OF HISTORY

THE soldier dies upon the field of battle ; and however great may be the anguish he experiences, it is generally soon over ; but the desolate hearts of his parents, and of his wife and children are filled with sorrow and hopelessness and lamentation for years. But these things are not made matters of history ; in the emblazonment of the achievements of the battle-field they are entirely passed over and forgotten ; it seems to be no part of the business, either of the ephemeral gazette, or of the more serious and permanent page of history, to keep a record of tears shed in private and of hearts that are bleeding and broken in retirement.

Thomas C. Upham. *The Manual of Peace, 1836.*

THE TRUE DOCTRINE

IF it can be proved that *defensive* wars are allowable, it would be altogether useless to pursue the inquiry any further, because under the name and pretext of defensive war, national contests of every description would be carried on. Every belligerent nation, with scarcely a single exception, scornfully rejects the imputation of being the original aggressor, and professes to prosecute its warlike measures for purposes of self-protection. And as long as we admit that defensive wars are allowable on Christian principles, so long we grant, for all practical purposes, everything which the advocates of war wish. The true doctrine is that human life, both in its individual and corporate state, as one and as many, is inviolable ; that it cannot be taken away for any purpose whatever, except by explicit divine permission ; and that war, in every shape and for every purpose, is *wrong*, absolutely *wrong*, wholly *wrong*. Any doctrine short of this will fall altogether powerless and useless upon the broad surface of the world's crimes and miseries ; it will dim the light of no sword ; it will wipe the tear of no widow or orphan. . . .

Ibid.

OBJECTIONS TO THE TEACHING OF LATIN AND GREEK

It is often remarked, and perhaps the remark is not *wholly* destitute of foundation, that the tendency of academical and collegiate education[1] is to infuse into the young mind principles at variance with the humble and benevolent spirit of the Gospel ; in a single word, the tendency is to *heathenise* it. . . . Some estimable men . . . have proposed some essential modifications in the course of instruction. . . . Among other things they would entirely exclude the study of the Latin and Greek languages and literature. And why ? Not because the classic languages, whether we consider their admirable structure or their close and diversified relations to the English language and to literature in general, are unworthy of attention ; but because, being deeply imbued with a violent and warlike spirit, they can hardly fail to impart something of that spirit to the susceptible minds of youth.

Ibid.

[1] "The only Englishmen who have evinced a remarkable genius in modern times, for the art of war—the Duke of Marlborough, Lord Peterborough, General Wolfe, and Lord Clive, were all trained in private schools."—Sydney Smith, *Ed. Review*, 1810.

WHAT A SPECTACLE!

No minister ought to rest, no minister ought to consider himself as having discharged his whole duty, until he has seen the members of his church formed into a peace society on the Gospel principle of *total abstinence*, renouncing for ever, and at all hazards, military enrolments, military musters, the payment of military fines, and all other efforts and contributions of a clearly military nature. What a spectacle would then be presented to the world ! Even impenitent and irreligious men would rejoice in it. Hope would arise in the darkened and depraved mind of the soldier. The eyes of experienced statesmen would be gladly directed to this transcendent beam of millennial light. Mankind would smile in their sorrows, and say, *It is indeed the star of Bethlehem.*

Ibid.

ADVICE TO QUEEN VICTORIA

A SECOND great object [the first was the education of the people] which I hope will be impressed upon the mind of this Royal lady is a rooted horror of war—an earnest and passionate desire to keep her people in a state of profound peace. The greatest curse which can be entailed upon mankind is a state of war. All the atrocious crimes committed in years of peace—all that is spent in peace by the secret corruptions, or by the thoughtless extravagance of nations, are mere trifles compared with the gigantic evils which stalk over the world in a state of war. . . .

I would say to that Royal child, worship God by loving peace. It is not *your* humanity to pity a beggar by giving him food or raiment—*I* can do that; that is the charity of the humble and the unknown. Widen you your heart for the more expanded miseries of mankind ; pity the mothers of the peasantry who see their sons torn away from their families ; pity your poor subjects crowded into hospitals, and calling in their last breath upon their distant country and their young Queen. Pity the stupid, frantic folly of human beings who are always ready to tear each other to pieces, and to deluge the earth with each other's blood—this is your extended humanity, and this the great field of your compassion. Extinguish in your heart the fiendish love of military glory, from which your sex does not necessarily exempt you, and to which the wickedness of flatterers may urge you. Say upon your death-bed,

" I have made few orphans in my reign—I have made few widows—my object has been peace. I have used all the weight of my character, and all the power of my situation, to check the irascible passions of mankind, and to turn them to the arts of honest industry : this has been the Christianity of my throne, and this the gospel of my sceptre ; in this way I have striven to worship my Redeemer and my Judge."

> Sydney Smith. *Sermon at St. Paul's, 1837.*

THE EXTREME PEACE DOCTRINE

SINCE the peace question has been before the public mind, those who affirm its right and expediency have naturally been met with objections more or less weighty. There are cases frequently put by the curious—moral problems, like those problems in arithmetic which in long winter evenings the rustics try the hardness of their heads in ciphering out. And chiefly it is said : Either accept this principle for better, for worse, carry it out to the end, and meet its absurd consequences ; or else, if you pretend to set an arbitrary limit, a " Thus far, no farther," then give up the principle, and take that limit which the common sense of all mankind has set, and which distinguishes offensive war as criminal, defensive war as just. Otherwise, if you go for no war, then be consistent, and give up self-defence in the highway, in your own house. Will you push it thus far ? Will you stick to your principle of non-resistance when your strong-box is broken open, when your wife and babes are insulted and slaughtered in your sight ? If you say yes, you only invite the robber and assassin ; and a few bloody-minded desperadoes would soon butcher the good.

In reply to this charge of absurdity on the extreme peace doctrine, as shown in the supposed consequences, I wish to say that such deductions consider only one half of the fact. They only look at the passive side of the friend of peace, only at his passivity ; they quite omit to consider his activity. But no man, it may be presumed, ever embraced the cause of peace and philanthropy for the sole end and satisfaction of being plundered and slain. A man does not come the length of the spirit of martyrdom without some active purpose, some equal motive, some flaming love. If you have a nation of men who have risen to that height of moral cultivation that they will not declare war or carry arms, for they have not so much madness left in their brains, you have a nation of lovers, of benefactors, of true, great and able men. Let me know more of that nation ; I shall not find them defenceless, with idle hands springing at their sides. I shall find them men of love, honour and truth ; men of immense industry ; men whose influence is felt to the end of the earth ; men whose very look and voice carry the sentence of honour and shame ; and all forces yield to their energy and persuasion. Whenever we see the doctrine of peace embraced by a nation, we may be assured it will not be one that invites injury ; but one, on the contrary, which has a friend in the bottom of the heart of every man, even of the violent and the base ; one against which no weapon can prosper ; one which is looked upon as the asylum of the human race and has the tears and the blessings of mankind.

In the second place, as far as it respects individual action in difficult and extreme cases, I will say, such cases seldom or never occur to the good and just man ; nor are we careful to say, or even to know, what in such crises is to be done. A wise man will never impawn his future being and action, and decide beforehand what he shall do in a given extreme event. Nature and God will instruct him in that hour.

Ralph Waldo Emerson. *War, A Lecture, 1838.   Printed in Æsthetic Papers, 1849.*

NOT THE CAUSE OF COWARDICE

THE cause of peace is not the cause of cowardice. If peace
is sought to be defended or preserved for the safety of the
luxurious and the timid, it is a sham, and the peace will
be base. War is better, and the peace will be broken. If
peace is to be maintained, it must be by brave men, who
have come up to the same height as the hero, namely, the
will to carry their life in their hand, and stake it at any
instant for their principle, but who have gone one step
beyond the hero, and will not seek another man's life ;
men who have, by their intellectual insight or else by
their moral elevation, attained such a perception of their
own intrinsic worth, that they do not think property or
their own body a sufficient good to be saved by such
dereliction of principle as treating a man like a sheep.

Ibid.

From Emerson's Journal, Dec. 12, 1835: "I strongly feel the inhumanity or unmanlike character of war, and should gladly study the
outward signs and exponents of that progress which has brought us to
this feeling." Nov. 25, 1838: "A company of soldiers is an offensive
spectacle." Oct. 30, 1841: "Can one nowadays see a soldier without a
slight feeling — the slightest possible — of the ridiculous ?"

PEACE CELEBRATIONS

AND is it thus ye welcome peace !
　　From mouths of forty-pounding bores ?
Oh cease, exploding cannons, cease !
　　Lest peace, affrighted, shun our shores !

Not so the quiet queen should come ;
　　But like a nurse to still our fears,
With shoes of list, demurely dumb,
　　And wool or cotton in her ears !

She asks for no triumphal arch ;
    No steeples for their ropy tongues ;
Down, drumsticks, down, she needs no march,
    Or blasted trumps from brazen lungs.

She wants no noise of mobbing throats
    To tell that she is drawing nigh :
Why this parade of scarlet coats,
    When war has closed his bloodshot eye ?

Returning to domestic loves,
    When war has ceased with all its ills,
Captains should come like sucking doves,
    With olive branches in their bills.

No need there is of vulgar shout,
    Bells, cannons, trumpets, fife, and drum,
And soldiers marching all about,
    To let us know that peace is come.

Oh mild should be the signs and meek,
    Sweet peace's advent to proclaim !
Silence her noiseless foot should speak,
    And echo should repeat the same.

Lo ! where the soldier walks, alas !
    With scars received on foreign grounds ;
Shall we consume in colour glass
    The oil that should be pour'd in wounds ?

The bleeding gaps of war to close,
    Will whizzing rocket-flight avail ?
Will squibs enliven orphans' woes ?
    Or crackers cheer the widow's tale ?

                    Thomas Hood.   *The Quakers'*
                    Conversazione, Hood's Own, 1839.

WAR CAN BE WILLED AWAY

WAR, by the common consent, and mere will of civilised man, has not only been divested of its most atrocious cruelties, but for multitudes, growing multitudes of individuals, has already been, and is, abolished. Why should it not be abolished for all ? Let it be impressed upon the heart of every one of you—impress it upon the minds of your children, that this total abolition of war upon earth is an improvement in the condition of man entirely dependent on his own will. He cannot repeal or change the laws of physical nature. He cannot redeem himself from the ills that flesh is heir to ; but the ills of war and slavery are all of his own creation. He has but to will, and he effects the cessation of them altogether.

> John Quincey Adams. *Oration
> at Newburyport, July 4, 1839.*

MORAL EVIL

THE chief evil of war ! What is it ? What induces us to place war at the head of human calamities ? In replying to these questions, I shall not direct you to the physical sufferings of war, however great or terrible. . . . What distinguishes war is, not that man is slain, but that he is slain, spoiled, crushed by the cruelty, the injustice, the treachery, the murderous hand of man. The evil is moral evil. War is the concentration of all human crimes. Here is its distinguishing, accursed brand. Under its standard gather violence, malignity, rage, fraud, perfidy, rapacity and lust. If it only slew men it would do little. It turns man into a beast of prey. Here is the evil of war, that man, made to be the brother, becomes the deadly foe of his kind ; that man, whose duty it is to mitigate suffering, makes the infliction of suffering his study and end ; that man, whose office is to avert and heal the wounds which come from Nature's powers, makes researches into Nature's laws, and arms himself with her most awful forces, that he may become the destroyer of his race. Nor is this all. There is also found in war a cold-hearted indifference to human miseries and wrongs, perhaps more shocking than the bad passions it calls forth. To my mind this contempt of human nature is singularly offensive. To hate expresses something like respect. But in war man treats his brother as nothing worth ; sweeps away human multitudes as insects ; tramples them down as grass ; mocks at their rights ; and does not deign a thought to their woes.

William Ellery Channing, D.D.
Lecture, 1838.

THE NOBLE ART

AND ever since historians writ,
    And ever since a bard could sing,
Doth each exalt with all his wit
    The noble art of murdering.

We love to read the glorious page,
    How bold Achilles kill'd his foe :
And Turnus, fell'd by Trojans' rage,
    Went howling to the shades below.

How Godfrey led his red-cross knights,
    How mad Orlando slash'd and slew ;
There's not a single bard that writes
    But doth the glorious theme renew.

And while in fashion picturesque,
    The poet rhymes of blood and blows,
The grave historian, at his desk,
    Describes the same in classic prose.

W. M. Thackeray. *From The Chronicle of the Drum, 1841.*

THE VIRTUES OF WAR

WAR crushes with bloody heel all beneficence, all happiness, all justice, all that is God-like in man. It suspends every commandment of the Decalogue. It sets at naught every principle of the Gospel. It silences all law, human as well as divine, except only that blasphemous code of its own, the *Laws of War*. If, in its dismal annals, there is any cheerful passage, be assured that it is not inspired by a martial fury. Let it not be forgotten—let it ever be borne in mind as you ponder this theme—that the virtues which shed their charm over its horrors are all borrowed of peace ; they are emanations of the spirit of love, which is so strong in the heart of man, that it survives the rudest assaults. The flowers of gentleness, of kindliness, of fidelity, of humanity, which flourish, in unregarded luxuriance, in the rich meadows of peace, receive unwonted admiration when we discern them in war, like violets shedding their perfume on the perilous edges of the precipice, beyond the smiling borders of civilisation. God be praised for all the examples of magnanimous virtue which He has vouchsafed to mankind ! . . . God be praised that Sidney, on the field of battle, gave, with dying hand, the cup of cold water to the dying soldier ! . . . The world constantly affords opportunities for deeds of like greatness. But, remember well that these are not the product of war. They do not spring from enmity, hatred and strife ; but from those benign sentiments, whose natural and ripened fruit, of joy and blessing, can be found only in peace. If at any time they appear in a soldier it is not *because*, but *notwithstanding* he is the hireling of battle. Let me not be told then of the virtues of war.

Charles Sumner. *The True Greatness of Nations, 1845.*

"The virtues with which nature has endowed men are only active in wartime. Whoever has no experience of war has no knowledge of men. Sordid and self-loving in his daily life, man becomes noble and self-sacrificing in wartime, because his only virtues are virtues of the warrior. . . . Poverty, chastity and humility, faith, hope, charity and endurance are the Christian virtues, but how many men can exemplify them in their daily lives? War puts them all within our reach; we are all, without effort, brought within reach of salvation."—René Quinton, *Soldier's Testament*, tr. Douglas Jerrold, 1930.

A HALF-CROWN SUBSCRIPTION

FEW people need to be told that associations exist up and down Christendom, having the ambitious object of abolishing war. Some go so far as to believe that this evil of war, so ancient, so ubiquitous, and apparently so inalienable from man's position upon earth, is already doomed ; that not the private associations only, but the prevailing voices of races the most civilised, is tending to confederation against it ; that sentence of extermination has virtually gone forth ; and that all which remains is gradually to execute the sentence. Conscientiously, I find myself unable to join in these views. Of all romances, this seems to me the most romantic. Consequently, when asked to become a member of any such association, I have always thought it most respectful, because most sincere, to decline. Yet, as it is painful to refuse all marks of sympathy with persons whose motives one honours, I design at my death to bequeath half a crown as the foundation-stone of a fund for extinguishing war ; the said half-crown to be improved in all time coming for the benefit of the aforesaid fund. . . . This half-crown (a fund that will overshadow the earth before it comes to be wanted, under the provisions of my will) is to be improved at any rate of interest whatever—no matter what ; for the vast period of the accumulations will easily compensate any tardiness of advance, long before the time comes for its commencing payment. . . .

Thomas de Quincey. *Miscellanies :
On War. Collective ed., 1845.*

A MAGNIFICENT AND ENNOBLING SCIENCE

IT is interesting to observe the steps by which (were it
only through impulses of self-defence, and with a view to
more effectual destructiveness) war exalted itself from a
horrid trade of butchery into a magnificent and enlightened
science. Starting from no higher impulse or question than
how to cut throats most rapidly, most safely, and on the
largest scale, it has issued even at our own stage of advance
into a science, magnificent, oftentimes ennobling, and
cleansed from all horrors except those which (not being
within man's power utterly to divorce from it) no longer
stand out as reproaches to his humanity.

Ibid.

A TRANSCENDENT ATMOSPHERE

WAR has a deeper and more ineffable relation to hidden
grandeurs in man than has yet been deciphered. To
execute judgments of retribution upon outrages offered
to human rights or to human dignity, to vindicate the
sanctities of the altar and the sanctities of the hearth—
these are functions of human greatness which war has
many times assumed, and many times faithfully discharged. But, behind all these, there towers dimly a
greater. The great phenomenon of war it is, this and this
only, which keeps open in man a spiracle—an organ of
respiration—for breathing in a transcendent atmosphere,
and dealing with an idea that else would perish—viz., the
idea of mixed crusade and martyrdom, doing and suffering,
that finds its realisation in a battle such as that of Waterloo
—viz., a battle fought for interests of the human *race*, felt
even where they are not understood ; so that the tutelary
angel of man, when he traverses such a dreadful field,
when he recalls the distorted features, counts the ghastly
ruins, sums the hidden anguish, and the harvests

" of horror breathing from the silent ground,"

nevertheless, speaking as God's messenger, " blesses it and calls it very good."

Ibid.

"He [De Quincey] was a pretty little creature, full of wire-drawn ingenuities; bankrupt enthusiasms, bankrupt pride; with the finest silver-toned low voice, and most elaborate gently-winding courtesies and ingenuities in conversation: ' What wouldn't one give to have him in a box, and take him out to talk!' (That was *Her* criticism of him; and it was right good)."—Carlyle, *Reminiscences*, 1881.

PLAIN AND FLAT

Ez fer war, I call it murder—
 There you hev it plain an' flat ;
I don't want to go no furder
 Than my Testament fer that ;
God hez sed so plump an' fairly,
 It's ez long ez it is broad,
An' you've gut to git up airly
 Ef you want to take in God.

'Tain't your eppyletts an' feathers
 Make the thing a grain more right ;
'Tain't afollerin' your bell-wethers
 Will excuse ye in His sight ;
Ef you take a sword an' dror it,
 An' go stick a feller thru,
Guv'ment ain't to answer for it,
 God'll send the bill to you.

Wut's the use o' meeting'-goin'
 Every Sabbath, wet or dry,
Ef it's right to go amowin'
 Feller-men like oats an' rye ?

I dunno but wut it's pooty
        Trainin' round in bobtail coats,
But it's curus Christian dooty
        This 'ere cuttin' folks's throats.

James Russell Lowell. – *The
Biglow Papers, 1846.*

Thomas Hughes (author of *Tom Brown's Schooldays* and *The Manliness
of Christ*) wrote in his Introduction to the first English edition of the
Biglow Papers (1859): "Had Mr. Lowell been an Englishman, no one
who knows his writings can believe for a moment that he would have
swelled the cry or strengthened the hands of the vain and mischievous
clique, who amongst us have of late years raised the cry of peace when
there is no peace."

PARENT AND CHILD OF EVIL

Wilberforce : Mr. Pitt has declared that peace is never
to be signed without indemnity for the past, and security
for the future. These are his very words.

Romilly[1] : Not as a politician, but as an arithmetician,
he knew when he uttered those words that they never
could be accomplished. War is alike the parent and the
child of evil. It would surpass your ingenuity, or Mr.
Pitt's, to discover any whatsoever which does not arise
from war, or follow war, or romp and revel in the midst
of war. It begins in pride and malice, it continues in
cruelty and rapine, it terminates in poverty and oppression.
Our bishops, who pray for success in it, are much bolder
men than our soldiers, who engage in it bayonet to bayonet.
For the soldier fights only against man, and under the
command of man : the bishop fights against the command
of God, and against God himself. Every hand lifted up
in prayer for homicide strikes him in the face.

Walter Savage Landor. *Romilly and
Wilberforce : Imaginary Conversations,
1846.*

[1] Romilly himself wrote (June 4, 1790): "I had the mortification, a
few days ago, of finding myself considered as a maintainer of the most
extravagant paradoxes, because I asserted that a war of any kind must
be to England a calamity; but that a victorious war would be the

greatest of all calamities. And this is thought a paradox after the experience of the glories, as they are called ... glories which produced no one solid advantage to this country; which did not add one single moment's happiness to the existence of any human being, but which were purchased by an immense debt, by infinite bloodshed, and, what was worse, which gave us false notions of our honour, and our dignity, and our superiority, of which we cannot be corrected but by the loss of much more treasure and much more blood."

CONTRARY TO HUMAN NATURE

" But it is contrary to human nature," say these gentlemen, " to the passions of men, that there should be no war. You must alter the creature himself first—make him another being."

How do they know ? . . .

Oh ! but we shall grow too commercial, too mechanical, and, above all, too effeminate, for want of occasionally blowing each other to bits ; of shrieking for water, and for termination to our misery, on fields of battle ; and of the fires, massacres, and worse horrors, of cities that are besieged.

Why so ?

J. H. Leigh Hunt. *Preface to 1849 edition of Captain Sword and Captain Pen.*

EXTRAORDINARY DOCTRINE

I deny that thirteen years of duration of peace is an additional argument why we should have an increase of our forces. And here I am very glad to call to my aid the opinion of a statesman who probably will be allowed by our opponents to be an authority in this matter. Towards the close of last session of parliament, Sir R. Inglis, the member for the University of Oxford, uttered this extraordinary doctrine—very extraordinary everywhere but at Oxford—that the longer you remained at peace, the greater the probability was that you would go to war. His idea seems to be that men in time of peace were only being fattened up for a speedy slaughter. Now, hear what Lord Palmerston said in reply to him :

" But I look to the general tendency of men's minds towards peace, and I differ from the hon. member for the University of Oxford, who thinks that the long duration of peace renders war more probable : I think, on the contrary, that the duration of peace renders its continuance more likely, and will make countries more disposed to settle their differences otherwise than by war."

Richard Cobden. *Speech at Manchester, Jan. 10, 1849.*

TO AROUSE THE PUBLIC WILL

WELL does John Quincey Adams say that mankind has but to *will* it, and war shall be abolished. . . . To arouse this powerful *public will*, which, like a giant, yet sleeps, but whose awakened voice nothing can withstand, should be our earnest endeavour. To do this we must never tire in exposing the true character of the war system. To be hated, it needs only to be comprehended ; and it will surely be abolished as soon as it is sincerely hated. See, then, that it is comprehended. Expose its manifold atrocities, in the light of reason, of humanity, of religion. Strip from it all its presumptuous pretences, its specious apologies, its hideous sorceries. Above all, let men no longer deceive themselves by the shallow thought that this system is a necessary incident of imperfect human nature, and thus continue to cast upon God the responsibility for their crimes. Let them see clearly that it is a monster of their own creation, born with their consent, whose vital spark is fed by their breath, and without their breath must necessarily die. Let them see distinctly . . . that war, under the law of nations, is an institution, and the whole war system is an establishment for the administration of international justice, for which the Commonwealth of

Nations is directly responsible, and which this Commonwealth can at any time remove.

Charles Sumner. *The War System
of the Commonwealth of Nations, 1849.*

THE RADICAL EVIL

THERE really resides in the heart of each of us a wild beast
which only waits the opportunity to rage and rave in order
to injure others, and which if they prevent it, would like
to destroy them. Hence arises all the pleasure in fighting
and war ; and it is this which gives the understanding, its
special keeper, always enough to do to overcome and to
hold it in some measure within bounds. One may indeed
call it the radical evil, with which those for whom a word
takes the place of an explanation may be contented.

Arthur Schopenhauer. *Parega
and Paralipomena, 1851. Tr. Ernest
Belfort Bax, 1888.*

ORIGIN OF ALL WAR

HISTORY from one end to the other relates simply of wars,
and the same theme is the subject of all the oldest works
of art, as also of the newest. But the origin of all war is
the desire to thieve ; hence Voltaire justly says, *Dans
toutes les guerres il ne s'agit que de voler.* So soon, namely, as
a people feels an excess of force, it falls upon its neighbour,
in order that, instead of living by its own labour, it may
appropriate the result of theirs, be it merely such as is
already existing, or be it that of the future in addition, to
be acquired by subjugating them. This furnishes the
material for the world's history and its heroic deeds. In
French dictionaries, under the word " *gloire,*" artistic and
literary fame should first be treated of, and then under
" gloire militaire " there should merely stand *voyez butin.*
It would seem in the meantime as though two very

religious peoples, the Hindoos and the Egyptians, when they felt an excess of force, did not for the most part employ it on robber campaigns, or heroic deeds, but on buildings which defy millenniums, and which make their memory honourable.

Ibid.

IN A SHORT SENTENCE

WHAT is war? I believe that half the people that talk about war have not the slightest idea of what it is. In a short sentence it may be summed up to be the combination and concentration of all the horrors, atrocities, crimes and sufferings of which human nature on this globe is capable. . . . Well, if you go into war now you will have more banners to decorate your cathedrals and churches. Englishmen will fight now as well as ever they did, and there is ample power to back them, if the country can be sufficiently excited and deluded. You may raise up great generals. You may have another Wellington and another Nelson, too ; for this country can grow men capable for every enterprise. Then there may be titles, and pensions, and marble monuments to eternise the men who have thus become great ; but what becomes of you and your country, and your children ?

John Bright. *Speech at Conference of the Peace Society, Edinburgh, Oct. 13, 1853.*

PEACE MORE NECESSARY TO FOREIGNERS

I BELIEVE there is no country in the world that benefits more by peace than England, though, materially speaking, peace is more necessary to every other country in Europe than to England.

Benjamin Disraeli, Earl of Beaconsfield. *In the House of Commons, July 21, 1854.*

NO GOOD IN WAR

You told me to tell you if I thought there was any good in war ; but I certainly cannot tell you any, I think it is a dreadful thing and it only causes great sorrows to many families.

> Kate Stanley[1] (aged 10). *To her mother.*
> *Nov., 1854. The Amberley Papers, 1937.*

[1] Afterwards Lady Amberley, mother of Bertrand Russell.

DECLINE OF A BARBAROUS PURSUIT

THE second greatest evil known to mankind—the one by which, with the exception of religious persecution, most suffering has been caused—is, unquestionably, the practice of war. That this barbarous pursuit is, in the progress of society, steadily declining, must be evident, even to the most hasty reader of European history. . . . The question arises, as to what share our moral feelings have had in bringing about this great improvement. And if this question is answered, not according to preconceived opinions, but according to the evidence we possess, the answer will certainly be that those feelings have had no share at all. For it will surely not be pretended that the moderns have made any discoveries respecting the moral evils of war. On this head nothing is now known that has not been known for many centuries. That defensive wars are just, and that offensive wars are unjust, are the only two principles which, on this subject, moralists are able to teach. These two principles were as clearly laid down, as well understood, and as universally admitted, in the Middle Ages, when there was never a week without war, as they are at the present moment, when war is deemed a rare and singular occurrence.

> Henry Thomas Buckle. *History
> of Civilization in England, 1855.*

CONCLUSION DRAWN FROM THE CRIMEAN WAR

We may draw at least this conclusion from the war which has broken out. I think what has occurred has shown that the arts of peace, practised by a free people, are not enervating. I think that the deeds which have been referred to, both of the commanders and the common soldiers, have shown that education has not a tendency to diminish, but to refine and raise the standard of the martial character. In these we may proudly recognise the might and prowess of a free and ancient people. These are all circumstances and conditions which are favourable to our confidence in the progress of civilisation and flattering to the consciousness of every Englishman.

> Benjamin Disraeli, Earl of Beaconsfield. *In the House of Commons, Dec. 15, 1855.*

RUSKIN REJOICES

I believe the war is at present productive of good more than of evil. I will not argue this hardly and coldly, as I might, by tracing in past history some of the abundant evidence that nations have always reached their highest virtue, and wrought their most accomplished works, in time of straitening and battle ; as, on the other hand, no nation ever yet enjoyed a protracted and triumphant peace without receiving in its own bosom ineradicable seeds of future decline. I will not so argue this matter ; but I will appeal at once to the testimony of those whom the war has cost the dearest. I know what would be told me, by those who have suffered nothing ; whose domestic happiness has been unbroken ; whose daily comfort undisturbed ; whose experience of calamity consists, at its utmost, in the incertitude of a speculation, the dearness of a luxury, or the increase of demands upon their fortune which they could meet fourfold without inconvenience.

From these, I can well believe, be they prudent economists, or careless pleasure-seekers, the cry for peace will rise alike vociferously, whether in street or senate. But I ask *their* witness, to whom the war has changed the aspect of the earth, and imagery of heaven, whose hope it has cut off like a spider's web, whose treasure it has placed, in a moment, under the seals of clay. Those who can never more see sunrise, nor watch the climbing light gild the eastern clouds, without thinking what graves it has gilded, first, far down behind the dark earth-line—who never more shall see the crocus bloom in spring, without thinking what dust it is that feeds the wild flowers of Balaclava. Ask *their* witness, and see if they will not reply that it is well with them and with theirs ; that they would have it no otherwise ; and would not, if they might, receive back their gifts of love and life, nor take again the purple of their blood out of the cross on the breastplate of England. Ask them : and though they should answer only with a sob, listen if it does not gather upon their lips into the sound of the old Seyton war-cry—"Set on."

John Ruskin. *Modern Painters,*
Pt. IV., *1856.*

"Warfare, bloodshed, slaughter, harshness, cruelty, were no longer objects of deprecation and repugnance, but were regarded as necessities for the ends to be achieved, and as acceptable and desirable. They were clothed with a certain poetic attraction, and even afforded a certain thrill like that of a religious mystery, so that one spoke of the beauty that lies in war and bloodshed, and of the heroic intoxication that in this way alone man can extol and enjoy."—Benedetto Croce. *History of Europe in the Nineteenth Century.* Tr. Henry Furst, 1931.

FAIR PEACE

PEACE, who tarriest too long ;
Peace, with delight in thy train :
Come, come back to our prayer !
Then shall the revel again
Visit our streets, and the sound
Of the harp be heard with the pipe,

When the flashing torches appear
In the marriage-train coming on,
With dancing maidens and boys :
While the matrons come to the doors,
And the old men rise from their bench,
When the youths bring home the bride.

Not decried by my voice
He who restores thee shall be,
Not unfavour'd by Heaven.
Surely no sinner the man,
Dread though his act, to whose hand
Such a boon to bring hath been given.
Let her come, Fair Peace ! let her come !
But the demons long nourish'd here,
Murder, Discord, and Hate,
In the stormy desolate waves
Of the Thracian Sea let her leave,
Or the howling outermost Main.

Matthew Arnold. *Merope, 1858.*

WAR SONG BY TENNYSON

THERE is a sound of thunder afar,
Storm in the south that darkens the day,
Storm of battle and thunder of war,
Well, if it do not roll our way.
Storm ! storm ! Riflemen form !
Ready, be ready to meet the storm !
Riflemen, riflemen, riflemen, form ! . . .

Let your reforms for a moment go,
Look to your butts and take good aims.
Better a rotten borough or so,
Than a rotten fleet or a city in flames !
Form ! form ! Riflemen form !
Ready, be ready to meet the storm !
Riflemen, riflemen, riflemen form !

Form, be ready to do or die !
    Form in Freedom's name and the Queen's !
True, that we have a faithful ally,
    But only the Devil knows what he means.
        Form ! form ! Riflemen form !
        Ready, be ready to meet the storm !
        Riflemen, riflemen, riflemen form !

> Alfred, Lord Tennyson. *First published in The Times, May 9, 1859.*

It would be unfair to leave the impression that Tennyson was an early Kipling. As once every schoolboy knew, he had a Vision (in *Locksley Hall*) of a future in which

> . . . the war-drum throbb'd no longer, and the battle-flags were furl'd
> In the Parliament of Man, the Federation of the World.

And earlier (in *The Golden Year*) there is:

>   Ah! when shall all men's good
> Be each man's rule, and universal Peace
> Lie like a shaft of light across the land. . . .

DRAMATIC SPECTACLES

IT is doubtful whether our soldiers would be maintained if there were not pacific people at home who like to fancy themselves soldiers. War, like other dramatic spectacles, might possibly cease for want of a " public."

> George Eliot. *The Mill on the Floss, 1860.*

WITHOUT NATIONAL FEELING

IN the old European system the rights of nationalities were neither recognised by governments nor asserted by the people. The interest of the reigning families, not those of the nations, regulated the frontiers. . . . In time of war, as there was no national cause at stake, there was no attempt to rouse national feeling. The courtesy of the rulers towards each other was proportionate to their contempt for the

L

lower orders. Compliments passed between the commanders of hostile armies ; there was no bitterness, and no excitement ; battles were fought with the pomp and pride of a parade.[1] The art of war became a slow and learned game.

> John Emerich Edward Dalberg-Acton,
> First Baron Acton. *Nationality : Home and Foreign Review, 1862.*

[1] "Instead of a small number of well-trained professionals championing their country's cause with ancient weapons and a beautiful intricacy of archaic manœuvre, sustained at every moment by the applause of their nation, we now have entire populations, including even women and children, pitted against one another in brutish mutual extermination, and only a set of blear-eyed clerks left to add up the butcher's bill."— Winston Churchill, *My Early Life.*

WEAK AND FRUITLESS

I HAVE been shown in the files of the War Department a statement of the Adjutant-General of Massachusetts that you are the mother of five sons who have died gloriously on the field of battle. I feel how weak and fruitless must be any words of mine which should attempt to beguile you from the grief of a loss so overwhelming. But I cannot refrain from tendering to you the consolation that may be found in the thanks of the Republic they died to save. I pray that our heavenly Father may assuage the anguish of your bereavement, and leave you only the cherished memory of the loved and lost, and the solemn pride that must be yours to have laid so costly a sacrifice on the altar of freedom.

> Abraham Lincoln. *To Mrs. Bixley of Boston, Nov. 21, 1864.*

CHRISTIANITY NOT PHILANTHROPY

CHRIST, therefore, is not merely the originator of philanthropy ; and indeed the Church has sustained another part on earth besides that of the Sister of Charity. She has not merely sat by sick-beds, and played the Lady Bountiful to poor people, and rushed between meeting armies on the field of battle to reconcile the combatants by reminding them of their brotherhood. Christianity is not quite the mild and gentle system it is sometimes represented to be. Christ was meek and lowly, but He was something beside. What was He when He faced the leading men among His countrymen and denounced them as a brood of vipers on their way to the infernal fires ? That speech which has been quoted above, " I am not come to send peace but a sword," will appear, when considered, to be the most tremendous speech ever uttered. Burke's wish that the war with France which he foresaw might prove a *long* war has been stigmatised as horrible. It was certainly an awful wish ; it may well cause those who look only to physical and immediate happiness to shudder ; but from Burke's premises it was justifiable. Christ's solemn resolution to persevere in what He felt to be His mission, in spite of the clearest foreknowledge of the suffering and endless bloodshed which His perseverance would cause to that race of which He was the martyr, was grounded on a similar confidence that the evil was preparatory to a greater good, and that if some happiness was to be sacrificed, it would be the price of a great moral advance. But the resolution was notwithstanding a most awful one, and should impressively teach us not to confound Christianity with mere philanthropy, not to suppose that what is shocking is of necessity unchristian, not to confound warmheartedness, bonhomie, or feminine sensibilities with the Enthusiasm of Humanity.

Sir John Seeley. *Ecce Homo, 1866.*

GOD WINKS

WE may surely wink at a few things for the sake of the public interest, if God Almighty does ; and if He didn't, I don't know what would have become of the country—

Government would never have been carried on, and many a good battle would have been lost. That's the philosophy of the matter, and the common sense too.

> George Eliot. *Sir Maximus Debarry* in *Felix Holt, 1866.*

YOUR PALLID ARMY FOLLOWS

Pass, pass, ye proud brigades, with your tramping sinewy legs,
With your shoulders young and strong, with your knapsacks and your muskets ;
How elate I stood and watch'd you, where starting off you march'd.

Pass—then rattle drums again,
For an army heaves in sight, O another gathering army,
Swarming, trailing on the rear, O you dread accruing army,
O you regiments so piteous, with your mortal diarrhœa, with your fever,
O my land's maim'd darlings, with the plenteous bloody bandage and the crutch,
Lo, your pallid army follows.

> Walt Whitman. *The Return of the Heroes, 1867.*

THE VERY IRONY OF FATE

That which invests war, in spite of all the evils that attend it, with a certain moral grandeur is the heroic self-sacrifice it elicits. With perhaps the single exception of the Church, it is the sphere in which mercenary motives have least sway, in which performance is least weighed and measured by strict obligation, in which a disinterested enthusiasm has most scope. A battle-field is the scene of deeds of self-sacrifice so transcendent, and at the same time so dramatic, that, in spite of all its horrors and crimes, it awakens the most passionate moral enthusiasm. But this feeling, produced by the thought of so many who have sacrificed their life-blood for their flag or for their chief, needs some definite object on which to rest. The multitude of nameless combatants do not strike the imagination. They do not stand out, and are not realised, as distinct and living figures conspicuous to the view. Hence it is that the chief, as the most prominent, becomes the representative warrior ; the martyr's aureole descends upon his brow, and thus, by a confusion that seems the very irony of fate, the enthusiasm evoked by the self-sacrifice of thousands sheds a sacred glow around the very man whose prodigious egotism had rendered this sacrifice necessary.

W. E. H. Lecky. *History of European Morals, 1869.*

THE SCHOOL OF HEROIC VIRTUES

Now war, which brings with it so many demoralising influences, has, at least, always been the great school of heroism. It teaches men how to die.[1] It familiarises the mind with the idea of noble actions performed under the influence not of personal interest, but of honour and of enthusiasm. It elicits in the highest degree strength of character, accustoms men to the abnegation needed for simultaneous action, compels them to repress their fears and establish a firm control over their affections. Patriotism, too, leads them to subordinate their personal wishes to the interests of the society in which they live. It extends the horizon of life, teaching men to dwell among the great men of the past, to derive their moral strength from the study of heroic lives, to look forward continually, through the vistas of a distant future, to the welfare of an organisation which will continue when they have passed away.

Ibid.

[1] It also teaches them how to kill. "It is more than habit which makes us hold that there is a moral difference between killing a man in battle and killing the same man from motives of greed and revenge. This belief

finds strong moral support in the good effects which war has on moral character. Some men it brutalises and hardens, but the Christian soldier is a familiar and genuine type. It is good for most of us to be brought face to face with hardship and the peril of death; and the discipline of war sometimes produces, not only the admirable virtue of courage, but qualities still more precious—obedience, loyalty, self-sacrifice and even tenderness—in a greater degree than the routine of Peace."—The Rev. James H. F. Peile, M.A., Bampton Lectures, 1907.

A MELANCHOLY CONCLUSION

It had been boldly predicted by some of the early Christians that the conversion of the world would lead to the establishment of perpetual peace. In looking back, with our present experience, we are driven to the melancholy conclusion that, instead of diminishing the number of wars, ecclesiastical influence has actually and very seriously increased it. We may look in vain for any period since Constantine in which the clergy, as a body, exerted themselves to repress the military spirit, or to prevent or abridge a particular war, with an energy at all comparable to that which they displayed in stimulating the fanaticism of the Crusaders, in producing the atrocious massacre of the Albigenses, in embittering the religious contests that followed the Reformation. . . .

The peace principles, that were so common before Constantine, have found scarcely any echo except from Erasmus, the Anabaptists, and the Quakers ; and although some very important pacific agencies have arisen out of the industrial progress of modern times, these have been, for the most part, wholly unconnected with, and have in some cases been directly opposed to, theological interests.

Ibid.

INCONSISTENCY

I am often accused of inconsistency ; but believe myself defensible against the charge with respect to what I have said on nearly every subject except that of war. It is impossible for me to write consistently of war, for the groups of fact I have gathered about it lead me to two precisely opposite conclusions.

When I find this the case, in other matters, I am silent, till I can choose my conclusion : but, with respect to war, I am forced to speak, by the necessities of the time ; and forced to act, one way or another. The conviction on which I act is, that it causes an incalculable amount of avoidable human suffering, and that it ought to cease among Christian nations ; and if therefore any of my boy-friends desire to be soldiers, I try my utmost to bring them into what I conceive to be a better mind. But, on the other hand, I know certainly that the most beautiful characters yet developed among men have been formed in war ;—that all great nations have been warrior nations, and that the only kinds of peace which we are likely to get in the present age are ruinous alike to the intellect, and the heart.

John Ruskin.   *The Crown of Wild Olive*, *1870*.

TOWARDS PERMANENT PEACE

THE war[1] just commenced so recklessly will, perhaps, make a large contribution towards permanent peace by showing that in these latter days it can only be prosecuted under conditions too horrible, both in their certainty and in their severity, for men to accept. This is the only solace we can discover in it—namely, a possibility that war may die by its own hands.

The Illustrated London News.
July 23, 1870.

[1] The Franco-Prussian War in which England was neutral. "We sit by," wrote Sir Robert Morier, with the vivacity which prevented his rise in a service in which opinions may neither be strongly expressed nor strongly held, "we sit by like a bloated Quaker, too holy to fight, but rubbing our hands at the roaring trade we are doing in cartridges and ammunition."—W. H. Dawson, *The German Empire*, 1917.

OUR MISTAKE

MAKE your theories now ! Cry up progress, the enlighten-
ment and good sense of the masses, and the peacefulness
of the French people ! I can assure you that here one
would be strangled if he were so ill-advised as to preach
peace. Whatever happens, we have had a set-back for a
long time. . . .

Ah, we intellectuals ! Humanity is far from our ideal !
Our great mistake, our fatal mistake, is to believe it our
equal and to treat it accordingly.

Gustave Flaubert. *To George
Sand. Aug. 3, 1870.*

ENGLAND AND GERMANY

THE times in which we live are critical times, and he who
embitters the feelings of one nation against another incurs
fearful responsibilities. The temper of the English people
—I mean the true aristocracy of the English people—has
hitherto been most dignified ; their action worthy of a
great and sorrowing nation. England is neutral ; and
what else could she have been . . .

There need be no formal alliance between England and
Germany. The two nations are one in all that is essential,
in morality, in religion, in love of freedom, in respect for
law. They are both hard workers, hard thinkers, and,
when it must be, hard hitters too. In the whole history of
modern Europe Germany and England have never been
at war ; I feel convinced they never will be, they never
can be. We have both our weak and our strong points, and
we know it ; but it is neither English nor German to
thank God[1] that " we are not like other people."

Max Müller. *Letter in The Times,
Aug. 29, 1870.*

[1] "It was in this war that a peculiarly repulsive habit of the Prussian
showed itself, as far as I am aware, for the first time; I mean the habit
of ascribing all their victories to the direct favour of Almighty God.

. . . *Punch* was not far wrong when it parodied old King William's telegraphic messages to his wife during the 1870 campaign in the following words:

> ' By grace divine, my dear Augusta,
> We've had another awful buster;
> Ten thousand Frenchmen sent below,
> Praise God from whom all blessings flow.' "

—C. F. R. Fletcher, *The Germans, Their Empire, and How They Have Made It*, 1914.

THE HOPEFULLEST FACT

BISMARCK,[1] as I read him, is not a person of " Napoleonic " ideas, but of ideas quite superior to Napoleonic ; shows no invincible " lust of territory," nor is tormented with " vulgar ambition," etc. ; but has aims very far beyond that sphere ; and, in fact, seems to me to be striving with strong faculty, by patient, grand, and successful steps, towards an object beneficial to Germans and to all other men. That noble, patient, deep, pious, and solid Germany should be at length welded into a nation and become Queen of the Continent, instead of vapouring, vainglorious, gesticulating, quarrelsome, restless, and over-sensitive France, seems to me the hopefullest public fact that has occurred in my time.

Thomas Carlyle. *Letter to The Times, Nov. 11, 1870.*

[1] "Bismarck, whose persona of hardness made him appear a man of iron to the outside world, was referred to by his wife, who had experienced the part of the personality behind the persona, as ' a poor sick duck.'"—Robert H. Thouless, *General and Social Psychology*.

ALMOST AMUSING

THIS day I thought that from the point of view of the history of humanity, it is very interesting and almost amusing for a sceptic with regard to progress to note in this year, 1871, that brute force, in spite of years of civilisation, in spite of sermons on the brotherhood of nations, and even in spite of treaties for the foundation of an European balance of power, brute force, I say, can assert itself and *prevail*, as in the times of Attila, without more hindrances.

> Edmond de Goncourt. *Journal,*
> *Jan. 1, 1871.*

CONTEMPLATING WAR FORENSICALLY

CHRISTIANITY does not admit, indeed, but utterly denounces and condemns the motives which lead to war,—selfish ambition, rapacity, tyranny, and vanity ; but the condemnation of one side is the justification of the other ; these very motives give the right of resistance to one side. And, inasmuch as the Church has no authority to decide which is the right side,—is no judge of national questions or of national motives, not having been made by her Divine Founder a " judge or a divider " in this sphere, the Church cannot, in her ignorance, exclude the other side either. The Church therefore stands neutral, and takes in both sides ; that is to say, both sides fight within the bond of Christian unity. She only contemplates war forensically, as a mode of settling national questions, which is justified by the want of any other mode.

> J. B. Mozley, D.D. *Sermon preached*
> *before the University of Oxford, Sunday*
> *morning, March 12, 1871.*

A MIRACULOUS OUTBREAK

THERE is a mediatorial function which pervades the whole dispensation of God's natural providence, by which men have to suffer for each other, and one member of the human body has to bear the burden and participate in the grief of another. And it is this serious and sacred function which consecrates war. Without it, indeed, what would war be but carnage ; with it, war displays, in spite of its terrible features, a solemn morality. The devotion of the individual to the community stands before us in a form which, while it overwhelms and appals, strikes us with admiration. That the nation may rise the individual sinks into the abyss ; he vanishes as a drop that waters the earth, yet he does not murmur ; it is his function, it is his appointment, it is an end to which he is ordained ; the member is bound to the body, the unit exists for the good of the whole. In a battle itself, a mass moves, advances, wins, and occupies without one look to its gaps ; a remorseless identity carries it through it all ; the whole is the same, while the parts disappear at every step ; and the great unit moves on without a pause to its goal. . . .

War is thus elevated by sacrifice ; by the mixed effect of glory and grief. There is in it that action just before death which so interests the human mind. All that a man does upon this extreme boundary of vision appeals to us ; what he said, or did, how he looked, his expressions and signs upon the verge of that moment awaken our curiosity ; it seems as if he were *in* another world, when he was so *near* one. So in war there is just that conflict of splendid action upon the very edge of life, which rouses curiosity and emotion ; the figures move upon the extreme horizon, in another instant they are below it ; yet the flame of energy mounts the highest upon the moment of the eclipse. There is a miraculous outbreak of power and will, which gathers all into a point : then all is over, and the man is gone.

Idem.

TRY PEACE

" Put up the sword ! " The voice of Christ once more
Speaks, in the pauses of the cannon's roar,
O'er fields of corn by fiery sickles reaped
And left dry ashes ; over trenches heaped
With nameless dead ; o'er cities starving slow
Under a rain of fire ; through wards of woe
Down which a groaning diapason runs
From tortured brothers, husbands, sons

Of desolated women in their far-off homes,
Waiting to hear the step that never comes !
O men and brothers ! let that voice be heard.
War fails, try peace ! Put up the useless sword.

John Greenleaf Whittier.
Disarmament, 1871.

THE TOUCH OF THE WHIP

IF the stupidity, negligence, laziness and improvidence of
States did not lead them into war, it is difficult to say to
what degree of abasement the human race might descend.
Thus war is one of the conditions of progress, the touch of
the whip which prevents a country from falling asleep by
forcing self-satisfied mediocrity out of its apathy. Man is
kept going only by effort and strife. . . . The day when
humanity became a great peaceful Roman Empire with
no more enemies outside itself would be the day in which
morality and intelligence would incur the greatest dangers.

Ernest Renan.[1] *La Réforme
Intellectuelle et Morale, 1871.
Extract tr. Enid McLeod, 1938.*

[1] "Ce soir, chez Brébant, on se met à la fenêtre, attirés par les acclamations de la foule sur le passage d'un régiment qui part. Renan s'en retire
vite, avec un mouvement de mépris, et cette parole: ' Dans tout cela, il
n'y a pas un homme capable d'un acte de vertu! '
"Comment, d'un acte de vertu? lui crie-t-on, ce n'est pas un acte de
vertu, l'acte de dévouement qui fait donner leur vie à ces privés de gloire,
à ces innommés, à ces anonymes de la mort!"—Edmond de Goncourt,
Journal, Aug. 23, 1870.

WAR NO LONGER POSSIBLE

WAR belongs essentially to the *ancien régime*. It presupposes
a great absence of self-interest since, after the victory, those
who are chiefly responsible for it—I mean the dead—do
not enjoy it. It is the opposite of that lack of self-sacrifice,
that greediness in claiming individual rights, which is the
spirit of our modern democracy. With such a spirit as this,
war is not possible.

Ibid.

THE HABIT OF PEACE

THE habit of peace would grow upon men, as does, unhappily, the habit of war. If an entire generation could grow up without having ever seen war, it would in all probability be thought of with such an intense aversion, that nations would recoil in horror from sending forth their sons, either to massacre, devastate, and plunder others, or to be themselves killed upon the field of battle or sent back mangled and shattered to their homes. Peace would have become habitual, and rulers or public men who tried to break it would be looked upon, not only abroad, but in their native countries, with the detestation they deserve. Armies and navies will then become useless burdens. The scientific skill which now employs itself in the multiplication and refinement of engines for the rapid destruction of human beings will turn to worthier pursuits. We shall dwell, not only in actual tranquillity, but—what is second only in importance—in security, confidence, and mutual friendship.

Lord Amberley. *Can War be Avoided.*
Fortnightly Review, May, 1871.

In this essay "he suggested, in some detail, a League of Nations closely analogous to that which now exists, or rather to that which President Wilson hoped to create."— *The Amberley Papers*, ed. Bertrand and Patricia Russell, 1937.

SOME CUNNING PHRASE

IT is a painful and terrible thing to think how easy it is to stir up a nation to war. Take up any decent history of this country from the time of William III. until now—for two centuries, or nearly so—and you will find that wars are always supported by a class of arguments which, after the war is over, the people find were arguments they should not have listened to. It is just so now, for unfortunately there still remains the disposition to be excited on these questions. Some poet, I forget which it is, has said :

" Religion, freedom, vengeance, what you will,
    A word's enough to raise mankind to kill ;
    Some cunning phrase by faction caught and spread
    That guilt may reign, and wolves and worms be fed."

" Some cunning phrase by faction caught and spread "
like the cunning phrase of " The balance of power," which
has been described as the ghastly phantom which the
Government of this country has been pursuing for two
centuries and has never overtaken. " Some cunning
phrase " like that we have now of " British interests."
Lord Derby has said the wisest thing that has been uttered
by any member of this Administration during the discussions on this war when he said that the greatest of
British interests is peace.

> John Bright. *Speech at Birming-
> ham, Jan. 13, 1878.*

The poet whom Bright "forgot" was Byron. The third line should
read: "Some factious phrase by cunning caught and spread."—*Lara*, viii.

THE RIGHT TO LIVE

THE fact . . . that we have almost to cast about in certain
cases for an explanation of the established belief in the
sacredness of human life, shows how deeply rooted that
belief is unless where some counter-belief interferes with it.

On the other hand, it is equally noticeable that there
are counter-beliefs which, under conditions, do neutralise
it, and that certain other beliefs, which form its proper
complement, have very slight hold on the mind of modern
Christendom. It is taken for granted that the exigencies
of the state of war, whether the war be necessary or not
for saving the state from dissolution, absolutely neutralise
the right to live. We are little influenced by the idea of the
universal brotherhood of men, of mankind as forming one
society with a common good, of which the conception may
determine the action of its members. In international

dealings we are apt to suppose that it can have no place
at all.

Thomas Hill Green. *Lectures on the
Principles of Political Obligation, delivered
1879-80. Printed in Philosophical Works.*

WRONG-DOING

OUR conclusion then is that the destruction of life in war
(to say nothing of other evils incidental to it with which
we are not here concerned) is always wrong-doing, with
whomsoever the guilt of the wrong-doing may lie ; that
only those parties to a war are exempt from a share in the
guilt who can truly plead that to them war is the only
means of maintaining the social conditions of the moral
development of man, and that there have been very few
cases in which this plea could be truly made. In saying
this it is not forgotten, either that many virtues are called
into exercise by war, or that wars have been a means by
which the movement of mankind, which there is reason for
considering a progress to higher good, has been carried on.
These facts do not make the wrong-doing involved in any
way less so. . . . It may be that, according to the divine
scheme of the world, such wrong-doing is an element in a
process by which men gradually approximate more nearly
to good (in the sense of a good will). We cannot think of
God as a moral being without supposing this to be the case.

Ibid.

FALSE INTELLIGENCE

YOU remember, gentlemen, what happened at the outbreak
of the great war between France and Germany in 1870.
At that time there existed for a few days a condition of
things which produced in that case excitement of expectation as to the points upon which the quarrel turned ; and
you remember that a telegram was sent from Berlin to

Paris, and was published in Paris, or rather, if I recollect aright, it was announced by a Minister in the Chamber, stating that the King of Prussia, as he was then, had insulted the ambassador of France by turning his back upon him in a garden, where they had met, and refusing to communicate with him. The consequence was an immense exasperation in France ; and the telegram, which afterwards proved to be totally and absolutely false, was a necessary instrument for working up the minds of the French people to a state in which some of them desired, and the rest were willing to tolerate, what proved to be a most disastrous war. That war never was desired by the French nation at large, but by false intelligence heat was thrown into the atmosphere, party feeling and national feeling to a certain extent were excited, and it became practicable to drag the whole nation into the responsibility of the war. I remember well at that time what passed through my mind. I thought how thankful we ought to be that the use of methods so perilous, and so abominable —for the word is not too strong—never could be known in our happy country. Yes, gentlemen ; but since that time false telegrams about the entry of the Russian army into Constantinople have been sent home to disturb, and paralyse, and reverse the deliberations of Parliament, and have actually stopped these deliberations, and led experienced statesmen to withhold their action because of this intelligence, which was afterwards, and shortly afterwards, shown to be wholly without ground. Who invented that false intelligence I do not know, and I do not say. All I say is that it was not sent from Constantinople. It was telegraphed in the usual manner ; it was published in the usual manner ; it was available for a certain purpose. . . .

That was not the only, nor was it the most important case. You remember—I am now carrying your recollections back to the time of the outbreak of the war with Afghanistan, and if you recollect the circumstances of that outbreak, at the most critical moment we were told that the Ameer of Afghanistan had refused to receive a British Mission with

insult and with outrage, and that insult and outrage were
represented as at once enlisting our honour and reputation
in the case, as making it necessary to administer immediate
chastisement. I do not hesitate to express my full belief
that without that statement the war with Afghanistan
would not have been made, would not have been tolerated
by the country. . . . That intelligence was sent. We were
never undeceived about it until we were completely
committed to the war, and until our troops were in the
country. The Parliament met ; after long and most
unjustifiable delays the papers were produced, and when
the papers were produced and carefully examined, we found
that there was not a shred of foundation for that out-
rageous statement, and that the temper and pride of the
people of this country had been wrought up, and the spirit
of wrath fomented and kindled in their bosoms, by intelligence that was false intelligence, and that somebody
or other—somebody or other having access to high quarters,
if not dwelling in them—had invented, had fabricated for
the evil purpose of carrying us into bloody strife.

> William Ewart Gladstone. *In the
> House of Commons, April 2, 1880.*

A FACTOR IN GOD'S PLAN

EVERLASTING peace is a dream, there is not one more
beautiful, and war is a factor in God's plan of the world
. . . without war the world would sink into materialism.

> Helmuth Karl Bernhard Graf von
> Moltke. *To Prof. Dr. Bluntcshli, Dec.
> 11, 1880.*

AN HALLUCINATION?

THERE is no fixed character appertaining to War which
seems to promise it a permanence superior to that which
might, at one time, seem to have attached to institutions

now obsolete and discredited. . . . In all stages and states of society, the appetite for War and the methods of conducting War, have reflected, with considerable exactness, the aggregate features and tendencies of the then existing civilisation, though the extraordinary energy which, at the present day, enriches every field of exertion, availing itself of the latest physical innovations and discoveries, seems to impart to War, among other things, an appearance of freshly-springing activity, which may be wholly an hallucination, and in no way an augury of its longevity.

> Sheldon Amos. *Political and Legal Remedies for War, 1880.*

INCITING A POET

It occurred to me that your marvellous powers of expressing well-justified anger might be fitly used at the present time in condemnation of our filibustering atrocities all over the world. You have, I doubt not, been in a chronic state of indignation daily intensified by our doings in Afghanistan, in Zululand, in the Transvaal, and on a smaller scale in other places. There never was, I think, an opportunity for a more scathing exposure of the contrast between our Christian creed and pagan doings, our professed philanthropy and our actual savagery.

> Herbert Spencer. *To Algernon Charles Swinburne, Mar. 7, 1881.*

The poet could not see his way to oblige. It is a pity. Spencer possibly had in mind something in the style of Swinburne's *An Appeal*, which begins characteristically:

> Art thou indeed among these,
> Thou of the tyrannous crew,
> The kingdoms fed upon blood,
> O queen from old of the seas,
> England, art thou of them too
> That drink of the poisonous flood,
> That hide under poisonous trees?

TO ENSURE TRUE PEACE

No government will nowadays admit that it maintains an army in order to satisfy occasionally its passion for conquest. The army is said to serve only defensive purposes. This morality, which justifies self-defence, is called in as the government's advocate. This means, however, reserving morality for ourselves, and immorality for our neighbour, because he must be thought eager for attack and conquest if our state is forced to consider means of self-defence.—At the same time, by our explanation of our need of an army (because he denies the lust of attack just as our state does, and ostensibly also maintains his army for defensive reasons), we proclaim him a hypocrite and cunning criminal, who would fain seize by surprise, without any fighting, a harmless and unwary victim. In this attitude all states face each other to-day. They presuppose evil intentions on their neighbour's part and good intentions on their own. This hypothesis, however, is an *inhuman* notion, as bad as and worse than war. Nay, at bottom, it is a challenge and motive to war, foisting as it does upon the neighbouring state the charge of immorality, and thus provoking hostile intentions and acts. The doctrine of the army as a means of self-defence must be abjured as completely as the lust of conquest. Perhaps a memorable day will come when a nation renowned in wars and victories, distinguished by the highest development of military order and intelligence, and accustomed to make the heaviest sacrifice to these objects, will voluntarily exclaim, " We will break our swords," and will destroy its whole military system, lock, stock, and barrel. Making ourselves defenceless (after having been the most strongly defended) from a loftiness of sentiment—that is the means towards genuine peace, which must always rest upon a pacific disposition.

Friedrich Nietzsche. *The Wanderer and his Shadow,* 1886. *Tr. Oscar Levy.*

BETTER TO PERISH

THE so-called armed peace that prevails at present in all countries is a sign of a bellicose disposition, of a disposition that trusts neither itself nor its neighbour, and, partly from hate, partly from fear, refuses to lay down its weapons. Better to perish than to hate and fear, and twice as far better to perish than to make oneself hated and feared—this must some day become the supreme maxim of every political community !—Our liberal representatives of the people, as is well known, have not the time for reflection on the nature of humanity, or else they would know that they are working in vain when they work for " a gradual diminution of the military burdens." On the contrary, when the distress of these burdens is greatest, the sort of God who alone can help here will be nearest. The tree of military glory can only be destroyed at one swoop, with one stroke of lightning. But, as you know, lightning comes from the cloud and from above.

Ibid.

THE GREAT WAR AND AFTER

PROBABLY in the next great war the questions which have accumulated during the last half-century and more, will all be given their answers at once. Some hates moreover will crave for satisfaction ; much envy and greed will be at work ; but above all, and at the bottom of all, there will be the hard sense of necessity. Whole nations will be in the field ; the commerce of the world may be on the sea to win or lose ; national existence will be at stake ; men will be tempted to do anything which will shorten hostilities and tend to a decisive issue. Conduct in the next great war will certainly be hard ; it is very doubtful if it will be scrupulous, whether on the part of belligerents or neutrals ; and most likely the next war will be great. But there can be very little doubt that if the next war is unscrupulously waged, it also will be followed by a reaction towards increased stringency of law. . . . At any rate it is a matter of experience that times, in which International Law has been seriously disregarded, have been followed by periods in which the European conscience has done penance by putting itself under straiter obligations than those which it before acknowledged.

> William Edward Hall *International Law. Preface to 3rd ed., 1889.*

GOD WILL SEE TO IT

WITHOUT war no State could be. All those we know of arose through war, and the protection of their members by armed force remains their primary and essential task. War, therefore, will endure to the end of history, as long as there is multiplicity of States. The laws of human thought and of human nature forbid any alternative, neither is one to be wished for. The blind worshipper of an eternal peace falls into the error of isolating the State, or dreams of one which is universal, which we have already seen to be at variance with reason. . . .

It is important not to look upon war always as a judgment from God. Its consequences are evanescent ; but the life of a nation is reckoned by centuries, and the final verdict can only be pronounced after the survey of whole epochs. . . .

Most undoubtedly war is the one remedy for an ailing nation. . . . The grandeur of war lies in the utter annihilation of puny man in the great conception of the State, and it brings out the full magnificence of the sacrifice of fellow-countrymen for one another. In war the chaff is winnowed from the wheat. . . .

What a disaster for civilisation it would be if mankind blotted its heroes from memory. The heroes of a nation are the figures which rejoice and inspire the spirit of its youth, and the writers whose words ring like trumpet blasts become the idols of our boyhood and our early manhood.

He who feels no answering thrill is unworthy to bear arms for his country. . . .

But it is not worth while to speak further of these matters, for the God above us will see to it that war shall return again, a terrible medicine for mankind diseased.

Heinrich von Treitschke. Lectures, 1892.
Tr. Blance Dugdale & Torben de Bille, 1916.

THE SUBLIMITY OF WAR

WE live in a warlike age ; the over-sentimental philanthropic fashion of judging things has passed into the background, so that we can once more join hands with Clausewitz in calling war the forceful continuation of politics. All the peacemakers in the world will never make the political powers all of one mind, and until they are, the sword will be the only arbiter. We have learned to perceive the moral majesty of war through the very processes which to the superficial observer seem brutal and inhuman. The greatness of war is just what at first sight seems to be its horror—that for the sake of their country men will overcome the natural feelings of humanity, that they will slaughter their fellowmen who have done them no injury, nay, whom they perhaps respect as chivalrous foes. Man will not only sacrifice his life, but the natural and justified instincts of his soul ; his very self he must offer up for the sake of patriotism ; here we have the sublimity of war. When we pursue this thought further we see how war, with all its brutality and sternness, weaves a bond of love between man and man, linking them together to face death, and causing all class distinctions to disappear. He who knows history knows also that to banish war from the world would be to mutilate human nature.

Ibid.

THE NORMAL CONDITION

WE behold the condition of Europe. For many years past peace has been rather an appearance than a reality. Possessed with mutual suspicions, almost all the nations are vying with one another in equipping themselves with military armaments. Inexperienced youths are removed from parental direction and control to be thrown amid the dangers of the soldier's life ; robust young men are taken from agriculture, or from ennobling studies, or trade, or the arts, to be put under arms. Hence the treasures of States are exhausted by the enormous expenditure, the national resources are frittered away, and private fortunes impaired, and this, as it were, armed peace, which now prevails, cannot last much longer. Can this be the normal condition of human society ?

Leo XIII. *Encyclical Letter on The Reunion of Christendom*,[1] *June 20, 1894.*

[1] Qt. A Primer of Peace and War, ed. Charles Plater, 1915.

THE CRITIC AS PEACEMAKER

THE Manchester school tried to make men realise the brotherhood of humanity, by pointing out the commercial advantages of peace. It sought to degrade the wonderful world into a common market-place for the buyer and the seller. It addressed itself to the lowest instincts, and it failed. War followed upon war, and the tradesman's creed did not prevent France and Germany from clashing together in blood-stained battle. There are others of our own day who seek to appeal to mere emotional sympathies, or to the shallow dogmas of some vague system of abstract ethics. They have their Peace Societies, so dear to the senti-mentalists, and their proposals for unarmed International Arbitration, so popular among those who have never read history. But mere emotional sympathy will not do. It is too variable, and too closely connected with the passions ; and a board of arbitrators who, for the general welfare of the race, are to be deprived of the power of putting their decisions into execution, will not be of much avail. There is only one thing worse than Injustice, and that is Justice without her sword in her hand. When Right is not Might, it is evil. . . .

As long as war is regarded as wicked, it will always have its fascination. When it is looked upon as vulgar, it will cease to be popular. The change will of course be slow, and people will not be conscious of it. They will not say " We will not war against France because her prose is perfect," but because the prose of France is perfect, they will not hate the land. Intellectual criticism will bind Europe together in bonds far closer than those that can be forged by shopman or sentimentalist. It will give us the peace that springs from understanding.

Oscar Wilde. *The Critic as Artist, 1894.*

RESOLUTIONS

THAT this Conference, while disclaiming any purpose of laying down rules for the conduct of International Arbitration, or of suggesting the special methods by which it should proceed, desires to affirm its profound conviction of the value of the principle of International Arbitration, and its essential consistency with the Religion of Jesus Christ.

That this Conference welcomes the indications of a more enlightened public conscience on the subject of International Arbitration, and desires to call the attention of all Christian people to the evidence of the healthier state of feeling afforded by the action of Legislatures, and in the increasing literature on the subject.

That this Conference, believing that nothing more strongly makes for peace than a healthy and enlightened public opinion, urges upon all Christian people the duty of promoting by earnest prayer, by private instruction, and by public appeal, the cause of International Arbitration.

Resolutions 41, 42, 43.
Lambeth Conference, 1897.

THE PROUD INSTINCTS OF AN IMPERIAL RACE

THE King of all the ages, the Lord of Hosts, is the " Prince of Peace." Surely when He speaks of peace, He means *peace* ; He means the tempers of peace, the moderation and self-restraint of peace, the strong sense of equity, the curbing of ambition, the aversion to boastfulness, and violence, and insolent self-assertion, which are the conditions and pledges of peace. What will He say, at His judgment seat, of the great and swelling words of pride and defiance of which history is full? What will He say of those national anti-pathies and hatreds, so lightly and easily kindled, so obstinate when once kindled, so unreasoning, so ignorant, so absolutely proof to argument or remonstrance, which have turned the fairest lands of this world into fields of blood ? Will He accept, at the bar of Eternal justice, as a plea for precipitate and needless wars, the " proud instincts of an imperial race ? " No, if we know anything of the mind of Jesus Christ, He will not.

R. W. Church, *Dean of St. Paul's.*
The Message of Peace, 1897.

NOTHING ELSE TO LOOK FOR

MEN look forward to a universal war, and now that self-interest, that is the Devil himself, is believed to be the paramount and practical law of life, there is nothing else to look for. Perhaps we may need the horrors of a universal war to teach poor blundering mankind that self-interest is not the master idea of nations, but their degradation and destruction. It is terrible that such lessons need to be taught by the crime of war. There is the real problem for thought, and it involves both God and man.

Stopford Brooke. *Diary, Jan. 1, 1898.*
Life and Letters, by L. P. Jacks, 1917.

TO STOP FIGHTING, STOP FIGHTING

IF a man drinks, and I tell him that he can himself stop drinking and must do so, there is some hope that he will pay attention to me ; but if I tell him that his drunkenness forms a complex and difficult problem, which we, the learned, will try to solve in our meetings, all the probabilities are that he, waiting for the solution of the problem, will continue to drink. The same is true of the false and intricate scientific, external means for the cessation of war, like the international tribunals, the court of arbitration, and other similar foolish things, when we with them keep in abeyance the simplest and most essential means for the cessation of war, which is only too obvious to anybody. For people who do not need war not to fight we need no international tribunals, no solution of questions, but only that the people who are subject to deception should awaken and free themselves from that spell under which they are. The means for the abolition of war consists in this, that the men who do not need war, who consider a participation in war to be a sin, should stop fighting.

Leo Tolstoi. *Carthago Delenda est, 1898.*

A BAD TIME COMING

I SYMPATHISE in your feelings and your aims, but not in your hopes. . . . In people's present mood nothing can be done in that direction.

Now that the white savages of Europe are overrunning the dark savages everywhere—now that the European nations are vying with one another in political burglaries—

now that we have entered upon an era of social cannibalism in which the strong nations are devouring the weaker— now that national interests, national prestige, pluck, and so forth are alone thought of, and equity has utterly dropped out of thought, while rectitude is scorned as "unctuous," it is useless to resist the wave of barbarism. There is a bad time coming, and civilised mankind will (morally) be uncivilised before civilisation can again advance.

Such a body as that which you propose,[1] even could its members agree, would be pooh-poohed as sentimental and visionary. The universal aggressiveness and universal culture of blood-thirst will bring back military despotism, out of which after many generations partial freedom may again emerge.

Herbert Spencer. *To Moncure
D. Conway, July 18, 1898.*

[1] "The war between the United States and Spain was weighing heavily on the consciences of many thoughtful Americans, among whom was Mr. Moncure Conway, who asked Spencer whether it would not be possible to form a concert of eminent men, who, whenever a peril of war arose, should meet as a ' supreme court of civilisation ' and determine the right and wrong, before any declaration of war took place."— *Life and Letters of Herbert Spencer*, by David Duncan, LL.D., 1908.

CHRISTIAN CHARITY

ONE of the Christian precepts that were impressed upon us in our early youth as of great importance, and that are glorified in millions of sermons, is : " Love your enemies, bless them that curse you, do good to them that hate you, and pray for them which despitefully use you and persecute you." It is a very ideal precept, but as useless in practice as it is unnatural. So it is with the counsel, " If any man will take away thy coat, let him have thy cloak also." Translated into terms of modern life, that means : " When some unscrupulous scoundrel has defrauded thee of half thy goods, let him have the other half also." Or, again, in the language of modern politics : " When the pious

English take from you simple Germans one after another of your new and valuable colonies in Africa, let them have all the rest of your colonies also—or, best of all, give them Germany itself. And, while we touch on the marvellous world-politics of modern England, we may note in passing its direct contradiction of every precept of Christian charity, which is more frequently on the lips of that great nation than of any other nation in the world.

Ernst Haeckel.[1] *The Riddle of the Universe, 1899. Tr. Joseph McCabe.*

[1] "Some one once put to him the following question: If in some way you could address a question to the Universe and be assured of a truthful answer, what question would you ask? Haeckel remained for some moments absorbed in thought, and then he said, 'The question I would most like to see answered is this: Is the Universe friendly?'" —James H. Breasted, *The Dawn of Conscience*, 1933.

AN AMERICAN VIEW

I DO not like to talk about the Boer war, it is too painful. To think of England, which I love and admire so much, and which is so full of beauty, being filled with mourning at this season ! When I do speak of the war my language becomes unfit for publication, and I therefore will not write of it to you. Talking of the Philippine war has the same effect upon me, and I have therefore ceased to write about McKinley. Every one who believes in the divine government of the world must believe that God will eventually take up the case of fellows who set unnecessary wars on foot, and I hope he won't forgive them. . . .

Kipling[1] has long been to me a most pernicious, vulgar person. I only admire one thing of his, " The Recessional." He may have written other things as good, but I don't read him. I think most of the current jingoism on both sides of the water is due to him. He is the poet of the barrack-room cads.

Edwin Lawrence Godkin.
To Miss Dawson, Dec. 23, 1899.

[1] 'E 'ath a notion that the War
Was a Imperial beano, gave

By a 'eroic people for
A people twenty times as brave . . .
Johnnies 'oo talked so bloomin' well
That when they spoke it made you cry,
An' blew each other into 'Ell
All out of Christian charity.
An' cracked the movin' patriot wheeze,
An' patronised "this world so wide,"
An' 'eld each other's arteries
An' so on, till each other died. . . .
                    T. W. H. Crosland, *The Five Notions.*

REMEMBER MAJUBA !

THE crowds who shouted to the departing troops " Remember Majuba ! " displayed the same passion as the lowest savages who make blood-revenge a primary duty. And the pride of mastery which prompts the Indian to wear as a trophy the scalp of his fallen foe, is the same in nature as that which will hear of nothing less than taking the chief city of a conquered nation. Is the sentiment of the prize ring—" I am stronger than you are "—so very noble ?

Herbert Spencer. *To The Morning
Leader, Feb. 5, 1900.*

Spencer reprinted this letter, with others, in *Various Fragments* (enlarged edition, 1907). "I reproduce them here," he says, "as a permanent record of my feelings respecting a war by which Great Britain has been discredited in every way—discredited in its intelligence, since a task regarded as small and easy has proved to be a task costing more in men and money than was ever before expended in the space of a year—discredited in its military capacity, since two hundred thousand trained soldiers have been required to conquer thirty to forty thousand untrained burghers—discredited in its honour, since, after disclaiming the desire for goldfields and territory it has taken both—and further morally discredited, since its character for love of liberty and desire to maintain the freedom of small nationalities has been for ever lost."

1900—1913

So shaken as we are, so wan with cares
Find we a time for frighted peace to pant,
And breathe short-winded accents of new broils.
>   Shakespeare. *Henry IV.*

PEACE NIGHT

THE evil revelry was no illusion of my pro-Boer brain.
Hall, an ardent fighter, came back sick and furious, more
than I was. Macpherson, a fierce Scot, was as disgusted.
Inspector Palmer was dark as pitch. It was the utter
abandonment which was so revolting. The faces lose
human expression. The girls are simply " loose." The
hideous look comes, which marks the end of human nature.

Surely, we might have just had the shadow of the past
to restrain us. We might have realised what we had come
through. There are the dead. And then, the old English
thing was to be too strong to let all barriers go. And some
faint touch of generosity might have been shown for those
who are beaten, and who are signing away their lives. The
ugliness of our joy is so appalling : the fat City men gone
mad. We must turn some corner and get away from this :
we must recover some tone and control. I know that our
nerves are high strung ; but our girls must not lead us
downhill.[1]

Henry Scott Holland, D.D.
To Dr. Talbot, Bishop of
Winchester, June, 1902.

[1] Not thus doth Peace return,
A blessed visitant she comes;
Honour in his right hand
Doth lead her like a bride.
Southey, *Carmen Aulica.*

MAN A FIGHTING, NOT A REASONING, ANIMAL

OUR permanent enemy is the rooted bellicosity of human
nature. Man, biologically considered, and whatever else
he may be into the bargain, is the most formidable of all
beasts of prey, and, indeed, the only one that preys
systematically on his own species. We are once for all
adapted to the military status. A millennium of peace would

M

not breed the fighting disposition out of our bone and marrow, and a function so ingrained and vital will never consent to die without resistance, and will always find impassioned apologists and idealisers.

Not only men born to be soldiers, but non-combatants by trade and nature, historians in their studies and clergymen in their pulpits, have been war's idealisers. They have talked of war as of God's court of justice. And, indeed, if we think how many things besides the frontiers of states the wars of history have decided, we must feel some respectful awe, in spite of all the horrors. Our actual civilisation, good and bad alike, has had past wars for its determining condition. Great-mindedness among the tribes of men has always meant the will to prevail, and all the more so if prevailing included slaughtering and being slaughtered. . . . The blessings we actually enjoy, such as they are, have grown up in the shadow of the wars of antiquity. The various ideals were backed by fighting wills, and when neither would give way, the God of battles had to be the arbiter. A shallow view this, truly ; for who can say what might have prevailed if man had ever been a reasoning and not a fighting animal ? Like dead men, dead causes tell no tales, and the ideals that went under in the past, along with all the tribes that represented them, find to-day no recorder, no explainer, no defender.

William James. *At Universal Peace Congress, Boston, 1904.*

PREVENTIVE MEDICINE

WE do ill, I think, therefore, to talk much of universal peace or of a general disarmament. We must go in for preventive medicine, not for radical cure. We must cheat our foe, circumvent him in detail, not try to change his nature. In one respect war is like love, though in no other. Both leave us intervals of rest ; and in the intervals life goes on perfectly well without them, though the imagination till dallies with their possibility. Equally insane when once aroused and under headway, whether they shall be aroused or not depends on accidental circumstances. How are old maids and old bachelors made ? Not by deliberate vows of celibacy, but by sliding on from year to year with no sufficient matrimonial provocation. So of the nations with their wars. Let the general possibility of war be left open, in Heaven's name, for the imagination to dally with. Let the soldiers dream of killing, as the old maids dream of marrying.

But organise in every conceivable way the practical machinery for making each successive chance of war abortive. Put peace men in power ; educate the editors and statesmen to responsibility. . . . Seize every pretext, however small, for arbitration methods, and multiply the precedents ; foster rival excitements, and invent new outlets for heroic energy ; and from one generation to another the chances are that irritation will grow less acute and states of strain less dangerous among the nations. Armies and navies will continue, of course, and fire the minds of populations with their potentialities of greatness. But their officers will find that somehow or other, with no deliberate intention on any one's part, each successive " incident " has managed to evaporate and to lead nowhere, and that the thought of what might have been remains their only consolation.

Ibid.

NON-RESISTANCE

THE gross world finds this an impossible doctrine ; and the Christian Churches, with the exception of one or two small societies, accept, justify, and sanctify the conduct of wars, at least wars of self-defence ; and self-defence is often secured by striking the first blow. I must confess, though this may appear a wild dream, that I do not find sheer impossibility in the vision of a non-resisting society growing into a nation and being left unmolested in its peaceful integrity by the other nations of the world.

Leonard, Lord Courtney of Penwith.
The Diary of a Church-goer, 1905.

WHAT NOBLER ROLE?

IT is vain to seek peace if you do not also ensue it. I hold that the growth of armaments is a great danger to the peace of the world. A policy of huge armaments keeps alive and stimulates and feeds the belief that force is the best, if not the only solution of international differences. It is a policy that tends to inflame old sores. And I submit to you that as the principle of peaceful arbitration gains ground it becomes one of the highest tasks of a statesman to adjust these armaments to the newer and happier condition of things. What nobler role could this great country assume than at the fitting moment to place itself at the head of a league of peace, through whose instrumentality this great work could be effected?

Sir Henry Campbell-Bannerman, G.C.B.
Dec. 21, 1905. In the Albert Hall.

THE PRELUDE

REAL war is a very different thing from the painted image that you see at a parade or review. But it is the painted image that makes it popular. The waving plumes, the gay uniforms, the flashing swords, the disciplined march of innumerable feet, the clear-voiced trumpet, the intoxicating strains of martial music, the pomp, the sound, and the spectacle—these are the enticements to war and to the profession of the soldier. They are not what they were. But they still form a popular prelude to a woeful pandemonium. And when war bursts out it is at first, as a rule, but a small minority even of the peoples engaged that really sees and feels its horrors. The populace is fed by excitements ; the defeats are covered up ; in most countries the lists of killed and wounded are suppressed or postponed ; victories are magnified ; successful generals are acclaimed, and the military hero becomes the idol of the people.

Francis W. Hirst. *The
Arbiter in Council, 1906.*

THE PRESS AND ARMAMENTS

WHEREVER the press is under official control, or is corrupt, or is largely in the hands of syndicates, possibly run by contractors, all manners of plausible lies can be circulated in regard to the inadequacy of national armaments, and reports are easily spread of tremendous preparations or threatening movements by other countries which require still more tremendous counter preparations on our part. The public does not investigate rumours, nor can it, as a rule, test the statements officially made ; and so until the weight of taxation becomes oppressive it suffers itself to be misled by the idea that the greater its army or its navy, the greater is its security. Then there is always a crowd of fools who think after the writers in the cheap press, imagining that huge armaments stimulate industry and so actually increase the prosperity of the nation.

Ibid.

TRUST ONE ANOTHER

SEVENTEEN years ago I said, " my aim is, above all, the maintenance of peace." History, I venture to hope, will do me the justice that I have pursued this aim unswervingly ever since. The main prop and base for the peace of the world is the maintenance of good relations between our two countries, and I shall further strengthen them as far as lies in my power. The German nation's wishes coincide with mine. The future will then show a bright prospect and commerce may develop among the nations who have learnt to trust one another.

The German Emperor, William II.
At the Guildhall, London, Nov. 13, 1907.

THAT SPIRIT

WELCOME you ? Why, no Englishman but welcomes you !
We rejoice to meet our brother Christians wherever we
can. We are glad to find you are heart to heart with us in
the main things of human life and human existence. We
are all the better for meeting here this afternoon. Our
hearts are warmed by your cheerful countenances, and
may that good spirit of unity, that spirit of love, that spirit
of brotherhood, that spirit of unanimity, be poured upon us
from on High ; and may it be that when children yet
unborn look back to the days that have been they will stand
in astonishment at the contemplation of men fighting and
cutting each other's throats.

The Very Rev. Dean Barker of Carlisle.
Conference at Holborn Restaurant of Repre-
sentatives of English and German Churches,
June 1, 1908.

NOT FAR OFF

THE Burgomaster of Munich said the other day when he
was over here that war between Germany and England
would be a crime, and Mr. Lloyd George said quite
recently that the day was not far off when the nation that
lifts up a sword against a nation would be treated as though
it had committed a felony. If these are the utterances of
statesmen, then surely those who stand forward as the
ministers of the gospel of Jesus Christ must be perpetually
insistent in their proclamation of the necessity for learning
war no more.

The Rev. Dr. John Clifford.
Meeting at Albert Hall, June 1, 1908.

A UNIVERSAL LEAGUE OF PEACE

AT the Hague Conference a year ago a memorial in favour
of peace was presented by the Churches of Great Britain,
Europe and America. It was in accepting this memorial

that the President, His Excellency M. Nelidoff, remarked that " too much must not be expected from this Conference ; it has taken nineteen hundred years of Christianity to give us the first International Peace Conference, and this is only the second that has been held."

The first Conference of the Churches of Christendom in the interests of International Peace has not yet been convened. That such a Conference is not only desirable, but even imperative must be admitted by all who, in sincerity, pray " Our Father . . . Thy Kingdom come, Thy will be done on earth," and who earnestly desire to fulfil the prophecy of the Angel-song at Bethlehem— " Glory to God in the Highest, and on earth peace, goodwill towards men."

Surely the time is now fully come when the professed followers of the Prince of Peace, the religious leaders of every land, should unite to form themselves into a Universal League of Peace, and to make impossible for the future the crime and wickedness of war.

J. Allen Baker, M.P. *Foreword to Peace and the Churches,*[1] *1908.*

[1] Souvenir volume of the visit to England of the representatives of German Christian Churches.

RESOLUTION

THE Conference, while frankly acknowledging the moral gains sometimes won by war, rejoices in the growth of higher ethical perceptions which is evidenced by the increasing willingness to settle differences among nations by peaceful methods ; it records, therefore, its deep appreciation of the services rendered by the Conferences at The Hague, its thankfulness for the practical works achieved, and for the principles of international responsibility acknowledged by the delegates ; and, finally, realising the dangers inseparable from national and commercial progress, it urges earnestly upon all Christian peoples the duty of allaying race-prejudice, of reducing by peaceful arrangements the conflict of trade interests, and of promoting among all races the spirit of brotherly co-operation for the good of all mankind.

Lambeth Conference, 1908.

THE CHURCH'S DUTY

SHE [the Church] is built upon the charter of the Sermon on the Mount. . . . I cannot help feeling that it is her duty, in her corporate capacity, and through the mouthpieces whom she chooses in order to express her thoughts to the men of her time, it is her duty to declare fully and frankly that war is not Christian, a survival merely of the natural man and of the older order, and she should therefore entirely withdraw her sanction from taking part in war, and from making preparation for war. She should have the courage to say that as a Church she disapproves of great armaments as much as she disapproves of fighting ; and that she believes it is the function of a Christian state, whenever it becomes really Christian, to act on the mighty principle of peace and love, which can conciliate the world not by being prepared for war but by frankly not being prepared, and by making it plain that, as a country even, she has decided to suffer rather than to fight, or even to contemplate the possibility of fighting.

The Rev. Dr. R. F. Horton. *At the Seventeenth Universal Congress of Peace, London, July 27, 1908.*

SYMPATHY AND SUPPORT

PEACE is the great interest of the civilised world, and everything which promotes it—whether it be by the education of public opinion . . . or by the conclusion of Arbitration Treaties, or by the efficient maintenance of defensive armaments—should have the sympathy and support of all who have the welfare of humanity at heart.

Arthur James Balfour. *Message to the Seventeenth Universal Peace Conference, 1908.*

INCREDIBLE

IT really seems incredible, when you begin to reflect upon it, that it should be necessary in the twentieth century of the Christian era to hold a meeting in a civilised country to protest against the expenditure by Christian communities of £400 millions a year upon preparing one nation to kill another. It is still more amazing that the leaders of nations should be more engrossed upon the perfecting and the rendering more deadly of the machinery of human slaughter than with setting up some tribunal for the possible adjustment of disputes between nations. You read a good many newspapers, and you find that there are more columns devoted to canvassing and examining the mechanism of slaughter than to the problem of peace.

The Rt. Hon. David Lloyd George. *In the Queen's Hall, July, 28, 1908.*

LIP SERVICE

To urge the advantages and to advocate the maintenance of peace might seem to be, what it certainly ought to be, an otiose and a superfluous task. Of all the deities in the Pantheon there is none to whom mankind, now as always, is more ready to pay the homage of lip service than to the goddess of peace. We are, indeed, often told by apologists for the existing state of things that the colossal armaments which are inflicting an immeasurable and ever-growing burden upon mankind are in themselves a safeguard, and indeed the best insurance against war. Now, it is said that your fighting units are numbered not by the thousands but by the million ; that every four or five years your battleships increase in bulk of displacement and in the perfection of their armaments ; the very completeness of the mechanism of destruction, the vastness of the scale upon which it is organised, must prevent statesmen and diplomatists from ever again contemplating the outbreak of war with a light heart.

> The Prime Minister (Mr. Asquith).
> *At the Seventeenth Universal Peace Con-
> ference, July 31, 1908.*

DA CAPO

IT is pretty generally admitted that the present rivalry in armaments with Germany cannot go on in its present form indefinitely. The net result of each side meeting the effort of the other with similar effort is that at the end of a given period the relative position of both is what it was originally, and the enormous sacrifices of both have gone for nothing. If it is claimed that England is in a position to maintain the lead because she has the money, Germany can retort that she is in a position to maintain the lead because she has the population, which must, in the case of a highly organised European nation, in the end mean money. Meanwhile, neither side can yield to the other, as the one so doing would, it is felt, be placed at the mercy of the other, a situation which neither will accept. There are two current solutions which are offered as a means of egress from this *impasse*. There is that of the smaller party, regarded in both countries for the most part as dreamers and doctrinaires, who hope to solve the problem by a resort to general disarmament, or, at least, a limitation of armament by agreement. And there is that of the larger and more practical party who are quite persuaded that the present state of rivalry and recurrent irritation is

bound to culminate in an armed conflict, which, by
definitely reducing one or other of the parties to a position
of manifest inferiority, will settle the thing for at least
some time, until after a longer or shorter period a state of
relative equilibrium is established, and the whole process
will be recommenced *da capo*.

Sir Norman Angell. *The Great
Illusion, Nov., 1909.*

QUESTIONS

Is it true that wealth and prosperity and well-being depend
on the political power of nations, or, indeed, that the one
has anything whatever to do with the other ?

Is it true that one nation can gain a solid, tangible
advantage by the conquest of another ?

Does the political or military victory of a nation give
any advantage to the individuals of that nation which is
not still possessed by the individuals of the defeated nation ?

Is it possible for one nation to take by force anything
in the way of material wealth from another ?[1]

Is it possible for a nation in any real sense to " own "
the territory of another—to own it, that is, in any way
which can benefit the individual citizens of the owning
country ?

If England could conquer Germany to-morrow, completely conquer her, reduce her nationality to so much
dust, would the ordinary British subject be the better
for it ?

If Germany could conquer England, would any ordinary
German subject be the better for it ?

The fact that all these questions have to be answered
in the negative, and that a negative answer seems to outrage common sense, shows how much our political axioms
are in need of revision.

Ibid.

[1] "If I am returned, Germany is going to pay restitution, reparation
and indemnity, and I have personally no doubt we will get everything
out of her that you can squeeze out of a lemon and a bit more. . . . I

propose that not only all the gold Germany has got, but all the silver and jewels she has got shall be handed over. All her pictures and libraries and everything of that kind should be sold to the neutral and Allied world, and the proceeds given to paying the indemnity."—Sir Eric Geddes, Speech at Cambridge, Dec. 9, 1918.

A VERY SAD FACT

REMEMBER . . . that as far as human experience goes, a reign of peace does not breed men less inclined for intrigue or for quarrelling, or for trying to get the better of each other. Human nature in Southern India, where peace has reigned for two generations, has not been altered. Again, take Italy from 1715 to the outbreak of the Napoleonic Wars. The peninsula was lapped in peace, but men degenerated instead of improved, and no one will dare to say that Florence and Venice in 1790 presented a worthier spectacle than Florence and Venice in less peaceful times. In truth, universal peace, whether produced by a universal Empire, or by some accident, does not breed worthier men and women. That is not a pleasant fact. On the contrary, it is a very sad fact, but it is one which we are bound to face, for if we do not face it we shall delude ourselves with shams and shadows.

J. St. Loe Strachey.
A New Way of Life, 1909.

IS THERE NO HOPE?

MUST the world, then, continue fighting, and is there no hope for peace, or, to put it in another way, is that deep and instinctive desire for peace which unquestionably is implanted in the minds of the best of human beings a snare and a delusion? How naturally arises in every woman's heart an echo of the old song:

" Oh, were I King of France,
        Or better, Pope of Rome,
I'd have no fighting men abroad,
        No weeping maids at home."[1]

Is that cry always to be denied ? We are far from saying
that it must be, and far from denying that war is a terrible
evil. That it dominates the world as it does is a riddle
which we have not the power to solve, and which we will
make no pretence at explaining. All we can do is to
point out to our countrymen that they must face the fact
that war is the law of the civilised world quite as much as
of the uncivilised, and that mankind has as yet found no
other way of settling which will is to prevail when what
we have termed a clash of wills takes place between communities who believe themselves equal in physical force.
Such a clash of wills among nations is as certain to take
place from time to time in the future as in the past. We
delude ourselves if we think that arbitration and the reign
of peace and reason constitute one of the ways by which
the British nation may escape from the anxieties and
difficulties which now beset it. That door is closed, at
any rate for this generation, and he is no true friend to his
country who pretends otherwise.

Ibid.

[1] Oh, if I were Queen of France, or, still better, Pope of Rome,
  I would have no fighting men abroad, no weeping maids at home.
   All the world should be at peace; or if kings must show their might,
   Why, let them who make the quarrels be the only ones to fight.
                    Charles Jefferies, *Jeannette and Jeannot.*

THE KING AND TOM

Now when the king went forth to arms
Trumpets played him shrill alarms,
Trumpets played with golden throats,
Triumph, gladness, in their notes.

But when Tom went out to battle
Clear-eyed springs began to prattle ;
Murmured, too, the fields of grain
Words of anguish, words of pain.

Lord eagles round the banner fly
Where the village crosses swing.
Tom is wounded—left to die.
But unscathed returns the king.

And when through gleaming gates he rode
Golden dawning yonder glowed ;
Bells set chiming far and wide
On the sunny countryside.

And when the peasant's pit was made,
Rustled trees in distant glade,
Chimes came through the oak-grove stealing
Of blue-bells and of lilies pealing.

Marya Konopnicka. c. 1909.
Tr. from Polish by Paul Selver.

ARMAMENTS

ARMIES and navies exist and increase solely under the plea that these are the best, and indeed the only, means of ensuring peace.

We deal with [two of] the axioms urged in their justification.

First : " To be prepared for war is the surest way to secure peace."

Answer : If only one nation " prepared," this axiom would be sound ; but when one arms others follow, and the fancied security vanishes, rivalry between nations ensues, and preparation, so far from promoting peace, sows suspicion and jealousy, developing into hatred, the prolific seed of future wars between nations hitherto peacefully disposed. . . .

Second : " Our armaments are intended only for our own protection, and are no menace to other nations ; they make for peace."

Answer : So say all the armed nations, and it is true that every nation regards and proclaims its own armaments as instruments of peace only, because these are meant to protect her from the existing armaments of other nations ; but just as naturally every nation regards every other nation's armaments as clearly instruments of war, and not of peace, because these may attack her. . . .

Thus armaments . . . on land or on sea, so far from preserving peace, inevitably become in time one of the chief, if not the greatest of all, causes of war, since they sow the deadly seeds of mutual suspicion.

> Andrew Carnegie. *Armaments and their results, 1909.*

"Colonel A. C. Yates, M.P., wrote . . . from the Athenæum Club to *The Times* [Dec. 27, 1910] to complain that Mr. Carnegie had called war a degrading evil. ' Does Mr. Carnegie,' he asked, ' really understand human nature and the immutable laws which govern and guide it? Is the grand law of the "selection of the fittest" to give way to the miserable mediocrity of compromise fostered by charity? '"—Graham Wallas, *The Great Society.*

A CURIOUS MENTAL MIXTURE

THE war against war is going to be no holiday excursion or camping party. The military feelings are too deeply grounded to abdicate their place among our ideals until better substitutes are offered than the glory and shame that come to nations as well as to individuals from the ups and downs of politics and the vicissitudes of trade. . . .

Modern war is so expensive that we feel trade to be a better avenue to plunder ; but modern man inherits all the innate pugnacity and all the love of glory of his ancestors. Showing war's irrationality and horror is of no effect upon him. The horrors make the fascination. War is the *strong* life ; it is life *in extremis* ; war-taxes are the only ones men never hesitate to pay, as the budgets of all nations show us. . . .

At the present day, civilised opinion is a curious mental
mixture. The military instincts and ideals are as strong
as ever, but are confronted by reflective criticisms which
sorely curb their ancient freedom. Innumerable writers
are showing up the bestial side of military service. Pure
loot and mastery seem no longer morally avowable motives,
and pretexts must be found for attributing them solely to
the enemy. England and we, our army and navy authorities repeat without ceasing, arm solely for " peace."
Germany and Japan it is who are bent on loot and glory.
" Peace " in military mouths to-day is a synonym for
" war expected." The word has become a pure pro-
vocative, and no government wishing peace sincerely
should allow it ever to be printed in a newspaper. Every
up-to-date dictionary should say that " peace " and
" war " mean the same thing, now *in posse*, now *in actu*.
It may even reasonably be said that the intensely sharp
competitive *preparation* for war by the nations is *the real
war*, permanent, unceasing ; and that the battles are only
a sort of public verification of the mastery gained during
the " peace " interval.

> William James. *The Moral Equivalent
> of War, 1910.* (*Memories and Studies, 1911.*)

THE HIGHER ASPECTS OF MILITARY SENTIMENT

IN my remarks, pacificist though I am, I will refuse to
speak of the bestial side of the war *régime* (already done
justice to by many writers) and consider only the higher
aspects of militaristic sentiment. Patriotism no one thinks
discreditable ; nor does any one deny that war is the
romance of history. But inordinate ambitions are the soul
of every patriotism, and the possibility of violent death
the soul of all romance. The militarily patriotic and
romantic-minded everywhere, and especially the pro-
fessional military class, refuse to admit for a moment that
war may be a transitory phenomenon in social evolution.
The notion of a sheep's paradise like that revolts, they say,

our highest imagination. Where then would be the steeps of life ? If war had ever stopped, we should have to re-invent it, on this view, to redeem life from flat degeneration.

Reflective apologists for war at the present day all take it religiously. It is a sort of sacrament. Its profits are to the vanquished as well as to the victor ; and quite apart from any question of profit, it is an absolute good, we are told, for it is human nature at its highest dynamic. Its " horrors " are a cheap price to pay for rescue from the only alternative supposed, of a world of clerks and teachers, or co-education and zoophily, of " consumers' leagues " and " associated charities," of industrialism unlimited, and femininism unabashed. No scorn, no hardness, no valour any more ! Fie upon such a cattleyard of a planet ! . . .

This natural sort of feeling forms, I think, the inner-most soul of army writings. Without any exception known to me, militarist authors take a highly mystical view of their subject, and regard war as a biological or sociological necessity, uncontrolled by ordinary psychological checks and motives. When the time of development is ripe the war must come, reason or no reason, for the justifications pleaded are invariably fictitious. War is, in short, a permanent human *obligation*.

Ibid.

Major F. Yeats-Brown (*Dogs of War*, 1934) thinks that "War represents the deep and honourable craving of man for the supernatural." After which it is puzzling to come upon him saying, "For a moment my mind turns back to my *guru*, who told me long ago that ' wars are mass-perversions of sexual desire.' I see that more clearly now, although not fully."

A THREAT TO WAR

THE value of war for the political and moral development of mankind has been criticised by large sections of the modern civilised world in a way which threatens to weaken the defensive powers of States by undermining the warlike spirit of the people. . . .

This strongly-marked love of peace is due to various causes.

It springs from the good-natured character of the German people, which finds intense satisfaction in doctrinaire disputations and partisanship, but dislikes pushing things to an extreme. . . . We are always inclined to assume that disputes between States can find a peaceful solution on the basis of justice without clearly realising what *international* justice is.

An additional cause of the love of peace, besides those which are rooted in the very soul of the German people, is the wish not to be disturbed in commercial life. . . .

Universal military service, too, contributes to the love of peace, for war in these days does not merely affect, as formerly, definite limited circles, but the whole nation suffers alike. All families and all classes have to pay the same toll of human lives. Finally comes the effect of that universal conception of the times—the idea that war in itself is a sign of barbarism unworthy of an aspiring people, and that the finest blossoms of culture can only unfold in peace. . . .

We regard our warlike preparations as an almost insupportable burden, which it is the special duty of the German Reichstag to lighten as far as possible. We seem to have forgotten that the conscious increase of our armaments is not an inevitable evil, but the most necessary precondition of our national health, and the only guarantee of our international prestige. We are accustomed to regard war as a curse, and refuse to recognise it as the greatest factor in the furtherance of culture and power.

> Friedrich von Bernhardi. *Deutschland und der nächste Krieg, 1911. Tr. Allen H. Powles, 1912.*

A BIOLOGICAL NECESSITY

THIS desire for peace has rendered most civilised nations anæmic, and marks a decay of spirit and political courage such as has often been shown by a race of Epigoni. . . .

Every one will, within certain limits, admit that the endeavours to diminish the dangers of war and to mitigate the sufferings which war entails are justifiable. It is an incontestable fact that war temporarily disturbs industrial life, interrupts quiet economic development, brings widespread misery with it, and emphasises the primitive brutality of man. It is therefore a most desirable consummation if wars for trivial reasons should be rendered impossible, and if efforts are made to restrict the evils which follow necessarily in the train of war, so far as is compatible with the essential nature of war. All that the Hague Peace Congress has accomplished in this limited sphere deserves, like every permissible humanisation of war, universal acknowledgment. But it is quite another matter if the object is to abolish war entirely, and to deny its necessary place in historical development.

This aspiration is directly antagonistic to the great universal laws which rule all life. War is a biological necessity of the first importance, a regulative element in the life of mankind which cannot be dispensed with, since without it an unhealthy development will follow, which excludes every advancement of the race, and therefore all real civilisation.

Ibid.

PEACE RELAXES, WAR BRACES

ALL petty and personal interests force their way to the front during a long period of peace. Selfishness and intrigue run riot, and luxury obliterates idealism. Money acquires an excessive and unjustifiable power, and character does not obtain due respect :

> " Man is stunted by peaceful days,
> In idle repose his courage decays.
> Law is the weakling's game,
> Law makes the world the same.

> But in war man's strength is seen,
> War ennobles all that is mean ;
> Even the coward belies his name."
> —Schiller : *Braut v. Messina.*

" Wars are terrible but necessary, for they save the State from social petrification and stagnation. It is well that the transitoriness of the goods of this world is not only preached, but is learnt by experience. War alone teaches this lesson."[1]

War, in opposition to peace, does more to arouse national life and to expand national power than any other means known to history. It certainly brings much material and mental distress in its train, but at the same time it evokes the noblest activities of the human nature. . . .

Frederick the Great recognised the ennobling effect of war. " War," he said, " opens the most fruitful field to all virtues, for at every moment constancy, pity, magnanimity, heroism and mercy, shine forth in it ; every moment offers an opportunity to exercise one of these virtues."

Ibid.

[1] Kuno Fischer, *Hegel*, i, p. 737.

THE EVENING NEWS, *MARS AND PEACE*

As I correct these proofs I receive from a correspondent the leading article cut from an evening paper (the *Evening News*) . . . Mars urges that there is one way of getting rid of the passions which make war :

" ' How shall I do that ? ' asked Peace.

" Mars smiled grimly. ' I don't think you would care for the job,' he said.

" ' But I can be very brave in a good cause,' said Peace eagerly. ' Tell me what I must do.'

" ' Well,' said Mars, ' I should begin by exterminating the human race.'

" ' Yes, you would,' said Peace ; ' but I shall do better. I shall educate them.'

" ' Thank goodness,' said Mars with a sigh ; ' then I'm safe for another thousand years at least.' "

Sir Norman Angell. The Great Illusion, 3rd ed., 1911.

THE NEEDED SPARK

THE Emperor of Russia in 1819, seemingly divining that world peace was near, invited the nations to meet in conference. Surveying the world to-day, the most striking figure seen is another Emperor, the German Emperor, who has recently celebrated his twenty-fifth year of peaceful reign, his hands unstained with human blood—a unique record. Hence Germany's astounding progress educationally, industrially and commercially, proving that the greatest of all national blessings is peace. . . .

Let us suppose that the Emperor were now to invite the chief civilised nations to confer upon the best means of ensuring world peace, which his own Empire has enjoyed so long. That they would attend and listen is certain. Success I believe certain to follow. All seems so easy, too easy perhaps ; but pray remember that the great inventions, discoveries, and steps forward have been achieved at last by seemingly slight and trifling advances, because the ground has been well prepared. Most great advances have appeared to burst upon us suddenly in their perfection. So it will probably be with the change from barbarous war to civilised peace. One small spark oft creates the flame. The German Emperor holds in his hand the torch, and should apply the needed spark.

Andrew Carnegie Speech at the unveiling of the bust of Sir W. R. Cremer, at the Hague, Aug. 29, 1913.

1914—1918

THEY come like sacrifices in their trim,
And to the fire-ey'd maid of smoky war,
All hot and bleeding, will we offer them.

Shakespeare.   *Henry IV., Pt. I.*

1911—1913

They come like sacrifices in their trim,
And to the fire-ey'd maid of smoky war,
All hot and bleeding, will we offer them.

Shakespeare.   Henry IV., Pt. i.

ANNOUNCEMENT

THE twenty-first Universal Peace Congress will be held from the 15th to the 19th of September, 1914, in the handsome buildings in which the Austrian Parliament meets.

International Peace Bureau,
Berne, April 15, 1914.

A STATE OF WAR

THE following statement was issued from the Foreign Office at 12.15 this morning :

Owing to a summary rejection by the German Government of the request made by His Majesty's Government for assurances that the neutrality of Belgium will be respected, His Majesty's Ambassador at Berlin has received his passports, and His Majesty's Government has declared to the German Government that a state of war exists between Great Britain and Germany as from 11 p.m. on August 4.

The Times, Aug. 5, 1914.

WHAT WE ARE FIGHTING FOR

IF I am asked what we are fighting for, I reply in two sentences. In the first place to fulfil a solemn international obligation, an obligation which, if it had been entered into between private persons in the ordinary concerns of life, would have been regarded as an obligation not only of law but of honour, which no self-respecting man could possibly have repudiated. I say, secondly, we are fighting to vindicate the principle—which in these days when force, material force, sometimes seems to be the dominant

377

influence and factor in the development of mankind—we are fighting to vindicate the principle that small nationalities are not to be crushed, in defiance of international good faith, by the arbitrary will of a strong and overmastering Power.

Herbert Henry Asquith (*Prime Minister*). *In the House of Commons, Aug. 6, 1914.*

UNTOUCHED

UNTIL a few days ago I believed, I think in common with most Englishmen, that our country would adopt in this crisis an attitude of strict neutrality. In my view neither the original quarrel nor the remoter conflicts arising out of it ought to have been regarded as involving ourselves. With the whole of the racial struggle between Serbia and Austria we have not the least interest, with the loathsome murder or the passionate retribution. It was not worth the life of a single British sailor.

Yet country after country has stepped in ; first Russia, because she wished to protect Serbia ; then Germany, because she wished to protect Austria, and was bound by treaty. Then France was compelled by her alliance to support Russia. And so from one end of Europe to the other arose the portent of unwilling and unenthusiastic millions marching to slaughter at the orders of their incompetent governors.

But at least England was free from any treaty obligation to enter into this war, or to take either side in the struggle. We had a right to the hope and belief, which a week ago were general, that our rulers would be able to keep us out of it. A week ago there was no war fever to hamper the keepers of the peace.

But within the last few days we have suddenly discovered that our hands were not, as was alleged, unfettered after all. Over and over again we had been told by the friends of the Entente Cordiale that it only meant a bond of friendship with France. We now know, what we always suspected, that it carried with it the duty of enmity to Germany.

That is why Sir Edward Grey's appeal to " honour " leaves many of us untouched. . . .

> C. P. Trevelyan.[1] *From a Letter to his Constituents on leaving the Government, Aug. 7, 1914.*

[1] Now Sir Charles.

A PEACEFUL DISPOSITION

FOR forty-three years our people has maintained peace. Wherever a danger of war arose in other lands, our nation has exerted herself to assist in removing or diminishing it. Her ideal was peaceful work. She has contributed a worthy share to the cultural wealth of the modern world. She has not dreamed of depriving others of light and air. She desired to thrust no one from his place. In friendly competition with other peoples, she has developed the gifts which God has given her. Her industry brought her rich fruit. She won also a modest share in the task of colonisation in the primitive world, and was exerting herself to offer her contribution to the remoulding of Eastern Asia. She has left no one, who is willing to see the truth, in doubt as to her peaceful disposition. Only under the compulsion to repel a wanton attack has she now drawn the sword. . . .

The Holy God carries on His work to its goal, even through the storm and horror of war, and permits no human wickedness to defeat His purpose.

> *Address of the German Theologians to the Evangelical Christians abroad, Aug., 1914.*

THE SPY SCARE

No official warning has apparently been given to the public to report at once to the police any one with a foreign accent who is found walking through the country with an apparently quite aimless purpose, but in reality to take notes for use in Germany. I heard only yesterday of a man who had been shot at an important town in the south, caught in the act of attempting to poison the water supply.[1] It was not reported in the papers. We who are dependent on public water supplies throughout the country ought to be on the alert.

> Canon H. D. Rawnsley. *Letter to Manchester Guardian, Aug. 27, 1914.*

[1] A good example of the preposterous rumours afloat at this period.

YOUTH ENVIED

I ENVY you young people your youth. They have put up the age limit for the Army, but I march, I am sorry to say, a good many years even beyond that. But still our turn will come. It is a great opportunity. It only comes once in many centuries to the children of men. For most generations sacrifice comes in drab weariness of spirit to men. It has come to-day to you ; it has come to-day to us all, in the form of the glory and thrill of a great movement for liberty, that impels millions throughout Europe to the same end. It is a great war for the emancipation of Europe from the thraldom of a military caste, which has cast its shadow upon two generations of men, and which has now plunged the world into a welter of bloodshed. Some have already given their lives. There are some who have given more than their own lives. They have given the lives of those who are dear to them. I honour their courage, and may God be their comfort and their strength.

> The Rt. Hon. David Lloyd George. *In the Queen's Hall, Sept., 1914.*

TO THE ELDERS

O YOUNG men that shed your blood with so generous a joy for the starving earth ! O heroism of the world ! What a harvest of destruction to reap under this splendid summer

sun ! Young men of all nations, brought into conflict by
a common ideal, making enemies of those who should be
brothers ; all of you, marching to your death, are dear
to me. Slavs, hastening to the aid of your race ; Englishmen fighting for honour and right ; intrepid Belgians who
dared to oppose the Teutonic colossus, and defend against
him the Thermopylae of the West ; Germans fighting to
defend the philosophy and the birthplace of Kant against
the Cossack avalanche. . . .

You are doing your duty, but have others done theirs ?
Let us be bold and proclaim the truth to the elders of these
young men, to their moral guides, to their religious and
secular leaders, to the Churches, the great thinkers, the
leaders of socialism ; these living riches, these treasures of
heroism you held in your hands ; for what are you
squandering them ? What ideal have you held up to the
devotion of these youths so eager to sacrifice themselves ?
Their mutual slaughter ! A European war ! A sacrilegious
conflict which shows a maddened Europe ascending its
funeral pyre, and, like Hercules, destroying itself with its
own hands !

> Romain Rolland. *Au-dessus de la Mêlée,*
> *Sept. 15, 1914. Tr. E. K. Bennett. (Above*
> *the Battle, 1916.)*

SON TO MOTHER

THEN I want to write to you about something else, which,
judging from bits in your letters, you haven't quite understood : why I should have volunteered for the war ? Of
course it was not because of any enthusiasm for war in
general, nor because I thought it would be a fine thing to
kill a great many people or otherwise distinguish myself.
On the contrary, I think that war is a very, very evil thing,
and I believe that even in this case it might have been
averted by a more skilful diplomacy. But, now that it has
been declared, I think it is a matter of course that one
should feel oneself so much a member of the nation that

one must unite one's fate as closely as possible with that
of the whole. . . .

This war seems to me, from all that I have heard, to
be something so horrible, inhuman, mad, obsolete and in
every way depraving, that I have firmly resolved, if I do
come back, to prevent such a thing from ever happening
in the future.

Franz Blumenfeld. *Sept. 23, 1914.*
German Students' War Letters. Tr.
A. F. Wedd, 1929.

FROM A SPECIAL CORRESPONDENT

I HAVE seen not a few of the wounded from the battlefields.
After talking to the soldiers who have come to Glasgow
to be nursed in Stobhill Hospital, vivid impressions have
been imprinted on my memory by the passionate declama-
tions of those brave men who have been helping to keep
the " Huns " at bay.

Many of them were emphatic as to the " brutality of
the German hogs." The Highlanders especially seemed
deeply incensed by the treachery and barbarism of the
enemy. They are handing over this legacy of righteous
hatred to the men who are taking their places in the
firing-line.

Every new man is told how the Germans have funked
the fair fight, how they have tied women to their artillery
and thus advanced because they knew the British would
not fire. They have been warned, too, about the frequent
appearance of the white flag—the flag which they say is
unfurled over hidden trenches of hand machine-guns.

The Sunday Chronicle, Sept. 27, 1914.

THE AGONY COLUMN

To Clergy. Sermons supplied each week. New, fresh,
simple, and drawing lessons from the present war. Send
for list and specimen, sixpence.—Page St., Westminster.

Will any one contribute £5 per week to help keep wife and family while I go to kill some Germans ? Otherwise impossible. I am a crack shot and good horseman.— Box F. 832.

The Times, Oct. 6, 1914.

VISION

AN amazing story of a night vision is published here [Petrograd]. It is in a letter sent by a Russian general with the army operating in East Prussia.

"While our troops were in the region of Suwalki," writes the general, " the captain of one of my regiments witnessed a marvellous revelation. It was 11 o'clock at night and the troops were in bivouac. Suddenly a soldier from one of our outposts rushed in and called out the captain. The latter went with the soldier to the outskirts of the camp and witnessed an amazing apparition in the sky. It was that of the Virgin Mary with the infant Christ on one arm. The other arm pointed to the west. All the soldiers knelt on the ground, and gazed fervently at the vision. After a time the vision faded away, and in its stead came a great image of the Cross shining against the dark sky. Slowly it faded away."

The Star, Oct. 9, 1914.

THE GERMAN PROFESSOR

RESENTING the action of the Aberystwyth College authorities in bringing back Dr. Ethé, the German professor, hundreds of people held a meeting of protest yesterday. A huge red ensign marked the meeting-place.

A remark by one of the councillors that " they did not want any of their enemies in Aberystwyth " was followed by Dr. Harries, an ex-mayor, advising the meeting " to give all enemies twenty-four hours' notice to quit." A procession was formed and a visit paid to the house of Dr. Ethé.

The crowd swarmed through the garden to the door, planted the red ensign on the step, and gave their message. Professor Marshall, who had arrived, made a comment on the conduct of the crowd and was roughly handled.

The crowd later marched to the house of Dr. Schott, who claims to be of British birth. The notice to quit was delivered. A visit was then paid to hotels in search of German waiters, and afterwards to local barbers and a pawnbroker.

Dr. Ethé has left the town and other Germans have promised to go at once.

The Daily Mail, Oct. 15, 1914.

"The pension paid Professor Ethé by the governors of Aberystwyth College produced strong protests at the meeting of the Aberystwyth Council. . . . Professor Edward Edwards made an appeal to the ' good sense and sporting instincts ' of the members not to persist in their refusal. Dr. Ethé, he said, had for years paid part of his salary into the pension scheme, and there was a legal obligation on the part of the college to pay him. . . . Councillor H—— said he did not know what to think of a man who came to the council to advocate consideration for a dirty Hun, and Alderman —— said the professors at the college did not live in the same sphere as the average man, and had got into the habit of treating ordinary mortals of the town with contempt."— *Western Mail,* May 10, 1916.

UTTERED IN VAIN

As soon as we were able from the height of Apostolic dignity to survey at a glance the course of human affairs, our eyes were met by the sad condition of human society, and we could not but be filled with bitter sorrow. For what could prevent the soul of the common Father of all being most deeply distressed by the spectacle presented by Europe, nay, by the whole world, perhaps the saddest and most mournful spectacle of which there is any record ? . . .

Moved by these great evils, we thought it our duty, at the very outset of our Supreme Pontificate, to recall the last words of our Predecessor, of illustrious and holy memory, and by repeating them once more, to begin our own Apostolic Ministry ; and we implored kings and rulers

to consider the floods of tears and of blood already poured
out, and to hasten to restore to the nations the blessings of
peace. . . . We implore those in whose hands are placed
the fortunes of nations to hearken to our voice. Surely
there are other ways and means whereby violated rights
can be rectified. Let them be tried honestly and with good
will, and let arms meanwhile be laid aside. It is impelled
with love of them and of all mankind, without any personal interest whatever, that we utter these words. Let
them not allow these words of a friend and a father to be
uttered in vain. . . .

> Benedict XV. *Encyclical Letter,*
> " *Ad Beatissimi,*" *Nov. 1, 1914.*

" *IT IS TRUE ALSO* "

IF any British worker wishes to realise for himself the
unscrupulous ferocity of the war-drunken people of Germany, let him read the German books and the German
papers. It is not only that the German soldiery have
mutilated children, outraged and tortured women, and
murdered wounded or aged men : it is not only that
German airmen have dropped bombs upon the streets of
Ostend and Antwerp and Paris : it is not only that the
Kaiser's ruffians have ravaged and ruined a neutral
country ; but it is true also that the great mass of women
and men in Germany are half mad with eagerness to set
fire to the streets of London and to murder wholesale
unarmed English women and children and men.

> Robert Blatchford. *The Clarion,*
> *Nov. 20, 1914.*

A DIFFERENT TALE

UP till a few weeks back, besides the facts of advance or
retreat, there was little news to read except instances of
German barbarity, such as the sack of Louvain, or stories
of German soldiers running because they disliked British

" cold steel." . . . About the courage of the German troops, our own soldiers have told a different tale. Line by line they have advanced in the dense formations which were part of the German accepted tactics, and again and again they have come forward without shrinking to almost certain death.

> A. H. D. Steel-Maitland, M.P. *Germany*
> *and England, Dec., 1914.* (*Printed in*
> *War and the Citizen, 1917.*)

FRATERNISATION

" FRENCH and German soldiers who had fraternised between the trenches at Christmas subsequently refused to fire on one another and had to be removed and replaced by other men." Amid the vast stream of war news which nowadays flows all over our newspapers I chanced to find that little paragraph in a corner of a halfpenny evening journal. It seems to me the most important item of news that I have read since the war began.

" Patriotism " and " war " are not human facts. They are merely abstractions ; they belong to the sphere of metaphysics, just as much as those ancient theological conceptions of Godhead and the Trinity, with their minute variations, for the sake of which once Catholics and Arians so gladly slew and tortured each other. But as soon as the sunshine of real humanity makes itself felt the metaphysics of patriotism and war are dissipated as surely as those of theology. When you have reckoned that your enemy is not an abstraction but a human being, as real a human being as you are yourself, why want to kill him any more than you want to kill yourself ? Patriotism and war are seen for what they are, insubstantial figments of fancy which it is absurd to materialise and seriously accept.

> Havelock Ellis. *Impressions and*
> *Comments, Jan. 9, 1915.* (*Published*
> *1921.*)

AN ATROCITY STORY

IN its issue of yesterday the *Labour Leader* published copies of letters which have passed between its editor and the Hon. E. Lyttelton, Headmaster of Eton, with respect to an article by Dr. Lyttelton in the January number of the *Hibbert Journal*, beginning with the sentence, "A friend writes from Devonshire that in his village is a Belgian child with her two hands cut off." In response to a request for further particulars of the atrocity, Dr. Lyttelton writes :

"Dear Sir,—I made a statement, as you see, on the authority of a friend, but since the article was written I find that the report cannot be substantiated. Another one from quite a different quarter has also broken down. I am writing to the *Hibbert Journal* to contradict the statement. I should be glad if you would do so in your journal."

The Daily News, Jan. 29, 1915.

An Anthology of Atrocities (real and invented) would be easy to compile, though it would make dull reading. There is a sameness about atrocities. The most novel is credited to the Spanish General Morillo, who at Santa Fé in 1816 had "all the females who were accomplished in literature, of whom there were many," hanged or shot. The commonest, according to written record, is "tossing the baby" on spear, pike or bayonet. In October, 1937 (says Mr. Carleton Beals, *Current History*, January, 1938), they were at it in Santo Domingo—"tossing babies on bayonets, clubbing women to death, and jabbing men with three-pronged daggers." One who has handled a rifle with fixed bayonet, and a baby, inclines to the opinion that baby-tossing is too skilled and arduous a sport ever to have been really popular with tired soldiers.

UNIMAGINABLE

MOST Englishmen have inferred—often in spite of strong pacific bias—that an evil and a peril so great can only be met by counter-violence, and that a terrible necessity has put a stop for the time to any attempt to conform to the moral ideal of peace. The assumption is so natural, and is made with such sincerity, and in countless instances is

supported with such generous heroism, that no pacifist
who refuses to make it can withhold his sympathy from
a great many of its adherents.

Why then do we not all make it ?

With the Christian who still stands by the testimony of
non-resistance, the fundamental matter is that the law,
example and spirit of our Lord Jesus Christ absolutely
forbids him to make such an assumption. . . .

I hold that Christ's recorded words are quite conclusive
as to His will ; but I do not press the point. I am content
to say that I cannot imagine Christ . . . ambushing a party
of German conscripts and turning a machine-gun on them.
Neither can I imagine Christ rushing upon a German lad,
who runs shrieking for his life . . . and plunging His
bayonet into the lad's back until the point comes out at
his breast.

> W. Blair Neatby. *The Christian
> and War, March, 1915.*

AN ABSURDITY AS WELL AS A CRIME

When this war ends, probably every nation in Europe will
feel such an intense weariness of the struggle that no great
war will be probable for another generation. The problem
is, so to alter men's standards and outlook that, when the
weariness has passed away, they shall not fall back into
the old bad way, but shall escape from the nightmare into
a happier world of free co-operation.

The first thing to make men realise is that modern war
is an absurdity as well as a crime, and that it can no longer
secure such national advantages as, for example, England
secured by the Seven Years' War. After the present war,
it should be easy to persuade even the most ignorant and
high-placed persons of this truth.

But it is even more necessary to alter men's conceptions
of " glory " and " patriotism." . . . If a better and saner

world is to grow out of the horror of futile carnage, men must learn to find their nation's glory in the victory of reason over brute instincts, and to feel the true patriotism which demands that our country should deserve admiration rather than extort fear. . . . If the statesmen will play their part, by showing that war is not inevitable, there is hope that our children may live in a happier world, and look back upon us with the wondering pity of a wiser age.[1]

> Bertrand Russell. *Is a Permanent Peace Possible? Atlantic Monthly, March, 1915.*

[1] "If I were a betting man and were laying a bet, I should think the odds in favour of a big war within the next ten years about 3 to 1. If not in the next ten years, sooner or later, I am afraid there will be a war. I think it will go on until Western Europe is reduced to chaos. Industrialism and ordinary government would disappear. The countryside would be full of marauding gangs of disbanded soldiers who would turn into bandits. All sanitary services would have gone to pieces. There would be widespread starvation."—Bertrand Russell, in an interview, *The Star*, March 24, 1938.

A FEW BARS OF MUSIC

THERE is a region where words stumble after truth, like children chasing a rainbow across a meadow to find the pot of fairy gold. Multitudinous volumes stuffed with the cant of pacifism and militarism will never explain to us the nature of peace and war. But a few bars of music may sometimes make clear things which all the moralists, and divines, and philosophers—even the poets themselves for the most part, though they come nearer to it at times than the rest—have struggled vainly to show us in their true proportions. The songs of a nation, its national anthems —if they be truly national and not merely some commissioned[1] exercise—are better interpreters than State papers. A man will learn more of the causes of wars, perhaps even of the rights and wrongs of them, by listening to the burst and fall of the French hymn, the ebb and surge of the Russian, in Tschaikovsky's famous overture, than he ever will from books or speeches, argument or oratory.

> F. S. Oliver. *Ordeal by Battle.*
> *June, 1915.*

[1] An uncommissioned exercise appeared in *The Times* of Sept. 14, 1914. "A correspondent, 'A.C.A.' whose initials recall the schooldays of a good many officers in His Majesty's Forces, sends us the following marching songs to old tunes, written, as he says, in the simplest words possible, and such as a private soldier might think and write for himself." No. 6, to be sung to the air of "Here's to the Maiden," contained the following verse:

> Here's to Lord Kitchener, brown with the sun,
> Gentle, persuasive, and balmy,
> Giving his orders and getting them done,
> All that he wants for the Army —
> Give him a shout,
> Lengthen it out,
> Tell friends and enemies what we're about.

A COLOSSAL SANITARY JOB

" THE once decent thing "(said Boon) " that we men who sit at home in the warm can do is to dwell on the horrors and do our little best to make sure that never, never shall this happen again. And that won't be done, Wilkins, by leaving War alone. War, war with modern machines is a damned great horrible trampling monster, a filthy thing, an indecency ; we aren't doing anything heroic, we are trying to lift a foul stupidity off the earth, we are engaged in a colossal sanitary job. These men who go for us into the trenches, they come back with no illusions. They know how dirty and monstrous it is. They are like men who have gone down for the sake of the people they love to clear out a choked drain. They have no illusions about being glorified. They only hope they aren't blood-poisoned and their bodies altogether ruined. And as for the bracing stir of it, they tell me, Wilkins, that their favourite song now in the trenches is :

Nobody knows how bored we are,
Bored we are,
Bored we are,
Nobody knows how bored we are,
And nobody seems to care.

Meanwhile you sit at home and feel vicariously ennobled."

Reginald Bliss (H. G. Wells).
Boon, 1915.

"Whether the phrase ' the war to end war' was my contribution to
the world or not, I cannot now remember. My mistake was in attributing
any common sense to mankind. To-day the huge majority of people in
the world think no more about the prevention of war than a warren of
rabbits thinks about the suppression of shot guns and ferrets. They just
don't want to be bothered about it. It is amazing how they accept the
things that will presently slaughter them."—H. G. Wells, *The Way the
World is Going*, Oct. 2, 1927.

UNCONTROLLED EXPLOSIONS

AT University College on Thursday Professor Morgan
continued his series of lectures on " Five Months with the
British Expeditionary Force." Speaking of the swearing
in which men indulge when going into action, he said it
was one of the effects of uncontrolled explosions of nerve
force which must occur in periods of tense excitement,
operating in this case on the vocal organs.

There was no impiety in such profanity, as it was wholly
subconscious, and in most cases the men would be most
surprised to learn that they had uttered so much as an
exclamation during the time.

Sunday Times, June 20, 1915.

"Our armies swore terribly in Flanders," cried my Uncle Toby—
"but nothing to this."—Laurence Sterne, *Tristram Shandy.*

TRENCH DIALOGUE

" If on this theme I think aright,
    There are five reasons why we fight :
    Because it's wet, because it's dry,
    And any other reason why."

" Go easy, soldier, don't get sore.
    Remember what we're fighting *for*."

" For little Belgium, for the King,
    For this and that and t'other thing . . .
    All very sound, all very fine !
    But somehow no concern of mine.
    Besides, this show is not as billed :
    We do not fight—we just get killed.
    Before I clap my eyes on Fritz
    The odds are I'll be blown to bits."

" Before he catches sight of you
    The odds are he'll be catsmeat too."

" O grave, where is thy victory ?
    What bloody fools we mortals be ! "

                                        Anon, *1915*.

KILLING AND DYING

THE peculiar twofold effect of war manifests itself in another manner. At the first glance there seem to be two characteristics distinguishing war : we are determined to kill and we are ready to die. The readiness to sacrifice their lives for an idea is considered by almost all human beings as an act denoting moral superiority. . . . On the other hand, readiness to kill another has always been considered to denote moral degradation. Thus it might be thought that there is a case of superiority and inferiority pitted against each other, and that it is to some extent left to the individual to choose whether he will bring out the good or the bad side of war the more strongly ; indeed, that it perhaps depends only upon the personality of the individual soldier whether war has a morally invigorating or a brutalising effect upon him.

In practice this twofold possibility has never been lost sight of, and even now we can read in almost every newspaper in every European country that our soldiers to-day are a " band of heroes uplifted by war," and those of the enemy " a rabble of war-brutalised soldiery." Putting such thoughtless comparisons aside, we might still think there is something genuinely good in war. We must reject such considerations, however, for the one thing characteristic of war is the desire to kill. *Only in war* may we kill our fellow mortals unpunished. . . . Man may sacrifice himself, however, for the utmost possible diversity of objects. Christ sacrificed Himself for mankind, Lucretia herself for her honour, Winkelried himself for the deliverance of his country, Thelka herself for love's sake. Doctors sacrifice themselves for the sake of investigating the plague, mothers for their children, children for their parents, and " noble characters " in general for their fellow-men. In short, every one in his life has abundant opportunity for self-sacrifice, and there is no need for him to select just that particular method of it which necessitates his first endeavouring to sacrifice as many others as possible.

> G. F. Nicolai. *The Biology of War.*
> *Written 1915-6. Tr. from the German by*
> *Constance and Julian Grande. Published*
> *1919.*

HOLY HATRED AND HOLY LYING

HATRED and lying have become holy ; and no effort is spared to proclaim hatred and contempt as brutally as possible, whether by means of derisive proclamations dropped by airmen (often strongly reminiscent of the

" heroic speeches " of the Trojan war), or by official proclamations. Discerning people may merely smile at these, but by the people they are believed ; and for a long time a great many really did look upon their enemies as contemptible, inferior and divided amongst themselves. . . .

The British army was supposed to be just a pack of riffraff with nothing better to show for themselves than " speed records in running away," and pinning all their faith to stone-throwing Basutos, or Afghans with their clubs. . . .

Then followed a whole series of calumnies, some of them the traditional ones in use from time immemorial, some of them new ones, often absolute inventions, but also sometimes containing a grain of truth, although mostly a quite harmless grain. Probably every war since the thirteenth century has begun with the ever successful attempt to persuade the masses that their wicked enemy has been poisoning wells. . . .

And now for the *gouged-out eyes*. . . . The most careful investigations were instituted, in Germany by Provost Dr. Kaulmann of Aix-la-Chapelle and by an unnamed writer on the staff of the *Vorwärts*. The last-named even offered a reward of fifty kronen for any information as to an authenticated case . . . yet not one . . . was brought to light. . . . Large sections, even of the educated German public, still believe that in Belgium German soldiers had their eyes gouged out.

Again, in Denmark and elsewhere Belgian children are said to have been exhibited whose eyes the Germans were alleged to have gouged out. . . .

The ugly aspect of these calumnies is that on both sides they are *increasing*.

Ibid.

A CERTAIN THEORY

WAR is made—this war has been made—not by any necessity of nature, any law beyond human control, any fate to which men must passively bow ; it is made because

certain men who have immediate power over other men
are possessed by a certain theory. Sometimes they are fully
conscious of this theory. More often, perhaps, it works
in them unconsciously. But it is there, the dominating
influence in international politics. I shall call it the
governmental theory, because it is among governing persons
—emperors, kings, ministers, and their diplomatic and
military advisers—that its influence is most conspicuous
and most disastrous. But it is supported also by historians,
journalists, and publicists, and it is only too readily adopted
by the ordinary man, when he turns from the real things
he knows and habitually handles to consider the unknown
field of foreign affairs. Very briefly, and, therefore, crudely
expressed, the theory is this : " The world is divided,
politically, into States. These States are a kind of abstract
Beings, distinct from the men, women and children who
inhabit them. They are in perpetual and inevitable
antagonism to one another ; and though they may group
themselves in alliances, that can be only for temporary
purposes to meet some other alliance or single Power.
For States are bound by a moral or physical obligation to
expand indefinitely each at the cost of the others. They are
natural enemies, they always have been so, and they always
will be ; and force is the only arbiter between them. That
being so, War is an eternal necessity. As a necessity, it
should be accepted, if not welcomed, by all sound-thinking
and right-feeling men. Pacifists are men at once weak and
dangerous. They deny a fact as fundamental as any of the
facts of the natural world. And their influence, if they have
any, can only be disastrous to their State in its ceaseless and
inevitable contest with other States."

G. Lowes Dickinson. *The
War and the Way Out, 1915.*

A PROPHECY

If, on the other hand, we and our allies should win, the
outlook is no more promising, if the diplomats are to have
their way. We, in that case, shall endeavour finally to

crush the German Powers, as they are determined finally to crush us. . . . In either case, the state of Europe will be the old bad state : the piling up of armaments, at the cost of the continued poverty and degradation of the mass of the people, the destruction of all hope and effort towards radical social reform, and, when the time comes, as in this case it infallibly will, the new war, the new massacre, the new impoverishment, the perpetual and intolerable agony of a civilisation for ever struggling to the light, for ever flung back by its own stupidity and wickedness into the hell in which at this moment it is writhing. Lord, how long, how long ?

Ibid.

GOD AND MR. BOTTOMLEY

TO-DAY, in my fifty-fifth year, and after about as strenuous a life as any man of that age has ever lived—I believe in God. . . . The great World-war has done it. In War there is a mighty alchemy, transmuting the base metal of human experience into the pure currency of Faith. . . .

Many years have come and gone since the death of Christ. The world has marched on. We are nearer the solution of its Mystery than ever we have been before. We are at the Gates, pleading for admission. But before they are opened, there is a final test to pass. The Devil—the Spirit of Evil—is pulling us back, crying, " Stay with me. I, too, am a God—the God of Blood and Iron—of Lust and Rapine—of Sword and Flame. I kill women and children and old men. I mutilate and torture. I destroy cathedrals and churches. I shoot nurses. I torment the wounded. I fire on hospitals. I am the God of Frightfulness, and *my* angels are the Imps of Hell. Stay with *me*." And Germany has said—" We will." In other words, she is not *ready*.

But God is in no hurry. He has many worlds besides this one to attend to. After all, we are but a mere speck in the Solar System—and there are millions of other systems

with billions and trillions of other worlds composing them.
So He leaves it to us to fight it out—according to our own
inclinations. But He makes it manifest that when *we* are
ready, He is. Nay, that He is waiting for us. And *that* is
the meaning of the war. The nations of the earth are sorting
themselves out. In the old words, some will be chosen and
others will be left. It is for the Anglo-Saxon race to see
that it is chosen.

Horatio Bottomley.[1] *In the*
Sunday Pictorial, Oct. 24, 1915.

[1] The late Horatio Bottomley was a popular patriot. His weekly
newspaper articles (invariably described in advance as "powerful")
heartened the civil population at this period, and his well-attended public
lectures were profitable to him. His financial character, however, was
not spotless, and after the war he languished in gaol.

LARGER VISION

OFTEN when warring for he wist not what,
An enemy-soldier, passing by one weak,
Has tendered water, wiped the burning cheek,
And cooled the lips so black and clammed and hot ;

Then gone his way, and maybe quite forgot
The deed of grace amid the roar and reek ;
Yet larger vision than loud arms bespeak
He there has reached, although he has known it not.

For natural mindsight, triumphing on the act
Over the throes of artificial rage,
Has thuswise muffled victory's peal of pride,
Rended to ribands policy's specious page
That deals but with evasion, code, and pact,
And war's apology wholly stultified.

Thomas Hardy. *Often when Warring,*
(Moments of Vision.) 1915.

CONFINED TO CLERGY

THE Bishop of London[1] conducted a remarkable inter-cession service attended by a great part of the clergy of London, at St. Martin-in-the-Fields, yesterday. The object of the service, to use the Bishop's own words, was " to wait upon God and to ask what is the meaning of the awful chastisement which has happened to the world, and especially where our own nation is concerned." The service was confined to clergy, none of the general public being admitted.

A similar gathering of the clergy of the diocese of Worcester was held recently, and the Bishop said on Sunday that " the answer that came to those 500 praying men was that all this happened because the world had forgotten the majesty of God."

Manchester Guardian, Nov. 24, 1915.

[1] "The Bishop of London photographed in khaki with determined but Christian expression."—*Quoth the Raven, An Unofficial History of the War.* E. V. L. and G. M., 1919.

SUFFICIENT FOR THE CATHOLIC

THE Sermon on the Mount contains the summary of Christ's ethical teaching and therein nothing is more prominently taught than love for enemies, pardon for offences, submission to injury, the abandonment of rights whether of persons or property. A special series of bene-dictions is invoked on those who embrace this course of conduct. But war is essentially insistence on rights, exaction of reparation, resentment against ill-treatment. War is therefore unchristian.

To this the general reply, sufficient for the Catholic who knows that the Church is his appointed infallible guide in morals as well as in faith, is that war cannot be unchristian because, if it were, the Church would have grievously and permanently erred in a capital point of morality.

The Rev. J. Keating, S.J. *Morality and War. A Primer of Peace and War, 1915.*

BRINGING IT HOME

ALMIGHTY GOD does not want war ; on the contrary He
has set up on earth a means of perpetuating with clearness,
certainty and force amongst the changing generations, the
principles of Christianity, the perfect observance of which
would render war impossible and unthinkable. But He
permits this terrible scourge, as He permits other consequences of sin and of the rejection of revealed truth, to
bring home to His erring children the folly of abandoning
His plans and disobeying Him. Men have the power,
denied to brutes, of living by reason and law ; if they
choose to live by passion and instinct they cannot wonder
that they fall into brute conditions. International relations
have to be lifted into the region of reason and justice if
civilisation is to be preserved.

Ibid.

A STRINGENT MORAL PRECEPT

IT is important to remember that we have the duty of
loving our enemies *even during the time of war*, at all events,
negatively. We must on no account treat them unjustly
in thought, word or deed. This is a stringent moral
precept, but one which is too often thrown to the winds
during conflicts between States. Few things are more
deplorable than the torrent of hatred fostered by a considerable section of the Press in all countries on such
occasions.

Charles Plater, S.J., M.A.
A Primer of Peace and War, 1915.

DEEP-LYING UNITY

NOR need the precept of charity make us hesitate to pray
for the material success of our arms in a just cause. That
such prayers should be offered by both sides need cause no

perplexity, and shows no lack of true religious feeling. On the contrary, both parties supposing their cause to be just, the conflict of prayer really points to a deep-lying unity, an allegiance to what is right, which is the best guarantee of future peace when misunderstandings have been cleared away. But since men are apt to be prejudiced in judging their cause to be just, the best thing is for both sides to pray for *what God sees to be a just peace.*

Ibid.

" UPON THIS WE ARE ALL AGREED "

WHEN history pronounces judgment on the guilt for this most horrible of all wars and its duration, it will disclose the terrible mischief caused by ignorance and hypocrisy. As long as the evasion of their guilt and ignorance is maintained by foreign rulers and their mentality governs enemy nations, any offer of peace from our side would be a folly which would prolong the war. All disguises must first be dropped. . . .

The war can only be terminated with a peace which, according to human judgment, offers us security against its repetition. Upon this we are all agreed. This is our strength and will continue to be so.

Herr von Bethmann-Hollweg.
In the Reichstag, Dec., 1915.

FIGURES TO DATE

THE Prime Minister, in a written answer to Mr. Molteno, gives the following particulars of the total British casualties in all fields of operations up to January 9 :

France	400,510
Dardenelles	117,549
Other Theatres	31,408
Total	549,467

January 29, 1916.

A NEW PERSPECTIVE

OPINIONS differ on the subject, but I have come back from France convinced that there is more direct evidence of true religion in the army than out of it at present, and in France than England. Men who have been looking death in the eyes as closely as our soldiers have in all these terrible months cannot fail to obtain a new perspective upon life. . . . The Church will, in my judgment, have a greater spiritual opportunity after the war than she has had for generations ; will she be worthy of it ?

The Rev. R. J. Campbell, D.D.[1] *Visits to our Troops in France, Feb., 1916.*
(In *War and the Citizen, 1917.*)

[1] Now a Canon. As a journalist his only serious rival was Horatio Bottomley. It has been suggested that this competition was responsible for Bottomley's conversion. (See p. 396.) The reverend gentleman contributed a weekly article ("another splendid message to the nation") to the *Illustrated Sunday Herald.* "Deep down in every one of us is the urge to give ourselves as fully as possible at the bidding of the ineffable somewhat that we feel has the right to require the sacrifice."—From an advertisement of a forthcoming article, "Why We Envy Our Glorious Dead," Nov. 5, 1915.

FIRST BRITISH CONSCRIPTS

THE Proclamation calling up the first classes of British conscripts was circulated yesterday throughout the kingdom. Forty thousand are to be posted in the London district alone.

Daily News, Feb. 10, 1916.

"This committee [The National Committee of the No-Conscription Fellowship] was prosecuted in May, 1916, for the publication of a leaflet, *Repeal the Act. . . .* Each member was fined £100 in default of two months' imprisonment. . . . It was at this trial that the Crown Prosecutor (Mr. Bodkin) said that *War would become impossible if the view that war was wrong, and that it was wrong to support the carrying on of war, was held generally.* For trying to circulate this statement as a poster a peace propagandist was afterwards heavily fined."—Margaret E. Hirst, *The Quakers in Peace and War,* 1923.

PACIFISM AND CRANKS

ONE of the most natural and obvious consequences of war is a hardening of the boundaries of the social unit and a retraction of the vague feelings towards international sympathy which are a characteristic product of peace and intercommunication. Thus it comes about that pacifism and internationalism are in great disgrace at the present time ; they are regarded as the vapourings of cranky windbags who have inevitably been punctured at the first touch of the sword ; they are, our political philosophers tell us, but products of the miasm of sentimental fallacy which tends to be bred in the relaxing atmosphere of peace.[1] Perhaps no general expressions have been more common since the beginning of the war, in the mouths of those who have undertaken our instruction in the meaning of events, than the propositions that pacifism is now finally exploded and shown always to have been nonsense, that war is and always will be an inevitable necessity in human affairs as man is what is called a fighting animal, and that not only is the abolition of war an impossibility, but should the abolition of it unhappily prove to be possible after all and be accomplished, the result could only be degeneration and disaster.

Biological considerations would seem to suggest that these generalisations contain a large element of inexactitude. The doctrine of pacifism is a perfectly natural development, and ultimately inevitable in an animal having an unlimited appetite for experience and an indestructible inheritance of social instinct. Like all moral discoveries made in the haphazard, one-sided way which the lack of co-ordination in human society forces upon its moral pioneers, it has necessarily an appearance of crankiness, of sentimentality, of an inaptitude for the grasp of reality. This is normal and does not in the least affect the value of the truth it contains. Legal and religious torture were doubtless first attacked by cranks ; slavery was abolished by them. Advocacy by such types does not therefore constitute an argument of any weight against their doctrines, which can adequately be judged only by some purely objective standard. Judged by such a standard, pacifism, as we have seen, appears to be a natural development, and is directed towards a goal which unless man's nature undergoes a radical change will probably be attained. That its attainment has so far been foreseen only by a class of men possessing more than the usual impracticability of the minor prophet is hardly to be considered a relevant fact.

W. Trotter. *Instincts of the Herd in Peace and War.* Feb., 1916.

[1]"Peace, like all other virtues, begets its own peculiar counterfeits. The man who really lives on a lower plane than that of every-day fact is able to persuade himself that he moves on a higher plane; and in peace-time we live amid a world of bubbles which nothing short of national disaster can completely explode."—G. G. Coulton, *Pacificist Illusions,* 1915.

BARBED OATS

BARBED oats are the latest instruments of offence invented by Germany. The far-reaching devilishness of the German methods of warfare is illustrated by an order our War Office (says the *Daily Express*) has had to issue to responsible officers in charge of cavalry and other mounted forces. Every bushel of oats now has to be examined carefully before it is used. It has been discovered that some of the sacks of oats purchased in the United States contained little pieces of steel, shaped like oats, and painted yellow. These are barbed, and a horse that swallowed one would have little chance of life. The placing of the barbed oats in the food is no doubt the work of Germans who have obtained employment in American granaries in order to kill our horses at 3,000 miles range.

The Cardiff Express, March 3, 1916.

TRUTHS IN WARTIME

Mr. A. Ponsonby, M.P., quoted the following illustration at a Glasgow meeting on Sunday as to how lies were manufactured by the press. After the fall of Antwerp the *Kölnische Zeitung* published this :

When the fall of Antwerp got known the church bells (in Germany) were rung.

A Paris paper, the *Matin*, altered it thus :

According to the *Kölnische Zeitung* the clergy of Antwerp were compelled to ring the church bells when the fortress was taken.

The London *Times* went one better with this :

According to what the *Matin* has learned from Cologne, the Belgian priests who refused to ring the church bells when Antwerp was taken have been driven away from their places.

An Italian paper, the *Corriera della Sera*, then took a part in the fabrication by stating that :

According to what *The Times* has heard from Cologne *via* Paris, the unfortunate Belgian priests who refused to ring the church bells when Antwerp was taken have been sent to hard labour.

The *Matin*, which began the yarn, concluded it thus :

According to the information of the *Corriera della Sera*, from Cologne, *via* London, it is confirmed that the barbaric conquerors of Antwerp punished the unfortunate Belgian priests for their heroic refusal to ring the church bells by hanging them as living clappers to the bells with their heads down.

The Labour Leader, March 30, 1916.

IF

If after I am dead
On goes the same old game,
  With monarchs seeing red
And ministers aflame,

And nations drowning deep
In quarrels not their own,
And people called to reap
The woes they have not sown . . .
If all we who are slain
Have died, despite our hope,
Only to twist again
The old kaleidoscope—
Why then, by God ! we're sold !
Cheated and wronged ! betrayed !
Our youth and lives and gold
Wasted—the homes we'd made
Shattered—in folly blind,
By treachery and spite,
By cowardice of mind
And little men and light ! . . .
If there be none to build
Out of this ruined world
The temple we have willed
With our flag there unfurled,
If rainbow none there shine
Across these skies of woe,
If seed of yours and mine
Through this same hell must go,
Then may my soul and those
Of all who died in vain
(Be they of friends or foes)
Rise and come back again
From peace that knows no end,
From faith that knows not doubt,
To haunt and sear and rend
The men that sent us out.

Eliot Crawshay-Williams. *From
A Soldier's Testament, 1916.*

IN A QUITE NOVEL DEGREE

THE Archbishop of Canterbury presided over a meeting
at Queen's Hall yesterday in connection with the movement
for the national revival of family prayers. A letter was
read from the Archbishop of York expressing the most
hearty sympathy with the movement. Lord French wrote :
" My experience in this war assures me that the teaching of
religious leaders in this country has already borne good
fruit." The Archbishop of Canterbury said that from what
he had learned and heard on the battle fronts of France
and Flanders he had the impression that in a quite novel
degree, and in a way which a short time ago would have
seemed impossible, men were thinking deeply of the
privileges, the problems, and the mysteries of prayer.

Daily News, June 6, 1916.

The Archbishop of Canterbury was right.

> Though I was windy out in France
> (like all the rest) I took my chance,
> but kept a guard upon my tongue
> when prayers were said or hymns were sung. . . .
>
> Daniel George, *Roughage*, 1935.

THESE GLORIOUS DAYS

" DOES any one suppose that linen drapers' assistants will
return to the shops after the war, content to hand laces to
women ? " asked the Bishop of London at Church House
yesterday. " Of course not ! " said Dr. Ingram. " I hope
we shall see men who have learned to live men's lives in
these glorious days refusing to have anything but a man's
life after the war."

The Cardiff Express, June, 1916.

SHIRKER

A MAN of 24 who sought to evade military service by dressing in a knickerbocker suit, with Eton collar, and posing as a schoolboy, has been fined 40s. at Liverpool and handed over to the military authorities.

The Cardiff Express, June 22, 1916.

THE MAKING OF A CRISIS

WAR between two nations under modern conditions is impossible unless you get a large number of people in each nation excited and afraid. Now, people can only be made excited and afraid in large masses by springing something on them suddenly which they do not altogether understand. War-mongers know this well enough in every country. That is the real objection to secret diplomacy. It enables the war-mongers to work up excitement and fear. They allow it only to be known that a crisis has occurred, " negotiations are proceeding, but a deadlock is feared." Nobody knows what is happening, what the real question is, what the worst is to be feared. " Panic on the Stock Exchange " is the inevitable newspaper placard in our streets—a little straw which shows how the psychological wind must blow in a nation before it can be induced to go to war. Suddenly we are told that the crisis is acute. Into this atmosphere of fear, ignorance, doubt, excitement, a complicated international question is flung to us in the speech of a politician which gives us the minimum of evidence and explanation and the maximum of patriotic and fear-inspiring *clichés*. Naturally, when that point is reached, ninety-nine people out of every hundred will take the lead given by " the people in authority." Peace and war no longer depend upon finding a reasonable settlement in a dispute, but upon whether in some country those in authority do or do not want war.

Leonard Woolf. *International
Government, 1916.*

EFFECT ON THE YOUNG

THE increase in juvenile offences is not peculiar to England.
Judging from reports in German newspapers, the increase
has been much more serious in Germany than here. In
some cases the number of young criminals has increased
fourfold during the war, and very stringent steps have been
taken by the German authorities in the hope of checking
this serious state of affairs.

The causes of the increase in offences are fairly obvious.
First and foremost is the decrease in parental control owing
to the absence of many of the fathers with the forces or at
work at a distance from their homes. Many of the mothers
have failed to control their children, sometimes because
they are occupied in public work, sometimes through
carelessness or giving way to drink. Again, the lack of
teachers has led to want of individual attention, and the
taking over of school buildings for military purposes has
necessitated the shortening of school hours in many places,
with the result that children have had more time than
usual for wandering the streets. . . . Moreover, the war has
caused a certain spirit of adventure to be in the air.
Children hear from their relatives and friends thrilling
accounts of trench warfare and other excitements, and
many of the offences that they have been committing are
really the result of childish imitation. All these are more
or less inevitable results of the war.

G. A. Aitken, M.V.O. *Juvenile
Offences. Oct., 1916. (Printed in
War and the Citizen, 1917.)*

A DENIAL FROM BERLIN

THE English wireless service is spreading the loathsome
and equally ridiculous report that the German authorities
use the bodies of dead soldiers for industrial purposes and
for extracting from them lubricating oils and food for hogs.

The English reports quote as their authority a report published in the *Lokalanzeiger* describing the mill where the carcases are transformed into oil. The German expression used in this report was " Kadaver," which, as everybody conversant with German knows, is never used for human bodies, but only for the carcases of animals. The *Lokalanzeiger*, commenting upon this last performance of anti-German propaganda, calls it the " acme of stupidity."

Manchester Guardian, April 23, 1917.

APPEAL BY THE POPE

TOWARDS the end of the first year of war We addressed to the nations who are at grips the most earnest exhortations, and, further, We indicated the road to be followed in order to reach a peace which would be stable and honourable for all. Unhappily, Our appeal was not heard, and the war continued desperately for another two years, with all its horrors.

It became even more cruel, and spread upon the face of the earth, upon the sea, and even into the sky ; and on defenceless cities, on tranquil villages, on their innocent populations, were seen to descend desolation and death.

And now any one can imagine how the sufferings of all would be multiplied and aggravated if yet more months, or worse still, more years, were to be added to this blood-stained time. Must the civilised world be nothing more than a field of death, and shall Europe, so glorious and flourishing, rush to the abyss, as if dragged by some universal madness, and lend a hand in her own destruction ?

Benedict XV. *To the Leaders of the Belligerent Peoples, Aug. 1, 1917.*

"Several of the replies of Governments will be found in Muller [*Das Friedenswerk der Kirche in den Letzten Drei Jahrhunderten*]. The belligerents in each case restated the familiar vindication of their own cause and the familiar malediction of their adversaries. The Austrian reply was the most favourable, the principal Allied Powers, newly reinforced by the United States, were unyielding."—John Eppstein, *The Catholic Tradition of the Law of Nations*, 1935.

REVEILLE

In the place to which I go,
    Better men than I have died,
Freeman friend and conscript foe,
    Face to face and side by side,
    In the shallow grave abide.

Melinite that seared their brains,
    Gas that slew them in a snare,
War's inferno of strange pains,
    What are these to them who share
    That great boon of silence there ?

When like blood the moon is red,
    And a shadow hides the sun,
We shall wake, the so-long dead,
    We shall know our quarrel done,—
    Will God tell us who has won ?

Ronald Lewis Carton.
Steel and Flowers, 1917.

INDELIBLE MARK

The heroic example set by those who have so gallantly given their lives for King and Country in this greatest of all struggles will leave an indelible mark upon the new generation. It is for those who have the care of the children in their hands and near their hearts to see that the lesson is not thrown away, and that in the New England that will arise when the war is ended, the people shall be ready to use wisely the liberties and privileges that will have been won afresh for them.

The Rt. Hon. Neville Chamberlain, *Director-General of National Service, ex-Lord Mayor of Birmingham.*[1] *Introduction to War and the Citizen, 1917.*

[1] Now Prime Minister of England. Speaking at a National Government Rally at Kettering, on July 2, 1938, he said: "When I think of those

four terrible years and I think of the 7,000,000 of young men who were cut off in their prime, the 13,000,000 who were maimed and mutilated, the misery and the suffering of the mothers and the fathers, the sons and the daughters, and the relatives and the friends of those who were killed, and the wounded, then I am bound to say again what I have said before, and what I say now, not only to you but to all the world—in war, whichever side may call itself the victor, there are no winners, but all are losers."

FIRESTEP CONVERSATION

" EARTH has not anything to show more fair
    (I gather from some poems I have read)
Than the great privilege we soldiers share
    Of fighting for our country till we're dead."—

" If fighting for one's country only meant
    The sort of thing the poets have to say ! . . .
I heard my country calling, and I went :
    I feel my reason urging, and I stay ! "—

" War wouldn't be so bad (though at its best
    It never was the blessing and the boon
That elderly civilians suggest)
    If both sides weren't fed up with it so soon."—

" War lasts too long. It should be bright and brief,
    All over in a month at the outside.
Then soldiers might get killed in the belief
    That they'd done something useful, having died."

Anon. 1917.

A LIGHT

ALREADY I have comprehended a light which never will filter into the dogma of any national church : namely, that one of Christ's essential commands was : Passivity at any price ! Suffer dishonour and disgrace, but never resort to arms. Be bullied, be outraged, be killed ; but do not kill. It may be a chimerical and an ignominious principle, but there it is. It can only be ignored ; and I think pulpit professionals are ignoring it very skilfully and successfully indeed.

> Wilfred Owen. *Letter, June, 1917.*
> *Qt. in Memoir prefixed to The Poems*
> *of Wilfred Owen.   Ed. Edmund*
> *Blunden, 1931.*

THE LANSDOWNE LETTER

We are now in the fourth year of the most dreadful war the world has ever known, a war in which, as Sir W. Robertson has recently informed us, the killed alone can be counted by the million, while the total number of men engaged amounts to nearly 24 millions. Ministers continue to tell us that they scan the horizon in vain for the prospect of a lasting peace. And without a lasting peace we all feel that the task we have set ourselves will remain unaccomplished.

But those who look forward with horror to the prolongation of the War, who believe that its wanton prolongation would be a crime, differing only in degree from that of the criminals who provoked it, may be excused if they, too, scan the horizon anxiously in the hope of discovering there indications that the outlook may, after all, not be so hopeless as is supposed. . . .

Some of the Allied claims for territory will probably become unattainable. Others, again, notably the reparation due to Belgium, remain, and must always remain, in the front rank : but when it comes to the wholesale rearrangement of the map of South-Eastern Europe, we may well ask for a suspension of judgment, and for the elucidation which a frank exchange of view between the Allied Powers can alone be judged. . . .

> Lord Lansdowne.   *Letter in*
> *Daily Telegraph, Nov. 29, 1917.*

"The publication of this letter encouraged thousands of people who had been longing and praying for some honourable way of ending the frightful slaughter. . . . At the same time there poured forth, as might have been expected, a flood of invective and an incredible mass of abusive correspondence, which, though largely incoherent, was marked by a violence rare in English political life. In fact, the abuse could not have been stronger had the writer been an open traitor. . . ."—Lord Newton, *Lord Lansdowne*, 1929.

WAR WEARY

It must be so—it's wrong to doubt—
The voluntary system's best.
Your conscript, when you've dragged him out,
Has not the Happy Warrior's zest.

Because it seemed the thing to do,
I flocked with other volunteers,
But—well, I don't mind telling you
I didn't bargain for three years.

Though we obeyed the Higher Law,
And though we have our quarrel just,
Were I permitted to withdraw
You wouldn't see my arse for dust.

Anon. *1917.*

FOOD HOARDING

Miss Marie Corelli, the novelist, was fined £50 at Stratford-on-Avon to-day for acquiring food in excess of ordinary requirements. The prosecution alleged that the offences occurred during September and November. The household consisted of seven persons, and was entitled to receive 32 lb. of sugar. Counsel said he was instructed that she obtained 183 lb. of sugar, independent of preserving sugar to which she was entitled. . . . A police constable alleged that during one month 83 lb. of sugar and 43 lb. of tea had been signed for by the butler. . . .

Manchester Evening Chronicle,
Jan. 1, 1918.

"The King's appeal to his people for a two minutes' silence in honour of the Victorious Dead on the anniversary of the Armistice will rank

in future ages as the most notable incident in the history of the war. In the midst of the selfish greed, ingratitude, recklessness, frivolity and extravagance of the time the voice of the noblest monarch in the world strikes clear with something of a grand reproach in its tenderness, etc."
—Miss Marie Corelli in the *Daily News*, Nov. 12, 1919.

FOUR QUOTATIONS

"THE act is in God's hands, as is our whole struggle. He will decide on it and we will leave it to Him. We must not argue with His ordering."

" We owe it to those who have given themselves in the holy cause to endure to the end and to abstain from grumbling, pessimism and carping criticism, taking as our watchword, ' Shall not the Judge of all the earth do right ? ' "

" Because the cause in which we are fighting is the cause of right we may fearlessly ask God to pardon our faults and to bless our efforts."

" We stand firm, faithful to our task and to the fulfilment of our duty. There is no doubt on which side lies the right ; therefore this conflict has become a holy conflict."

Two [of these quotations] are from the Kaiser's speeches. Two are from Captain the Rev. Frederick Guest's *Hints to Clergy and Ministers* for their sermons next Sunday, issued on behalf of the National War Aims Committee.

Daily News, June 4, 1918.

THE ARMISTICE

THUS, Mr. Speaker, at 11 o'clock this morning came to an end the cruellest and most terrible war that has ever scourged mankind. I hope we may say that thus this fateful morning came to an end all wars.

David Lloyd George.

As the Prime Minister has said, there is nothing we can do under conditions so unexampled than for the House to acknowledge our gratitude to Almighty God. (Subdued cheers.)

H. H. Asquith.

My Fellow Countrymen : The armistice was signed this morning. Everything for which America fought has been accomplished. It will now be our fortunate duty to assist by example, by sober, friendly counsel, and by material aid in the establishment of just democracy throughout the world.

Woodrow Wilson, Nov. 11, 1918.

CELEBRATIONS

On November 11th they said, " We are so happy ! We will show it and romp." They did, and were happier still. On November 12th they said, " We were so happy last night ! We must romp again." They made gestures more violent, lit fires, knocked hats off and charged each other in the streets. Were they happy ? Perhaps. But I know I came between two men, facing each other, with the sulky semi-consciousness of bulls in their eyes, and with split lips and dripping noses. On November 13th they said, " We must pump up jollity to the last dregs of all." They rushed about, dragging cannon to batter in doors of hotels, tore clothes off the backs of women, and tied one, it is said, to a lamp-post and danced round her. I deduce that they were not so happy.

Desmond MacCarthy. Written
November, 1918. (Experience, 1935.)

APPROXIMATE RESULT

Mr. Macpherson (Under-Secretary for War) stated, in reply to Mr. R. Runciman (L. Cleveland), that the military casualties in the Expeditionary Forces in the different theatres of war were necessarily incomplete, and he was afraid that some time would elapse before the exact figures could be given. But up to November 10, 1918,

the figures, including the Dominion and Indian troops, in
the various theatres of operation were as follows :

Total Casualties . 3,049,971	
Officers (killed, wounded, and missing) ..	142,614
Men	2,907,357

Manchester Guardian, Nov. 20, 1918.

"It is generally supposed that the total military and naval deaths
amount to between ten and thirteen millions. One authority reckons
as follows: Known deaths, 10,004,771; presumed deaths, 2,991,800 ;
total, 12,996,571."—C. R. M. F. Cruttwell, *A History of the Great War*, 1934.

OUT OF THESE RUINS

In spite of the vast material destruction, in spite of the
blotting out from the book of life of practically one whole
generation of men, in spite of the unmeasured misery
which has reigned and reigns still over the greater part
of Europe, in spite of the gigantic difficulties of the task
before us ; in spite of the great war-harvest of evil and the
exhaustion of brain and spirit in most of the victorious
nations as well as in the vanquished, our war has ended
right ; and we have such an opportunity as no generation
of mankind has ever had of building out of these ruins a
better international life and concomitantly a better life
within each nation. I know not which thought is the more
solemn, the more awful in its responsibility : the thought
of the sacrifice we survivors have asked or exacted from our
fellow-men ; or the thought of the task that now lies upon
us if we are not to make that sacrifice a crime and a mockery.

Gilbert Murray.
Creighton Lecture, Nov., 1918.

ARMAGEDDON AND AFTER

We fought at Armageddon for the freedom of the world !
   I fought, and you fought, and here our bones lie mixed.
By the master-hands which held us, eastward and westward
   hurled

We were shattered, we fell down, for the place and time
  were fixed. . . .

Millions we marched ; and the rattle of the drums
  Drowned the rattle of our chains, and the shouting held
    our ranks.
For sweet to our ears was " The conquering hero
    comes,"
  And sweet to our hearts " A grateful Country's
    thanks. . . ."

We fought at Armageddon for the freedom of mankind :
  I fought, and you fought, and here our bones lie
    strewn.
The flesh is stript from off us, the chains remain behind,
  And the Freedom that we fought for is an unremembered
    tune.

                                    Laurence Housman.
                                  The Heart of Peace, 1918.

THE SENSE OF RECTITUDE

In the war of 1914-1918 each of the belligerents was
animated by a passion of certainty that its participation
was unavoidable and its purpose good and noble ; each
side defended its cause with arguments perfectly convincing
and unanswerable to itself and wholly without effect on the
enemy. Such passion, such certitude, such impenetrability
were obviously products of something other than reason,
and do not in themselves give us any information as to the
objective realities of the distribution of justice between the
two sides. The sense of rectitude is in fact and manifestly
a product of mere belligerency, and one which a nation
may confidently expect to possess, no matter how nefarious
its objects may ultimately appear to be in the eyes of
general justice. The fact that such a sense of rectitude is a
universal and inevitable accompaniment of war, and as

                                                    o

strong in a predatory and criminal belligerent as in a generally pacific one, gives us a convenient measure of the extent to which prejudice must prevail in warfare.

> W. Trotter. *Instincts of the Herd : Postscript of 1919.*

THE PROCESS OF SUBLIMATION

WE can see the line along which war must eventually disappear even without any active human interference. Its two causes are already decaying. The excessive birth-rate is falling, and necessarily falls with every rise in culture. Excessive industrialism has likewise passed its climax ; there is no more world left to fight for ; and with the regularisation of industrial and commercial activities, or the whole material side of life, the economic cause of war falls away, and the energy thus released is free for sub-limation into other and possibly more exalted forms of human activity.

Whether we are to-day approaching the first great step in this process of sublimation is still open to doubt. War is so young in the world, its fascination remains so strong, and Man, though he seems so delicate, has proved so tough, and so remarkably impervious to facts. When, indeed, we contemplate Man in the spirit in which the author of *Job* contemplated Behemoth, the Hippopotamus, we may well exclaim in wondering awe :

He is chief of the ways of God :
And who can measure the thickness of his skull ?

> Havelock Ellis. *The Origin of War : The Philosophy of Conflict, 1919.*

PEACE TREATY

I

THROUGH the door at the end appear two huissiers with silver chains. They march in single file. After them come four officers of France, Great Britain, America and Italy.

And then, isolated and pitiable, come the two German delegates, Dr. Muller, Dr. Bell. The silence is terrifying. Their feet upon a strip of parquet between the savonnerie carpets echo hollow and duplicate. They keep their eyes fixed away from those two thousand staring eyes, fixed upon the ceiling. They are deathly pale. They do not appear as representatives of a brutal militarism. The one is thin and pink eye-lidded : the second fiddle in a Brunswick orchestra. The other is moon-faced and suffering : a privat docent. It is all most painful. . . .

Suddenly from outside comes the crash of guns thundering a salute. It announces to Paris that the second Treaty of Versailles has been signed by Dr. Muller and Dr. Bell. Through the few open windows comes the sound of distant crowds cheering hoarsely. And still the signature goes on. . . .

Hon. Harold Nicolson. Peace-
making : Diary. June 28, 1919.

PEACE TREATY

II

From the tennis lawn you can hear the guns going,
    Twenty miles away,
Telling the people of the home counties
    That the peace was signed to-day.
To-night there'll be feasting in the city ;
    They will drink deep and eat,
Keep peace the way you planned you would keep it
    If we got the Boche beat.
Oh, your plan and your word, they are broken,
    For you neither dine nor dance ;
And there's no peace so quiet, so lasting,
    As the peace you keep in France.

You'll be needing no Covenant of Nations
    To hold your peace intact.
It does not hang on the close guarding
    Of a frail and wordy pact.

When ours screams, shattered and driven,
    Dust down the storming years,
Yours will stand stark, like a grey fortress,
    Blind to the storm's tears.

Our peace . . . your peace . . . I see neither :
    They are a dream, and a dream.
I only see you laughing on the tennis lawn ;
    And brown and alive you seem,
As you stoop over the tall red foxglove,
    (It flowers again this year)
And imprison within a freckled bell
    A bee, wild with fear.

Oh, you cannot hear the noisy guns going :
    You sleep too far away.
It is nothing to you, who have your own peace,
    That our peace was signed to-day.

                    Rose Macaulay, *June 28, 1919.*

1920—

THE time of universal peace is near ;
Prove this a prosperous day, the three nook'd world
Shall bear the olive freely.

Shakespeare. Anthony and Cleopatra.

ABOLISH OR REDUCE ARMAMENTS

In the general restoration of justice and reconciliation of nations it is much to be desired that all nations enter without misgiving into a general society, or rather family, for the purpose of protecting their individual independence and for the preservation of order. Such a comity of nations is recommended amongst other reasons, by the widely felt need of abolishing or reducing military armaments which weigh so heavily on the resources of the State ; and in this way war with its train of evils will be entirely avoided or at least rendered less menacing, and the liberty and territorial integrity of every nation safeguarded.

Benedict XV. *Encyclical Pacem Dei Munus Pulcherrimum of May 23, 1920.*

HOPES DEEPLY STIRRED

We commend to all Christian peoples the principles which underlie the League of Nations, the most promising and the most systematic attempt to advance towards the ideal of the family of nations which has ever been projected. It has deeply stirred the hopes of those who long for peace on earth and increase of fellowship. But if any such League is to have success it will need the enthusiastic and intelligent support of millions of men and women.

Randall Davidson, D.D., *Archbishop of Canterbury. Encyclical Letter, Lambeth Conference, Aug. 7, 1920.*

A SUICIDAL CHARACTER

The general judgment of mankind upon war is that it is a scourge of the nations, which, along with famine and pestilence, makes up the dread trinity of human woes.

This estimate rests on considerations which have certainly not lost in force in modern times.

War is organised destruction of the harvest of civilisation and of those who produce it. It impoverishes a country in two ways—by diverting labour from productive to unproductive tasks, and by annihilating wealth which had previously been accumulated by peaceful industry. It also sets at naught the civilised doctrine of the sanctity of human life, and replaces the beneficent efforts of science to save and husband life by measures which directly or indirectly sweep away whole masses of population. The ever-increasing efficiency of the instruments and methods of destruction has still more decidedly given to modern warfare an aspect of folly and clothed it with a suicidal character. The conquerors, hardly less than the vanquished, have emerged from the World War bleeding, dazed, exhausted, and doomed to shoulder almost intolerable burdens.

W. P. Paterson, D.D. *Encyclopædia of Religion and Ethics : Art. War, 1921.*

ONLY LITERATURE

AGAIN and again between these catastrophes of blood and terror the cry rises up for reconciliation of the peoples and for peace on earth. It is but the background and the echo of the grand happening, but, as such, so necessary that we have to assume its existence even if, as in Hyksos, Egypt, in Bagdad and Byzantium, no tradition tells of it. Esteem as we may the wish towards all this, we must have the courage to face facts as they are—that is the hallmark of men of race-quality, and it is by the being of these men that *alone* history is. Life if it would be great, is hard ; it lets choose *only* between victory and ruin, not between war and peace, and to the victor belong the sacrifices of victory. For that which shuffles querulously and jealously by the side of the events is only literature—written or thought or lived literature—mere truths that lose themselves in the moving

crush of facts. History has never deigned to take notice of
these propositions.

> Oswald Spengler. *Der Untergang
> des Abendlandes, 1922. Tr. Charles
> Francis Atkinson, 1928.*

"Here is the majestic Spengler, star of the declining West: ' I see
further than others. . . . Destiny depends on quite other, robuster forces.
Human history is war history. . . . Barbarism is that which I call strong
race, the eternal warlike in the type of the beast-of-prey man.'

"Violence, greed, injustice, are raw, red and real; liberty, happiness,
peace, are ' ineffective dreams.' Now the trouble with this stuff is not
so much the savagery we read into the words as their vagueness and
lack of meaning. ' Barbarism is that which I call blab blab, the blab
blab in the type of blab man.'"—Stuart Chase, *The Tyranny of Words*, 1938.

*

IN THE NATURE OF THINGS

WAR is force carried to the slaughter of innocent people
wholesale, organised by States without any court of justice
or appeal to a higher power, and aiming on each side at
the subjugation of the opposing nation to the will of the
conqueror. From the very circumstances of the case, when
once it begins between modern great States the whole of
each nation is, as far as possible, mobilised against the whole
of the other, and neither side can afford to forgo any action
which might lead to an advantage over the other. Thus
it comes about, and in the nature of things is bound to come
about, that one after another the scruples of humanity and
the dictates of the Christian conscience are thrown aside
and war becomes more and more ruthless.

> *Christianity and War. Report presented
> to C.O.P.E.C.,*[1] *April 5-12, 1924.*

[1] Conference on Christian Politics, Economics and Citizenship.

A MORE DIFFICULT QUESTION

CADET and O.T. Corps form a more difficult question.
. . . They are definitely a preparation for war, and seem
to many incompatible with an educational training towards
peace as the higher ideal. The value which is claimed for

them is that they teach discipline, keenness, a proper pride and helpfulness to others in the highest degree ; they afford healthy exercise and an opportunity of service. Many who encourage and are active in the movement have no intention to stimulate the spirit of militarism. . . . " Si vis pacem, para bellum " may or may not be a sound practical maxim, it cannot, when the preparations include the young, be said to create an atmosphere which exalts the virtue of peace.

Ibid.

RECOMMENDATIONS

The Conference recommends :

1. That the Christian Churches should in their public testimony and with all their influence oppose all policies that provoke war, and support all conditions in the relations of nations favourable to peace, and the agencies which promote peace.

2. That they should unreasonably condemn, and refuse to support in any way, a war waged before the matter in dispute has been submitted to an arbitral tribunal, or in defiance of the decision of such a tribunal.

3. That they should exert all their authority in securing protection from all forms of persecution for those whose conscience forbids their rendering any kind of war-service.

4. That by study of the New Testament in the light of the guidance of the Spirit, they should seek to reach a common Christian conscience in regard to war.

5. That they should cultivate such intimate fellowship with the Churches of other lands that through the one Church of Jesus Christ the spirit of reconciliation shall triumph over all national prejudices, suspicions, and enmities, and that the churches of many lands may unitedly formulate a Peace-Programme which can be commended to all who profess and call themselves Christian, so that Christ shall reign as Prince of Peace.

6. That the Churches should hold these principles, not

only in times of peace, when their practical denial is not threatened, but that also, when war is imminent, they should dare to take an independent stand for righteousness and peace, even if the Press and public opinion be at the time against them.

Ibid.

COLOSSAL FUTILITY

I MAINTAIN that by far the most tragic thing about war is not its immorality, nor its cruelty, but its manifest and colossal futility and imbecility. I maintain that war achieves no single object of advantage in the high sense to any one, nor does it attain any one of the supposed aims for which it is waged.

Lord Ponsonby. *Now is the Time, 1925.*

TRAGIC DISPARITY

THE age of competitive armaments and competitive alliances culminated in the " world war," a monstrous struggle without intrinsic purpose, involving nation after nation in a conflict whose initial issues were obscure to them and irrelevant to their interests. Mankind has never witnessed so tragic a disparity between means and ends. The struggle could not be localised because the nations were so interdependent, so bound up with one another. All the great nations of the world were embroiled, not because a single issue divided them but because a single system held them fast. Nothing was common save the catastrophe. In the words of Viscount Grey, " it was a victory of war itself over everybody who took part in it."

R. M. MacIver,
The Modern State, 1926.

WAR CRIES

" Liberty " and " Justice " have always been reckoned expensive words, but that " Civilisation " could cost as much as I forget how many millions a day came as a surprise to many thoughtful taxpayers. . . . " You are fighting for civilisation," cried the wisest and best of those leaders who led us into war.[1] . . . Startled by this sudden enthusiasm for an abstraction in which till then politicians and recruiting-sergeants had manifested little or no interest, I, in my turn, began to cry : " And what is civilisation ? " I did not cry aloud, be sure : at that time, for crying things of that sort aloud one was sent to prison.

Clive Bell. *Civilisation, 1928.*

[1] Mr. Winston Churchill, at Theydon Bois, on August 26th, 1938, said, "It would be a mistake if any foreign Power supposed that Britain was no longer capable, if need be, of bearing her part with other nations in defending the title-deeds of civilised mankind."

WAR RENOUNCED

The High Contracting Parties solemnly declare in the names of their respective peoples that they condemn recourse to war for the solution of international controversies, and renounce it as an instrument of national policy in their relations with one another.

The High Contracting Parties agree that the settlement or solution of all disputes or conflicts of whatever nature or of whatever origin they may be which may arise among them shall never be sought except by pacific means.

Articles 1 and 2 of the Pact of Paris, 1928.

"The United Kingdom is now linked with 60 out of 66 other states in the world (including the self-governing Dominions of the British Crown and the Kingdom of Egypt) by the Pact of Paris for the Renunciation of War as an instrument of National Policy, and with 56 of these by the further and more positive bond of common membership in a formal association of states, the League of Nations . . . ." Arnold J. Toynbee, *A Study of History.* Vol. 1. 1934.

Such subtle covenants shall be made
Till peace itself is war in masquerade.
John Dryden, *Absalom and Achitophel.*

THE END OF DREAMS

WE are getting to the end of our visioning
The impossible within this universe,
Such as that better whiles may follow worse,
And that our race may mend by reasoning.

We know that even as larks in cages sing
Unthoughtful of deliverance from the curse
That holds them lifelong in a latticed hearse,
We ply spasmodically our pleasuring.

And that when nations set them to lay waste
Their neighbours' heritage by foot and horse,
And hack their pleasant plains in festering seams,
They may again,—not warely, or from taste,
But tickled mad by some demonic force.—
Yes. We are getting to the end of dreams !

Thomas Hardy. From Winter Words, 1928.

ENLISTING THE MORAL JUDGMENT OF HUMANITY

THE Conference affirms that war as a method of settling international disputes is incompatible with the teaching and example of Our Lord Jesus Christ.

The Conference believes that peace will never be achieved till international relations are controlled by religious and ethical standards, and that the moral judgment of humanity needs to be enlisted on the side of peace. It therefore appeals to the religious leaders of all nations to give their support to the effort to promote those ideals of peace, brotherhood and justice for which the League of Nations stands.

The Conference welcomes the agreement made by leading statesmen of the world in the names of their respective peoples, in which they condemn recourse to war for the solution of international controversies, renounce it as an instrument of national policy in their relations with one another and agree that the settlement of all disputes which may arise among them shall never be sought except by pacific means ; and appeals to all Christian people to support this agreement to the utmost of their power and to help actively, by prayer and effort, agencies (such as the League of Nations Union and the World Alliance for Promoting International Friendship through the Churches) which are working to promote goodwill among the Nations.

When nations have solemnly bound themselves by Treaty, Covenant or Pact for the pacific settlement of international disputes, the Conference holds that the Christian Church in every nation should refuse to countenance any war in regard to which the government of its own country has not declared its willingness to submit the matter in dispute to arbitration or conciliation.

The Conference believes that the existence of armaments on the present scale amongst the nations of the world endangers the maintenance of peace, and appeals for a determined effort to secure reduction by international agreement.

Resolutions 25, 26, 27 and 28, Lambeth Conference, July-Aug., 1930.

AT LOVE GREEN

WHEN grandees feasted have, to see the abhorred
heeltaps and damaged dainties to the board
come cringing back agrees not with their taste—
eat they will not, and yet they would not waste.
Then to the butler's or the cook's discreet
back comes the charwoman on stealthy feet,
and in a bag receives, and bears away,
the spoiling relics of a splendid day.
Time bears (my Lord) just such a bag, and deft-
handed is he to pouch whatever's left

from bygone exploits when their glories fail.
I knew a time when Europe feasted well :
bodies were munched in thousands, vintage blood
so blithely flowed that even the dull mud
grew greedy, and ate men ; and lest the gust
should flag, quick flesh no daintier taste than dust,
spirit was ransacked for whatever might
sharpen a sauce to drive on appetite.
From the mind's orient fetched all spices were—
honour, romance, magnanimous despair,
savagery, expiation, lechery,
skill, humour, spleen, fear, madness, pride, ennui. . . .
Long revel, but at last to loathing turned,
and through the after-dinner speeches yawned
those who still waked to hear them. No one claps.
Come, Time, 'tis time to bear away the scraps !
Time came, and bent him to the priestlike task.
Once more Love Green beheld its farmers bask
in former ruin ; home-come heroes, badged
with native mud, to native soil repledged
limbs that would lose their record, ten years hence,
whether they twinged for tillage or defence.
No longer was the church on week-days warmed
that special liturgies might be performed ;
war-babies, too, now lost their pristine glamour,
and were as bastards bid to hold their clamour.
So Time despatched the feast ; some items still
surpassed his pouch, though ; one of these, the bill.
Many, for this, the hind who pinched and numb
faced the wet dawn, and thought of army rum ;
many the mother, draggled from childbed,
who wept for grocer's port and prices fled ;
and village Hampdens, gathered in the tap,
forsook their themes of bawdry and mishap
to curse a government which could so fleece
on spirits under proof, and call it Peace.

                                    Sylvia Townsend Warner.
                                    Opus 7, 1931.

THE REQUIREMENTS OF RIGHT REASON

SINCE the unbridled race in armaments, which on the one
hand is the consequence of international rivalry, and on the
other is the cause of enormous expenditure taken out of the
resources available for the public well-being, is not the least
of the reasons for the present crisis, We cannot refrain from
renewing and making Our own the grave warning of Our
Predecessor. We deplore the fact that it has not yet been
heeded and We exhort you, Venerable Brethren, to employ
every means at your disposal through preaching and through
the Press to enlighten men's minds and to incline their hearts
to the requirements of right reason, and even more, of the
law of Christ.

Pius XI. *Apostolic Letter Nova
Impendet of Oct. 2, 1931.*

THE FOULEST THINGS

Two things are incredible to me. That a generation which
has known war should submit to preparation for another.
And that if and when it comes our spiritual leaders will
fail us again as badly as they failed us in 1914-1918. Yet,
why not? The alchemy of war produces other compounds
as strange as a priest justifying war because it is Christ-like
and a scientist discovering that it improves the stock.[1]
There is a sense in which it is true and bitter that in a war
the foulest things are those which take place in the mind.

Storm Jameson. *No Time
Like the Present, 1932.*

[1] In his Rectorial address in 1931 to the students of Aberdeen University
Sir Arthur Keith said: "Nature keeps her human orchard healthy by
pruning; war is her pruning-hook. We cannot dispense with her services.
This harsh and repugnant forecast of man's future is wrung from me."

AN EMBARRASSING SIGHT

I SCARCELY know how it is, but a priest inciting to war is an embarrassing sight. Any soldier who suffered under a bellicose chaplain will confirm this feeling. In *The Times* Recruiting Supplement of this same year (1915) prelates and parsons play at sergeants so finely that *The Times* commends them, and adds : " Nor has there ever been any real doubt as to the view of the Nonconformist Churches —although many members are known to be opposed to war. It is recognised, however, that the usual standards of conduct cannot apply to this war."

1916. This year a great stroke delivered by William Cunningham, Archdeacon of Ely, in Great St. Mary's at Cambridge. " The most specious of modern false prophets are those who have come forward as conscientious objectors at local tribunals ; they look not for Divine guidance now in the great struggle in which our nation is engaged, but at the recorded Divine commands in days gone by, and insist that the Divine word, given once for all, is binding on us for all time. . . . He did not say one word of His own about killing, but He did speak of the wickedness of hating. The Christian soldier may be thoroughly chivalrous, and may in the course of his duty kill many men whom he does not hate. . . . It is the spirit of hatred that Christ would have us exorcise ; while the false prophet endeavours to make a Christian code out of the Sermon on the Mount."

Ibid.

THIS HARMFUL POSTULATE

WAR alone brings up to its highest tension all human energy and puts the stamp of nobility upon the peoples who have the courage to meet it. All other trials are substitutes, which never really put men into the position where they have to make the great decision—the alternative of life or death. Thus a doctrine which is founded upon this harmful postulate of peace is hostile to Fascism. And thus hostile to the spirit of Fascism, though accepted for what use they can be in dealing with political situations, are all the international leagues and societies which, as history will show, can be scattered to the winds when once strong national feeling is aroused by any motive—sentimental, ideal, or practical.

Benito Mussolini.
Encyclopedia Italiana, 1932.

THE ALTAR OF A NON-ENTITY

THE ends for which wars are fought are not concrete but abstract ; they are such ends as national prestige, national honour, national security, ends begotten of pride and born of fear. And these nations whose prestige must be flattered, whose honour must be safeguarded, whose security must be guaranteed, are not real things at all but figments. They are the embodiment of a debased Hegelianism, which holds that the State is a real entity and that its well-being is more important than that of its individual citizens. To it individuals, generation after generation, must be subordinated, and to its alleged welfare men and women must be sacrificed. . . .

How long, we cannot help wondering, will men continue to sacrifice their lives and happiness on the altar of a non-entity ?

C. E. M. Joad.
Under the Fifth Rib, 1932.

PEACE IS NOT REST

WE are spiritual beings, whose lives are realised in a material medium. Our peace will be secured not by ignoring or evading the fundamental conflict of life, but by recognising it, by immersing ourselves in it, by so adapting ourselves to the conditions it imposes on us as to transform and redeem them—in a word, by gradually substituting sustained tolerance and control for spasmodic upheavals and concussions.

Peace is not rest, nor heavenly dream, nor a " pure " idea ; its only value on parchment is to remind us to establish it. Peace is order-evoking energy, the idea realised ; and, since all our activities are expressed at last in relation to materials, its aim is that ultimate prosperity in which the world's resources will be humanised, to achieve their highest significance in a life to which all men contribute and in which all share.

Basil de Selincourt. *Towards Peace and other Essays, 1932.*

FUROR TEUTONICUS

THE *Nordic* demonic element is different from that of other races. The *Nordic* demonic element is heroic. It culminates in scorn of death. Light and darkness in the Germanic soul likewise. Light : *Siegfried*. Darkness : *Hagen*. But this *Hagen* has nothing ugly, dwarfish, contemptible about him, this *Hagen* is true as a king and true as a soldier. The Germanic element is heroic. It permeates primeval life, which is *life*, even when it is death. . . . Life, death . . . equal, more : One. The eternal truth : to die is to live again. . . . Nature ! The Myth, the song of dying, that is to say, of self-renewing Nature !

German heroes do not fear death. They seek it as an adventure on the battlefield, prize the entry into Valhalla, scorning to die in bed. . . .

The discord, light and darkness, the demonic, the terrible ; the primæval wildness in the Teuton ! The *furor* (in turn to more modern times). But this *furor teutonicus* is heroic too. . . .[1]

Erich Czech-Jochberg. *Deutsche Geschichte, National-Sozialistich gesehen, 1933.*

[1] Qt. "Friends of Europe" Publications, No. 63, 1938.

SO A GOD . . .

I THINK war wrong. I also think it silly. Sometimes a comedian in a theatre will do something so divinely irresponsible, so completely and gorgeously silly, that one sinks back into one's seat in helpless laughter. A few minutes later he does it again . . . and then again . . . and again. Gradually one ceases to laugh. So a god, to whom the death of a man was no more than to man the death of a fly, must once have laughed uproariously at man's invention of war . . . and grown weary of laughing . . . and then wished that the absurd little creatures would hit upon something else as gorgeously comic.

I think war silly. I think that war is the ultimate expression of man's wickedness and man's silliness. There are times when I think that its childish silliness is even more heart-breaking than its wickedness.

A. A. Milne.
Peace with Honour, 1934.

MODERN WAR

LET him [the virile Patriot] think of war in terms of Profiteers, Embusqués, Nepotism, Job-wangling, War Diaries, Propaganda, Rumours, Spy-mania, Honours Lists, Staff Appointments, Patriotic Songs, " Combing Out," White Feathers, Business as Usual, and Keeping the Home Fires Burning ; Hatred and Malice and all Uncharitableness ; and then Lies and Lies and still more Lies, and the apotheosis of all the Bottomleys, Kreugers and Stravinskys of the world. That is modern war. Leave out the ten million dead soldiers ; we can be brave and hearty about " our gallant boys "—*dulce et decorum est pro patria mori* ; but add a few hundred thousand mutilated women and a few hundred thousand starved children . . . and then reflect that this is only the beginning of it. This is only a comparatively short Four Years' War. There are still sixteen

years of post-war virility to come. Crushing taxation ;
shackles on liberty from which we shall never again be
free ; millions of unemployed in whom hope is almost
dead ; a rising generation in whom hope was never born ;
and anarchy and autocracy fighting a last desperate battle
among the ruins. . . .

Ibid.

THE DEVIL'S RAINBOW

AN adequate defence force is the treasure lying at the foot
of the devil's rainbow : it moves away and away until
civilisation follows it over the precipice. But this will not
hinder the government. We shall before long be in a
position to burn and poison many more foreigners than we
can at present, and to destroy foreign towns and works of
art more promptly and thoroughly. No one wishes to do
this, but it is all that rearmament can do. Mutual fear will
increase, and sooner or later we, or the enemy of the
moment, will get the jumps and take the initiative. It is
a toss-up whether we ruin his capital before he ruins
London, but both of us have a good chance of succeeding
almost simultaneously, and neither of us have much chance
of making peace afterwards.

E. M. Forster. *Notes on the Way.*
Time & Tide, June, 1935.

NURSERY RHYME

WHAT puffs and patters,
What clicks and clatters,
I know what, oh what fun !
It's a lovely Gatling gun ![1]

*Military Mother Goose (A German
Book of Nursery Rhymes), 1935.*

[1] Qt. *Education in Nazi Germany,* by *Two English Investigators,* 1938.

A NUISANCE

It is the habit of statesmen to-day to lead their peoples as generals lead their armies—from behind. They no longer enunciate principles, or outline policies, which they invite men and women of like mind to support ; their skill lies in ascertaining the greatest wish, the greatest fear, or the greatest prejudice of the greatest number, and building a " platform " round it. . . .

Politicians either know nothing of foreign affairs themselves, or are convinced that the electors aren't interested in them, and that they must give the public what it wants, so they content themselves with paying lip-service to peace in an occasional peroration, while they leave the experts to their job of getting ready for the next war.

There is no way of altering that, of achieving a real peace policy, unless those who are opposed to war become vocal and declare the faith that is in them. In other words, we must make a nuisance of ourselves.

The Very Rev. H. R. L. Sheppard.
We say " No," 1935.

NO MORE HUMAN BEINGS

How far the process of spiritual and intellectual preparation for war must be carried, a Nazi German, Herr Friedrich Sieburg, in his book *Es werde Deutschland* makes clear. . . .

" There are to be no more private Germans. Each is to attain significance only by his service to the state and to find complete self-fulfilment in its service. Thus to express it in more emphatic terms, there are to be no more human beings in Germany, but only Germans."[1]

All this has a certain consistent logic in it. Modern war cannot be waged by normally civilised men : men must therefore be de-civilised. And modern propaganda, using school and church and press and cinema, is quite capable of doing it.

Sir Norman Angell. *Preface to Peace, 1935.*

¹ Herr Herman Gauch, in his book, *Neue Grundlagen der Rassenforschung*, published in 1933, declares that the real distinction is not between the human race and other animals, but between the Aryan race and other animals, including all the other human races.

FOR THE CHILDREN

THE duty of all Germans is, in Hitler's own words, " not to seek out objective truth in so far as it may be favourable to others, but uninterruptedly to serve one's own truth." Things like the Versailles Treaty should be used to work up " blazing fury and passionate hate."

All printed matter from the child's primer to the last newspaper, every theatre, every cinema, every advertisement pillar, every hoarding, must be pressed into the service of this single great mission until the anguished prayer of our confederated patriots, " Lord set us free," is transformed in the brain of the tiniest child into the fervent prayer, " Almighty God, bless our arms in the future : be just as Thou hast ever been, decide now whether we yet deserve our freedom ; Lord bless our battles."

Ibid.

THAT "BUT"

WHILE . . . it is difficult to be absolutely against war, it is the easiest thing in the world to be *conditionally* against war ; to say " Oh, yes, we are against war, war is horrible, vile, wasteful, detestable—*but*——" And then up comes the word honour, or the defence of your women and children. Your politicians will always be able to provide you with that *but*, however bad the claim may be, and however much they themselves may have been the foolish cause of it. They can always provide you with a case if they want you to " see red." But both those words, in connection with war, have become a lie. You cannot defend your honour in war, because war forces you to do dishonourable things. You might as well talk of defending your reputation for honesty by thieving. You *cannot*, in modern war, defend your women and children. In future wars, they will be the main objective of the enemy, in order to break down the morale of the nation. Henceforth all nations alike are committed, by the developments of modern war, to wholesale attack on the weak, the unarmed, and the defenceless. In such a process of war no honour is left, and certainly no Christianity. Therefore for peace-makers to object to war conditionally is useless. The only useful thing to do is to say *now*, in time of peace, " We will not have war ever again ! "

> Laurence Housman. *Christ and Cæsar*,
> (*St. Martin's Review.*) *Oct.*, *1935.*

RISKS

PACIFISM certainly has its risks. But so has militarism ; and the risks of militarism are far greater than those of pacifism. Militarism cannot fail to lead us into war, whereas pacifism has a very good chance of preventing war from breaking out.

The nations of the world live within a malevolently charmed circle of suspicion, hatred and fear. By pursuing a policy of pacifism, and only by pursuing a policy of pacifism, we can break out of the circle. One generous gesture on the part of a great nation might be enough to set the whole world free. More than any other nation, Britain is in a position to make that gesture. " To make it," protest the militarists, " is to court disaster." But to go on preparing for war and thereby rendering war inevitable is also to court disaster—disaster more certain and more complete.

Which is better, to take a risk for a good cause, or to march to certain perdition for a bad one ?

Aldous Huxley. *What are you going to do about it ? 1936.*

THE GERMANIC NORDIC SOUL

THE spirit of attack is the spirit of the Nordic race. It works in their blood, like an untamable craving. It is the spirit of eternal setting forth, everlasting preparedness ; it reaches out to farthest destinies and conquers a world not for the sake of possession but for the sake of conquering. . . . It is a great incomprehensible spirit, which urges and overcomes ; it is the best of the occident, this soul of the Nordic race, this spirit of attack. To this spirit the great hour is never the hour of victory, of triumph ; posssession is already a disappointment. The Mediterranean soul may be elated in the hour of victory, to the Germanic Nordic soul it has already a bitter taste.[1]

Dr. Helmut Stellrecht. *Wehrerziehung des deutschen Jugend (Military Education of German Youth), 1936.*

[1] Qt. *Education in Nazi Germany*, by *Two English Investigators*, 1938.

WHY CALL IT " WAR " ?

MAN going to war at the present time is as a man fighting with his bare hands against a ten-thousand horse-power machine of his own making. He is comparable to an infant attacking a steam-roller. Logically this is possible ; actually it is beyond his nature as a human creature ; and if he insists upon attempting it he can only look forward to the fate that attends a physical impossibility. It is possible to fall six feet without serious damage : that is what man did before gunpowder. It is possible to fall twelve feet and to survive : that is what Europe did a hundred years ago. It is possible for a whole family to fall from the roof of its house, and some will live to tell the tale—as in 1914. But it is not possible for human beings to jump over Shakespeare's Cliff and to resolve anything in so doing except the problem of existence ; and the fall from Shakespeare's Cliff to the sands below is what war is to man to-day. It is an act of race suicide. . . .

Incidentally, if war has become race suicide by a perfectly natural process of evolution, why should we continue to call it " war " ? Why not clear our minds of cant and have the courage to say " race suicide " ? It would help us to stop deceiving ourselves. The effect upon the peoples of Europe, if politicians everywhere cut " war " from their vocabularies, and spoke always of " race suicide " instead, might be enormous.

Max Plowman.
The Faith Called Pacifism, 1936.

APPALLING FRANKNESS

I PUT before the whole House my own views with an appalling frankness. From 1933 I and my friends were all very worried about what was happening in Europe. You will remember that at the time the Disarmament Conference was sitting in Geneva. You will remember at that time there was probably a stronger pacifist feeling running through this country than at any time since the war. I am speaking of 1933 and 1934. You will remember the election at Fulham in the autumn of 1933, when a seat which the National Government held was lost by about 7000 votes on no issue but the pacifist. You will remember perhaps that the National Government candidate, who made a most guarded reference to the question of defence, was mobbed for it.

That was the feeling in the country in 1933. My position as the leader of a great party was not altogether a comfortable one. I asked myself what chance was there—when that feeling that was given expression to in Fulham was common throughout the country—what chance was there

within the next year or two of that feeling being so changed
that the country would give a mandate for rearmament?
Supposing I had gone to the country and said that Germany was rearming and that we must rearm, does anybody
think that this pacific democracy would have rallied to
that cry at that moment? I cannot think of anything that
would have made the loss of the election from my point
of view more certain.

> Lord Baldwin. *In the House
> of Commons, Nov. 12, 1936.*

ACTING LIKE SAVAGES

IT is a specious cry—arm against Fascism and war; it
brings in anti-Fascists and anti-militarists, lovers of justice,
liberty, democracy and peace, all bent on this sinister
suicide pact, all set to kill the thing they love. Wars to
end war only give war a fresh lease of life; sanctioned and
accepted once more, unchained and let out for yet another
run, the encouraged and pampered monster goes growling
on its maniac way, the stronger after each orgy for the
next . . . No giving war a respectable name, or a noble
name, or a fine high-faluting name, or even a name that
makes it sound sensible and necessary, is going to alter
its character as a lunatic civilisation-destroyer; its respectable name is, indeed, an added danger, since it thus
entraps the good, and is haloed by their honourable intentions. Leave it to the brigands, and it will appear
nakedly what it is, a senseless herd ferocity, condemned by
all decent people; let decent people themselves accept
it, and it begins to wear a plausibly sanctimonious air, as
if a cannibal orgy were to be attended by bishops and got
up to look like a church service. . . .

This business of acting like savages because other people
do is a mistake that all savages make. It gets civilisation
nowhere. . . . Civilised experiments have not always
worked in a savage world, but they have always been worth
while; they have made landmarks, they have been looked

back on later as pioneering achievements, like the first flights in the air. Pioneers have not always survived to see what comes of their experiments ; but if no one made them, nothing would come of them. The point about the disarmament experiment is, what is the alternative ? War and more war, stupid and cruel destruction, the savage dancing his tribal dance, whooping in his feathers, tomahawk and war-paint, until the jungle swallows him up and the world as we know it crashes in ruins.

Rose Macaulay.
Aping the Barbarians, 1937.

DISILLUSIONMENT

IT is but necessary to notice the disillusionment that has overcome many of our greatest soldiers, to realise that European politicians will be forced to find some other methods of settling their disputes, if civilisation is to be allowed to proceed along its path. Lord Kitchener has been quoted by Lady Oxford and Asquith as having said that " War is futile in settling international disputes." Lord Allenby, in his last public speech, stressed that " The gains of war are dead-sea fruit," whilst many other military experts, amongst whom are Field-Marshal Sir William Robertson, spoke in the same vein. Similarly, Captain Liddell Hart, the military correspondent of *The Times*, writes in his book, *Europe in Arms*, " The burden of defence has increased while the security afforded has decreased." What then is the cause of this pessimism amongst fighting men ? Why also does Lord Lothian write, " Can Europe possibly survive with twenty-six sovereign states armed to the teeth, and with tariffs to the sky ? " The arms and the tariffs are created for the good of their people by politicians basing their calculations upon the accepted theories of our day. Mr. Baldwin has warned us that another great European conflict will bring our civilisation tumbling down with a crash as great as that of the mighty Roman Empire—but surely if modern war is merely a question of defence, which means security (and the statesmen of all countries assure us continually about this) how can mere defence threaten us with destruction?

Captain Philip S. Mumford.
Patriotism True and False, 1937.

UTTERLY INCONCEIVABLE

IN his recent book, *What it Means to be a Christian,* the Bishop of Gloucester lays down the following maxim in regard to the problems of Christian morality : " I do not think that a good Christian wants casuistry. It is far better that you should give a man a simple rule of conduct. I would suggest the following : that a man should ask himself what Christ would have done in the circumstances. Every one is able to read and ponder over the life of Christ, and to be inspired by His teaching and example. If he aims at that, I do not doubt that his conduct will be right." Applying that maxim to modern war, the answer is plain and inevitable. To me at least it is utterly inconceivable that Christ could be the pilot of a bombing aeroplane, or could drench helpless cities in mustard-rain. I cannot believe that any Christian can regard such a suggestion as arguable. Yet if not, since *qui facit per alium facit per se,* the question is settled : war in its modern methods is intolerable for the Christian : we will not fight.

Canon C. E. Raven.
We Will Not Fight, 1937.

WASTAGE

WHEN I read, in a *Times* leader on the proposed new Air Force, the bland statement that " its rate of wastage would certainly be high," I begin to question the right of myself or any other woman to create human beings who may be exposed to suffering even more dreadful than that which I witnessed two decades ago. Is it my son's destiny, ten years hence, to become part of that Air Force's "wastage"—unconsidered human debris, thrown on the scrap-heap of the next war's poisoned and mutilated victims?

Vera Brittain.
Why I Stand for Peace, 1937.

"The military preparation of the woman is the basis for the protection of the young, which is the most important of all the war-tasks of the woman. The right to matrimony will have to be made contingent upon evidence of ability for this task."— *Wehrerziehung, Military Education for Women,* 1935.

BRITTLE FELICITIES

ANY one who rejects unconditionally the grotesquely brutal, savage and humourless assault on civilisation known as war, may, surely, be called a genuine pacifist. He may reject it for a number of reasons ; he may be a person of civility and sensibility, who will not abet the destruction of the glories of human culture—the bombing, e.g., of Athens, Venice, Florence, Rome, Chartres, Oxford and Cambridge, and a thousand other brittle felicities—not to mention (for it is mentioned oftener) the disgusting torture and mutilation of thousands of even more brittle, though less beautiful, human beings everywhere, and the brutalisation and shoddy degradation of mind liable to accompany the perpetration and moral justifying of these excesses. Is it so rare to consider any risk preferable to deliberately undertaking these revolting savageries and reducing Europe to a scrap-heap of cultureless and insanitary debris ? But do not let us dehumanise pacifism by calling it superhuman.

Letter in Time and Tide, Nov. 6, 1937.

THE FUTURE

WHAT sort of future are we trying to create for ourselves and for our children ? Is it to be better or worse than that which we have inherited ?

Are we trying to make a world in which the peoples that inhabit it shall be able to live out their lives in peace of mind and in the enjoyment of a constantly rising standard of all that makes life worth living, of health and comfort, of recreation and culture ? Or are we preparing for ourselves a future which is to be one perpetual nightmare, filled with the constant dread of the horrors of war, forced to bury ourselves below ground and to spend all our substance upon the weapons of destruction ?

> The Rt. Hon. Neville Chamberlain, *Prime Minister. At the Lord Mayor's Banquet, Guildhall, Nov. 9, 1937.*

THIS BARBARIC STUFF

EXTRACT from the new text-book for Hitler Youth :

" Such a death sets a seal on life and is an inspiration for those who come after.

" It is repugnant to the heroic man that death on the battle field should be made the occasion for lamentations and sentimentality."

What do young men who may be cut down in the flower of youth say to this vicious dope ? Who are " those who come after " ? Don't they want to die as youths, too ?

What is Dr. Hellmut Stellrecht, the author of this monstrous doctrine, doing on the earth ? And why didn't Hitler get himself killed when he was a corporal ?

At a time when we are reverencing and honouring the Empire's dead and repledging ourselves to see they did not sacrifice themselves in vain, this barbaric stuff is doubly obnoxious.

> *The Sunday Chronicle, Nov. 14, 1937.*

OUR GIRLS

WE must make it quite clear to our girls what the military education of a people really means : they must understand that we need a generation of women, who do not look upon the soldiering activities of their menfolk as a necessary evil, but as a sacred duty.

National-Sozialistische Mädchenerziehung,
National-Socialist Girls' Education, Feb.,
1937.

MATHEMATICS

A WIDELY used arithmetic book, of which 718,000 copies are in circulation (*Examples in Mathematics for higher classes in the new Elementary School,* by Johannes Rasziej, Bruno Wisch and Albert Hollman) has a novel device of a few words of comment or story to lead up to different sets of problems.

" My father owns a house. His five tenants and he form a peaceful little community. He is about to calculate the cost for household necessities, cleaning, etc., when he realises that an enemy is abroad and he must prepare for defence."

Problems then follow dealing with the expense of cleaning and preparing attics for air-raid precautions, installing sand bins, medical supplies, etc. . . .

Naturally the Air Force offers opportunities for calculations of all kinds.

" A squadron of 46 bombing aeroplanes throws bombs at an enemy town. Every aeroplane carries 500 bombs weighing 1500 kilogrammes each. Calculate the weight of all the bombs together. How many fires will the bombs start if every third explodes and every twentieth causes a fire ? "

Two English Investigators, Education in
Nazi Germany, 1938.

UNIVERSITY EDUCATION

" WHAT is the purpose of university education ? " asks the Rector of Frankfurt University, Dr. Ernest Krieck. " It is not objective science which is the purpose of our university training, but the heroic science of the soldier, the militant and fighting science."

The Rector of Frieburg University bears this out : his solemn address to the students at the opening of the first session includes the following :

" The honour and the fate of the nation to which the students are bound will in the future demand that their whole existence shall be bound up with military service."

Ibid.

A THREEFOLD CORD

MY position is this. I feel about war much as the pacifist feels, but I do not think as he thinks. I am opposed to pacifism, not in spite of being a Christian, but because I am a Christian. I believe that St. Paul and St. Peter in the position they adopt express the mind of Christ. I find the general mind of the Church all down the centuries opposed to pacifism, and pacifism the eccentricity of the few. The chief supporters of pacifism in the early centuries are almost invariably people of high character, but notoriously eccentric in other ways ; and I think the same thing true to-day. Moreover, when we appeal to reason and fact, pacifism again fares badly. Scripture, tradition and reason form a threefold cord which is not quickly broken, and the Great War has not seriously strained it.

> The Rev. H. L. Goudge, D.D., *Canon of Christ Church. A Sermon preached before the University of Oxford, Sunday morning, Jan. 30, 1938. Published as pamphlet, April, 1938.*

WHOSE FAULT ?

No Christian has ever supposed that war was anything but an evil, or that it could create the reign of righteousness and truth. All that it can do is to render that creation possible ; and, if a just war is followed by an unjust and vindictive peace, it has been fought in vain. But whose fault is that ? Certainly not the soldier's.

Ibid.

NOT COMMITTED

FOR those who adopt the rigorist interpretation of the commandment " Thou shalt not kill," the pacifist position is proved ; and no more remains to be said. But most Christians are unable to accept an interpretation which seems to them to conflict both with the main line of the Church's tradition and with sanctified common sense. They would agree with the Archbishop of York in holding it to be one of the errors of humanism to treat life upon the earth as absolutely sacrosanct ; and they would accept his statement of the position in the Church Assembly on February 5, 1937 : " He remembered the words, ' Fear not them which kill the body, and after that have no more that they can do.' If it was not a wholly intolerable injury that he should be killed because he chose to uphold some cause which he thought right and which involved that result, neither was it on the other side an intolerable injury if in the same process he took the life of another man. Christians were not committed to the position that in no circumstances whatsoever might they take the life of their own brother. The conditions which might justify it must be watched with the utmost vigilance, but if life was not the most precious thing to him, neither was it in his brother man ; and it might be his duty in pursuing what was of higher value than life, to take his as well as to give his own. It could be a Christian duty to kill."[1]

This important pronouncement helps to clear the issue, which is sometimes clouded by utterances such as that of Lord Daryngton in the same debate, when he said " it was wrong to quote the words ' greater love hath no man than this, that a man lay down his life for his friend,' and then to say that man had committed a crime and was really a murderer."[2] As Dr. Temple said, " The pacifist was not denying that it might be their duty to die for their country ; the only question was whether it could be their duty to kill for their country."[3]

Percy Hartill, B.D. *Pacifism and Christian Common Sense. April, 1938.*

[1] Report of Proceedings of Church Assembly, Vol. xviii, No. 1, p. 196.
[2] Ibid., pp. 180-1.
[3] Ibid., p. 195.

USING FORCE

In regard to the quantity of force being commensurate with the end to be achieved, it is sufficient to state baldly the facts of the extent to which force was used in the Great War. Ten million soldiers were known to have been killed or died of wounds ; another three millions were presumed dead ; twenty million were wounded ; nine million children were made orphans ; five million wives became widows ; ten million refugees were driven from their homes ; and in the aftermath of the war millions more suffered through the ensuing disease and economic disasters. Such is the measure of the force which was used in four and a half years of modern warfare. Is it unfair to ask the non-pacifist what good purpose was or could have been fulfilled with which such a use of force could be in any way commensurate ?

Ibid.

GOD AND GUNS

" The great need of England to-day is God, not guns, the Bible, not bombs," declared Mr. A. Lindsay Glegg at an Albert Hall rally of the Scripture Union yesterday, to celebrate the English Bible's fourth centenary.

A congregation of about 10,000, including hundreds of

children, heard Sir Thomas Inskip, Minister for the Co-ordination of Defence, and other speakers, plead for a revival of Bible reading in daily life.

Sir Thomas said that the influence of the Bible on the character of our forefathers was the foundation of Britain's greatness.

"We hope and pray that that greatness may be preserved, but it will be preserved and strengthened only if this generation can maintain and develop the habit of reading the Bible," he said.

The Observer, April 10, 1938.

"Sir Thomas Inskip, Minister for Co-ordination of Defence, speaking yesterday at a garden party at Stokes Bay, held by the women's section of the Gosport and Alverstoke Constitutional Association, referred to the tendency of some to emphasise the gaps in our defence, and said: 'We are getting the men and we are getting the guns.'"—*The Times*, June 23, 1938.

Herr Bürckel, Commissioner for Austria and Gauleiter of the Saar, speaking at Stuttgart on Aug. 31, 1938, said: Better standards of living are a better blessing than cannon grenades. Our mothers and the French mothers did not bear their sons to let them be slaughtered for some foreign affair.—*Reuter*.

A VOICE FROM SOUTH AFRICA

WE build bombing planes for defence and dare not ask ourselves too searchingly what defence may mean in this connection. Let us face it. Man is preparing to do what he has never done before, to murder (there is no other word) on a tremendous scale, defenceless children. That knowledge and the acquiescence in the preparation that is likely to have this end, little as we may desire it, must have a tremendous effect for the bad on our psychology and our moral values. Whether it is done in the name of liberty, democracy or what you will, it still remains a blood sacrifice of the innocent to the god of nationalism, it still remains the foulest thing that man has comtemplated or done.

T. O. W. *The Daily Tribune*,
Natal, April 30, 1938.

NEVER AGAIN

THE motto " Never again war " is also my motto. Therefore, I am making Germany strong and secure, and am
placing her upon her own feet. . . . But the motto must
be " Never again war " and " Never again civil war,
class warfare or internal strife."

> Adolf Hitler. *Speech in the*
> *Lustgarten, Berlin, May 1, 1938.*

THAT TRANQUILLITY AND PEACE

GERMANY and Italy have left behind themselves the
Utopias to which Europe blindly entrusted its fortunes in
order to seek between themselves and to seek with others
a régime of international co-operation which may erect
more effective guarantees of justice, of security, and of
peace equitable for all. We can reach this only when the
elementary rights of each people to live, to work and
defend itself are loyally recognised, and the political
equilibrium corresponds to the reality of the historical
forces which constitute it and determine it. We are convinced that it is on this road that the nations of Europe
will find that tranquillity and peace which are indis-
pensable for the preservation of the very basis of European
civilisation.

> Benito Mussolini. *May 8, 1938.*

FREE TRIPS ABROAD

A WAR is always attractive because it offers a city clerk
the chance of donning a uniform and wearing puttees and a
chance for travel *gratis*, while an armistice or peace is always
desirable after three or four years in the trenches because it
offers the soldier a chance to come back home and wear
civilian dress and a scarlet necktie once more. Some such
excitement humanity evidently needs, and if war is to be

avoided, governments may just as well recruit people between twenty and forty-five under a conscript system and send them on European tours to see some exposition or other once every ten years. The British Government is spending five billion pounds on its Rearmament Programme, a sum sufficient to send every Englishman on a trip to the Riviera. The argument is, of course, that expenditures on war are a necessity while travel is a luxury. I feel inclined to disagree : travel is a necessity, while war is a luxury.

Lin Yutang. *The Importance of Living, 1938.*

MICKEY MOUSE, PEACEMAKER

THE tremendous importance of humour in politics can be realised only when we picture for ourselves . . . a world of joking rulers. Send, for instance, five or six of the world's best humorists to an international conference, and give them the plenipotentiary powers of autocrats, and the world will be saved. As humour necessarily goes with good sense and the reasonable spirit, plus some exceptionally subtle powers of the mind in detecting inconsistencies and follies and bad logic, and as this is the highest form of human intelligence, we may be sure that each nation will thus be represented at the conference by its sanest and soundest mind. . . .

But we don't even have to have a conference of international humorists to save the world. There is a sufficient stock of this desirable commodity called a sense of humour in all of us. When Europe seems to be on the brink of a catastrophic war, we may still send to the conferences our worst diplomats, the most " experienced " and self-assured, the most ambitious, the most whispering, most intimidated and correct and properly scared, even the most anxious to " serve " mankind. If it be required that, at the opening of every morning and afternoon session, ten minutes be devoted to the showing of a Mickey Mouse picture, at which all the diplomats are compelled to be present, any war can still be averted.

Ibid.

A REMINDER FROM AMERICA

THE Secretary of State, Mr. Cordell Hull, yesterday issued in the form of a statement to the Press a reminder to the 63 signatories of the Kellogg-Briand Pact. . . .

Mr. Hull began his statement by saying that the Government of the United States had been following the recent developments in Central Europe with close and anxious attention. He then recalled the signing of the Kellogg-Briand Pact a decade ago,[1] and added :

" That pledge is no less binding now than when it was entered into. It is binding upon all parties. We cannot shut our eyes to the fact that any outbreak of hostilities in any part of the world injects into world affairs the factor of general disturbance. The ultimate consequence no man can foresee, but it is liable to afflict all nations with incalculable and permanent injuries."

The Times, May 30, 1938.

[1] See p. 428.

IN FULL AGREEMENT

MR. A. HENDERSON asked the Prime Minister whether, in view of recent developments in Central Europe, His Majesty's Government would associate themselves with the recent declaration made by Mr. Cordell Hull, on behalf of the United States Government, that the Kellogg-Briand pact remains binding on all parties to seek the pacific settlement of disputes.

Mr. Chamberlain (Birmingham, Edgbaston, U.).—His Majesty's Government are in full agreement with the views expressed by Mr. Cordell Hull in his declaration of May 28. I need hardly add that they for their part are fully resolved to respect the obligations which they entered into in signing the Pact of Paris. (Hear, hear.)

The Times, June 2, 1938.

COLLECTIVE ACTION

LORD CECIL to-day gave the Nobel Lecture, according to the statutes of the Peace Prize, before a distinguished audience, including the King and Queen of Norway, the Crown Prince and Crown Princess, and members of the Cabinet, the Storting, and the Diplomatic Corps.

Comparing the world with the situation six years ago, " the contrast is terrible " [he said]. " Again we see rising the idea that might is right, that mercy and tolerance are only symptoms of feebleness, and that the old conception of blood and iron is the only thing to trust. The question is : Can we prevent war ? Let us be sure we can. . . .

" The difference between uncontrolled nationalism and international co-operation depends, not necessarily on the forms of government prevailing in different States, but on the spirit in which Governments operate. In the end, however, I am confident that a free Government is the best for free people. I have no doubt that ideas of peace and co-operation will ultimately triumph, and I am sure that by the combined efforts of peace-loving people they can be made to triumph now, before Europe has again plunged into a fresh blood-bath."

The Times, June 2, 1938.

KIND WORDS

MR. CHURCHILL, M.P., speaking for the League of Nations Union in Birmingham last night, said that the idea that dictators could be appeased by kind words and minor concessions was doomed to disappointment.

Volcanic forces were moving in Europe, he continued, and sombre figures were at the head of the most powerful races. The dictator countries were prepared night and day to advance their ambition, if possible by peace, if necessary by war. He was under the impression that we and other countries stood in great danger. For four years Germany

had been arming with might and main. There had never
been seen such an outpouring of the munitions of war. At
the present time we were sheltered to some extent by the
strength of the French Army, but the German numbers
were overtaking it, and in the next few years they would
be much more numerous. We had our own Navy, happily
still supreme in the European Mediterranean, but our air
forces, on which so much depended, so far from overtaking
Germany, were actually falling farther and farther behind.
Britain must rearm at the earliest possible moment ; we
must stand by the League Covenant, which alone justified
a great rearmament ; and on the basis of the Covenant we
must unite with other countries desiring freedom and
peace.

The Times, June 3, 1938.

DETERMINED TO MAINTAIN PEACE

M. DALADIER, the Prime Minister, speaking at Lyons to-day,
declared that France counted on the moderation and the
spirit of conciliation of all nations to solve the dangerous
problems of the day. " We also count," he added, " on
our firmness to save Europe from recourse to violence."

M. Daladier said :

" France is determined to remain true to herself. She
will not renounce any of the great hopes which for centuries have animated men and nations, and which have
given to history its deeper meaning. She will not yield to
the delirium of an epoch which is overthrowing all accepted
values.

" She will not say of liberty that it is worthless, of dignity
that it is illusory, of justice that it is deceptive. She will
not allow force to become the arbiter of all human
relationships.

" We are determined to maintain peace, for our love for
it consists neither of renunciation nor of weakness. We do
not regard it as a precarious benefit which must be bought
every day by fresh concessions to the spirit of domination.

P

" Inspired by peace, we have already overcome many perils. We shall meet others on our path, but we shall surmount them, too, if we remain united."

The Daily Telegraph, June 6, 1938.

DIVIDED COUNSEL

But is there no absolute point of view ? Can we not find somewhere written up in letters of fire or gold—" This is right. This wrong ? "—a moral judgment which we must all, whatever our differences, accept ? Let us then refer the question of the rightness or wrongness of war to those who make morality their profession—the clergy. Surely if we ask the clergy the simple question : " Is war right or is war wrong ? " they will give us a plain answer which we cannot deny. But no—the Church of England, which might be supposed able to abstract the question from its worldly confusions, is of two minds also. The bishops themselves are at loggerheads. The Bishop of London maintained that " the real danger to the peace of the world to-day were the pacifists. Bad as war was, dishonour was far worse." On the other hand, the Bishop of Birmingham described himself as an " extreme pacifist. . . . I cannot see myself that war can be regarded as consonant with the spirit of Christ." So the Church itself gives us divided counsel—in some circumstances it is right to fight ; in no circumstances is it right to fight. It is distressing, baffling, confusing, but the fact must be faced ; there is no certainty in heaven above or on earth below.

Virginia Woolf. *Three Guineas, 1938.*

ONE OF THE BEST DETERRENTS

The Women's Voluntary Services, organised under the Dowager Lady Reading, will enable women to serve their country and at the same time save themselves from those

" thousand deaths " that are undergone when danger
evokes no active and intelligent response. A useful part
can be given to half a million women upon that " home
front " where they will all, willy-nilly, find themselves
when the supreme hour arrives. That every such post
should be visibly filled would be one of the best deterrents
for an enemy who might be tempted to test our defences.

Observer (leading article),
June 19, 1938.

" The militarisation of the women, of the entire female part of the
population, is nothing less than one of the greatest tasks of this century."
—*Deutsche Kämpferin,* Military Education of Women, 1936.

ONLY NOW

Lord Halifax, Secretary of State for Foreign Affairs, who
was the guest of honour at the annual dinner of the Royal
Institute of International Affairs at Grosvenor House last
night, said that we were only now appreciating the cata-
clysmic effect of war and learning that it unsettled at least
as much as it settled. All nations to-day were in consequence interested, in varying degree, but to a far greater
extent than formerly, in foreign policy. The common folk
of every nation wanted peace. They realised that if peace
was to be secured relations of contentment must be established between nations, and that the foreign policy of all
nations was the instrument through which these efforts
would either succeed or fail. Whereas war used to be able
to find some sort of rough solution for practical differences
between nations, in these days, when the disturbing factors
were intangible ideas respecting no international boundaries,
it was realised that war was a very uncertain remedy.

The Times, June 22, 1938.

KEEPING UP ONE'S SPIRITS

THE Prime Minister addressed a mass meeting at a National Government rally in the grounds of Boughton House, Kettering, the home of the Duke of Buccleuch, on Saturday night. The Duke of Buccleuch presided and several Midland M.P.s were on the platform.

Mr. Chamberlain, who declared that at no time in his life had he enjoyed better health and better spirits, said : ". . . . When I look round the world I must say I am appalled at the prospects. War, accompanied by horrible barbarities, inflicted either wittingly or unwittingly upon civilian populations is going on to-day in China and much nearer to us in Spain. Almost every week we hear rumours of war on this question or on that in other parts of the world, and all the principal nations are spending their precious savings on devising and manufacturing the most efficient instruments for the destruction of one another. I wonder whether, since the world began, has it ever seen such a spectacle of human madness and folly ?

The Times, July 4, 1938.

THE LESSONS OF THE PAST

NOT all people are reasonable in a world whose nerves are on edge ; and, as Mr. Chamberlain observed, public opinion is not without influence even in countries where there is no expression of free opinion. When Mr. Chamberlain justifies his determination to " strain every nerve to prevent a repetition of the last Great War in Europe " by reference to the appalling casualties and the common subsequent misery of every belligerent, his audience at home and farther afield might well remember the many hospitals still filled with patients who should be a living warning to any system of government not to forget the lessons of the past.

The Times (leading article), July 4, 1938.

MORAL PRINCIPLES

THE use of armed force in defence of international law is
held to be justified in a statement issued on behalf of the
Archbishop of York and other leaders of the Church of
England. . . .

The signatories are : The Archbishop of York, the
Bishops of Bath and Wells, Bristol, Carlisle, Chelmsford,
Derby, Dover, Lichfield, St. Asaph, Southwark, Southwell,
the Deans of Chichester and Exeter, the Provost of Wake-
field, and the rector of Birmingham (Canon Guy Rogers).

The statement . . . is as follows :

We who sign this statement represent a great multitude
who have been rendered anxious about the moral basis
of foreign policy and rearmament as a result of the recent
trend of events. It is to many people far less evident than
it was three years ago on what moral principles foreign
policy should be based, and in what conditions it may be
justifiable to have recourse to armed force. . . . It seems
to be assumed that our country would resort to war in self-
defence, which is generally understood to include defence
of the territorial integrity of the British Empire ; from
that we do not dissent, though we should wish the decision
whether a *casus belli* exists to rest with an impartial
authority, unless a territorial aggression has actually taken
place.

But we wish to affirm with all possible emphasis that
there is clearer moral justification for the use of armed force
in defence of international law than for a war of the old
type in defence of territorial possessions or economic
interests. And we are far from satisfied that this order of
moral priority is universally accepted by our fellow citizens
or by the Government. . . .

There is a real moral case for a repudiation of the use of
armed force altogether ; but our country has not been
persuaded that it is sound. There is no moral case for
building and maintaining armaments without clear moral
principles to direct their use. We are anxious lest the
recent trend of events should develop into a drift away

from all moral principles, and result in an acceptance of
sheer expediency as the guide of our action. . . .

The Times, July 7, 1938.

THE HIGHER WORLDLINESS

THERE appears in your columns to-day a statement as to
the use of armed force in defence of international law. It
is weightily signed by men whom I am not worthy to
criticise, including the Archbishop of York and nine
diocesan bishops. While anxious statesmen, striving for
peace, may have doubts, most of those who welcome the
higher worldliness in international affairs will approve it.
Stalin in a moment of moral exaltation might have added
his signature, for in the statement there is no mention of
Christ or appeal to Christian ideals.

I had thought that leaders of the Church of England,
even when gravely preoccupied by the complexities of a
supremely difficult world situation, existed to preach
Christ and to proclaim Christian principles. Have the
signatories forgotten that their Master, if the Gospel
according to St. Matthew be accurate, believed that He
could have had " more than twelve legions of angels " to
protect Him from arrest : that, repudiating the use of
force, He went to the Cross, a typical saint of non-resistance ?

Some of us believe that, according to the Gospel, the
kingdom of righteousness will come through the innocent
suffering of good men. We do not see it coming as the
result of a policy which in the end might only too easily
lead to our attempting to drop high explosive bombs on
the women and children of Berlin.

The Bishop of Birmingham.
Letter to The Times, July 7, 1938.

CONFUSION OF THOUGHT

To talk about going to war to enforce international law
illustrates the confusion of thought which now exists, for
the very first object of the " reign of law " is to substitute

police action against the individual for war as the sanction behind law. We have had experience of one vast war fought by a collection of democracies from 1914 to 1918 to defend freedom against autocracy and to maintain the sanctity of treaties. Most people now feel that while the cause was just the remedy was almost as fatal as the disease, and that a war for the principle of the League of Nations is not likely to produce ultimately more satisfactory results than a war for Woodrow Wilson's 14 points, which included the League of Nations. . . . Mankind is not going to be benefited by multiplying carnage and destruction a thousandfold for the sake of questions which will immediately be swallowed up in the vast and catastrophic issues which will be raised by general war. That is where the conflict of moralities arises and why it is no solution to declare that we ought always to be ready to go to war on moral issues—though admittedly there are times when war rather than retreat is the lesser of two evils.

> Lord Lothian. *Letter to The Times, July 8,*
> *1938 (printed in the issue of July 13, 1938).*

SOBER RESPONSIBILITY

WE spoke as if our civilisation was very securely based. There had been other civilisations than ours. Tutankhamen was forgotten till he was dug up, and it was very possible that the things which protected our civilisation were more slender than we sometimes thought. Therefore it was right that we should, in a spirit of sober responsibility —not by any means in a spirit of depression, but in a spirit of determination—pass this Finance Bill. He agreed that there was much about which we could be cheerful. This country had resources of character, courage, and history which would see it through. But let them make no mistake ; if we and the world did not succeed in finding some way to stop the folly of this ever-increasing expenditure on armaments, then the future which we were preparing

for our children was one at which we might shudder.
(Cheers.)

Sir John Simon. *In the House of
Commons, July 15, 1938. Reported
in The Times, July 16, 1938.*

ONIONS INSTEAD OF GUNS

LORD BALDWIN was speaking at the Astley Horticultural
Society's Show, held in the grounds of Astley Hall, his
Worcestershire home, at which he presented the prizes.

" One wonders," he said, " if there will ever be sufficient
sanity in this world between nations, when they will cease
to make large guns, and instead will compete against each
other in growing the biggest onions. It would be a wiser
world and would serve a more useful purpose."

The Times, Aug. 2, 1938.

ADMITTEDLY REMOTE

THE scientific study of human nature, especially in its social
aspect, is only in its infancy. As Dr. Glover[1] forcibly pointed
out a few years back, the causes of war are at least as much
psychological as economic. Repression and frustration in
early life engender unconscious cruelty whose natural outlet
is violence, and mass suggestibility, under the influence of
propaganda, generates an irresistible mass hysteria, a
neurosis of society. Theoretically, at least, it is possible to
plan a system of education which would allow the natural
impulses to be expressed instead of repressed, thus removing
the dangerous because unconscious mainspring of violence,
and making it possible to harness the deep psychological
forces to construction instead of destruction ; and one which
instead of fostering suggestibility and material respect for
authority as such, would encourage critical reflection and a
healthy distrust of propaganda. A society educated thus
would be a new kind of society, of its very nature much less

inclined to make war than ours. Admittedly this is remote ; but is it more remote than was our electric age from the age of Galvani or of Ampère, or even of Faraday ? To apply scientific method to the study and control of human nature, new techniques and a new approach are necessary ; but there is no reason to suppose that it cannot be done, and many reasons for supposing that in doing so lies the world's chief hope of emerging from chaos and frustration.

The Times. Leading article, Aug. 18, 1938.

[1] Dr. Edward Glover, *War, Sadism and Peace*, 1933.

MORAL REARMAMENT

THE strength of a nation consists in the vitality of her principles. Policy, foreign as well as domestic, is for every nation ultimately determined by the character of her people and the inspiration of her leaders ; by the acceptance in their lives and in their policy of honesty, faith, and love as the foundations on which a new world may be built. Without these qualities, the strongest armaments, the most elaborate pacts, only postpone the hour of reckoning.

The real need of the day is therefore moral and spiritual rearmament. A growing body of people in this and other countries are making it their aim. It is a work in which all men and women, in all countries and of all races, are called to share and have power to help. Were we, together with our fellow men everywhere, to put the energy and resourcefulness into this task that we now find ourselves obliged to expend on national defence, the peace of the world would be assured.

Baldwin of Bewdley, Salisbury, Amulree, Birdwood, F. M., William Bragg, Clarendon, Cork and Orrery, Admiral of the Fleet, Desborough, Kennet, Lytton, J. W. Mackail, Milne, F.M., W.D. Ross, Sankey, Stamp, Stanmore, Trenchard, Marshal of the R.A.F.

Letter to The Times, Sept 10, 1938.

IN THE INTEREST OF PEACE

I TOOK very serious measures on May 28 : 1. The strengthening of the Army and the Air Force was on my order considerably increased forthwith, and immediately carried out. 2. I ordered the immediate extension of our fortifications in the west. I may assure you that since May 28 the most gigantic fortifications that ever existed are under construction there. . . . After completion it will comprise 17,000 armoured and concrete fortifications. Behind this front of steel and concrete, which is laid out in three, and partly in four, lines of a total depth of up to 50 kilometres, there stands the German people in arms. These most gigantic efforts of all times have been made at my request in the interest of peace.

Adolf Hitler. *Speech at Nuremberg,*
Sept. 12, 1938.

FANTASTIC AND IDIOTIC

BEHIND all the intricacies and discussions and multitudinous conjectures that have been whirling round the central problem of the Czech-German dispute has stood, dimly limned but unmistakably recognisable, the spectre of Armageddon—a large-scale, perhaps world-wide, war springing from a local racial difference in Central Europe. And the conviction is everywhere felt that war on this issue would be a folly and a crime, and that humanity would be heading for the madhouse if the nations of the most densely populated Continent of the world were really going to bomb one another to pieces on account of the troubles of some three and a half million folk in the pleasant land of Bohemia. Granted that their destiny is a matter of real importance, granted that many implications radiate outward from this central problem, and granted that principles and national

ambitions are involved, it would still be fantastic and idiotic
that their troubles should become the occasion for mankind
to plunge into general hostilities.

The Times, Sept. 15, 1938.

THE STAND

HERE we make the stand. Here we vow and dedicate ourselves utterly, if it should be required, to bear out that
stand to the last breath. We shall undertake this and do it
if we must so that the security of freedom shall be redeemed ;
and that bounds shall be set to open tyranny in such fashion
as history shall for ever record and generations to come
remember with thankfulness for as long as any freedom
lives upon this earth.

J. L. Garvin. *The Observer, Sept.
25, 1938.*

" IF I WERE CONVINCED "

HOWEVER much we may sympathise with a small nation
confronted by a big, powerful neighbour we cannot in all
circumstances undertake to involve the whole British
Empire in war simply on her account. If we have to fight
it must be on larger issues than that. I am myself a man of
peace to the depths of my soul. Armed conflict between
nations is a nightmare to me, but if I were convinced that
any nation had made up its mind to dominate the world by
fear of its force I should feel that it must be resisted. Under
such a domination the life of people who believe in liberty
would not be worth living.

The Rt. Hon. Neville Chamberlain.
Broadcast Address, Sept. 27, 1938.

ON MORE FRIENDLY TERMS

THE memorandum and the map were handed to me at
my final interview with the Chancellor, which began at
half-past ten that night and lasted into the small hours of
the morning. . . . For the first time I found in the
memorandum a time limit. Accordingly, on this occasion
I spoke very frankly. I dwelt with all the emphasis at my
command on the risks which would be incurred by insisting
on such terms, and the terrible consequences of a war if war
ensued. I declared that the language and the manner of
the document, which I described as an ultimatum rather
than a memorandum, would profoundly shock public
opinion in neutral countries, and I bitterly reproached the
Chancellor for his failure to respond in any way to the
efforts which I had made to secure peace.

In spite of these plain words, these conversations were
carried on on more friendly terms than any that had yet
preceded them, and Herr Hitler informed me that he
appreciated and was grateful for my efforts, but that he
considered that he had made a response since he had held
back the operations which he had planned, and that he had
offered in his proposal to Czechoslovakia a frontier very
different from the one which he would have taken as the
result of military conquest.

> The Rt. Hon. Neville Chamberlain.
> *In the House of Commons, Sept. 28, 1938.*

" OUT OF THIS NETTLE "

" IT'S all right this time," Mr. Chamberlain is reported to
have said last night. And when he set out from Heston on
this early, moist morning the mood of these words was still
in him. Whatever grave formality there may have been
about his two previous aerial departures, it was quite lost
to-day.

No weighed and solemn words this time from the Prime

Minister, instead, " If at first you don't succeed, try, try again "—and a tag from Shakespeare to cap it—" Out of this nettle, danger, we pluck this flower, safety." Then a broad grin of contentment—there is no other word for it—and as he stood on the steps of the 'plane, having wrung countless friendly hands, one saw his eyes searching for yet another friend to whom to flourish his hat. Even after that, when the doors were closed and the 'plane slowly swung across the onlookers, there he was at the window, smiling and waving. " If at first you don't succeed. . . ." By that hearty, youthful motto he showed the belief that was in him and in the nation.

Much of the success of this send-off (and it was a huge success) was due to Sir John Simon. . . .

Dr. Kordt, of the German Embassy, was there again, and Count Grandi was a spectator this time, apparently as pleased as any one. M. Corbin, however, was not there, nor any of the French Embassy people. M. Jan Masaryk also was absent. Every one refused to regard this absence of the Czech Minister as a gloomy portent.

Manchester Guardian, Sept. 30, 1938.

The "tag from Shakespeare" will be found in *Henry IV.*, Pt. I., Act. 2, Sc. iii. *Enter* HOTSPUR, *reading a letter:* I tell you, my lord fool, out of this nettle, danger, we pluck this flower, safety. *The purpose you undertake is dangerous; the friends you have named uncertain; the time itself unsorted, and your whole plot too light for the counterpoise of so great an opposition.*—Say you so, say you so? . . . By the Lord, our plot is a good plot as ever was laid; our friends true and constant; a good plot, good friends, and full of expectation; an excellent plot, very good friends.

PEACE FOR OUR TIME

MY good friends, this is the second time in our history that there has come back from Germany to Downing Street peace with honour. I believe it is peace for our time.[1]

The Rt. Hon. Neville Chamberlain.
Speaking from a window to the crowd in Downing Street, Sept. 30, 1938.

[1] I hope that hon. members will not be disposed to read into words used in moments of some emotion, after a long and exhausting day, after I had

driven through miles of excited, enthusiastic, cheering people, something more than they were intended to convey. I do indeed believe that we may yet secure peace in our time, but I never meant to suggest that we would do that by disarming until we can induce others to disarm too. — Mr. Chamberlain in the House of Commons, Oct. 6, 1938.

" HERR HITLER DEFERRED "

THERE is no doubt that the evidence that Mr. Chamberlain offered concession from strength and not from weakness won him a respect that might not otherwise have been accorded. Meanwhile other authoritative voices were uplifted for peace: the President of the United States spoke out for humanity, and the Italian Duce, responding to the Prime Minister's leadership, acknowledged that peace is a supreme interest to dictators as to other national rulers. Herr Hitler deferred, as no man need be ashamed of doing, to the protest of the whole world against war.

The Times, Oct. 1, 1938.

" PEACE WITH HONOUR "

No one in this country who examines carefully the terms under which Hitler's troops begin their march into Czecho-Slovakia to-day can feel other than unhappy. Certainly the Czechs will hardly appreciate Mr. Chamberlain's phrase that it is " peace with honour."[1] The terms are a little better than the Godesberg ultimatum but not much.

Manchester Guardian, Oct. 1, 1938.

[1] "On n'a pas le droit de prostituer le beau nom de paix en l'accolant à ces opérations punitives."—Gabriel Peri, *l'Humanité*, Oct. 1, 1938.

AN AMERICAN VIEW

LET no man say too high a price has been paid for peace in Europe until he has searched his soul and found himself willing to risk in war the lives of those who are nearest and dearest to him. But no man who is honest will attempt to pretend to himself that a high price has not been paid. It is a price which enables a dictator who would willingly destroy the last vestige of democracy in Europe to claim with justice that he scored over the democracies of Europe the greatest diplomatic triumph of modern times—that he accomplished by a mere ultimatum what Bismarck failed to accomplish with armies.

New York Times, Oct. 1, 1938.

A CROWN OF THORNS

A GREAT injustice against a nation which has always served the cause of peace in Europe and the world and has gone to the extremes of self-denial to show its goodwill and desire for good relations with its neighbours. The Prime Ministers who after the Munich Conference went to their homes were welcomed as the saviours of peace. Not a glance was given at the treaties of alliance and no recognition was afforded to the alliances of Czecho-Slovakia and all the obligations arising from her international contracts.

All that Prague and the Czecho-Slovak nation received was a crown of thorns.

*Broadcast from Prague Wireless
Station, Oct. 1, 1938.*

A TALK WITH THE FÜHRER

MR. CHAMBERLAIN, receiving representatives of the British Press yesterday before his departure from Munich, said :
" I have always been of the opinion that if we could get

a peaceful solution to the Czechoslovak question it would open the way generally to appeasement in Europe.

"This morning I had a talk with the Führer, and we both signed the following declaration :

"We the German Führer and Chancellor and the British Prime Minister, have had a further meeting to-day and are agreed in recognising that the question of Anglo-German relations is of the first importance for the two countries and for Europe.

"We regard the agreement signed last night and the Anglo-German Naval Agreement as symbolic of the desire of our two peoples never to go to war with one another again.

"We are resolved that the method of consultation shall be the method adopted to deal with any other questions that may concern our two countries, and we are determined to continue our efforts to remove possible sources of difference and thus to contribute to assure the peace of Europe."

The Times, Oct. 1, 1938.

"I believe there are many who will feel with me that this declaration signed by the German Chancellor and myself is something more than a pious expression of opinion. In our relations with other countries everything depends on there being sincerity and good will on both sides. I believe that there is sincerity and good will on both sides, and that is why to me its significance goes far beyond its actual words. . . . No doubt I shall have plenty of critics who will say that I am guilty of facile optimism, and that a better plan would be to disbelieve every word that is uttered by rulers of other great States in Europe. I am too much of a realist to believe that we are going to achieve our paradise in a day. We have only laid the foundations of peace. The superstructure is not even begun."—Mr. Chamberlain in the House of Commons, Oct. 3, 1938.

"The agreement, as anybody can see, is not a pact at all. So far as the question of never going to war again is concerned it is not even an expression of the opinion of the two who signed the paper, it is their opinion of the desire of their respective peoples. I do not know whether the hon. member will believe me, or attribute to me also sinister designs, but I may tell him that the document was not drawn up by Herr Hitler but by the humble individual who now addresses this House."—Mr. Chamberlain, in the House of Commons, Oct. 6, 1938.

A TREMENDOUS OPPORTUNITY

His (Mr. Chamberlain's) last-minute personal efforts to save the peace of Europe have appealed to the imagination of the whole world and made suddenly visible and articulate that profound horror of war, of its wickedness and blindness as well as its misery, which has for long formed a bond of inward and unconscious union between all the people of the earth. He has in his hands the same instrument of world emotion that President Wilson had in 1918.

Is that emotion a passing thing or is it a deep, permanent conviction which Governments can be compelled to obey ? If it is a deep conviction, can Mr. Chamberlain be trusted to use it, to understand it, to see that peace means something better than mere running away from war, and that, however great the majority of people who want peace, they cannot have it unless they stand together as one ?

A tremendous opportunity is there : will it be used ?

> Dr. Gilbert Murray. *Letter to*
> *Manchester Guardian, Oct. 1, 1938.*
> (*Printed Oct. 4, 1938.*)

"The Prime Minister had opened a magnificent new opportunity and it should be used, not for making more bombs, gas masks, and shelters, but for directing the energies of the people away from destruction and to reconstruction, and for the people themselves to take advantage of it to force their Governments to reflect and express their own universal abhorrence of allowing the barbaric methods of violence and destruction ever to enter again into the relationships between nations." — Report of speech by Lord Ponsonby in the House of Lords, Oct. 4, 1938.

A BEQUEST

The Parliamentary representatives of the political parties forming the Government majority in the Czecho-Slovak Government appeal to the conscience of the French and British Parliaments at a time so painful for the Czecho-Slovak nation. We do so after the conference in Munich, where a decision was made about us and without us in a manner unparalleled in history. . . .

This is the painful fact which leaves an ineffaceable scar in our hearts, and so we turn our minds to-day to all the noble spirits of Europe and of the world, demanding that they should recognise our position.

We appeal to them to understand the moral revolution which has caused the punishment of a State and a nation which wanted nothing more than to fulfil its obligations, a nation which had real faith in the high principles of human co-operation, a nation which committed no other wrong than the desire to live in its own fashion in the cultural community of nations and States.

We bequeath our sorrow to the French and English people.

> President of Czecho-Slovak Chamber of Deputies and the Senate. *Telegram to the Speaker of the British House of Commons and to the President of the French Chamber of Deputies, Oct. 2, 1938.*

AN ARMED FUTURE

FOR a long period now we have been engaged in this country on a great programme of rearmament which is daily increasing in pace and in volume. Let no one think that because we have signed this agreement between the four Powers at Munich we can afford to relax our efforts in regard to that programme at this moment. (Loud Opposition laughter.) Disarmament on the part of this country can never be unilateral. (Loud Ministerial cheers.) . . .

We must renew our determination to fill up the deficiences that yet remain in our armaments and in our defensive precautions so that we may be ready to defend ourselves and make our diplomacy effective.

> The Rt. Hon. Neville Chamberlain. *In the House of Commons, Oct. 3, 1938.*

A REASONABLE FUTURE?

You may treat with Herr Hitler or not, but the only way you will win peace is by reasonableness. The only way to conquer evil is to put something better against it. Hatred is a destroyer which brings its own reward ; love is the only thing which is eternal, because it is constructive.

> George Lansbury. *In the House of Commons, Oct. 3, 1938.*

THE GREAT GERMAN FUTURE

FROM now on the German nation will shape its future in this community of will and destiny, and no power in the world will be able any longer to threaten this future. The German nation stands to-day in a solid unity from north to south, from east to west, all its members prepared to stand by each other and not to let themselves be separated. Your happiness to-day is the happiness of 75,000,000 people in the rest of the Reich, just as your sufferings until a few days ago were the sufferings of all. Now we enter into the great German future, and will in this hour thank the Almighty that He has blessed us on our way in the past and ask Him to lead us to good in the future. *Deutschland— Sieg Heil!*

> Adolf Hitler. *Speech at triumphal entry into Eger, Oct. 3, 1938.*

A TERRIBLE FUTURE?

WHEN he (M. Daladier) returned from Munich and witnessed the joy of the people of Paris at the knowledge that he had brought peace, he was filled with anxiety. Peace could not be won for ever, but had to be defended day by day. He would say, with all the strength of which he was capable, that if the country were to relax, and if the maintenance of peace were to be looked upon merely as an excuse for indifference, they would be heading rapidly for a terrible future.

Report of speech by M. Daladier,
Prime Minister of France, Oct. 4, 1938.

WHERE ARE WE GOING?

I WANT to speak of the future. We have to look where we are, and events are moving fast. . . .

I am in entire agreement with those who would push on to bring up those defences of which I spoke to a satisfactory point with the least possible delay. I would mobilise our industry to-morrow. . . .

There is one little thing—a straw—from which I have derived comfort. All the peoples of Europe have looked down into the volcano this last week, and they have begun to ask questions. I do not believe there is a country in the world, and I include Germany and Italy, where men are not asking : " Where are we going ? What is there in the policy of our leaders which has brought us to this vision ? "

When men begin to ask these questions they will never rest until they have had an answer.

Lord Baldwin. *In the House of Lords, Oct. 4, 1938.*

In God's name cheerly on, courageous friends,
To reap the harvest of perpetual peace
By this one bloody trial of sharp war.

Shakespeare. *Richard III.*

ACKNOWLEDGMENTS

THANKS are due to the authors and publishers concerned for permission to use extracts from the following copyright works : *The Great Illusion*, and *Preface to Peace*, by Sir Norman Angell ; *Armageddon and After*, and *Christ and Cæsar*, by Laurence Housman ; *Aristophanes and the War Party*, by Dr. Gilbert Murray ; *Memories and Studies*, by William James (by permission of Mr. Henry James and Longmans, Green & Co., Ltd.) ; *Towards Peace*, by Basil de Selincourt (Oxford University Press) ; *No Time Like the Present*, by Storm Jameson (Cassell & Co., Ltd.) ; *Three Guineas*, by Virginia Woolf (The Hogarth Press) ; *International Government*, by Leonard Woolf ; *The Modern State*, by R. MacIver (Oxford University Press) ; *Peacemaking*, by the Hon. Harold Nicolson (Constable & Co., Ltd.) ; *Instincts of the Herd*, by W. Trotter (Ernest Benn, Ltd.) ; *Peace with Honour*, by A. A. Milne (Methuen & Co., Ltd.) ; *The Decline of the West*, by Oswald Spengler (George Allen & Unwin, Ltd., who have also granted permission for the use of extracts from the authorised edition of the Works of John Ruskin) ; *Germany and the Next War*, by F. Von Bernhardi (Edward Arnold & Co.) ; *Civilisation*, by Clive Bell (Chatto & Windus) ; *Opus* 7, by Sylvia Townsend Warner ; *The Philosophy of Conflict*, by Havelock Ellis (Constable & Co., Ltd.) ; *The Importance of Living*, by Lin Yutang (Wm. Heinemann, Ltd.) ; *The Collected Poems of Thomas Hardy*, and *Ordeal by Battle*, by F. S. Oliver (MacMillan & Co., Ltd.) ; *Pacifism and Common Sense*, by Percy Hartill, B.D., and *The Case Against Pacifism*, by H. L. Goudge, D.D. (A. R. Mowbray & Co., Ltd.) ; *Under the Fifth Rib*, by C. E. M. Joad ; *A Soldier's Testament*, from *The Gutter and the Stars*, by Eliot Crawshay Williams ; *Intentions*, by Oscar Wilde (by permission of Mr. Vyvyan Holland) ; *Boon* and *The Way the World is Going*, by H. G.

Wells. *Let us Honour Peace*, by Captain Philip S. Mumford, Canon C. E. Raven, Vera Brittain, etc., (R. Cobden-Sanderson, Ltd.); *The Faith Called Pacifism*, by Max Plowman (J. M. Dent & Sons, Ltd.); *Politics*, by Heinrich von Treitschke (Constable & Co., Ltd.); *Arbiter in Council*, by Francis W. Hirst.

If by inadvertence or inability to trace the present owners of copyright any material has been used without authority, or if by oversight permission granted has not been duly acknowledged, apologies are tendered to all concerned.

Thanks are also due to T. C. Duncan Williams for assistance in proof-reading, and to Herbert Coates for the loan of his collection of press-cuttings for the years 1914-1918. Mention must be made of Amabel Williams-Ellis, Enid McLeod, Catherine Carswell, Flora Grierson, Elizabeth Sears, Rona Roberts, Guy Chapman, Edgell Rickword, Holbrook Jackson, J. P. Morrison, Alfred Stait, J. E. Walker, John and Margaret Bunting, Arthur Roberts, and H. Milner Gulland, who offered suggestions or gave practical help.

D.G.

INDEX OF AUTHORS

480